Additional Praise for *Investing Amid Low Expected Returns:*
Making the Most When Markets Offer the Least

"Antti has written an important book addressing the most critical challenge to investing for retirement – low prospective returns for the key asset classes. Reviewing extensive histories with humility and experienced judgment, Antti comes up with a balanced and yet optimistic outlook. Reasonable return streams remain for investors to diversify into; however, patience and good risk control will be required. This book is an encouraging read for investors!"

—Jeffrey Pichet Jaensubhakij, Group CIO, GIC

"I often describe Antti's previous book, *Expected Returns,* as the encyclopedia of empirical research of investment management. More than a decade later, Antti has once again written the quintessential guide to navigating the challenging low-return and high-volatility market environment that may lie ahead. He shares his deep understanding and insights into the various components driving returns and provides a clear framework to guide investors in constructing a portfolio to weather the storm."

—Yu (Ben) Meng, Chair of Asia Pacific of Franklin Templeton and
former CIO of CalPERS

"Antti provides a vital update to the canonical toolkit he presented in *Expected Returns*. The new book has even broader coverage, yet is more succinct. Investors who read this book will leave with a straightforward risk-return framework, a well-considered set of investment beliefs, a list of bad habits to avoid, and empirically good practices to follow. This book is the foundation of solid portfolio management for institutional and retail investors."

—Larry Swedroe, Chief Research Officer, Buckingham Wealth Partners

Investing Amid Low
Expected Returns

Investing Amid Low Expected Returns

Making the Most When Markets Offer the Least

Antti Ilmanen

WILEY

Published by John Wiley & Sons, Inc., Hoboken, New Jersey.
Published simultaneously in Canada.

For general information on our other products and services or for technical support, please contact our Customer Care Department within the United States at (800) 762-2974, outside the United States at (317) 572-3993, or fax (317) 572-4002.

Wiley also publishes its books in a variety of electronic formats. Some content that appears in print may not be available in electronic formats. For more information about Wiley products, visit our web site at www.wiley.com.

Library of Congress Cataloging-in-Publication Data is Available:

ISBN 9781119860198 (Hardback)
ISBN 9781119860211 (ePDF)
ISBN 9781119860204 (ePub)

Cover Design: Wiley
Cover Image: © Buena Vista Images/Getty Images

SKY10033130_021922

Dedicated to the young retirement savers across the world — who have been handed a bad draw — and to everyone working for their benefit.

Contents

Foreword

I know what you're thinking: another book?! What could Antti possibly have forgotten to say in his first 550-pager? I mean, you did read every page including the footnotes and the rather weak phoned-in Foreword, didn't you? Of course you did. Well, simply put, a lot happens in 10 years. Things happen in markets. Things happen in politics. Things happen in research. (Yes, we actually learn some stuff, and unlearn some stuff we thought we knew.)

For one, and you may have noticed this from the title of the book, markets have near ubiquitously gotten even more expensive. This has some potentially depressing consequences for the future, and, frankly, no option for dealing with this problem is particularly pleasant (save, we're all wrong, and stocks and bonds are actually dirt cheap right now – but don't hold your breath!). Globally, lower expected returns have no easy fix. But Antti, with some help from Stoics and St. Augustine, tackles this head-on in Part 1. Essentially the options are (a) take more risk so even with lower expected returns you can hit your goals (certainly counterintuitive as it's literally saying, "This looks worse than normal, so give me more," but some investors, with binding expected return floors they can't fall below, sometimes, hopefully reluctantly, need to do this); (b) ignore it and accept lower expected returns for the foreseeable future, don't "get cute" and try to ameliorate the problem, and just ride it out (I call this the "Jack Bogle" argument though, through our friendship, and with a twinkle in his eye, even Jack bragged to me a bit about selling some stocks in 1999–2000); or (c) find and incorporate other sources of expected return that either aren't very low now, or perhaps are compressed but are not correlated with the ones you invest in already (i.e build a better portfolio). Antti considers all these.

Another thing that happens after 10 years is – wait for it – we collectively have ten more years of data/history to learn from. While ten years is not enough time to seriously change our view of long-term expected returns (see my Foreword to Antti's first book on how hard this is), it's still the case that for some asset classes and strategies (e.g. illiquid ones), ten more years is a big fraction of their total histories, and thus it is still a pretty big deal to obtain them. And for other asset classes and strategies we have (not just Antti and me or AQR, though we've done our share, but the broader community of researchers) spent some of the past ten years building meaningfully longer histories by going back further in time. It's sometimes counterintuitive, and we recognize that older data may or may not be as relevant as current data, but as long as you've not yet peeked, new data further back in time is as much "out of sample" as future data. The credit premium, commodity premium, and especially style premia (aka alternative risk premia) are helpful data my colleagues and I (again it was not just us) are proud of having extended historically further back than previously known or at least widely available – in some cases now having nearly a hundred years of evidence (and in some really special cases even longer than that). To our satisfaction, and admittedly relief (you never know when going out of sample!), the older data provided yet more evidence that these premia are likely real and significant.

But, as excited as we are about more data – and you might not expect to hear this from a "quant" – more data doesn't always mean more "truth." Realized returns are noisy beasts over even time frames we'd all call long-term. As I've recently written about, changes in valuation can influence our estimates of realized (and expected future) returns a lot, over some surprisingly long time frames. (In one piece I show strategies like long-short value and just passive stock market exposure, starting out expensive and ending up even more expensive, have substantially distorted estimates of the natural expected return over even a seventy-year time horizon; see Asness (2021)). This Foreword is not the place for the details, but put simply, we believe that obtaining estimates of expected return that do not give undue credit for a strategy getting more expensive or undue blame for it cheapening (as rarely are either expected to occur in perpetuity going forward) is doable, yielding less biased (more accurate) and more precise (an underappreciated advantage) estimates for the future. But, none of this changes the sentiment that strategies getting very cheap or very expensive over the period studied do matter a ton in the real world over time horizons investors care about. We have often used the physics-envy term "time dilation" to refer to how long real life can seem while living it versus how short it can seem when checking out a backtest. It's easy to look at a good backtest in an intuitive robust strategy and examine its three- to five-year painful periods and think, "Of course I'd stick with it, it makes economic sense and look at the whole history!" But, I'm guessing, to none of our readers' surprise, it's a little harder to do live and real-time! To state the obvious, you need the best strategy you can stick with, not the even-better-in-theory strategy that you can't. You can influence that in two very different ways. You can alter your strategy, or come up with ways to put it in perspective that can help you stick with the best versions. We hope that, in particular, by explaining how distortive valuation changes can be, and coming up with concrete and useful ways to incorporate this into our estimates going forward, we can get both less biased and more precise estimates and, through the power of this argument, buck up some investors through deeper understanding. Luckily, Antti is a master teacher. In particular in Part 2 Antti brings his "twin perspectives" to bear, sharing tons of evidence, theory, and lived experience (we've both been doing this a while!) to help.

Antti and I have had many of the same teachers, from our days in graduate school to even our decades apart as researchers in the "real world," and especially learning from our colleagues over the past 10 years at AQR (not to mention AQR's "extended family" of academic consultants, co-authors, etc.). There's no getting away from the fact that this book is to some extent a reflection of Antti's beliefs, of my beliefs, and of AQR's beliefs. I say that for both disclosure, and because it's just true (not always the same thing! ☺) and something readers should know. While Antti and I don't agree on everything (for instance, he's Finnish and thinks going from a 190° Fahrenheit sauna to immediately roll around in the snow is "healthy"), we do agree on much more than we don't.

And this brings me to the uncomfortable (for me) topic of Antti sharing our stuff. Antti is, to put it politely, an "over-sharer." This is generally a good thing in a researcher. No hiding assumptions, lots of musing about the many reasons he could be wrong with an open mind, all good things. But, the crux here, he has a true natural bias to reveal some things we'd sometimes prefer to keep to ourselves for a while! But that's my problem, not yours. I think it is certainly good for you as the reader! Though, to be fair, we don't let Antti share everything. He goes pretty far herein, even further than his last book, but we do believe we have some sources of "alpha" (such a loaded word) that are still relatively unique and there we do clamp down on Antti a bit (not an easy task!). Maybe, if the pattern continues, we'll let him go even further for book number three in the year 2031.

OK, back to the book. Even though it starts with doom-and-gloom in terms of low expected returns, it doesn't end that way. Parts 2 and 3 cover a wide range of ideas to improve investor outcomes that don't rely on markets going up. Some are strategies not particularly rich or cheap (so not a tactical view) but just sources of expected return not correlated to the major ones and, we believe, endemically underutilized in most portfolios. But some are tactical. In particular, what we have deemed (back in 1999–2000 for you old timers) the "value spread" shows that, unlike so many other premia that appear expensive, the value premium, historically positive on average, seems record cheap now (a self-serving opinion and one that will date my Foreword!). Antti covers this (e.g. in Figure 6.3 and a few other places). But, given it's one of the only things I can think of that both has made money over the very long-term and is currently very cheap versus history, it deserves its own mention. When such a reversal will happen is, of course, always the most difficult part. But that we believe it will happen net from here is one of the only silver linings we find among a world of almost all low expected future returns, and, again, although self-serving (I got my kids' money way overweight on this one and they're starting to ask for portfolio reviews over dinner!), I think it's exciting enough to stress here even more.

Finally, there are also some often overlooked parts of the investment process – not as sexy as what to buy and when to buy (or sell) it, but still vital: things like risk management, portfolio construction, and even the mundane but vital area of trading costs and fees. Antti is steeped in both real world and theoretical experience in these areas and he, thankfully, doesn't neglect them. Needless to say, in a world of low expected returns going forward, obsessing over this stuff, always a good idea, goes up even more in importance. When the world is offering you less for showing up, giving up more on, say, a sloppy implementation that overtrades or takes many unintended bets, is a more serious offense than usual.

Summing up, the past 10 years have challenged many ideas and beliefs that were once considered conventional wisdom (e.g. contrarian valuation-based market timing has not worked well in a world of continually more expensive stocks), reinforced others that are too often overlooked (e.g. trading costs matter), and have thrust what were once nice ideas (e.g. ESG, another topic Antti brings great insight to) into the front ranks of importance.

This book covers all that, and, since it is, after all, Antti's work, does much more too. (Overly terse is not an insult that has ever been hurled at Antti, though I think this book is far easier going than the last wonderful but dense one.) As close as I am to these issues and the underlying research, I still learned from this book, and hope you all feel the same way and enjoy it as much as I did.

Cliff Asness
Managing and Founding Principal,
AQR Capital Management
November 2021

Part I

Setting the Stage

Chapter 1

Introduction

- Lower asset yields and richer asset prices have brought forward future returns. The payback time for the recent decades' windfall gains is approaching.
- Most assets are expensive compared to their history. It is not just bonds.
- Few investors have had the serenity to accept low prospective returns. Most hard choices have been delayed. Reaching for yield helps only so far.
- Good investing practices such as discipline, humility, and patience are timeless but become even more important in tough times. Focus on what you can control.
- This book's first part sets the stage. It puts the low expected return challenge and different investors' responses in broad historical context.
- The second part reviews the building blocks that may help improve long-run returns. It updates and extends evidence on market risk premia, illiquidity premia, style premia, and alpha.
- Those blocks still need to be put together. The third part covers portfolio construction, risk management, ESG, cost control, tactical timing, and bad habits.

1.1. Serenity Prayer and Low Expected Returns

Serenity Prayer versus St. Augustine's Prayer

The Serenity Prayer can give fresh insights when investors are beginning to face the challenge of persistent low returns, having been spoiled for a generation.

God, grant me the serenity to accept the things I cannot change,
the courage to change the things I can,
and the wisdom to know the difference.[1]

It is no news that historically low bond yields and high asset valuations point to a low *expected* return world. Meanwhile, many investors have gotten used to strong *realized* returns as rich assets have grown ever richer. Several market observers, myself included, have asked investors to acknowledge this disconnect and to adjust spending plans and investment plans accordingly.

Few investors have shown the "serenity to accept" the lower expected returns in the sense of moderating their future spending plans. Many more have shown "the courage to change" in moving into riskier investments when the market no longer offers the expected returns these investors have grown used to. Collectively, we are due for a disappointment as we cannot all buck the fate of lower expected returns. So it seems "the wisdom to know the difference" has been lacking.

A subset of retirement savers understand that they must save more now that the market offers less, and a few institutions are belatedly lowering their return expectations and planning belt-tightening. Most, however, keep delaying hard choices and follow the youthful St Augustine in praying: *Lord, make me chaste – but not yet.*

This take-risks-and-kick-the-can approach has worked quite well during the past decade – not least thanks to the generous central bankers, for whom even agnostic investors should praise in their evening prayers. The period since the Global Financial Crisis (GFC) has been a time of low growth, low inflation, low interest rates – low everything except *realized* investment returns, it seems. Some say this is because we borrowed returns from the future: not through standard borrowing (although plenty of that took place too) but rather through the windfall gains from ever-lower yields and ever-richer asset valuations. These boosted the post-GFC realized returns but promise even harder times for the rest of the 2020s and/or beyond.

Finally, many investors have adjusted neither their return expectations, nor investment plans, nor spending plans. Wishful thinking can be explained by "rearview-mirror" expectations: Since past returns have been healthy, why should we expect anything different from the future?

Extrapolating the strong market performance since the GFC as an indication of the future would be a wrong lesson to draw. We learn slowly from data, and even a decade is a short period to learn about long-run expected returns, especially if realized returns have been driven by large valuation changes.

While we should be humble about predicting returns, I believe that the next ten years will be characterized by low realized returns, not just by low *expected* returns. I hasten to add that when record-low cash rates are at the heart of the problem, going to cash is not the obvious answer. Any putative market timer will have to be very lucky to get the timing right.

So investors need to take risk to earn any rewards. It is especially important to do this efficiently and intelligently now that the rewards are likely to be meager. And investors should take risks with wide-open eyes when the risk of disappointment – fast or slow – is higher (more on the "how" soon).

---

[1]This variant is the best-known version of the Serenity Prayer, originally written by American theologian Reinhold Niebuhr. This version has been used in Alcoholics Anonymous meetings since the 1940s – a linkage that may turn out to be fitting in the future as investors must wean themselves from the addiction of easy money and related windfall gains. In any case, I felt elated when, on a snowy morning jog in early 2021, I saw the connection between my favorite inspirational quote and the low expected return challenge, a key theme in my planned book. For long, the working title of this book was *Investing with Serenity.* In the end I decided to emphasize low expected returns in the title, while highlighting the serenity angle in this Introduction.

Serenity Prayer Versus Outcome Bias

Investing with serenity is not only about calmly accepting low returns. It is about investing thoughtfully, understanding one's investment goals, and figuring out best ways to reach them. We need to make the most when markets offer the least. While on this journey, investors should focus more on the process than outcomes. This is another important connection between the Serenity Prayer and investor behavior. Outcome bias refers to the all-too-common tendency to equate the quality of a decision with the quality of its outcome.[2] Few investors serenely accept an extended period of disappointing performance. Yet, overreacting to past performance is not a recipe for long-run success.

When it comes to realized returns, luck dominates skill over months and even years. Good investments will have bad periods. In relatively efficient markets, competition means outperformance cannot be as reliable as we'd like. We can see consistently successful surgeons or engineers but observe that investors do not achieve comparable consistency – if we measure success by short-term outperformance.[3] Good investors are anchored by market outcomes and relatively close to 50/50 short-term odds around them. Odds of outperformance tend to increase with a longer horizon, but more slowly than many investors accept. A long-run positively rewarded strategy or a skillful investor can have painfully long bad patches. Equity markets do experience losing decades (most recently in 2000–2009) and even Buffett has suffered underperformance longer than a decade.

Statisticians say we may need decades to distinguish luck from skill in investing. Yet, most investors shrug and judge investments based on the past few years' performance – at most. Sadly, it is not enough. In reality, most of us cannot give investments as much patience as is rationally needed. Impatience leads to ill-timed capitulations at asset class level and wasteful fire/hire decisions in manager choices.

There are no easy solutions to this perennial challenge, but we can all try to do better. Investing with serenity is about investors and managers accepting what cannot be changed – that the outcomes over short and even quite long horizons are dominated by luck or randomness. Instead, judgments should focus on what can be controlled: improving expected returns by improving the investment process and decision-making quality.

I understand that this may sound preachy, especially given that some of the systematic style strategies I highlighted in my first book recently underwent several bad years.[4] Yet, this book emphasizes patience as one key investing virtue, so I cannot avoid the topic.

The message is not relevant only to my favorite strategies. More generally, serenity is all about consistent investing: Figure out what you believe in and try hard to stick with it. Inconsistently

---

[2]Judging a decision's quality by its ex-post outcome and not by the ex-ante process is called both "outcome bias" and "resulting fallacy" (Duke (2018)). Another related term is "hindsight bias" (seeing past events as more predictable than they really were; "I knew it all along"). Related work by Taleb (2001), Kahneman (2011), and Mauboussin (2012) highlights the difficulty of disentangling luck versus skill, as well as the common tendency to underestimate the role of luck in outcomes.

[3]For example, Warren Buffett's track record is about long-run success, not about implausible short-run consistency. Exceptions to this rule typically involve return smoothing (which conceal true economic fluctuations in private asset funds) or effective market-making gains (high-frequency liquidity provision strategies are partly behind the success of Jim Simons' most famous fund, Medallion, which is anyway closed to outside investors).

[4]This is why I could not publish a manuscript "Patience," now in Chapter 9. It would have sounded too self-serving and outright irritating to some suffering investors. So please don't think I consider patience easy. It is fair to ask underperforming managers if a systematic strategy is broken or a discretionary manager has lost her touch. But also know that, statistically speaking, we tend to rush to judgment too soon.

chasing different long-run successful strategies would likely turn out worse than sticking with one mediocre strategy.

1.2. Outline of This Book

Though the Serenity Prayer was written by a Christian theologian, its themes reflect seemingly universal ideals and its origins in the Stoic philosophy seem obvious. Witness the words of Epictetus two millennia ago:

> *The chief task in life is to identify and separate matters . . .*
> *which are externals not under my control,*
> *and which have to do with the choices I actually control.*[5]

Investment success requires good investment strategies *and* good investors. Good investors understand which matters they can control – and focus on these. In the outline for this book, I split the matters into three sections:

- Know your history – setting the stage, especially the low expected return challenge.
- Know your investment opportunity set – my focus here will be on long-run rewarded factors as building blocks.
- Know how to assemble the parts into the whole – through portfolio construction, risk management, ESG considerations, and cost control.

Prescriptions on good investing can be timeless. They are not different when returns are high or low. However, amid low returns, good investing matters even more.

Part I: Investment Winter Ahead

My generation has benefited from windfall gains in almost all asset classes over multiple decades when real yields have fallen and asset valuations have risen, thereby boosting the realized returns. The payback time is near – likely starting in the 2020s. Chapter 2 will stress that harsher investment conditions are ahead, whether through the slow pain of stingy coupons and dividends or the fast pain of losses when rich asset valuations revert to more normal levels.

This is not only a world of low *bond* yields. Virtually all long-only assets appear expensive compared to their own histories. The price of any asset is the sum of the market's expectation of future cash flows discounted to their present value. The common element in discount rates – the riskless rate – is near all-time low. Thus, equities and illiquid assets too appear to have expected returns near record lows; these are just not as visible as they are for bonds.

Figure 1.1 depicts the evolution of simple yield-based expected long-run real returns of US equities and bonds since 1900. The September 2021 real yields of 2.9% and -0.9% are at 2nd and 1st percentile, respectively, over a nearly 122-year window.

---

[5]Epictetus stressed that we cannot control what happens to us but we can control how we react to it. His near-contemporary Stoics Seneca and Marcus Aurelius emphasized similar themes, as did Viktor Frankl much later. More personally, I drew lifelong inspiration from how graciously my colleague Rory Byrne lived his last years before succumbing to a brain tumor at the age of 35 – his code was "Do your best with the cards you've been dealt." This book's subtitle reflects the same aspiration applied to the current market environment. I dedicated my first book to Rory's memory.

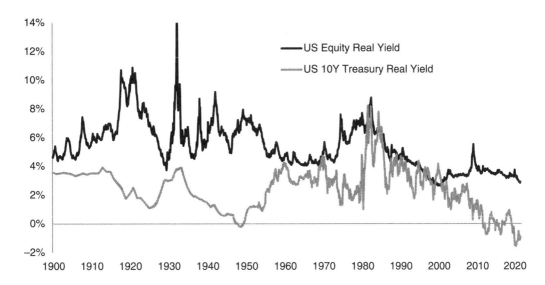

Figure 1.1 Simple Expected Real Return of US Equities and Treasuries, Jan 1900–Sep 2021
Sources: AQR, Robert Shiller's website, Kozicki-Tinsley (2006), Federal Reserve Bank of Philadelphia, Blue Chip Economic
Indicators, Consensus Economics. Notes: Equity is represented by the S&P500 stocks (before 1926 using Cowles data as in
Robert Shiller website). The equity real yield is the sum of income and growth proxies. Income is an average of two
measures: D/P ratio and half of the cyclically-adjusted E/P ratio (which uses smoother 10-year real earnings in the
numerator, and implicitly assumes 50% payout ratio), while growth is assumed to be 1.5% (long-run real EPS growth).
No mean reversion is assumed. The real bond yield is the 10-year Treasury yield minus survey-based or statistical inflation
forecast for a decade, as in Ilmanen (2011).

We cannot observe expected returns directly; we can only estimate them. Such estimates
are typically based on current market conditions (Figure 1.1 is just one example of this forward-
looking approach) or on historical average returns. We can complement either empirical approach
by theoretical considerations – or simply take discretionary views.

I will emphasize the long-term benefits of humility, especially with market timing. Short-
term market timing is hard but even ten-year return forecasts involve wide uncertainty bands.
The limits of our knowledge reflect the competitive nature of investing in relatively efficient
markets and thus limited return predictability. While we have increasing amounts of data, we still
live in a world of small data and low signal-to-noise ratios for all but high-frequency investment
strategies. If we contend that the world has structurally changed in recent decades, we have even
less data to work with.

After all that questioning of the reliability of expected return estimates, they may be the best
we have. So they should be used – with appropriate humility. That expected returns are low is a
fact. That realized returns will be low in the rest of the 2020s is merely an opinion.

Chapter 3 will provide historical context on asset allocation practices before describing
how the low return environment can hurt various investor types and how these investors have
responded. As noted above, many investors have shown more courage to increase investment risk
than serenity to adjust lower their spending plans. Serenity is about accepting reality as it is, and
doing one's best with it. Serenity is not the same as wishful thinking or unrealistic optimism.

The low return message may make me sound like a Cassandra, but I also have earned the
nickname Pollyantti for my penchant to seek silver linings in all kinds of bad news. The rest of
the Introduction includes my best set of silver linings – what we can control in this challenging
situation.

In any case, a key message from the happiness literature is that happiness equals the difference between reality and expectations. By moderating my readers' expectations on future returns, this book is likely to boost their long-run happiness. You're welcome.

Part II: Building Blocks to Improve Returns

While expected returns may vary over time, historical average returns give us useful information on which factors have been rewarded over the long run. And if the current valuations are not very far from historical averages, this evidence may also give a good estimate of future expected returns.

Research-oriented investment practitioners and academics have converged over time in their opinions *on which factors have been historically well rewarded*. Empirical evidence over recent decades or even longer histories point to certain asset class premia as well as certain style premia. Their past rewards have been sufficiently persistent, pervasive, and robust to be statistically and economically significant and beyond data mining concerns. Figure 1.2 highlights nine premia with almost a century of evidence; each will be discussed in Chapters 4 and 6. The bars show annual average compound returns over cash since 1926 (left y-axis), while the line shows Sharpe ratios (risk-adjusted returns, henceforth "SRs", right y-axis). Chapters 5 and 7 will also cover illiquidity premia and manager-specific alpha, but we do not have nearly century-long evidence to back them up.

The first bar is the global equity premium, 6.2% per annum, justly the most important source of return and risk for most investors. Yet, there are many other rewarded factors.

Three other asset class premia – the term premium (between long-dated government bonds and cash), the credit premium (between corporate credits and comparable government bonds), and the commodity premium (in a diversified basket of commodity futures) – earned 1.8–3.5% annual average rewards.

The list of rewarded factors has got longer in recent decades. Evidence on alternative risk premia, notably five style premia, has become more widely known. Favoring cheap assets (value), recently outperforming assets (in relative sense in momentum and in absolute sense in trend), high-income assets (carry), and stable or high-quality assets (defensive) are styles that have performed well within many asset classes – and better as a diversified composite shown here. The performance of long/short style premia is presented before trading costs and fees, which together with superior diversification explains the high SRs (ranging from 0.53 for value to 0.89 for trend).[6]

After costs and fees, style premia would have been lower, and the fact that these ideas are now widely known among investors ("their alpha has morphed into alternative beta") may further reduce forward-looking return estimates.

Investor interest in style premia – both long-only "smart beta" factor investing and long/short alternative risk premia variants – grew significantly in the 2010s. However, the disappointing performance in recent years – especially losses in the stock selection value strategy – led many investors to give up on style premia.

---

[6]The historical average return levels depend crucially on the leverage and volatility applied to these long/short strategies. Sharpe ratio (SR) is a more robust (scale-invariant) performance metric than average return. I will thus use SRs extensively, despite their own shortcomings. As a reminder, SR is the ratio of average over volatility for any investment's excess return over cash. Here I conservatively target bond-like 5% volatility per style, which gives 2.5% to 4.5% average premium per style.

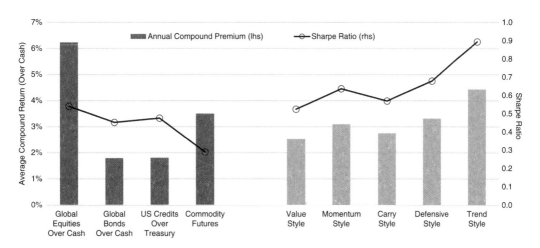

Figure 1.2   Annual Excess Returns and Sharpe Ratios of Main Asset Class Premia and Alternative Risk Premia, 1926–2020

Source: Data from AQR. Notes: Geometric means and Sharpe ratios of nine return series, which exclude cash return but are before subtracting trading costs and fees. Equities and (government) bonds are GDP-weighted multi-country composites. Credit is a US corporate portfolio over matching Treasury. Commodity is an equally-weighted portfolio of available commodity futures. The five long/short style premia use simple specifications applied in many asset classes (cf. Chapter 6 and Ilmanen et al. (2021a)) and one-month implementation lag, and are scaled to 5% volatility.

Historical evidence does not get better than for these nine premia. If you find differently, please let me know. For example, evidence on illiquidity premia in private assets or on the small-cap premium is more limited than many believe – a key topic in Chapter 5.

One way to view the long-term evidence in Figure 1.2 (and further empirical evidence later in this book) is as "base-rate information." Kahneman (2011) and Mauboussin (2009) discuss the common "base-rate neglect" where decision-makers focus too much on the specific situation at hand and ignore the general probabilities. Investors should recall that we all are prone to such neglect, even if they can overlay their specific information or views on top of base-rate information provided here. This book serves carrots and broccoli as the main items on the investment menu, not much of the sweet stuff.

Many investors count on manager-specific "alpha," but empirical evidence argues against confident predictions of positive alpha. Chapter 7 reviews evidence on active versus passive investing and methods for demystifying active manager returns.

I then summarize risk-based and behavioral forces that may explain various asset class and style premia, before asking questions like "Who is on the other side of these premia strategies?" or "How does one sustain conviction and patience in a chosen approach through its bad times?" (Chapters 8 and 9).

Finally, I go geeky in Chapter 10 and introduce the four equations that even equation-averse people should know about investing.[7] I also offer a brief tour of some key predictive techniques (e.g. time-series versus cross-sectional approaches to estimate expected returns).

---

[7] I found 30-odd years ago that I belong to the majority who naturally read text and gloss over equations in any article, while most of my peers in the Finance Ph.D. program were inclined to do the opposite. I hope that belonging to the majority has helped me serve better as a bridge between academia and practitioners.

Part III: Putting It All Together

Having written the mammoth book *Expected Returns* and soon afterwards joined AQR in 2011, I was aware I had focused on the already-overrated part of investment management, and I promised myself to do justice to the often-overlooked parts. So the first AQR paper I wrote – with my colleague Dan Villalon – was deliberately called "Alpha Beyond Expected Returns."

We began with a picture of apple harvesters (Figure 1.3) and the following introduction:

> *Investors spend much of their time on selecting active investments or active managers, which is nearly a zero-sum game. While doing so, they underutilize diversification, risk management, and effective implementation. We call these less glamorous activities collectively as sources of "alpha beyond expected returns" where alpha is loosely defined as improved risk-adjusted returns. In today's low-rate environment, it is even more important that investors do not let any source of alpha go to waste.*

> *If investing were compared to apple harvesting, the accompanying picture illustrates the classic mistakes made when reaching for the top (excessively focusing on expected returns), while missing the low-hanging fruit. Look at the poor quality of diversification – all apples in one basket. What should we say about risk management when the poor girl is standing under the ladder? And cost control is hardly impressive when we see one overseer and one active worker. Do not let your investment process be like this harvesting effort!*

> *More seriously, investors should strive to add value in every step of the investment process: expected return generation, portfolio construction, risk management, and cost-effective execution.*

The parallels are tasty, and this picture also serves as a good outline for the last section of this book: Putting It All Together. Chapters 12, 13, and 15 respectively focus on portfolio construction, risk management, and cost control.

Mean-variance optimization is a common workhorse in portfolio construction, despite its various pitfalls. I emphasize the role of constraints (on, say, illiquidity and leverage) in driving

Figure 1.3   Apple Harvesting Parable of Bad Investing Practices
Source: AQR. Originally from Penrose Chamber of Commerce (http://www.penrosechamber.org/). Text additions are our own.

actual asset allocation choices. When it comes to risk management, survival comes first. Cost consciousness is important but thoughtful investors do not minimize costs or fees but maximize net returns.

Even before those chapters, I present an ode to diversification. Diversification remains the one almost-free lunch in investing, though its costs include unconventionality and lesser intuition. Diversification is short stories and long evidence.

The hot topic of ESG (environmental, social, governance) investing deserves its own chapter. When judging its return impact, we don't have enough data and the world is changing, so priors matter a lot. Financial theory suggests that the world offers more trade-offs than win-wins in the long run. Still, ESG "sinners" may lag in a transition phase, and ESG-oriented investors may accept some long-run cost to virtue.

The last chapters argue that strategic diversification trumps tactical timing as a method of improving investment outcomes and that multiyear return chasing is a premier bad habit among investors.

These are the big-picture ideas, but there is inevitably much more to good investing. Given the broad subject, I largely keep a bird's eye view in this book but occasionally zoom in on selected details.

1.3. On Investment Beliefs

While this book describes what I consider good investing practice, it does *not* provide investment advice. This is not just a compliance disclosure, but it reflects both the appropriate humility on a challenging topic and my wish to help you stick with a plan. I try to provide useful information and insights for investment decision-making, but you (or your organization) must make your own choices.[8]

It is hard to come up with investment edges, but it is easy to forfeit those edges. Even if you had skill to identify return sources which give you an edge, you could waste them without patience, diversification, or risk and cost control. So while I have strong opinions on good long-run return sources (certain asset class and style premia) and on helpful investment practices, you need not share mine. Choose your own beliefs and try to stick with them.

I list next some of my core leanings when it comes to good investing. Each opinion below arguably errs toward humility and away from overconfidence, in order to enhance long-run performance. They are evidence-based opinions, as later chapters will attest.

- I prefer diversification over concentrated positions. One test of how much you really care about diversification is your willingness to use leverage to harness the power of multiple rewarded factors. Most investors say no and let equity market directional risk dominate their portfolio.
- I believe more in style premia than illiquidity premia as long-run return sources.

---

[8]There is always some tension between one-size-fits-all ideas of good practices and customization. This book leans toward the former as I share the broad ideas that I find relevant for most investors, whereas how you apply them depends on your specific beliefs, characteristics, and preferences.

In any case, there are many winding paths to investment success. Some paths involve very different investment choices from mine (e.g. more illiquids, more concentrated, more discretionary, more tactical . . .). This is as it should be and that's what makes a market. The only investment that everyone can simultaneously hold is the cap-weighted portfolio; all other strategies need someone on the other side.

- I prefer portfolio perspective on any investment over narrow framing. That is, I ask what this investment will do to my overall portfolio risk and return, not how it behaves alone: so, top-down rather than bottom-up.
- I prefer strategic long-term diversification over bold tactical timing. This preference reflects the powerful benefits of diversification, limited tactical return predictability, and the dangers of impatience.
- I prefer holding portfolios that are resilient across many different macro scenarios instead of portfolios that perform well when my investment view turns out to be right.
- In the same spirit, survival comes first in risk management. The chance to hit view-based jackpots is a luxury that for many comes at the cost of lower long-run returns. Risk management should ensure the ability to fight another day.
- I prefer probabilistic thinking over stories. The former emphasize uncertainty around future outcomes (as well as in judging past outcomes), while stories tend to anchor on one view.
- I prefer systematic investing over discretionary approaches. Besides providing discipline, systematic investing is more evidence-based and relies more on diversification. It comes with its own pitfalls, such as vulnerability to structural changes and less intuitive narratives.
- In sum, my investment beliefs favor humble forecasts and bold diversification.[9]

I get it, this may sound boring and too abstract. If good investing were easy, fun, and exciting, its fruits might really get "arbitraged away."

Miscellanea

I have already referred to my first book, *Expected Returns* (2011). I did not expect to write another book, but as I kept learning more in my AQR years, the temptation grew. The lockdowns and travel restrictions gave me an opportunity in 2020–21, and I took it.

The new book describes my matured vision on expected returns of various investments (Part II), but it also presents them in the broader historical context of the low-return challenge (Part I) and reviews how the pieces can be efficiently assembled (Part III). I try to keep this book shorter despite its broader subject matter. Admittedly, the bar was low as *Expected Returns* ran up to 550 pages.[10]

A few other points are worth highlighting:

- This book is mainly for professional investors and financial advisors but also contains many lessons to strategically-minded individual investors.
- I have talked to the majority of the world's largest institutional investors during the past decade(s) and even directly advised some of them. They all think about similar questions, but

---

[9]Inspired by Kahneman-Lovallo (1993) "Timid Choices and Bold Forecasts" which describes two mistakes in managerial decision-making that fortuitously tend to offset each other.
[10]One way to keep the page number down is by not including all the deserving references. I capped them near 500 and focused on more recent research – apologies to others. For excellent books with as broad coverage as this one, see Lussier (2013), Ang (2014), and Pedersen (2015). I also recommend viewing the *Words from the Wise* series in aqr.com, where we interviewed many luminaries (John Bogle, Charley Ellis, Robert Engle, Marty Leibowitz, Harry Markowitz, Richard Thaler, Ed Thorp, and Roger Urwin) who have influenced our thinking. For two other wonderful sets of interviews and profiles of modern finance giants, see Towle (2014) and Lo-Foerster (2021).

they can come up with different answers. I will cover some of these here but I will not name names, except for some discussion on publicly-known approaches like the "Norway Model," the "Endowment Model," and the "Canada Model."

• As noted in the Acknowledgments, this book owes a large debt to the work of my AQR colleagues. Admittedly, this book gives an AQR-colored vision on good investing, but I strive to give a balanced picture.

• As I want to avoid letting this book become dated soon, I will steer clear of hot topics at the time of writing, such as meme stocks, Robinhood, bitcoin, NFTs, and SPACs. I share the worry with other old fogeys that many get-rich-quick efforts will end in tears and may discourage a generation of investors from the more boring but necessary type of retirement saving and investing.

• On the many footnotes: I use them to improve the flow and to actively segment two kinds of readers – those who like footnotes and those who don't know what they are missing by not reading them.

Finally, I am well aware of the reputed headwinds that sequels frequently disappoint and that non-fiction books are becoming an outdated mode of communication. If I can provide enough insights and structure within two covers to help readers navigate the low-return challenge, I might overcome those twin gales. You'll be the judge.

Chapter 2

The Secular Low Expected Return Challenge

- Expected returns in all major asset classes have fallen to near historic lows.
- All assets' expected cash flows are discounted by a common riskless rate and myriad risk premia. When the common part of the discount rate is record-low, it is no wonder if "everything looks expensive."
- Past realized returns have remained solid thanks to the discount rate effect – repricing due to the very fall in required asset yields and resulting windfall gains.
- Rearview-mirror expectations may lull many investors into complacency, just when the challenge is the greatest.
- Low expected returns can materialize either through "slow pain" or "fast pain."

2.1. Broad Context

Savers and investors have enjoyed benign tailwinds for many decades, but the question now is between headwinds and no winds. Low expected returns for most assets will make it hard for pension savers around the world to reach their retirement goals and for many institutions to reach their spending goals. It may seem trifling to worry about cooling investment conditions at a time of global warming and pandemics, yet this counts as one of the most important generational challenges we face.[1]

---

[1] This book focuses on narrow investment issues, thus omitting big topics such as inequality and polarization, geopolitics, the impact of technological change, and a variety of environmental and other threats. Likewise, it does not cover the many positive developments which make some authors argue, with good data, that for most people there has been no better time in history to be alive than today. Still, the demographic challenge is growing. The boomer generation got the investment decades of windfall gains, while delaying the costly environmental and fiscal reckoning for which the young will ultimately bear the consequences. (Even the debates on climate change and inequality are influenced because low discount rates raise both the present-value costs of climate change and the measured current wealth inequality.)

Take defined-benefit pension plans. If we compare the value of institutional assets to liabilities, the majority of plans have been underfunded since the Global Financial Crisis (GFC). Many private sponsors are leaving the field.

Or take the defined-contribution pension savers. Simple arithmetic says that they earn their retirement pot either through their savings or through the investment returns on savings. When the markets are friendly and provide high returns over multiple decades, the miracle of compounding ensures that little saving is needed. When the markets are stingy and do not fulfil their role, saving must create the whole retirement pot.

Or take endowments that expect to spend 5% real because they are used to earning as much from the market. Markets will not deliver a given level of returns just because you need it. Unless you adjust your spending plans, you will eventually need to spend from your capital.

The broad policy issue is whether underfunded pension systems can afford paying the promised pensions in an ageing society. OECD estimates that the ratio between old-age (>65) and working-age population (20–64) rose in the US from 22% to 28% between 1990 and 2020 and will rise to 40% by 2050. Statistics look worse for the European Union: 22–34–56(%), while Japan has led the way with 19–52–81(%), and China is catching up quickly with 10–19–48(%).

To be fair, I – and many other so-called experts – have been warning about low expected returns for a while, but especially the US markets kept delivering quite generous returns through the 2010s. What gives?

Rich assets got richer as their discount rates fell. Forward-looking returns appear low compared to history wherever we look, and have done this for a long time. The GFC of 2008 brought global policy rates and bond yields to extremely low levels for a decade, and the more recent Covid-19 crisis of 2020 might ensure that they will remain low for long. It is wrong, however, to think that the low expected return challenge applies only to bonds; it is relevant for all asset classes. Low starting yields are most visible for government bonds, but we see for all asset classes (corporate bonds, equities, real estate, private equity) historically low yields and/or above-average valuations.

Why? Mechanically, every long-only asset can be priced as "Expected cash flows divided by a discount rate which reflects a riskless rate and some risk premia." Even if the expected cash flows and risk premia were near historical norms, the very low common (riskless) part of the discount rate can make everything expensive.

The fundamental backdrop to low yields is of course the persistent slow growth, low-inflation environment after the GFC, which has left major central banks battling deflationary forces with loose monetary policies (near-zero policy rates and quantitative easing). Attempts to tighten monetary policies have been quashed, most recently by the Covid crisis. Loose central bank policies are less an active choice and more a response to "wet logs economies" (where any tightening can cause recession or crashes) and to fundamental trends in demographics, globalization, and technology (which have caused lower inflation and natural real rates).

Near-zero or even negative yields on riskless bonds thus make all asset classes look historically rich. It is a world of low expected total returns rather than a world of compressed risk premia. This is a global challenge but likely worse for European and Japanese investors, due to especially low cash/bond yields as well as a tendency to hold large bond allocations.

This low expected return challenge may be underappreciated by many investors because realized returns have remained strong. The baby-boomer generation benefited from windfall gains over decades which sustained high returns even through the 2010s. These tailwinds cannot go on much longer, and it may soon be payback time. We may have been "borrowing returns from the future" as the windfall gains "brought future returns forward."

2.2. Rearview-Mirror Expectations, Discount Rate Effect, and Low Expected Returns

Forward-looking analyses point to historically low future returns due to low starting yields, even without any reversals in valuations. Investors who assess prospective returns from a rearview mirror of recent decades will have a more positive outlook but are likely to be disappointed. Extrapolating future returns from recent decades' realized returns is more typical for equity investors and illiquid-asset investors; bond investors have the benefit of visibility as lower bond yields stare them in the face.

Even for other asset classes, it is helpful to consider the bond-like logic that high starting yields and capital gains from repricing (falling yields, rising valuations) cause contemporaneously high realized returns – but also imply lower prospective returns thereafter, both because starting yields are now lower and because one cannot expect further windfall gains and might even worry about some reversal.

Figure 2.1 provides empirical analysis of the discount rate effect. It shows how changing valuations have influenced realized asset returns in a way that makes those past realized returns misleading proxies of prospective returns. The graphs give the big picture, but to understand the details you must read the footnotes.

It is commonly argued that the tailwinds from falling yields have boosted bond returns in recent years and decades. A simple numerical exercise in Figure 2.1 (Panel A) verifies this. Between 1981 and 2020, the average excess return of the 10-year Treasury over cash was 3.3%. We can estimate that 1.5% of this can be attributed to the sample-specific windfall gains caused by yields falling from 12.4% to 0.9%, so the excess return would have been 1.8% in a more neutral

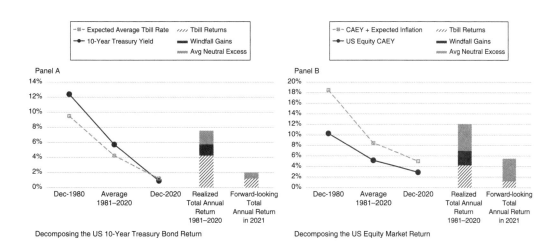

Figure 2.1 Discount Rate Effect: Windfall Gains in Realized Asset Returns Between 1981 and 2020

Sources: AQR, Bloomberg, Robert Shiller's website. Notes: See construction details for the return decompositions in footnotes below.

sample period.[2] Looking ahead, it would be foolish to extrapolate the 3.3% excess return experience, and even the 1.8% may be higher than today's yield curve suggests.

"Bond prices move inversely to (their) yields," we are often reminded. Not just *bond* prices! It is less widely understood that a similar discount rate effect applies to other asset classes, including equities. So let's go through the same arithmetic in Figure 2.1 (Panel B) for US equities. Between 1981 and 2020, the average excess return of the S&P500 index over cash was 7.8%. We can estimate that 2.7% of this (more than a third) can be attributed to the sample-specific windfall gains caused by the cyclically-adjusted earnings yield (CAEY) falling from 10.3% to 2.9%, so the excess return would have been 5.1% in a more neutral sample period.[3] Looking ahead, it would be foolish to extrapolate the 7.8% for the future; moreover, today's CAEY is well below the 40-year sample average 5.1%.

- Viewing total returns is even worse, as cash rates have fallen from double-digit levels to near zero. Figure 2.1 highlights the symmetry between the discount rate effects in bond and equity markets, as well as the dangers of rearview-mirror expectations in both asset classes.
- On the left-hand side in each panel, a line shows the trend decline in asset yields through the 40-year sample period. (To show total expected return, a dashed line in the second panel includes expected inflation besides the equity yield because the latter is naturally a real yield. I do not assume that the fall in expected inflation changed equity valuations, though.)
- On the right-hand side, the first stacked bar decomposes the realized total annual return over four decades into the average T-bill rate (4.2%), the windfall gains due to the asset yield decline, and the average ("neutral") excess return over T-bills beyond this windfall gain.
- The last stacked bar in each panel presents, more speculatively, the prospective return using the same decomposition. All components point to lower expected returns for both assets. The picture would be even more bleak if I were to assume capital losses from mean-reverting asset yields, but I won't. I simply assume that next decade sees average T-bill rates near 1% (in line with consensus forecasts and the Fed's term structure models), no more windfall gains, and a little lower "normal" excess return (due to the current yield curve slope and CAEY being lower than the past four-decade average).

---

[2]Specifically, I regress monthly excess bond returns on contemporaneous yield changes. The correlation is near −0.95 and the slope coefficient (−)5.3 gives the bond's average empirical duration. The product of the slope and the net yield change of −11.5%, pro-rated over 40 years, gives the annual windfall gain of 1.5%. The annualized regression intercept 1.8% is likely a better measure of the excess return investors expected on average during the sample period than the realized excess return. To bond geeks, this estimate likely understates the impact of yield changes by missing so-called convexity effects. To factor geeks, it is important to estimate the empirical impact of yield or valuation changes on contemporaneous returns (instead of just assuming a 1-for-1 relationship) because with many long-short factors such relationship is weak (see Ilmanen-Chandra-Nielsen (2015) and Asness (2016, 2021)). Finally, in the exercises quoted here, the results are robust whether I use raw returns or log returns (though the latter will have a lower average return, closer to the geometric mean) and whether I study monthly or annual changes.

[3]Here I regress monthly excess equity returns on contemporaneous changes in the CAEY (the inverse of "the Shiller CAPE"). The correlation is near −0.9 and the slope coefficient (−)14.6 gives the equity market's empirical sensitivity to its own discount rate changes. The product of the slope and the net yield change of −7.4%, pro-rated over 40 years, gives the annual windfall gain of 2.7%. So the windfall gains have been larger for equities than bonds despite a less extreme yield fall, thanks to equities' longer "duration." Comparing slope coefficients of −14.6 and −5.3 reminds that equities' distant cash flows give them a very long "duration" (in the sense of a high sensitivity to their own discount rate, not to bond yields). The annualized regression intercept 5.1% is likely a better measure of the excess return equity investors expected on average during the sample period. Annual windfall gains are larger for greater valuation changes and shorter historical windows.

Hopefully these examples convince readers how extrapolating the past four decades' asset returns can be doubly misleading. First, realized returns exceeded average expected returns due to the fall in asset yields, and second, today's starting yields are lower than the past sample average. The discount rate effect makes such extrapolative rearview-mirror expectations particularly dangerous because after major windfall gains from a repricing, many investors' subjective expectations rise just when objective prospective returns are lower (see Greenwood-Shleifer (2014)).

We cannot know whether the low expected returns will materialize through "slow pain" or "fast pain." In a slow-pain scenario, investors will clip low or non-existent coupons and dividends for decades and will no longer benefit from the tailwinds of ever-richer asset valuations. In a fast-pain scenario, we see mean reversion to historically more normal (higher) bond yields and (lower) risky-asset multiples, implying speedy capital losses followed by fairer returns thereafter.

As one casualty of the low-return world, *compound interest* may lose its status as the eighth wonder of the world. Compounding cannot help as much even over long horizons if we face persistent low returns.

How do we measure market's time-varying expectations of future returns? The most common approaches anchor on market yields. Figure 1.1 in the Introduction showed yield-based expected long-run real return estimates of US stocks and government bonds since 1900. The thick line in Figure 2.2 tracks their 60/40 combination. It is at all-time lows in 2021, below 2% and well below the 5% real return level typical of the 20th century. For portfolios with larger bond weightings (typical in Continental Europe and Japan), expected returns are even lower.

The dashed line shows for comparison the subsequent 10-year realized real return of the 60/40 portfolio. It illustrates that the yield-based estimate has some, albeit imperfect, ability to predict future returns (see Chapter 16). In recent decades, realized returns have exceeded expected returns partly thanks to the windfall gains, as both asset classes richened over time through their falling discount rates. The gap between the two lines has been exceptionally wide in recent years.

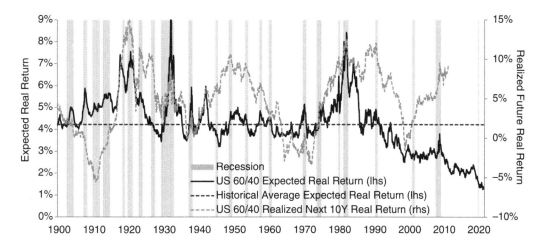

Figure 2.2   Expected and Realized Real Return of US 60/40 Stock/Bond Portfolio, Jan 1900–Sep 2021

Sources: AQR, Robert Shiller's website, Kozicki-Tinsley (2006), Federal Reserve Bank of Philadelphia, Blue Chip Economic Indicators, Consensus Economics, NBER. The 60/40 Expected Real Return is constructed from the stock and bond real yield series in Figure 1.1. The realized next 10-year real return for the 60/40 portfolio is based on the total returns of the S&P500 index and 10-year Treasuries, in excess of the realized inflation.

Recession periods are shaded. Clearly, recessions have become shorter and less frequent over time, giving a more benign macroeconomic backdrop.

There are many other ways to estimate expected returns. Some capital market assumption providers assume mean-reverting valuation changes over the forecast horizon, and make more bearish forecasts than shown here.

What about survey-based expected returns? Figure 2.3 shows the Survey of Professional Forecasters consensus predictions since 1992 of the next-decade average return for US equities and Treasury bills, as well as of the next-decade average inflation rate and 10-year Treasury yield. Notably, expected nominal equity returns halved from 10% to 5%, a larger drop than for expected bill returns (5% to 1.8%). Overall, all nominal and real return expectations were falling, which suggests that the decline in expected cash rates has been at the heart of the persistent richening of equities and other asset classes. Indeed, many measures of expected equity premium and term premium (over cash) do not show a similar downtrend over time.

We compare these economist forecasts later (in Figure 4.6) to the Graham-Harvey survey of Chief Financial Officers since 2000: Their next-decade equity return forecasts fall from 10% to 6% (but the equity-bond premium forecasts are relatively stable near 4%). Dahlquist-Ibert (2021) study a set of capital market assumptions providers since 2010 and find a mild decline in expected equity returns from above 6% to about 5%. They also find that these long-term forecasts exhibit a contrarian tendency, in contrast to Greenwood-Shleifer (2014) findings of extrapolative expectations (whose sample focuses on short-term forecasts by retail investors rather than professional forecasters).

Horizon matters: The yield-based approach seems most relevant for a ten-year horizon, while for longer horizons, starting yields and valuations matter less, whereas for shorter horizons, momentum and macro forces can be important.

Abnormally low cash rates today mean that while expected total returns are historically low, the expected excess returns of risky assets over cash may not be particularly low. Indeed, they are above average in many countries because expected nominal cash rates appear near zero or negative for several years out and the real cash rate is −1% to −2%. If the situation normalizes, say, by 2030, we may see again zero or mildly positive expected real cash rates and 2–3% inflation,

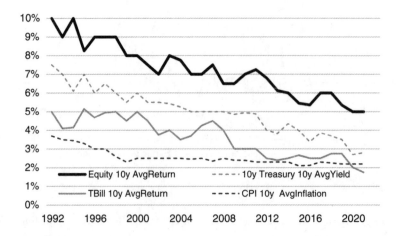

Figure 2.3 Falling Next-Decade Expectations on Everything, 1992–2021

Source: Data from Survey of Professional Forecasters, published by the Federal Reserve Bank of Philadelphia. Notes: Consensus forecasts of next-decade average annual inflation, average annual stock market and Treasury bill returns, and average 10-year Treasury yields over the coming decade.

in which case the same expected total return on equities would imply about 2% lower expected equity premium over cash.

2.3. How Low Are "Riskless" Long-term Yields from a Historical Perspective?

I start with the longest historical view in this book. We have better historical evidence on long-dated bond yields than cash yields, though information on maturity and credit quality is sparse before the 20th century. Homer-Sylla (2006) is the classic source on distant histories, but recent work by Schmelzing (2020) is worth displaying here. Figure 2.4 shows that nominal and real yields fell from double digits in the Middle Ages to near 3% around 1900. The inflation surprises especially in the 1970s brought nominal rates back to double digits before the extraordinary bond bull market of 1980 to 2020.[4]

Classic economic theory states that equilibrium real yields and real growth should be similar. Long-run empirical evidence seems nearly the opposite! I don't show here growth numbers but, roughly speaking, real economic growth was 0.0–0.1% per year for centuries before the Industrial Revolution, while the past two centuries have seen about 2% real annual growth in advanced economies. Thus, fast-growing centuries occurred amidst much lower real yields (and as one reconciling feature, more abundant capital).[5]

Figure 2.4 also shows that after centuries of little net inflation, the 20th century brought with it more persistent price rises, first near the two world wars. Later the Great Inflation in the 1970s was a scary early experience of the fiat money world, albeit mainly caused by spiking oil prices. The Great Moderation era since 1982 was characterized by lower macroeconomic volatility, disinflation, and global convergence toward 2% inflation. Inflation expectations also became less sensitive to labor market conditions and short-term inflation. It remains debated how much these benign developments reflected greater central bank independence and credibility (gravitational pull to their targets) versus mere luck.[6]

The Global Financial Crisis triggered widespread inflation concerns, given all the stimulus, yet the 2010s turned out to be a very disinflationary decade. A slow recovery led to worries of secular stagnation (growing debt and easier monetary policies were needed to sustain even moderate economic growth) and of "global Japanification" (Japan led the world by a couple of decades in demographics, excess savings, and its central bank's inability to generate inflation despite trying hard).

---

[4]Because equity markets were not yet developed, these bond yields may be our best estimates of return on capital until the 19th century. Several qualifiers are in order: These yields overstate expected and realized returns because default risk reduced income. It was reasonable to expect some default losses (not well quantified even ex post before the mid-1800s). On the other hand, capital was scarce, and only relatively creditworthy borrowers had access to it. The net impact on yields and returns is unclear.

[5]This evidence also contradicts Piketty's (2013) claim that the rate of interest (or broader investment return) always exceeds the rate of economic growth, "R-G." I will bypass this topic because we could have endless debates about which interest rate and which growth rate are relevant.

[6]This benign picture can be challenged. Let us not forget that we have seen three major recessions and several financial crises since 2000. And there is continued concern that central banks may have been *too* helpful, at least toward financial investors. The so-called Fed Put and its cousins may have boosted moral hazard and caused problems that we will have to pay down the road. Paraphrasing Hemingway, some problems arise first gradually, then suddenly.

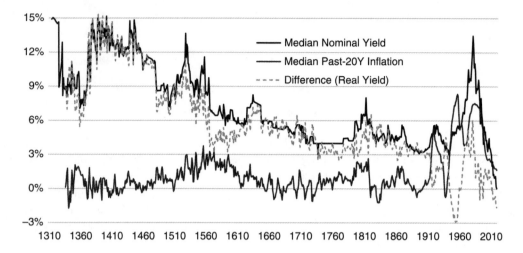

Figure 2.4 Falling Yields Over Centuries: Eight-Country Evidence Since 1300s
Source: Data from Paul Schmelzing's website. Notes: I take Schmelzing (2020) source data but add 2019–20, and I use past 20-year average inflation to proxy for expected inflation. I use eight-country medians to capture the global rates. (Medians are more resistant than means to outliers like French 50% yields amid Napoleonic wars or the 1900s hyperinflations.) The eight countries and starting years are Italy (1314), UK (1314), Germany (1326), France (1387), Spain (1400), Netherlands (1400), USA (1786), and Japan (1870). Among the six European states, only France existed when the time series began, so the loans in the early sample were to some rulers, princes, or cities. As capital markets evolved over time, loans were replaced by tradeable bonds, and for the past century, the dataset covers 10-year government bonds. Earlier, loan/bond maturity and credit quality varied over time and across countries.

After the Covid-19 crisis, even larger monetary and fiscal stimulus than seen after 2008 has revived inflation concerns. As long as economies are weakened by the virus and the lockdown effects or by precautionary saving, inflation pressures should be muted. But as economies normalize, some of the trends that kept a lid on inflation in the 2010s may give it an extra push in the 2020s (retreat from globalization, efficient supply management replaced by quest for buffers, political backlash to market capitalism and quest for redistribution, central bankers' greater openness to more inflation, and even demographics as the number of workers per retirees is declining). Eventually, all the stimulus and the debt will have to be repaid, while greater focus on the environment will add its own costs. I am not in the prediction business, but I agree that the odds of an upward surprise in inflation in the 2020s are meaningful.[7]

Focusing on US post-war data, nominal Treasury yields have exceeded inflation expectations, except for the last decade.[8] The required real yield was especially high in the 1980s, sometimes called "the bondholders' revenge" after decades of losses. Even after the decline in inflation

---

[7]Jorda-Singh-Taylor (2020) studies the long-run after-effects of previous pandemics and found lower real interest rates and mildly higher real wages. None of the earlier pandemics triggered as strong policy response as Covid-19, though.

[8]The negative global real bond yield seen in Figure 2.4 in the mid-1900s reflects the temporary high post-WWII inflations in several countries. Using more forward-looking statistical or survey-based measures of inflation expectations in the US, the 10-year Treasury yield only matched expected inflation in the late 1940s when Treasury yields were capped. Other studies that use last year's realized inflation find more episodes of negative real Treasury yields. However, this tended to happen after inflation surprises (say, in the 1970s) when survey-based inflation forecasts remained lower.

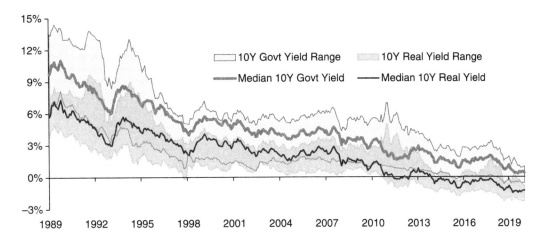

Figure 2.5 Global Bond Yield Decline and Convergence, 1990-2020
Sources: Bloomberg, Blue Chip Economic Indicators, Consensus Economics. Notes: Medians and max-min ranges of eight countries' 10-year government bond yields and real yields based on economist consensus forecasts of next-decade average inflation. Countries include the US, Canada, Australia, Japan, Germany, France, Italy, and the UK.

expectations ended in the early 2000s, real bond yields kept falling, and turned negative in the 2010s. As we will see in Chapter 4, real bond yields can be split into expected real cash rates and required bond risk premia. Both were clearly positive in the 1980s and both fell to zero and even negative levels in the 2000s.

Falling nominal and real yields are a global phenomenon; see Figure 2.5 where I zoom to the recent history. Indeed, many advanced countries have negative short rates and bond yields. Japan was early with near-zero bond yields, but several European countries have overtaken Japan, with many trillions (trn) of euros worth of debt earning mildly negative nominal yields.[9]

Many forces have contributed to the decline in real bond yields. The most relevant for this book is an explanation focusing on the imbalance between savings supply and investment demand. The "saving glut" hypothesis initially emphasized how trade surpluses and reserve accumulation in China and other emerging economies have boosted the global saving propensity and thus put downward pressure on real yields. Another source of saving glut is related to demographics and a growing need for pension savings in an ageing society.[10] Indeed, the low expected return challenge may raise saving rates if pension savers have a certain target for the retirement nest egg and they realize that juicy market returns will no longer do the work for them. The irony is that unattractive expected returns on financial investments may prompt more saving.

---

[9]It was generally believed that nominal yields cannot go negative as savers could just "put their cash under the mattress." So far, negative yields are seldom charged directly to retail savers, thereby limiting cash hoarding. If economic activity were to weaken further, central banks may consider new ways of pushing rates even more negative in a sustainable way. Apart from central bank policies, regulatory pressures such as liability matching or solvency capital requirements, and bonds' role as safe-haven negative-beta assets, can push private institutions to hold bonds even at negative yields.

[10]Both the reserve accumulation (e.g. Bernanke (2005)) and pension saving motives (e.g. Kopecky-Taylor (2020)) favor conservative assets like bonds (especially for the older pension savers and retirees), which points to low safe-asset yields but not to compressed risk premia. A third source of saving glut has recently been identified by Mian-Straub-Sufi (2020), that of the rich ("the 1%"). This last group is likely to save more and to favor riskier investments. It seems like a fruitful area of research to empirically compare the magnitudes and impacts of these different sources of excess savings.

Taking a societal perspective, the low expected return world is a way to make savers partici-pate in the burden-sharing post-GFC and now post-Covid. Saver-investors have benefited from richening asset valuations, but the low rates may eventually help (typically younger) borrowers more than savers. The ultimate pain is ahead for savers if future inflation eats up the windfall gains and the real value of their savings, while policymakers may keep short rates low for long in the spirit of economy-supporting financial repression seen after WWII (e.g. yield curve control or other capping of bond yields even as inflation rises).

2.4. Decadal Perspective on Investment Returns

I finish this chapter by complementing the forward-looking low expected return evidence with some backward-looking evidence, especially on the decade since my first book.

The conventional wisdom on decadal return patterns is contrarian: a bullish decade follows a bearish one, and so on. Table 2.1 shows that there is something to this notion: Most earlier decades of double-digit (excess-of-cash) returns for the S&P500 (the roaring 20s, 50s, 90s) were followed by disappointing decades. The best decade (50s) was followed by a double dip – first the lukewarm 60s, then the stagflationary 70s. Conversely, the three decades with the lowest excess returns (the bearish 30s, 70s, 2000s) were followed by strong decades. Yet, mean-reverting forces are not too strong as there was a strong successive pair in the 40s–50s and a weak one in the 60s–70s. And when we look at inflationary trends in bond and commodity performance, we see longer cycles: disinflationary 20s–30s, inflationary 60s–70s, disinflationary 80s–90s and 2010s. Only the 1940s and the 2000s saw positive excess returns for both bonds and commodities.

Looking at the 2010s from the century perspective, it is clear first that it was a disinflation-ary decade (bond rewards were well above average despite low starting yields, while commodity indices earned negative returns). The 2010s was also a benign decade for risky assets – especially for US large-cap stocks and even more for tech stocks. Virtually any kind of diversification away from the US 60/40 hurt performance: non-US stocks including emerging markets, hedge funds, alternative risk premia – all unhelpful in the 2010s. Yet, Table 2.1 shows that this is not something you should expect on every decade and perhaps least of all after a decade of a US large-tech–led bull market. The 2020s may turn out very differently. Time will tell if we are in for a Covid-scarred decade, another roaring 20s, or inflationary 70s, or something new.

Easy central bank policies (both low rates and quantitative easing) supported continued richening of already rich bonds, stocks, and all risky assets – whether liquid or illiquid. "The Fed put" became available to an increasingly broad range of assets whenever markets looked shaky, as the alternative of fast pain was too unbearable for policymakers. This also meant that any macro trends were cut short, which hurt trend-followers and macro traders. Meanwhile, reaching for yield worked better beyond the traditional liquid asset universe as investors shifted to riskier and less liquid assets (to achieve their return targets when traditional markets were now offering less).

Another major development has been the increasing global dominance of tech-oriented superstar platform companies. These include FAMAG (Facebook, Apple, Microsoft, Amazon, Google i.e. Alphabet) – the acronym covering the five largest US firms.[11] Investors believe(d) in the ever greater concentration of monopolistic profits among these disruptive firms, thanks

---

[11]Each FAMAG firm has a market capitalization in excess of $1trn, some even exceeding $2trn, in summer 2021. They count as five of the world's six largest companies, together with the Saudi Aramco (https://companiesmarketcap.com).

Table 2.1 Decadal Perspective of Realized Asset Class Returns (Geometric Mean Premia), 1921–2020

	S&P500	NASDAQ	Non-US Dev Equity	Emerging Equity	Global Equity	US Tsy10	Global Govt	Commodity	Real Estate	Hedge Funds	Cash
1920s	10.3%				5.5%	3.0%	1.8%	-6.3%			3.6%
1930s	1.4%				3.9%	3.5%	2.5%	-1.4%			0.4%
1940s	12.8%				13.4%	1.4%	1.0%	23.0%			0.6%
1950s	13.9%				16.2%	-0.5%	-0.1%	1.0%			2.3%
1960s	3.5%				2.1%	-1.4%	-0.6%	2.8%			4.6%
1970s	1.2%	8.2%	5.2%		1.7%	-2.7%	-1.6%	21.2%	7.1%		7.2%
1980s	4.5%	4.5%	7.0%		6.6%	2.3%	3.0%	-2.1%	1.2%		9.4%
1990s	12.4%	22.8%	3.2%	3.2%	8.8%	3.2%	5.3%	-0.8%	5.1%	9.6%	5.1%
2000s	-1.0%	-2.9%	1.1%	13.5%	-1.5%	4.0%	3.9%	7.3%	6.7%	3.2%	2.4%
2010s	13.2%	18.6%	4.9%	3.0%	9.8%	3.6%	3.6%	-4.1%	8.3%	3.1%	0.6%

Sources: AQR, Bloomberg. Notes: Compound average *excess returns over cash* for several asset classes. S&P500, NASDAQ and Tsy10 are US equity and bond indices. Developed non-US and emerging equities are unhedged MSCI indices in dollar terms. Global equities and government bonds are GDP–weighted averages of currency-hedged country index returns (AQR). Commodities are equal-weighted futures contracts (AQR). Real Estate averages US NCREIF and NAREIT equity indices and splices in housing returns in the 1970s. Hedge Funds averages HFR fund-weighted index and fund-of-funds index. The last column shows cash return for approximating total returns. Decades are from 1-to-0 (e.g. 1921–1930) to end with 2020.

to network effects, R&D edge, increasing returns to scale, and winner–takes-all outcomes. The presumption is that the dominating disrupters will not themselves be disrupted either by upstart competitors (which they can buy) or by policymakers/regulators (which they can influence with their vast cash pools and increasing political power). The shift from a physical world to a digital/virtual world was accelerated by Covid-19 and lockdowns, further aiding these companies.

Beyond the general asset richening, apart from inflationary assets, and growth/tech stock outperformance, the 2010s was characterized by the rise of ESG investing and private assets. In a humble discretionary view, I predict that the general asset richening, disinflationary trend, and growth stock outperformance will reverse in the 2020s, while the rise of ESG seems like the most certain trend to continue. Let us see in 2030 how I fared with this call.

Chapter 3

Major Investor Types and Their Responses to This Challenge

- Defined benefit pensions, individual pension savers, and university endowments are presented as three broad investor types facing the low-return challenge.
- Each investor type saves to meet some future liability or a spending plan. Beyond this common goal, there are many differences.
- Abundant market returns have allowed these savers to reach their goals with smaller contributions. This will change in a low-return world, for example, the private saver may need to double her saving rate. The challenge has already bitten for defined-benefit plans whose liabilities are marked to market.
- Historical overview of institutional asset allocations highlights decades-long shifts from bonds to equities and to alternative assets. Low expected returns have accentuated these trends (although some institutions have taken a more conservative stance).
- Reach-for-yield investing amid low rates has many historical precedents. It is understandable but hardly riskless.

This chapter gives institutional and historical context. Before explaining how the low expected return challenge hurts various investor types and how these investors are responding to this challenge, I take some steps back. I describe major investor types to help understand their typical investment approach. Historical perspective on their evolving asset class allocations provides context for their current responses.

3.1. Three Broad Investor Types

I will focus on three broad investor types as stylized examples, without going into details which vary within and across countries:

- Defined-benefit (DB) pension plan
- Individual pension saver in a defined contribution (DC) pension plan, such as 401k
- University endowment (as an example of wealth pools without explicit liabilities)

What Is Each Investor's Goal?

There are major differences between these stylized investors, but also major commonalities. In all cases, investors are saving today (delaying current spending) and investing for a cause: to eventually spend the money. The function is to shift cash flows over time. Pension savers try to efficiently fund their post-retirement consumption with some blend of their savings and the returns on those savings. At the individual level, it is a matter of spreading earnings from 30–40 working years to cover perhaps as many years of retirement spending.

All these asset pools exist to pay some kind of liability. For a DB pension plan, the liability is explicit and legally binding. For the individual DC saver, the liability takes the form of a stream of planned consumption. For an endowment, it is a stream of planned spending on diverse expenditures. These future plans may not be easily measured, they may not be legally binding, and they may be aspirational rather than the minimum level needed. Still, such spending needs have the economic characteristics of a liability.[1]

Basic Descriptions

In a DB plan, a sponsor – a public entity or a private company – sets up a retirement plan for its employees. The plan promises defined retirement benefits to the participating employees according to some formula (often tied to the salary in the final working years and the number of working years). The investment risk and longevity risk rest with the plan sponsor which may need to make additional contributions if initial contributions and investment returns result in underfunding.

- I need to provide some terminology on pension fund balance sheet: The market value of pension plan *assets* reflects the cumulative contributions and the investment returns earned on them (minus benefits paid out). The present value of projected plan *liabilities* reflects both accumulated benefit obligations and the impact of projected wage growth, as well as the discount rate used. The difference between the market value of plan assets and the present value of plan liabilities is the plan surplus or deficit (A-L). The corresponding ratio of the value of assets over liabilities is called the funding ratio (FR = A/L). When assets exceed / equal / lag liabilities in value (i.e. FR $>/=/<$ 100), the plan is described as overfunded / fully funded / underfunded.

---

[1]Larry Siegel has admirably described these commonalities in several papers. We co-authored in Ilmanen-Kabiller-Siegel-Sullivan (2017), but I might rather recommend Sexauer-Siegel (2013) and Podkaminer-Tollette-Siegel (2020).

- Many US corporate sponsors decided over time that their DB plans were too costly or risky for the firm, shifted toward DC plans, and thereby passed the investment and longevity risks to their employees. The share of private DB plan assets fell in a few decades from 76% to 32%. Meanwhile, many public sponsors have retained the appetite to underwrite DB plans, despite persistent underfunding challenges. One reason for this difference is accounting treatment which has made corporate DB plans discount their liabilities at market-based bond yields, while public DB plans can discount their liabilities at the expected return on assets. The higher and smoother discount rate for public plans makes their FR look less bad.

The individual pension saver in a DC plan gets some help from the sponsor/employer – the set-up of saving/investment plan, with hopefully a manageable number of investment options, and perhaps employer matches to the employee contributions. But, as noted, the investment and longevity risks belong to the employee, as does the crucial decision how much to save.

- DC savers are not generally as well off as DB plan participants, in part due to insufficient saving. The common message to DC savers is: Save more, work longer, invest smarter.
- Even bigger challenges lie in the post-retirement phase, where DC plans often lack one of DB plans' big draws, a guaranteed lifetime income. Investors show puzzlingly little interest in annuities, even though real annuities are the theoretically ideal riskless asset.

An endowment fund is a wealth pool donated over time to an educational entity or other nonprofit organization to help it cover its expenditures. The best-known endowment funds belong to large US universities, such as Harvard and Yale.

- Unlike pension plans, there are no binding liabilities, and the endowment may retain its capital in perpetuity while only spending the returns on it.
- A typical spending rule involves withdrawing each year 5% of the three-year moving average value of the endowment. Such a spending rule smooths the university spending somewhat from mark-to-market fluctuations but also protects the real value of the endowment capital as long as the real compound returns don't fall sustainably below 5%.

I drill now a bit deeper into the saving/contribution decision, investment decision, and typical response to changing conditions for each investor type. Then I look beyond these stereotypes.

How Much to Save/Contribute – and Who Decides?

The DB pensions may be designed to be fully pre-funded, not funded (pay-as-you-go), or partially funded. Even when pensions are intended to be pre-funded, sponsors have some flexibility on their contributions. The actual DB plan history is a story of generous pension promises and insufficient pension contributions, resulting in persistent underfunding (also reflecting increased longevity and unfavorable market outcomes).

The DB set-up may make individual pension savers think that the modest savings required from them, as little as a single-digit share of salary, are sufficient to fund their retirement security. Either the employer or the markets or a fairy godmother takes care of the rest. The fuzziness could make DB savers feel they have earned what is due to them, while bearing virtually no risk.

The reality is harsher for the DC saver, but the math is clearer. *You* are responsible for the amounts saved (though you may benefit from matching employer contributions), and you bear risk for the investment returns. We'll discuss the required savings rates later, but these are not in single digits, especially not in our world of low expected returns.

- Auto-enrollment and auto-escalation may nudge you to save more, while reasonable default choices (e.g. target-date funds) may help you in investment decisions.
- Decisions and risks belong to you, and market rollercoasters can provoke investment behavior that harms long-run results.
- You will not know at retirement whether you have saved enough or how much you can afford to consume. The longer you live, the more likely you are to outlive your pension savings.
- If your savings and the investment returns on them turn out to be insufficient, and it is too late to work more, you need to adapt and make do with a lower standard of living. Or you can hope to get support from family or elsewhere, echoing a DB plan's hope to get support from the state (pension insurance or a bailout) if the sponsor contributions do not suffice.

Which Investment Problem to Solve?

So investors save to meet some future spending goals. The old lifecycle hypothesis on consumption implies saving when income is high (peak working years) and dissaving when it is low (retirement). Some theories of lifecycle investing stress that also risk-taking patterns should vary with age. In particular, target-date funds apply the heuristic that investor risk appetite declines with age. They therefore follow an equity/bond glide path which shifts from roughly 90% equity weight in the individual DC saver's early working years to near 50% equity weight in the final working years.

Figure 3.1 gives an example of a stylized "through" (as opposed to "to") glide path, which continues to invest in equities beyond the retirement date but at declining weights until some conservative equity allocation level (here 30%) is reached.

One justification for this downward-sloping glide path is that the lifecycle asset allocation decision should include human capital which is arguably bond-like for many people outside financial careers. Thus, young investors with abundant human capital already have large bond-like allocations in their total portfolio and should focus investable holdings in equities, while old investors with less remaining bond-like human capital should hold more bonds. Another reason

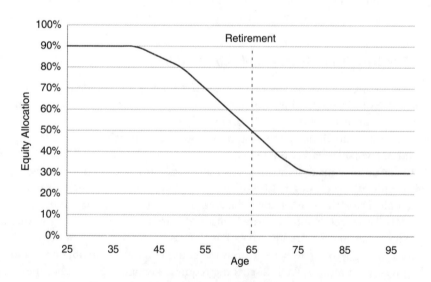

Figure 3.1   Equity Allocation in a Stylized Glide Path for a Typical Target Date Fund

is that young savers have greater flexibility to adjust the amount they work if they get a bad draw, which allows them to take more investment risk than near-retirees.[2]

Some institutions choose to invest in an asset that matches the liability, say a bond with a similar duration, to reduce the risk in asset-liability mismatch. Others prefer to invest in a riskier asset with a higher expected return, say equities, hoping that they need to save/contribute less to reach the liability or spending goal. Yet other institutions change their behavior over time: Many corporate DB plans were equity-oriented in the 1990s but shifted to bond orientation by the 2010s.

What determines which approach the investor takes? Why does one institution ignore liabilities and apply constrained mean-variance optimization on asset allocation, or in extreme simply maximize expected asset returns? Conversely, why does another institution focus on liabilities and apply constrained A-L *surplus* optimization, or in extreme simply match assets with liabilities (i.e. minimize the surplus volatility)?

There are many answers, the first being that the more risk tolerant sponsors choose the former, the more risk averse the latter. Moreover, when the liability is very explicit and binding, a set of fixed payments on a future date, it is likely to lead to liability-driven or surplus-oriented investing. The present value of liabilities also matters: the lower the discount rate that is applied on liabilities, the higher the present value of liabilities and the lower the surplus (A-L) and the funding ratio (A/L). Thus, surplus-oriented investing is more likely if accounting rules use market-yield-based discount rates (corporate DB plans) of 4% or less, rather than expected asset returns (public pension plans) of 7–8%; and likewise, if laws or regulations make the liabilities materially consequential for the sponsor (more so for corporate DB plans for whom low funding ratios imply punitive pension insurance charges).

In reality, many institutions make discretionary decisions and care about both the asset-only perspective and asset-liability perspective, and perhaps even about peer comparisons. Then there are three different risk measures that are relevant – total portfolio volatility, tracking error versus the liability (i.e. surplus volatility), and tracking error versus typical peer portfolios. The relative weights of these perspectives are rarely specified, but implicitly some priority choices are made.

How to Respond to Changing Conditions?

Asset allocation may evolve in a planned fashion with investor characteristics, such as funding ratio (as a proxy for wealth) or age (as a proxy for risk aversion). Somewhat confusingly, the DB plans and the DC saver use the term "glide path" in different meanings. Figure 3.1 showed the DC saver's age-dependent equity allocation, while Figure 3.2 focuses on a DB plan's equity

---

[2]See Bodie-Merton-Samuelson (1992) or Kritzman (2000) on how human capital effects can cause age-dependent risk aversion and thus overturn the classic Robert Merton result that investor risk aversion is constant over time. The literature offers many other glide path shapes. For example, Ayres-Nalebuff (2010) argues for even more downward-sloping glide path of equity-bond weights; they recommend that young people lever up equity exposures when their pension savings are still tiny, to have a more balanced total exposure to equity markets over time. (This is countered by general dislike of leverage as well as concern that a bad early experience may put off young investors from the whole idea of pension saving.) Others go the other way and favor an upward-sloping glide path to increase equity weight near retirement when the pension saving pot is largest; this has historically led to high average returns thanks to harvesting more equity premium (This is countered by the fact that it would make investors most vulnerable to sequencing risk – bad market outcome when the savings pot is large – which could lead to bad choices, such as when many near-retirees sold out their equity portfolios during the 2008–9 bear market.) Yet other ideas involve considerations beyond age, either reducing risk if benign market moves have helped investors reach their pension savings target earlier than expected or when some floor level of pension income is threatened. Broader analyses include social security, bequest motive, and so on.

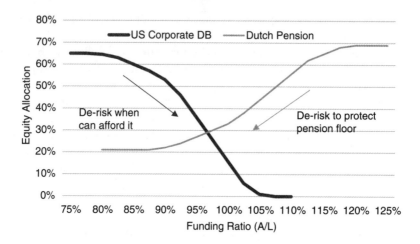

Figure 3.2   Stylized DB Pension Glide Paths: Starting from a Good Place and a Worse Place

allocation as a function of its funding ratio. It also highlights surprisingly different real-world glide paths across countries.

The US corporate DB plans have increasingly adopted a glide path approach where they shift their equity-bond allocations down when their asset/liability funding ratio improves from, say, 80% toward 100%. This may be counterintuitive and is indeed opposite to the textbook case or the behavior of Danish and Dutch pension funds. In these latter cases, DB plans start from overfunded levels (A/L FR > 100%) but must reduce their equity allocations if their funding ratio threatens to fall below 100%. They need to become dynamically more risk averse to ensure that some (subsistence) level of assets to cover liabilities is maintained.

Many US DB plans start from the bad place of meaningful underfunding (A/L FR << 100%), with limited sponsor ability to cover it with extra contributions. These plans cannot afford *not* to take risk, given the need to climb out of the hole, while large equity allocations increase the risk that they will fall into a deeper hole (more severe underfunding).[3] The DB glide path refers to pre-specified plans to de-risk if the funding ratio improves, say, starting from 65% equity allocation at 80% FR, shifting from equities to 50% bonds at 90% FR, and to no equities near full funding (100% FR).[4]

What if unexpected bad news happens? If the market returns disappoint and leave asset values lower than expected, or if the liability values turn out higher (due to a lower discount rate or higher expected longevity), the DB sponsor and the DC saver need to make up the difference. This requires further contributions from the DB sponsor and higher saving or longer working

---

[3]In an old joke, a big-city motorist is lost in the Irish countryside and asks a local farmer how to get to a big city. The farmer tries to give him directions, then gives up and says, "If I wanted to get there, I wouldn't start from here." Likewise, underfunded US DB plans only have bad choices, while the Dutch ones could have more rational choices.

[4]Such delayed de-risking echoes the young St. Augustine's prayer quoted in Chapter 1. Andonov-Bauer-Cremers (2017) and Broeders-Jansen (2021) present contrasting evidence of US public pension plan and Dutch pension plan behavior, traced back to their different regulations and the discount rate being based on the expected return on assets versus market yields. Underfunded public pension plans in the US are more likely to take more risk, while in Holland we see the opposite pattern. Leibowitz-Ilmanen (2016) covers different types of discount rates and how they influence funding ratios.

from the DC saver. Likewise, the endowment donors need to be even more generous. If this is not possible, the DB sponsor may need pension insurance or bailout support, while the DC saver and the endowment need to adjust their spending levels down.

Beyond the Three Stylized Investor Types

There are major differences within each of the three groups discussed previously. More importantly, there are other investors beyond our stylized examples. Loosely speaking, they fit into one group or a blend.

Insurance companies have clear liabilities. They are more uncertain than pension liabilities but can often be statistically estimated with high confidence. Insurers are heavily regulated to ensure they can cover insured payments, so many insurer types must hold conservative bond-oriented portfolios.

Individuals may save for other goals than pension, perhaps for a house or to send kids to college. In all cases, savers face trade-offs between safety, liquidity, and return.

There are other wealth pools besides endowments which lack explicit liabilities and thus act mainly like assets-only investors. Foundations have a similar nonprofit nature as endowments, but their goal is not tied to financing an entity. Another distinction is that a foundation is often established with a pot of money and no further funds may be added to it, whereas endowments can fundraise on an ongoing basis (arguably giving them a longer horizon). A family office is a little more mercenary; the goal is not to give the money away but to keep it in the family and grow it for the benefit of future generations, or at least spend it in a controlled fashion.

A sovereign wealth fund is often thought as a pension fund but is perhaps better viewed as a family office, albeit for a very large family; it is supposed to take care of national wealth for the benefit of future generations. Among my three stylized investor types, sovereign wealth funds are closest to endowments.

The boundaries between these groups can be fuzzy. Many public DB plans invest more like an endowment than a liability-oriented corporate DB plan. Likewise, rich households resemble endowments more than pension savers. They hold a pool of wealth, and binding liabilities do not drive their investment behavior.

3.2. History of Institutional Asset Allocation

Pre-WWII History[5]

Individual saving and investing have taken place for thousands of years, and the idea of diversification was recognized already in the Bible (Ecclesiastes 11:2) and the Talmud, but delegated and pooled investing through institutions has a much shorter history.

In the 1600s and 1700s, financial innovations like the joint stock company, the mutual fund, and the insurance company were developed in Holland and Great Britain to make risk pooling and diversification easier for wealthy individuals. Life insurance companies were the dominant institutional investors in Britain in the 1800s and held this status beyond WWII. Pension

---

[5]I was a history buff even before I became interested in investing. It has been a guilty pleasure to combine both interests, so I will provide a bit more historical context here than is strictly needed. For those interested in this intersection, I warmly recommend three books written in recent years: Will Goetzmann's (2016) *Money Changes Everything*, Philip Coggan's (2020) *More*, and Bill Bernstein's (2021) *The Delusions of Crowds*.

companies came later: The first US corporate pension plan was by American Express in 1875, while Bismarck's Germany led the way with national old-age pensions in 1889.

I focus here on the US and UK experiences. The major growth of pension companies is a post-WWII phenomenon. Individuals used to hold more wealth than institutions. Bonds, land, and private enterprises were bigger sources of wealth than public equities. Likewise, early institutional investing was very conservative, focusing on bond investments – the main questions were which bond sectors and how illiquid.[6]

Individual investing also dominated equity holdings and was primarily direct until the 1920s when mutual funds (or unit trusts in Britain) grew popular. Both individual and institutional investors on either side of the Atlantic began to tentatively increase their equity holdings during the roaring 1920s, encouraged by Edgar Lawrence Smith's (1924) book *Common Stocks as Long Term Investments*, with its evidence of equities' outperformance over more than half a century. One British investor, John Maynard Keynes (yes, the famous economist), took the lead in running the King's College Cambridge endowment with exceptional 57–75% equity allocations in 1920s–30s. Keynes also chaired a life insurance office whose equity allocations at 25% exceeded those of its peers.

Post-WWII History

The post-WWII asset allocation among US and UK institutional investors has been dominated by two big trends: first, shifting from fixed income to equity-dominated portfolios and, later, raising the weight of illiquid alternatives. Both shifts were led by large endowments in the US. Other endowments and foundations, public and private pension plans, and UK life insurance companies followed suit. Australian and Canadian institutions soon took the same path, while Continental European and Japanese institutions followed much later (and often still have more bond-oriented portfolios). But before these trends, I highlight the growing importance of institutional investing.

Increasing Institutionalization of Investing

Figure 3.3 tracks ownership shares in the US equity market since 1945. The shift from direct retail investing in equities to delegated institutional asset management has been dramatic. Around 1950, more than 90% of US equities were directly held by households. By 2020, mutual funds (including ETFs) had overtaken households, with each having just over 30% ownership share. Foreign investors and pension funds each hold a further 12–15% of the market.

Households still hold most of US stocks but more through mutual funds and pension funds than directly. Likewise, the pension funds' ownership share in Figure 3.3 may underestimate their role as they hold some of their equities through mutual funds and ETFs. Demographic changes have made pension funds the dominant institutional investor, even if they often invest through other managers. These trends are global, as the shift from retail stock holdings to institutional holdings began in the US but is also happening in other countries. For example, UK households' direct equity ownership share has fallen to about 10%.[7]

---

[6]See Chambers-Dimson (2016) and Morecroft-Turnbull (2019).

[7]This book will not drill into the history of investment vehicles or financial services, either the ancestry (the first common stock Dutch East India Company in 1602, the important development of limited liability in the mid-1800s, or the recent growth of ETFs), let alone the prospects for fintech, DeFi, and blockchain. Chambers-Dimson (2016) and Goetzmann (2016) are excellent introductions to financial history.

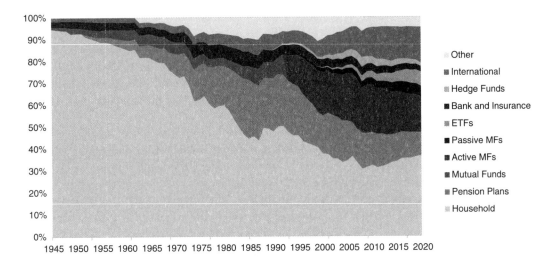

Figure 3.3   Evolving Equity Market Ownership Shares in the US, 1945–2020
Sources: Federal Flow of Funds, Z1/L223 report. Hedge fund share from HFR.

Figure 3.4   Evolving Asset Allocation for Large US Endowments, 1900–2017
Source: Data from Chambers-Dimson-Kaffe (2020). Notes: Equal-weighted average of twelve large endowments (Brown, Chicago, Columbia, Cornell, Dartmouth, Harvard, Johns Hopkins, MIT, Penn, Princeton, Stanford, Yale). The real estate weighting is boosted by one endowment's (Columbia's) large campus holdings in Manhattan. The weight series track broadly those of NACUBO's large endowments. Since the above hand-collected series ends in 2017, the NACUBO series has seen alternatives' weight grow further by 3% to 54% in 2020.

Shift from Bonds to Equities

Endowments were always relatively small but they were pioneers. Keynes's early role has already been noted. Figure 3.4 shows that, after WWII, the large US endowments raised their equity allocations to over 50% by the early 1950s.[8] US pension funds reached such levels only decades later, private plans earlier than public plans.

---

[8]See Chambers-Dimson-Kaffe (2020). This article contains a great review of US endowment investing practices since WWII, while the authors have earlier focused on Keynes's pioneering role in Chambers-Dimson (2015).

British pension funds grew large (aided by major tax benefits) and more equity-oriented (aided by revised actuarial thinking and legislative restrictions) even before their US peers. Ross Goobey is considered the early father of "the cult of equity." He headed Imperial Tobacco's pension fund for decades and boosted the equity allocation from 28% in 1953 to 96% in 1961. Other UK pension funds gradually followed Goobey's call, and equity allocations rose through the rest of the century (to 60–80% peak in the 1990s, depending on the source), before turning down with liability-driven investing.

Among US investors, growing equity allocations were motivated by the strong equity and weak bond performance after WWII. The shadows of the Great Depression and nearly 90% market drawdown receded from memories, while equities' historical edge was found again in the Fisher-Lorie (1964) analysis based on the new CRSP database.

Revised thinking played an equally important role. The fiduciary duty of endowment and pension trustees in the Prudent Man Rule had long been interpreted to require conservative single investments with little risk of loss. The novel Modern Portfolio Theory emphasized diversification as the primary risk management approach. Two influential reports commissioned by the Ford Foundation in the late 1960s helped change the institutional investing landscape. They encouraged equity-oriented investing as well as delegating asset management to specialized external managers. They also helped a more diversification-oriented reinterpretation of the Prudent Man Rule to be coded in both US endowment and pension legislation in the early 1970s.

The canonical 60/40 portfolio: I have tried to uncover the origins of the 60/40 portfolio with the help of many senior experts (Elroy Dimson, Charley Ellis, Don Ezra, Marty Leibowitz), and by now feel confident to answer "unclear." Here is the best I can offer.

As shown earlier, some pioneering institutions held a 60/40 portfolio already in the 1960s. Typical US private DB plan equity weights reached the 60% by the early 1970s. However, they fell below 50% during the 1973–74 bear market and regained 60% only in the 1990s. US public pensions long had trivial equity allocations (3% in 1959 and 14% in 1969), but when legal restrictions were lifted they gradually caught up and their equity weights exceeded 50% in the 1990s.[9]

A literature review reveals an early mention in Innocenti (1969), but 60/40 may have really become the conventional wisdom in the 1990s, and even then only in Anglo-American countries. The circularity of peer-chasing may have helped 60/40 cement its position as a natural anchor for institutional investing, but there may be a deeper reason. Marty Leibowitz has suggested that 60/40 offers a naturally acceptable risk/reward trade-off for many investors (9% average return and 9% volatility since WWII, with few historical drawdowns exceeding 20%).

The Rise of Illiquid Alternatives

The second major institutional asset allocation trend in our lifetime is the shift toward illiquid alternative assets. One can debate whether a traditional asset like real estate should count as an alternative but it surely is illiquid. And one can debate whether hedge funds or gold are illiquid or an asset class. But I count them in, together with private equity (buyouts and venture capital),

---

[9]See Clowes (2000), Federal Flow of Funds (Table L118), and Pensions and Investments surveys in Figure 3.5 in this chapter.

private credit, infrastructure, natural resources (farmland, oil and gas, timber, commodity futures), and a wide menu of even more esoteric investments (art, wine, cat bonds, music royalties, litigation finance, and so on). Among these, real estate, private equity, and hedge funds have grown into multi-trillion dollar asset classes.

As noted, the 1970s legislation allowed endowments to take more risk and not just larger equity allocations. Again, endowments led the way to alternatives. The approach has been dubbed the Endowment Model or the Yale Model, as it was pioneered by David Swensen's Yale Endowment since the mid-1980s and popularized through his books in the 2000s.

Among endowments, the largest ones were not only early but they seem to have been the most successful performance-wise, and they have continued to push to ever-higher alternatives allocations. While overall endowment allocations to alternatives rose from 5% in the early 1990s to nearly 30% recently, large endowments allocate twice as much. Figure 3.4 shows that the alternatives allocation for large endowments has exceeded 50% since the late 2000s (even excluding real estate). The largest subgroup allocations are near 20% for hedge funds and other liquid alts, 15% for private equity buyouts, and 10% for venture capital. Yale's alternatives allocation has even approached 80%. While Yale focuses almost exclusively on external managers, some Canadian pension plans have led the way in less costly internal management.

Many pension plans have followed endowments to large alternatives allocations, both in the US and other English-speaking countries. Alternatives allocations for global pension funds rose between 1995 and 2020 from 5% to 26% at the expense of all traditional asset classes.[10]

Other Trends

Beyond these big two, several smaller trends have emerged in institutional asset allocation:

Lower home bias: Globalization of equity and bond portfolios began latest in the 1980s, but still in the early 1990s, most institutions apparently held at least 90% of their portfolios in domestic assets. Since then, home bias has declined and country weights have converged toward global cap-weights, but only gradually.[11] Admittedly, international diversification inevitably leads to second-guessing after a decade when domestic assets outperformed (as we have seen with US investors after the 2010s).

Bifurcation: The 60/40 portfolio concept has become somewhat outdated by the growth of alternative allocations. Yet, there may be some wisdom of the crowds in the 60/40 portfolio as it has proven to be a quite challenging benchmark to beat.

Since 2000, some institutions – public DB plans, endowments, many international investors – kept raising their equity allocations or at least equity-cum-alternatives allocations, while others – corporate DB plans and insurance companies – shifted toward bond-oriented portfolios. Figure 3.5 contrasts the evolving asset allocations of US public and corporate DB plans since the mid-1980s.

---

[10]See Thinking Ahead Institute (2021). There are large differences across countries, with recent alternatives allocations in Switzerland (mainly real estate), Canada, the US, and Australia at 24–32%, compared to those in Japan, the Netherlands, and the UK at 8–12%. The rising alternatives allocations came mainly at the expense of equities. Overall bond allocations remained stable since many corporate sponsors moved DB plans toward bond-oriented investing, often on their way out of DB.

[11]See Thinking Ahead Institute (2021), pp. 34–35, for some estimates of home bias. Home bias matters more outside the US because other countries' weight in the global market portfolio is that much smaller.

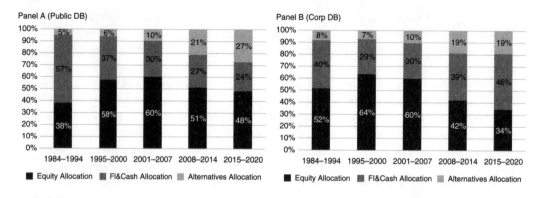

Figure 3.5   A-B Evolving Asset Allocation for US Public and Corporate DB Pensions, 1984–2020

Sources: Pionline until 2007, Center for Retirement Research for public DB since 2008, Milliman for corporate DB since 2008.

By coincidence, both groups had 60/30/10 allocation across EQ/FI/Alts for the middle period 2001–2007. Earlier, public DB plans had been more conservative than corporate DB. After 2006, a new accounting and regulatory environment (together with the scars from the GFC) pushed many corporate DB plans toward bonds and liability-driven investing.[12] Public DB plans acted more like endowments, retained more equity-oriented portfolios, and moved even more aggressively into alternatives. The one consistent trend for both corporate and public plans has been the rising allocation to alternatives, recently reaching 20% for corporate plans and 25% for public plans.

Broadening the limit of investable: What institutional investors consider investable has kept widening: from large and midcap stocks to small and micro-caps; or from US to non-US developed and emerging markets or even to frontier markets. At the same time, securitization in bond markets enhanced liquidity in many segments until it didn't (2008). Finally, investors no longer required liquidity for their whole portfolio and moved with abandon from listed/liquid assets into private assets.

Doeswijk-Lam-Swinkels (2014) have created a history of an investable global market cap portfolio, with asset class weights and returns going back to 1959. The investable market cap portfolio has seen reasonably stable 50/50 weights between equities and bonds over time, and other asset classes have had modest weights. Looser thresholds on investability could raise the weights of non-traditional asset classes.[13]

---

[12]Leibowitz-Ilmanen (2016) discusses corporate DB plans' shift after 2006 toward liability-driven investing and from DB to DC.

[13]Any such effort is plagued by data limitations and definitional challenges. I discuss these issues in Box 3.1 and in Chapter 5 (5.1). For pioneering work, see Ibbotson-Siegel (1983). In principle, the weights in this portfolio reveal the average investor's assets. The evolution of these weights over time reflects a combination of asset performance, net issuance, and evolving understanding of what is investable (e.g. securitization, improving liquidity, growing and better counted private assets).

Box 3.1   Global Market Portfolio

I will return to the topic of investable global wealth many times in the coming pages, but here are the broad results. Think loosely of $100 trn in global equities, $120 trn in global bonds, and much less – or much more – in other asset classes. Real estate is a great example where we may count the investable market as below $2 trn but the overall market as over $200 trn. The word "investable" is thus first-order important and leaves much room for debate.

- Global (listed) equity market cap is near $106 trn at the end of 2020, depending on definitions. Apart from asking whether micro caps and frontier-market stocks are investable, we can debate what to do with restricted stocks (China, Facebook, and others), cross-holdings, and so on. With strict definitions of what is investable, the US may be half of the market, but with looser definitions "only" 39%.[14]
- Fixed income markets are larger in nominal size than equity markets (though the higher volatility makes equities the more dominant drivers of most portfolios' risk and return). They are even larger if money markets, municipal debt, mortgage debt, and bank loans are included in the definition. Instead of $120 trn, the market size might be over $200 trn. However, some argue that debt does not count as net wealth at all but is a zero-sum side deal between a borrower and a lender. The US share of bond markets may be near 40%, or less if Chinese debt is counted at almost the same size, again depending on definitions.
- Investable private asset markets are still counted as well below $10 trn, when internally managed private assets are excluded. Preqin estimated that even including "dry powder" investable private assets amounted to $7.3trn in mid-2020 – buyouts $2.3trn and each of venture capital, growth/other-PE, private credit, real estate, and infrastructure/natural-resources near $1trn.
- We can debate all these numbers, let alone the value of human capital. But it is especially illuminating to recall that some observers estimate the value of global real estate at $200–300trn, as much as equities and bonds together. Limited liquidity in housing makes most of real estate "non-investable," while listed REITs and equivalents are counted as equity rather than real estate but amount to multiple trillions. Other private assets are important but smaller.
- Doeswijk-Lam-Swinkels (2014) have a higher standard of "investable", so their estimated global market portfolio amounts "only" to $160trn at end-2020 (up from $90trn in 2012). Using major indices like MSCI and Bloomberg Barclays, public equities are $60–70trn, public bonds $70–80trn, real estate and private capital about $7trn each.

(continued)

---

[14]Market sizes are US $41trn, China $12trn, EU27 $11trn, other developed markets $32trn, other emerging markets $10trn, based on the 2021 *SIFMA Capital Markets Fact Book*. My book has little to say about Chinese equity and bond markets, despite each having grown to become the second-largest in the world. Besides their growing size, their investability is improving. There are still capital restrictions to both directions, and the Chinese equity market is more influenced by its retail participants than many other markets. I will remind in Chapter 4 that China showcases how economic growth and equity market returns need not go hand in hand. At least, China offers potential for global diversification and active management.

- Gadzinski-Schuller-Vacchino (2018) ignore investability considerations and estimate the global capital stock broadly at over $500trn, mainly due to adding large estimates for private businesses and non-securitized loans.

    The above analysis focused on the assets and not on the asset owners or asset managers. Wealthy individuals/families and large institutions manage internally a large chunk of their capital (e.g. directly controlled firms and residential real estate), but they still delegate more than $100trn to external managers.
- PwC (2020) bravely estimates that the end-investor total assets in 2020 amount to $258trn.[15] Out of this $258trn, $112trn or 43% is delegated to external asset and wealth managers (specifically, $50trn to mutual funds and ETFs, $48trn to "mandates," and $14trn to alternative managers (hedge funds and private assets)). Out of mutual funds and mandates about 75% are actively managed, 25% passive; virtually all alternatives are active.
- A BlackRock study by Novick et al. (2017) focuses on global equities, then $68trn, and reports broadly similar findings. A majority 59% is internally managed and 41% delegated. Of the delegated part, 57% is managed actively.

How is the money managed? Active versus passive: For decades, most equity portfolios applied traditional active management (mainly discretionary stock picking), even if academic research argued that active managers may not be worth their fees. Performance measurement became possible from the 1960s onwards with benchmark indices and peer comparisons. Passive investing became a feasible option to active management in the 1970s, when the first index funds were launched. They were not an instant hit. The big shift from active to passive began only in the 2000s but has been inexorable since then (see Figure 3.6). The past 15–20 years have seen traditional active managers lose market share to index funds and ETFs, but also to even more active alternative managers (hedge funds and private equity).

How is the money managed? Other dimensions: My taxonomy of investment models in Figure 3.7 tries to capture the essentials of different popular investment models. It helps tie together several discussions from above.[16] Most institutions take for granted the equity-concentrated nature of their portfolio, but they differ in their choices on the role of illiquid assets and on external versus internal management. Among institutions that focus on liquid public markets, most rely heavily on external managers. I call this group loosely "60/40" (including investors with other stock/bond allocations).

[15]Individuals hold $165trn (high net worth individuals $88trn, mass affluent $77trn) and institutions $93trn (pension assets $50trn, insurance companies $34trn, SWFs $9trn). I am not sure how, say, housing and bank lending are treated; recall that broader definitions of housing and debt as wealth might imply even twice as large global wealth. Finally, such studies must beware double-counting, when pension funds pool money from individuals and then delegate their management to, say, mutual funds and hedge funds.
[16]A special issue of the *Journal of Portfolio Management* (2021) reviewed a variety of investment models, including several articles on Endowment and Canada models as well as our retrospective of the Norway Model (https://jpm.pm-research.com/content/47/5). Chambers-Dimson-Ilmanen (2021) included nearly the above taxonomy, while Koedijk-Slager (2021) presented another one.

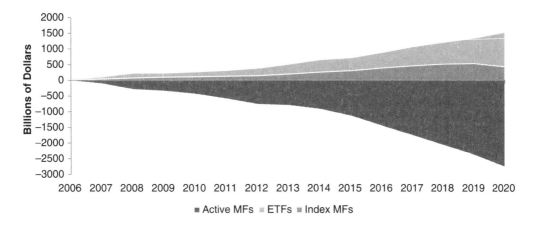

Figure 3.6   Cumulative Net Flows in Different US Mutual Fund Sectors, 2006–2020
Source: Data from Investment Company Institute.

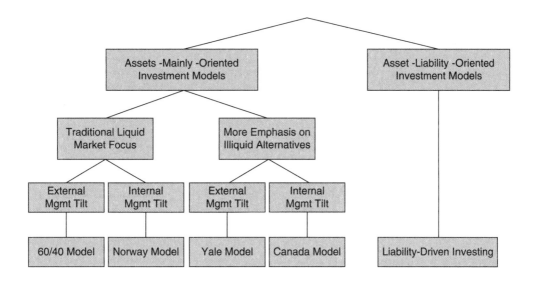

Figure 3.7   One Taxonomy of Investment Models

Large institutions with greater resources are more likely to manage internally a meaningful part of their assets. The best-known example is Norway's large (as in over $1trn) sovereign wealth fund[17] which manages more than 90% of its assets internally and at very low cost.

Among institutions that invest more extensively in illiquid assets, it is natural to differentiate the Endowment or Yale Model (based on large endowments) which relies on external managers versus the Canada Model (based on pioneers like Ontario Teachers and Canada Pension Plan)

---

[17]The proper name is Government Pension Fund Global (GPFG), which is managed by the NBIM under the stewardship of the Ministry of Finance. For disclosure, I advised Norway for a decade in an expert panel (a great learning experience to us all, thanks to the hosts and to my peers Andrew, Gerlof, and Sung!) and one year in a strategy council. I also coauthored an article "The Norway Model" with David Chambers and Elroy Dimson in 2012, and an update in 2021. As an aside, while NBIM is a successful active manager, its tracking error versus the benchmark is so low (0.3–0.4% in equities) that many would consider it more like an index fund. The illiquids allocation is only about 3% (in real estate).

which have brought much of illiquid asset management in-house. The latter approach requires both large resources and high labor compensation costs, yet remains much cheaper than external management.

The final investment model differs from the first four in its focus on asset-liability management. As discussed, some corporate DB plans and insurers hold bond-heavy portfolios and in extreme match the durations or even cash flows between their assets and liabilities. Such matching is harder for underfunded plans but may be feasible with the help of derivatives. A sponsor's end-game in such liability-driven investing is often to minimize risks related to its DB plan and maybe even to eventually close the plan.[18]

ESG theme: Last but not least, responsible or sustainable or "ESG" investing has experienced huge growth in recent years, and given climate change concerns this seems likely to continue. Many large institutions still care about their investments' expected returns and risk, but perhaps as much or more they care about their environmental impact. I will return to this topic in Chapter 14.

3.3. How Has the Low Expected Return Challenge Hurt Various Investor Types?

I only summarize how the pain has materialized for each of the three investor types. Remember that realized returns on stocks, bonds, and other assets have remained benign in recent decades, especially the 2010s, thanks to the windfall gains from ever lower yields and higher valuations. So the worst pain is likely still ahead.

DB Plans

For DB plans, the main way the problem shows up is in their underfunding. Many DB plans were well overfunded around 2000, but insufficient contributions amid persistently falling bond yields and increasing longevity estimates seemed to make deep underfunding a permanent state of affairs (see Figure 3.8). The average funding ratio (FR) of US corporate DB plans in the 2010s was 83%, having been above 100% in 2007, and approaching that level again in 2021.

The impact of lower yields has been milder for public DB plans whose assumptions on the expected return on assets determine the discount rate, but this has not saved their funding ratios. These expected returns have come gradually down to near 7%, restricted by the fact that more realistic (i.e. lower) assumptions would imply contributions that are politically unpalatable.[19] The sad fact is that even with the high discount rates, the average FR for US public pension plans fell from 102% in 2001 to 76% in 2010 and 72% in 2020.

Worse, there is a wide range of funding ratios across public DB plans. The lowest ones are well below 50% even with the expected-return-based discount rates. The more tangible question is how soon these funds will run out of money and what happens then.

---

[18]Yet another investment model would focus on more aggressive risk diversification than the first four which were dominated by equity market risk. This model could include risk parity or alternative risk premia strategies, but it is rarely used for the total portfolio.

[19]US public pension plans have been criticized for not using market yields, let alone Treasury yields, to discount liability values (Novy-Marx-Rauh (2009)); for having unrealistically optimistic return expectations (Andonov-Rauh (2020)); and for pushing into riskier and costlier alternative assets (Sharpe (2005), Lu et al. (2019), Ennis (2020)).

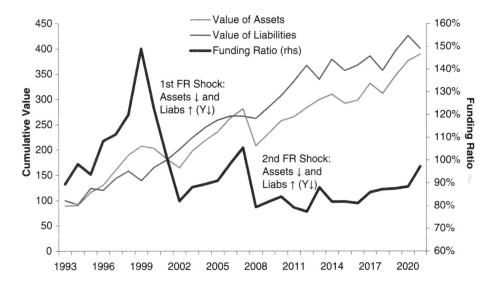

Figure 3.8   US Corporate DB Plans' Evolving Funding Ratio and its Two Parts, Dec 1993–Jun 2021
Sources: Milliman since 2000, earlier a proxy based on A&L returns as in Leibowitz-Ilmanen (2016).

Apart from the gradual deterioration in FRs, it is useful to highlight the worst experience to date. In 2008, the average FR of US corporate DB plans fell from 105% to 79% (and it has never really recovered since). This was a triple-whammy blow where asset values fell and liability values rose, while many sponsors had cash flow problems in their operating business (GFC, recession, and all that) and could hardly pay their pension contributions.[20] Meanwhile, some European pension plans – say, Danish and Dutch – remain better funded.

Why did all these things happen, and why the cross-country variation? Undoubtedly market outcomes were not as friendly in the decade following 2000. But even great performance in the 2010s could only go so far as to maintain the FRs inherited from the 2000s – liabilities grew at nearly the same pace. Indeed, extrapolating the 1990s experience contributed to today's problems, as many decision-makers wishfully assumed that market returns would take care of their pension promises. Overpromising future pensions and underdelivering contributions is easy both for politicians and corporate sponsors, when the bill comes due much later.

We must also acknowledge the role of path-dependence, such as accounting and regulatory environment, which gave public DB plans in the US more leeway than for corporate plans. I can highlight Danish luck in their regulator pushing pension funds to liability hedging in the mid-2000s when it was, with hindsight, still affordable. The same is to some extent true for Holland (though full duration hedging was rare). Together with more regular contributions, this has helped pension funds in both countries to remain close to fully funded, and it is no coincidence that these two countries consistently lead the Mercer ranking of the world's pension systems (see *Mercer CFA Institute Global Pension Index 2020*).

---

[20]For A-L-oriented investors, the 2008 scenario was arguably the perfect storm of calamities. In contrast, for institutions with an asset-only perspective, a scenario where risky assets fall and bond yields rise is even worse, as the portfolios' both main asset classes get hurt (and unlike the A-L-oriented investor, there is no corresponding benefit in falling liability values). It is useful for every investor to consider these two stress scenarios and try to ensure that their portfolios can survive them.

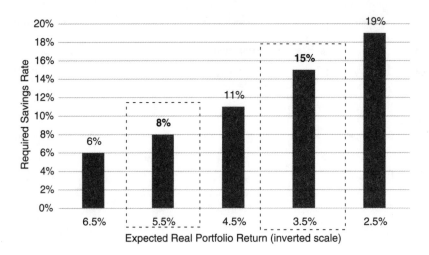

Figure 3.9   Annual Savings Rate Needed for 75% Replacement Rate
Source: Data from Ilmanen-Rauseo-Truax (2016), which includes the auxiliary assumptions behind this bar chart.

DC Savers

If you are an individual DC saver, you must shoulder the investment risk and the longevity risk in pension saving. The main impact of the low-return environment is that you must save a lot (more).

We estimate that the low expected return challenge requires *almost doubling of the savings rate needed* for a given retirement income target. Specifically, Ilmanen-Rauseo-Truax (2016) estimates that under plausible assumptions, a pension saver who targets 75% replacement rate of the final salary should put aside 8% of salary every year. This math worked for the base-case (median) outcome if markets offer 5.5% real return for a balanced stock/bond portfolio. Those were the good old days. If the future expected real return is 2% lower, that is, 3.5% for a balanced stock/ bond portfolio (no mean feat from today's starting yields), the required annual saving rate is 15% (see Figure 3.9).[21] Moreover, if the pension saver wants better than 50/50 chance of reaching the retirement target, the required annual saving rate can easily rise to 20%.[22]

Also note that any fixed rule for the decumulation phase, such as the popular 4% (real) annual withdrawal rate, will prove problematic when investment returns are sustainably lower. Your risk of outliving your savings increases meaningfully if expected returns are 2% lower, and even more so if you face an unlucky sequence of returns (low realized returns soon after the retirement when your pension pot is large, and you spend from this pot after the fall).

Such risks may not be enough to make young savers change their saving patterns . . . unless they are nudged with the help of some software which visually displays their likely aging. Hershfield et al. (2011) shows that seeing such pictures makes young people identify better with their

---

[21]This estimate assumed that pension savings need to cover 45% of the final salary. The remaining 30% to reach 75% replacement rate is expected to come from social security or from other sources. Break-even savings rate is one way to quantify the impact and to create a sense of urgency. There are more sophisticated approaches to quantify saving needs and decumulation policies, but even this simple example underscores the practical implications of lower expected returns.
[22]See Ilmanen-Truax-Rauseo (2016) and Ilmanen-Rauseo (2018), as well as Mitchell (2020) for post-Covid perspectives.

future selves and makes them choose higher retirement savings allocations. Such apps may be more helpful for our youngsters' long-run wealth than any instant trading apps.

I remind readers of the counterintuitive challenge – the need to save more just when the opportunity is less attractive, to reach a given retirement target. Moreover, collectively done, this effort could create a vicious spiral of ever-more saving and ever-higher asset valuations, "vicious" because it would aggravate the low-expected-return challenge.

Endowments

Wealth pools like endowments, if they do not consider their implicit liabilities, can look back approvingly to a history with relatively high realized asset returns. So far the main problems have been temporary, as with Harvard's forced sales of assets during the GFC. For most endowments, the recoveries have been fast enough (V-shaped), and smoothing in both illiquid asset valuations and in the spending rule has helped. Yet, critics have argued that the endowment model has not worked as well as expected, perhaps due to the high fees and the inability of all endowments to identify those top-quartile managers.[23]

The forward-looking picture is less pretty than the rearview mirror. Thoughtful endowments are asking whether they can continue with the 5% spending rule if the markets offer real returns nearer 3%. So far this has not been a reality, but endowments must soon consider their willingness to eat their endowment capital.

At least endowments have a choice to make. In contrast, US foundations are required to spend at least 5% of their capital annually to retain their tax-exempt status. The low expected return challenge is likely to force them to eat into their capital.

Overall, corporate DB plans have already taken the hit from the low expected returns, insofar as low bond yields raised their liability values and made the plans underfunded. Asset-oriented investors without explicit liabilities – both individual DC savers and endowments among our three main investor types – still have most of the pain ahead of them, once low asset returns materialize.

3.4. How Are Investors Responding to the Low Expected Return Challenge?

The risk-reward trade-off becomes crystallized when taking no risk gives you zero or negative return. In 2020, a large part of fixed-income markets traded at negative nominal yields and an even larger part at negative real yields. You can select a riskless investment and be guaranteed to see its real value erode over time, or you can buy riskier assets to earn higher expected return, but this comes with the risk of more adverse outcomes.

Most institutions have taken the latter course unless laws and regulations push them to the former. In short, public DB plans and endowments are trying to boost their portfolios' expected returns, while many corporate DB plans are leaving the field. Individual savers are hoping for

---

[23]Ennis (2020, 2021) stresses how poorly the endowment model fared since the GFC. Though to be fair, the US 60/40 was an incredibly tough benchmark to beat in the 2010s. Hammond (2020) and Lo et al. (2020) provide other negative empirical evidence over longer histories, while Beath et al. (2021) and Brown-Hu-Kuhn (2021) give a more positive picture. The debate continues.

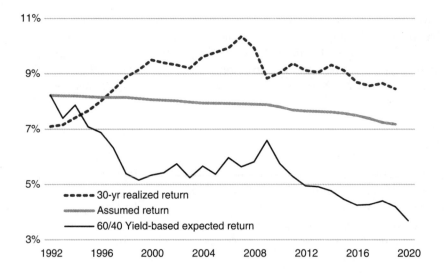

Figure 3.10   US State and Local Pensions' Assumed Returns Compared to 30-Year Trailing Realized Returns and Yield-based 60/40 Expected Returns, 1992–2020

Sources: Census of Governments in https://publicplansdata.org/quick-facts/national/#investments, Robert Shiller's website, Survey of Professional Forecasters. Notes: The 60/40 expected return is 60% of Shiller CAEY for the S&P500 index plus survey-based economist forecast of next-decade inflation and 40% of US 10-year Treasury yield.

the best. Some are saving more, others are buying lottery tickets in meme stocks and options, yet many are not investing very differently.

Figure 3.10 contrasts US public pension plans' average assumed/expected asset return (discount rate) over time to both their trailing realized return and to a yield-based estimate of a 60/40 portfolio's expected return.

Let's first compare the top two lines. Realized nominal returns have been so benign (8–10% 30-year trailing returns since the mid-1990s) that it may breed complacency and even make optimists wonder why these plans are lowering their expected returns. This is precisely the danger with rearview-mirror expectations when falling asset yields create large windfall gains (see Figure 2.1). Comparing the bottom two lines should remove any complacency. The lowest line shows that simple market-based expected asset return (for a 60/40 US stock/bond portfolio, based on Shiller earning yields and Treasury yields) has fallen much faster than the public pension plan assumed return. The gradual cuts in assumed returns from 8¼% to 7¼% have not been sufficient to prevent a wide gap from emerging between assumed returns and yield-based expected returns.

Public pension plans have closed this gap and justified their return assumptions by making riskier investments (larger equity and alternatives allocations, shifts from Treasuries to higher-yielding fixed income) and more optimistic return or alpha assumptions (vis-à-vis available market returns). Understandably, academic research on reach-for-yield investing is picking up.[24]

Pension plans have been between a rock and a hard place. While it is easy to criticize them, I do not know what were the least bad choices they could make, given the mismatch between their pension promises and (insufficient) contributions. One perspective is that corporate DB plans grasped the nettle while public DB plans kicked the can. Another is that corporate sponsors passed the challenge and key risks to their employees (DC), while public plans stayed the course and tried to offset lower expected returns by taking more risk.

---

[24]See Lu et al. (2019) and Campbell-Sigalov (2020).

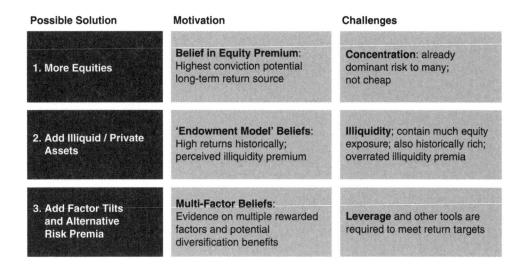

Possible Solution	Motivation	Challenges
1. More Equities	**Belief in Equity Premium**: Highest conviction potential long-term return source	**Concentration**: already dominant risk to many; not cheap
2. Add Illiquid / Private Assets	**'Endowment Model' Beliefs**: High returns historically; perceived illiquidity premium	**Illiquidity**; contain much equity exposure; also historically rich; overrated illiquidity premia
3. Add Factor Tilts and Alternative Risk Premia	**Multi-Factor Beliefs**: Evidence on multiple rewarded factors and potential diversification benefits	**Leverage** and other tools are required to meet return targets

Figure 3.11   Three Institutional Answers to the Low Expected Return Challenge

Nothing is new under the sun. Wealthy Dutch investors in 1600–1700s responded to lower government bond yields by increasing their allocations to riskier assets, notably real estate (see Korevaar (2021)). Later, the 1850s fall in UK yields led to life assurers' allocation shifts from consols (perpetual annuity government bonds) to debentures (mainly on railways and docks), which offered 50–150 bps more yield than consols but a material default risk. Turnbull (2017, p. 97) describes: "This is arguably the first example of a phenomenon that reoccurs in actuarial history: long periods of falling long-term interest rates (for example, in Britain in 1930–1945) tended to compel institutions to bet their way out of their potential unprofitability by increasing investment risk rather than locking in a loss."

What are investors actually doing? Figure 3.11 shows the common ways institutional investors have tried to keep earning 5% real returns when the market offers much lower expected returns: (1) more equity-like risk-taking (including taking more risk within equities and credits); (2) more illiquid private assets; (3) more factor-based investing. I will discuss all of these in the next chapters and argue that they are all evidence-based. That is, historically these approaches have enhanced portfolio returns. Other approaches that are more beliefs-based than evidence-based (that is, less supported by empirical evidence or academic consensus) have become less popular. These include traditional active management through stock picking as well as market timing.

Figures 3.4 and 3.5 showed that institutional investors have significantly raised their allocations to alternative assets (illiquid/private assets). Banks estimate that quant investing allocations doubled to nearly 10% during the 2010s. What about higher equity allocations? Figure 3.5 suggests declining institutional allocations to public equities, but this picture may be partly misleading. More of the equity beta now comes in alternatives (e.g. private equity and hedge funds have meaningful beta exposures) or in fixed income ("going down the credit curve"). Meanwhile, the equity-to-bond reallocations by many corporate DB plans involved with liability-driven investing have offset higher equity allocations by other institutions (sovereign wealth funds and DB pension plans).

To be clear, all investors cannot simultaneously increase their equity exposures. Someone needs to take the other side. More generally, we cannot collectively hide from the low expected returns. We need the "serenity to accept what cannot be changed" – and at least consider adjustments to spending plans and not just to risk-taking plans.

Part II

Building Blocks of Long-Run Returns

Chapter 4

Liquid Asset Class Premia

- Cash rates near zero (or negative) reflect a combination of low expected inflation and negative expected real rates. "Low for longer" has been the post-GFC reality.
- The equity premium and other asset class premia are the most important long-run return sources for most investors.
- At the time of writing (2021), equities look cheap versus cash but promise below-average total or real returns for the coming decade(s). New analyses explore the robustness of historical equity returns, various decompositions, forward-looking analyses, and relations to economic growth.
- Government bond yields are obviously low, but yield curves remain upward-sloping. Survey-based bond risk premia are low, reflecting negligible inflation risk premia, bonds' safe-haven role, as well as central bank asset purchases.
- Credit spreads are below historical norms. Evidence is updated on realized credit premia for investment-grade and high-yield bonds, on excess returns for "fallen angels" and for short-dated bonds, and on active fixed-income managers.
- The long-run commodity premium is not predictable from spreads or valuations. A diversified portfolio of commodity futures has historically earned 3–4% over cash. This may seem like magic when single commodities averaged 0% over cash.

Part II covers long-run return sources, first focusing on asset class returns. Every long-only investment's total return can be decomposed into riskless cash return (reward for time) and some return premia (reward for risks). After briefly discussing cash returns, this chapter covers four market risk premia (liquid asset class premia for equities, government bonds, credits, and commodities). Chapters 5–7 then turn to illiquidity premia, long/short strategies through the lens of publicly known alternative risk premia (value, momentum/trend, carry, and defensive styles), as well as proprietary alpha.

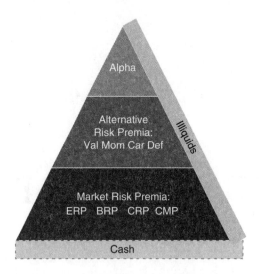

Figure 4.1   Pyramid of Long-Run Return Sources

These return sources were described in detail in Ilmanen (2011). It will be a blessing to many readers that this new book will not go as much into the weeds. I will only update some data and summarize the highlights of the extensive research literature from the past decade.

The pyramid in Figure 4.1 represents any portfolio's return as a blend of all these contributing components.[1] It is possible to demystify a discretionary manager – or the whole hedge fund industry – by estimating how much its long-run performance reflects each component. Even institutions that do not invest much in systematic strategies have become increasingly interested in understanding better the underlying return sources of their portfolio and its constituent managers. I'll return to this quest in Chapter 7 (7.3).

4.1. Riskless Cash Return

This anchor to all investment returns warrants special focus because its abnormal level is at the heart of the low expected return challenge we all face. A couple of decades ago the perception of the "normal cash rate" in the US was near 4%, reflecting expected inflation of 2–3% and an expected real rate of 1–2%. At the time of writing, the US stands out among major economies by offering a near-zero cash rate instead of a negative one.[2]

---

[1] The origins of this pyramid are in the old beta-alpha decomposition of portfolio returns, which was extended in Berger-Crowell-Kabiller (2008) to include the middle layer, which in turn was later used and extended by others. I add illiquids to the side (as they may reflect all kinds of premia as well as alpha) and cash at the base to capture all sources of portfolio returns.

[2] I remain deliberately loose on "which cash rate?" The term covers money market rates with high credit quality. Maturities can range from overnight to a year, but it is common to use one-month rates in historical studies. Main cash rates include policy rates (e.g. Fed funds), Treasury bill rates, collateralized repo rates, and various bank rates. (We are just seeing a transition from LIBOR-based rates to other benchmark rates.) The spreads between different money market rates are narrow in calm times but can widen dramatically in troubled times like 2008. The long-run results in this book are generally robust to the use of either low Treasury bill rates or somewhat higher bank rates.

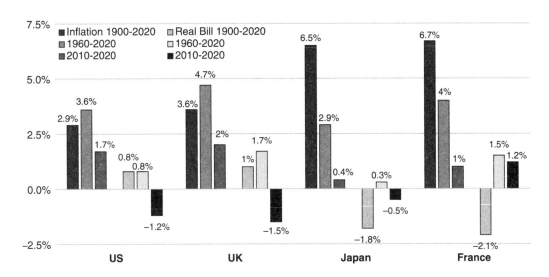

Figure 4.2 Average Inflation and Real Cash Return 1900–2020

Source: Data from Dimson-Marsh-Staunton (2021). Copyright © Elroy Dimson, Paul Marsh, and Mike Staunton. Notes: This bar chart shows G5 countries without Germany. German experience looks similar to France, excluding the 1923 hyperinflation.

It is easy to observe the current cash rate but the expected cash rate over the next decade or longer is not directly observable. To estimate future average cash returns, we can study some combination of survey evidence, market forwards/futures or bond yields (possibly contaminated by term premia), historical averages, term structure models, or macroeconomic estimates.

We gain better insights by separately studying the expected inflation and expected real cash rate. While both parts are historically low today in most economies, the negative real cash rates are even more exceptional and are expected to normalize over time. Covid scars may keep these rates lower for longer, but the consensus expectation is that within a decade we should see real cash rates drift to positive levels.

Figures 4.2 and 4.3 explore very long cash rate histories, split to two parts.

Starting with inflation, Chapter 2 and Box 4.1 highlight the Great Inflation in the 1970s and the disinflation since 1982. Expected long-term inflation became increasingly well anchored at lower levels, following actual inflation undershoots. The story of the past 25 years is that US (and UK) inflation drifted from near 3% to near 2%, while staying below 2% in the euro-area, and below 1% in Japan despite the BoJ's efforts to achieve a higher inflation.

Main explanations include the disinflationary impact of globalization (cheaper labor), technology, as well as central bank independence. A few decades after major central banks won the war against inflation, their concern flipped toward insufficient inflation and the dangers of deflationary recessions.

Turning to expected real cash rates, they have sometimes been negative amid high inflation (around the two world wars and the first oil crisis), but being recently negative amid low inflation is exceptional.[3] Globally, the long-run average real cash rate has been near zero but nearer +1% in the US since 1900 (see Figures 4.2 and 4.3). The persistently negative values since 2008 have been quite a contrast to the US peak values of 3–4% in the 1980s and even in 2000.

---

[3] Real rates are often computed by subtracting past (year's or smoothed) realized inflation from current Treasury bill rates. Negative real rates may then reflect inflation surprises (if the inflation spike is expected to normalize soon). I prefer to use survey-based inflation expectations that are available in the US since the mid-20th century (see Figure 4.3 for economists' one-year-ahead inflation expectations).

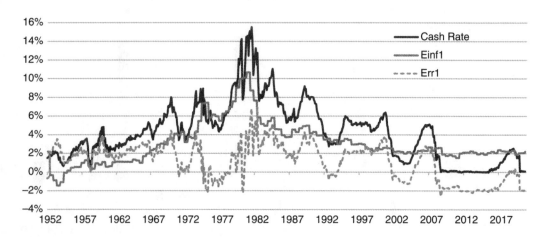

Figure 4.3 US Cash Rate Split into Expected Inflation and Expected Real Return, 1952–2020
Source: Data from Livingston Survey, conducted and published by the Federal Reserve Bank of Philadelphia. Notes: "Err1" is
the difference between the short-term Treasury bill ("cash") rate and the economist consensus forecast of next-year inflation
("Einf1").

Box 4.1   A Brief History of Inflation

The very long-run story is one of near zero net inflation over centuries or millennia,
where bouts of high inflation (often during war times) were offset by bouts of deflation.
The last century has seen higher and more persistent inflation – following the end of the
gold standard in the 1930s and especially after the introduction of fiat (paper) money in
1971. (The interim period of the Bretton Woods regime was a quasi gold standard where
major exchange rates were largely fixed and the dollar was tied to gold at a $35 price.) The
period 1973–82 of twin oil crises saw high, even double-digit, inflation rates in advanced
economies. The mountain shape of (a largely unexpected) rise and fall in inflation between
the 1950s and 1990s, visible in Figure 4.3, leaves its mark on all studies of historical real
asset returns.

  Hyperinflation is a relatively rare event, especially in advanced economies. The
countries that lost the two world wars suffered later from bouts of hyperinflation, most
famously Germany in 1923. Since 1950, only emerging economies have experienced
hyperinflation – Argentina, Brazil, and Zimbabwe are among the infamous poster boys.

  The challenge in modeling even the US inflation is that the process clearly has changed
over time. Until the end of the gold standard, zero inflation (random walk prices) was a reasonable base case. Since WWII, the inflation process became more persistent, and random
walk inflation became a plausible base case by the 1970s. After the Volcker disinflation and
increasing central bank credibility, inflation expectations became well anchored near 2%.
This is not just a US story. Since 2000, most economies have experienced low and stable
or falling inflation rates. (However, as I submit the manuscript to the publisher in October
2021, inflation levels have just risen to multi-decade highs.)

Economists have explored the fundamental reasons behind the exceptionally low real short rates. One strand of literature tries to estimate the evolution of R*, the natural or neutral real policy rate consistent with stable inflation and output at equilibrium level. The main theoretical drivers of R* are productivity and demographics.[4] The slowdown in both has certainly contributed to the low real rates, and there is little sign that these trends are turning.[5] Another driver, the saving glut, was discussed in Chapter 2.[6]

Forecasting gradual normalization (i.e. a rise) in nominal and real rates is a commonly held base case. It seems plausible and in line with market pricing. After more than two decades of well-anchored inflation expectations, the inflation outlook seems exceptionally uncertain in 2021. That said, a similar rising-rate forecast has been made for at least a decade, and yet policy rates kept staying "low-for-longer."

As a technical aside, if you are a *currency-hedged investor*, your own domestic cash rate anchors the returns. If you are from a country with high short rates, you will earn more for a given asset than another investor from a country with low/negative short rates. You earn from hedged foreign assets *your* own cash rate and *their* excess return over cash. (Thus, for currency-hedged foreign bonds, the relative curve steepness is crucial.) You also cannot lever total returns or real returns but only excess returns over cash. If you instead hold unhedged foreign assets and if exchange rates do not change (a big if, though a random-walk assumption is a decent base case), the expected total return is the same for you as for the foreign asset's domestic holder.

4.2. Equity Premium

The equity risk premium is clearly the most important risk premium both for real-world investors and in the academic literature. According to one-factor asset pricing models like the Capital Asset Pricing Model (CAPM), it is the *only* premium that influences assets' expected returns. Public equities are the largest allocation in many investor portfolios. The equity premium dominates these portfolios' risk even more because equities are more volatile than most other asset classes and because the premium is also embedded in many assets outside public equities (e.g. high-yield bonds, hedge funds, private equity).

---

[4]This book covers demographic effects only briefly. The theoretical and empirical messages on how aging influences economies, asset returns, and premia are simply too mixed or weak. Slow-moving demographic trends might matter a lot, but we cannot really judge it statistically. The broad ideas are that aging tends to reduce inflation and economic growth, while the pension saving for the largest baby-boomer cohorts may boost asset prices and their dissaving hurt assets. Even these patterns are debated in the literature (e.g. Bakshi-Chen (1994), Poterba (2001), Ang-Maddaloni (2003), Goyal (2004), Arnott-Chaves (2012), Kopecky-Taylor (2020)). It is also open whether asset prices are influenced more by global or local aging trends.

[5]Vollrath (2020) estimates that most of the decline in US GDP-per-capita growth in the 21st century reflects slower human capital growth, as the multi-decade positive impact from women's higher labor force participation and the baby boomers' working age dissipated. Secondary reasons included slower productivity growth due to the shift from manufacturing to service economy as well as some firms' increasing market power. Rachel and Summers (2019) emphasize secular stagnation concerns and argue that the neutral real rate would have fallen even more in the absence of expansive fiscal policies and growing contingent liabilities related to aging. Other explanations to low real cash rates stress the saving glut channel (motivated by the high saving rates of workers in China and the rich in West), precautionary saving motive after the scars of the GFC and the Covid crisis, as well as modern tech companies' low investment needs (see e.g. Hamilton et al. (2016)).

[6]Beyond these "real" factors, central banks' monetary policy stance – whether through targeted policy rates or quantitative easing – could also have a larger impact than standard theories suggest. See Borio et al. (2017).

Empirical analysis can focus either on the *historical realized premium* (can still debate which equity index – the large-cap S&P500 or a broader US index or an even broader global index; over which period – how distant histories remain relevant; whether over cash or long-term bonds; whether arithmetic or geometric mean) or on a *forward-looking premium* (often estimated based on some valuation ratios or discounted cash flow models, again leaving room for debate).

The historical average is a more relevant measure of future equity premium if we believe the required premium is constant over time and has not been impacted by any major structural changes. The forward-looking premium is more relevant if the required premium varies over time. Such time variation is evident from the wide historical range of, say, the cyclically adjusted earnings yield (20% in the early 1920s versus 2.5% in 2000) or the dividend yield (falling from 7.5% to 1% during the same period).

In this chapter, I summarize updated evidence on historical returns and new research on forward-looking equity returns. Chapter 8 will cover theoretical underpinnings and Chapter 16 tactical market timing. My first book, the CFA Institute Research Foundation 2012 collection of articles *Rethinking the Equity Risk Premium*, as well as the yearbooks by Professors Ibbotson, Dimson–Marsh–Staunton, and Damodaran provide more detail.

Historical Equity Premium

Historical equity market performance is commonly reported either in excess of inflation, cash (Treasury bills), or bonds (long-term Treasuries) – called the real equity return, equity risk premium, and equity-bond premium, respectively. The key statistic is either the annual arithmetic or geometric average return, or a risk-adjusted return such as the SR (arithmetic average return in excess of cash, divided by its volatility). The best resource on historical equity premia are Dimson–Marsh–Staunton yearbooks, which by 2021 cover up to 90 countries, though 32 included in the main results and "only" 21 having the full 121-year history, 1900–2020. For global equities, the total annual compound return or geometric mean is 8.3% (9.7% arithmetic mean[7]). The corresponding real return is 5.3% (6.7%), equity premium over US bills 4.4% (5.9%), equity premium over bonds 3.1% (4.3%), and SR 0.35.[8]

Figure 4.4 shows four different performance metrics for five multi-country composites: World (the middle bar), its split to the US and World-ex-US, and an alternative split to Developed

[7]The difference between arithmetic and geometric means is approximately half the variance of returns. If equity market volatility is 16%, this so-called variance drain or volatility drag is about 1.3% ($\approx 0.5 * 16\%^2$). Geometric mean captures better the historical multiperiod compound return, but it is debatable which measure is better for forward-looking analysis. Theoretical models like a one-period CAPM point to the use of arithmetic mean. Over a multi-period window, the arithmetic mean estimates the expected average terminal wealth across many possible outcomes, while the geometric mean estimates the expected median terminal wealth. With estimation errors, a longer horizon points to geometric mean. Finally, for a small part of a regularly rebalanced portfolio, arithmetic mean is more apt.

[8]This study focuses on unhedged equity holdings, but my multi-country analysis of currency-hedged equity investing gives very similar results. I use a narrower set of countries but country-specific cash rates. Recall that each country's equity return over the local cash rate is a good approximation of currency-hedged excess return. See Boudoukh et al. (2019) for more on currency hedging.

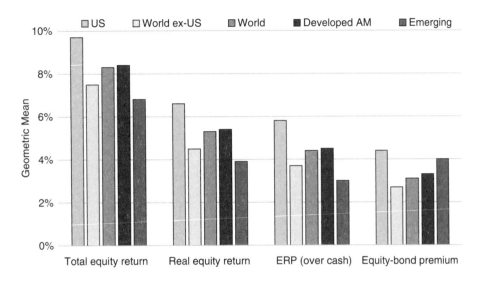

Figure 4.4 Average Compound Returns and Premia for Global Equities, 1900–2020
Source: Data from Dimson-Marsh-Staunton (2021). Copyright © Elroy Dimson, Paul Marsh, and Mike Staunton.

and Emerging Markets.[9] Whichever metric we use, equities have a proud history behind them, with statistically and economically significant positive premia.[10]

The US equities clearly outperformed other countries (6.6% versus 4.5% real return 1900–2020, and more dramatically 11.3% versus 4.4% 2010–20). The authors' decomposition shows that the long-run US edge comes primarily from the much faster real growth of dividends (1.9% in the US versus near zero elsewhere). In contrast, average dividend yields or net valuation changes did not differ much between the US and non-US equities, and net real exchange rate changes had little impact.

Developed markets outperformed emerging markets by most metrics, partly due to including the US, to having a smaller volatility drag, and to avoiding large losses in Japanese and Chinese emerging markets in the 1940s. Since the 1950s, emerging markets have outpaced developed markets (largely thanks to Asian tiger equities which earned 4% annual real returns since the 1960s, which more than offset mildly negative real returns from Brazil and India).

Dimson-Marsh-Staunton (2021) shows that long-run equity premia over inflation, cash, and bonds are positive for all 21 countries with a full history since 1900. Only South Africa and Australia earned higher real returns than the US. The worst long-run performers were Austria, Italy, and Belgium with 1–3% real returns.

Figure 4.5 shows per-decade equity premia over cash for the five composites. The overall picture is very positive. The 1950s was the best decade, while the 1980s and the 2010s compete for the runner-up spot. The 1910s was the worst decade (all composites had negative premia and

---

[9]Dimson-Marsh-Staunton (2021) classifies countries as emerging markets following MSCI classifications since 1987 and earlier if they had below-$25k per-capita-GDP at 2010-equivalents. Emerging markets represent 43% of the world GDP in 2020 but only 14% of equity markets – partly reflecting exclusions and restrictions (state-owned enterprises, cross-holdings, restricted founder holdings).

[10]Over the long history, equity premia are clearly statistically significantly different from zero. Conveniently, the t-statistic of the mean equals the Sharpe ratio multiplied by the square root of time. Since $\sqrt{121} = 11$, 11 times the US SR of 0.40 implies a t-statistic as high as 4.4. Other SRs are somewhat lower, 0.35 for the World and Developed Markets, 0.29 for World-ex-US, and 0.25 for Emerging Markets.

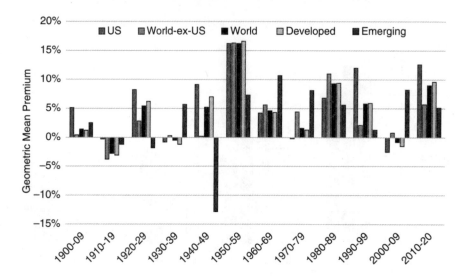

Figure 4.5 Decadal Perspective on the Equity Premium Across Regions
Source: Data from Dimson-Marsh-Staunton (2021). Copyright © Elroy Dimson, Paul Marsh, and Mike Staunton.
Notes: Unhedged total returns of all composites over US bills (geometric means).

even worse real returns), due to WWI and the Spanish flu. Emerging markets' 12% annual loss in the 1940s was by far the worst experience, as Japanese and Chinese equities lost most or all of their value.

Equity investing is thus hardly riskless. Major equity indices have long-run annual volatilities between 16% and 20% (emerging markets 23% and single stocks much higher). Even that successful US market has seen its share of risks. One way to quantify risks is through the depth or length of drawdowns. Figure 8.1 and Table 13.1 (later in the book) track the cumulative drawdowns from the previous peak for the S&P500 excess return over cash. The maximum drawdown occurred during the Great Depression (1929–32), with an 84% peak-to-trough fall. The longest periods below the past peak were 1968–86 and 1929–45. The largest post-war drawdowns involved the market losing half of its value near 1974, 2001, and 2008.

Despite these large interim losses, the long-run cumulative returns from equity investing have been compelling (see Figure 4.11); even the big drawdowns look like blips along the upward march if one can take the luxury of a long horizon.

Dimson-Marsh-Staunton (2021) focuses on real returns rather than equity premia. The longest period of negative real return was exceptionally short in the US, only 16 years.[11]

---

[11]The myth that stocks have little risk over the long run is supported by the statistical fact that the annualized volatility gets lower with horizon. (This partly reflects the fact that the unexpected part dominates short-horizon returns while the positive expected part matters more over long horizons; any mean reversion tendency reinforces this effect.) This myth has gained most public attention from Jeremy Siegel's empirical argument that US equities always beat inflation, bills and bonds at long horizons. (The US equity-bond premium has seen longer bouts of negative performance than the real return, recently a 20-year period ending in March 2020.) Siegel's argument is certainly country-specific and apparently also period-specific. The picture looks different in the 1800s, with a clearly lower equity premium in the US, thanks to relatively high bond and cash returns during that century, perhaps reflecting higher default risk (no riskless government bonds. . .). The lower premium was evident already in Siegel (1994) and Arnott-Bernstein (2002), but McQuarrie (2021) argues that these early studies had overstated equity returns and understated bond returns in the 1800s. McQuarrie finds *no* equity-bond premium between 1793 and 1921(!) before the familiar large premium emerges over the next 60 years.

For most other countries, the real drawdowns in the 20th century could extend much longer than in the US, for example, Germany 55 years, Japan 51 years, the UK and the World 22 years.

Before turning to forward-looking returns, I want to emphasize that historical average returns almost certainly overstate the prospects of future returns. I have highlighted the twin effect of past windfall gains boosting past realized returns and today's starting yields being lower. But since this is such an important topic, let me reiterate.

Equities give a leveraged exposure to economic growth but as importantly they are very long-duration assets. Stock markets reflect the expected discounted value of all future cash flows of currently listed companies, and the discount rate is crucial for long-duration assets. Discount rate news may matter even more than growth news, and the discount rate on equities has kept falling over time. Many forces have contributed to the gradual (not steady!) structural repricing of equities.[12] I have stressed the role of windfall gains in past realized returns and the likelihood that future returns will no longer be cushioned by further windfall gains from repricing (recall Figure 2.1).

Forward-looking Equity Premia (or Real Yields)

Yield-based expected return for equity markets is often based on either a simple dividend discount model (dividend yield plus growth) or the cyclically adjusted earnings yield (CAEY). Fancier versions explore the role of share buybacks, more refined measures of growth, as well as possible mean-reversion or structural changes in valuation or growth metrics. The expected return is for an unstated horizon but typically used for about a decade. Importantly, it is a real return because inflation could be added to both sides of the equation.

In the classic dividend discount model (DDM), the expected real return on equities is given by $\mathbf{E(R)} \approx \mathbf{DY} + \mathbf{g} + \mathbf{E(\Delta V)}$, where DY = dividend yield, g = trend growth in real dividends per share (DPS) or earnings per share (EPS), and $E(\Delta V)$ = expected change in valuation multiples.

Assuming no mean-reversion, $E(\Delta V) = 0$, then $\mathbf{E(R)} \approx \mathbf{DY} + \mathbf{g}$. This "income plus growth" is the Gordon growth model. It implicitly assumes a constant payout ratio (k = D/E), a constant growth rate (for g_{DPS} and g_{EPS}), and a constant number of shares, so no net buybacks ($g_E = g_{EPS}$). As explained below, I assume 1.5% compound growth rate based on century-long historical data.

If we make a restrictive further assumption that the retained earnings grow at the cost of capital, then E(R) equals the earnings yield.[13] Since annual earnings are very volatile, forward-looking analyses commonly use the CAEY. CAEY can either be a proxy for long-run real equity

---

[12]The discount rate is influenced by interest rates and required equity premia. Other things like good liquidity and good institutions/governance can help equity values both from numerator and denominator sides. Leverage explains some of equities' higher long-term return than GDP growth, but a long-run discount rate effect has also contributed. Equity markets hardly existed before the industrial revolution but the prices would have been lower given much slower expected growth and high discount rates (capital scarcity, less diversification ability, lower liquidity).

[13]Under this assumption, the value of the firm is insensitive to the payout ratio k because whether the firm reinvests earnings and generates profits equal to its return on equity, or it distributes them to investors with a market-wide cost of capital E(R), both the firm and the shareholders earn the same rate of return.

return (as in Figure 4.9) or half of it could be used to proxy for the long-run income yield (as in Figure 1.1, a more stable expected return series).[14]

It is interesting to contrast these yield-based "objective" return forecasts with survey-based "subjective" return forecasts. My first book and Greenwood-Shleifer (2014) emphasize that these appear inversely related. Subjective expectations are often optimistic after a major bull market when market valuations are high and objective return prospects low. This is easy to interpret as irrational exuberance (or a cycle of greed and fear) moving market prices away from fair value. Extrapolative expectations are more pronounced in retail than institutional or economist surveys and when the forecast horizon is short (say, one year and not a decade).

Figure 4.6 shows that the equity market (nominal next-decade return) expectations of economists (since 1992), of CFOs (since 2000), and of capital market assumptions providers (since 2010) have all declined over time. For comparison, the dashed line shows the "objective" market-yield-based forecast CAEY (which is a real return, so we add the consensus forecast of next-decade inflation to it). The details differ, but the downward trend is evident in all series. In contrast, estimates of equity *premia* over bonds or cash show little trend over this period (not shown). Overall, these surveys appear more rational than retail surveys, which exuded optimism in 2000 and turned more bearish after the market had fallen.[15]

I assume the long-run real growth of earnings-per-share or dividends per-share to be 1.5%, based on more than a century of US data. The literature shows limited predictability in these growth rates, so a historical average may be the best forecast. Equity pricing reflects very long horizons so the expected growth rate should move very slowly. That 1.5% assumption seemed generous a decade ago, especially when international evidence suggested a lower growth rate. However, since then we have seen dividend and earnings growth outpace output growth. The 2010s were more benign to capital than to labor.

Figure 4.7 tracks the cumulative real growth of US GDP per capita, dividends per share, and earnings per share since 1900. The main message from the longest sample is that DPS and EPS growth rates have not quite matched the GDP-per-capita growth rate, but all have long-run values of 1.5–1.9%.[16]

---

[14]Again, CAEY is the inverse of the better-known "Shiller CAPE" or the cyclically adjusted price/earnings ratio (CAEY = 1/CAPE). CAPE divides the current (real) market price with 10-year average (real) earnings. Since past decade's earnings are on average five years "stale" today, we may make CAEY more comparable to the current earnings yield by scaling it up by 1.075 (if we assume 1.5% annual trend growth in real EPS, then 5 * 1.5% = 7.5%). The simplest use of CAEY is as a real expected return measure by itself, but it would have implied extremely wide variations in real equity yields, even exceeding 20% in 1920s/30s. We could also replace DY with 0.5*CAEY as a proxy for the broad income yield, effectively assuming a long-run payout ratio of 0.5. (Arguably, either way of using CAEY is more robust to the buyback revolution than the DY+g model. CAEY reflects some mix of dividend income and growth, with a possibly time-varying payout ratio k.) Finally, some observers may use exceptionally high or low current CAPE or CAEY to indicate return potential from mean-reverting $E(\Delta V)$; as noted, I assume no mean reversion here.

[15]Survey expectations on long-run total equity returns in Figure 4.6 are mostly between 5% and 7% in the 2010s. Looking at a few other survey sources may be interesting. Andonov-Rauh (2020) report about 9% return expectations among US public DB plans, the higher level perhaps justified by a multi-decade horizon. Giglio et al. (2021) report about 6% return expectations among Vanguard mutual fund investors, but a Natixis Investment Managers' 2019 survey of individual investors reveals double-digit return expectations in all countries, including the US (see Huber (2021)). Apparently, the Vanguard clients do not drink the same Kool-Aid as other retail investors.

[16]In contrast, Kuvshinov-Zimmerman (2021) reports that global stock market capitalization grew in line with GDP between 1870 and the 1980s (more due to net issuance than higher stock prices), but thereafter grew much faster – mainly due to the rising profit share of the listed sector but also due to lower discount rates.

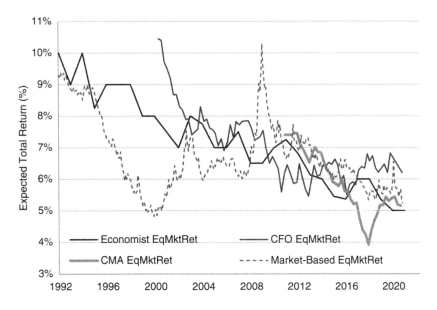

Figure 4.6 Subjective and Objective Long-Run Return Expectations for the US Equity Market
Sources: Survey of Professional Forecasters (FedPhiladelphia) for economist survey, Duke (FedRichmond) for CFO survey, Dahlquist-Ibert (2021) for CMA (capital market assumptions), Robert Shiller's website, Blue Chip Economic Indicators, Consensus Economics. Notes: "Market-Based EqMktRet" is the sum of CAEY (proxy for expected real return) and consensus forecast 10yr inflation rate.

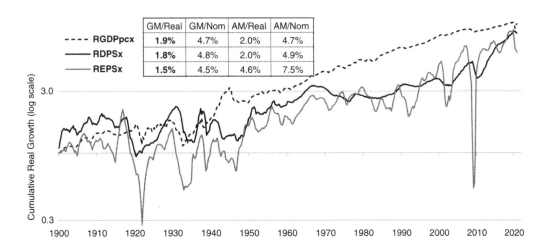

Figure 4.7 US Economic/Dividend/Earnings Growth, 1900–2020
Sources: Robert Shiller's website, FRED (Fed St. Louis). Notes: DPS and EPS on the S&P500 index and its predecessors.

It is notable that the EPS series is by far the most volatile, so while it has the lowest geometric mean it has clearly the highest arithmetic mean. This difference may contribute to the perception that the 1.5% growth estimate is stingy. It is important to specify how we measure earnings growth. The text box highlights that adding back inflation and the volatility drag gives a long-run nominal arithmetic mean EPS growth of 7.5%. Further, any estimates of aggregate earnings (as opposed to per-share earnings) have tended to grow faster (see the dilution topic below);

Table 4.1   US Economic/Dividend/Earnings Growth, 1900–2020 and Subperiods

	1900–2020	1900–1940	1941–1980	1981–2020
RGDPpcx	1.9%	1.6%	2.5%	1.6%
RDPSx	1.8%	1.4%	1.0%	2.9%
REPSx	1.5%	0.5%	2.1%	1.9%

Sources: Robert Shiller's website, FRED (Fed St. Louis) database.

they can also better match the full GDP growth over time. Finally, some observers argue that the conservative GAAP reported earnings should be replaced by operating earnings (excluding write-offs), analysts' forward-looking earnings, or national accounts profits, all of which tend to be higher if not necessarily faster growing than the GAAP earnings.

There is also a fair concern that the increasing use of share buybacks reduces the share count over time and thus may boost EPS growth (even when there is no change in aggregate earnings growth). Table 4.1 splits the long history into three parts and shows that the real EPS growth has been mildly faster (2%) during the past forty years that coincide with heightened buyback activity. The faster EPS growth may also reflect a benign political environment and capital market environment. Market power of large firms has increased, with greater industry concentration and larger profit shares, while globalization and technology trends have given a supportive backdrop. Still, a shift from 1.5% to 2% would not change the big picture.

Even amidst the high use of buybacks, dividend growth gained pace in the 2010s, pushing the long-run real DPS growth estimate above real EPS. Recall, however, the evidence from the Dimson-Marsh-Staunton (2021) that outside the US the long-run real DPS growth has been near zero. Thus my 1.5% estimate for real payout growth may still be a good long-run anchor for this important but hard-to-pin-down "g."

Admittedly, the low expected return challenge and many other problems would be lessened if future economic and payout growth turns out to be faster than I assume. How to improve long-run growth rates is a very important question but beyond this book.

Trying to Refine the Expected Return Estimates

You may want to skip ahead if buybacks, dilution, and return decomposition do not particularly interest you. I will now provide some color on more advanced and perhaps tedious topics of expected equity returns. I confess that while research in this area feels important, it often brings more questions than clarity. That said, the recommended sources are AQR Portfolio Solutions Group (2017a), Straehl-Ibbotson (2017), and L'Her et al. (2018).

The goal is to refine the forward-looking analysis through better yield estimates (how to look beyond dividend yields), better growth estimates (which input series to use and how), more granular decompositions, and considering mean reversion versus structural changes. The first three refinements are interrelated and they contribute to the puzzlingly weak empirical relationship between equity returns and economic growth (see Box 4.2).

Ultimately, we have too little empirical data to judge which models best predict future long-run growth or returns. The decisions rely on art as much as science, priors matter, humility is needed, and model averaging is a good idea.

Refinement 1: Broader income yield including buybacks

One important way to relax the Gordon growth model is to allow the number of shares to vary over time, with a knock-on impact on k and g_{EPS}. This relaxation is important because the US equity markets saw a gradual net issuance worth 2% annually for much of the 20th century, diluting the ownership share of existing shareholders. This 2% dilution implied that real EPS growth rate was near 1% when the aggregate real earnings growth rate was near 3% (see next section).

These patterns changed after share buybacks (repurchases by the issuing firm) became increasingly popular since the 1980s.[17] Dividend yields fell sharply both due to true richening and to the buyback surge. As many firms replaced dividends with share buybacks, the naïve payout ratio (k = D/E) fell from 60% to 43%. Broader income yields that include net buybacks besides dividends have been more stable over time, and thus more robust to the structural change in the use of buybacks.

The simple "DY+g" model has arguably understated expected equity market returns since the 1980s. Other implications are that the dilution rate (ΔS or net issuance) has gradually edged from almost 2% to near zero, and the g_{EPS} growth rate has increased faster than g_E. Straehl-Ibbotson (2017) derives the following expected return equation for broad payouts: $E(R) \approx NTY + g_{TPagg}$ where NTY = net total (payout) yield and g_{TPagg} = growth in real *aggregate* total payouts.[18]

Figure 4.8 tracks over time the net total yield and its three components: dividend yield, gross buyback yield, and gross issuance yield. Both the dividend yield and the net total yield have trended lower over time, while the rise in gross buyback yields has been partly offset by a more negative gross issuance yield.

Refinement 2: Growth estimates differing between DPS and GDP

The long-term *per-share* dividend or earnings growth has historically lagged *aggregate* dividend or earnings growth by up to 2% annually. This gap largely explains the slower real growth of DPS or EPS (1–1.5% p.a. for 1900–2009 in the US) than real GDP-per-capita (near 2%) and real GDP (above 3%). The gap has been even wider globally.[19] One intuition is that part of economic growth accrues to new enterprises rather than existing shareholders in listed firms (see more in Box 4.2).

---

[17]Net issuance is the difference between gross equity issuance and gross buybacks. Some studies prefer to quote net buybacks, which is just the inverse of the net issuance. For forward-looking analysis, either metric can be expressed as annual or in smoothed (cyclically adjusted) form, say, as 10-year average. Net buybacks can be measured in different ways – through the number of shares outstanding, Treasury stock changes, cash flow data, or index divisor changes. Some measures are relevant for indices with a fixed number of constituents while others include new issuance. Some measures include other cash flows returned to investors besides net buybacks, such as cash mergers and acquisitions, and their treatment of buybacks tied to employee stock options may vary. Likewise, aggregate effects such as delistings, IPOs, index reconstitutions, or debt may be included or excluded. These details are well beyond this book.

[18]The net total payout yield adds to the dividend yield the net buyback yield (or subtracts net issuance, ΔS). If this ΔS adjustment is made in the income (carry) part, it is important for consistency to then add to it the growth of aggregate total payouts, not of the per-share payouts. Straehl-Ibbotson (2017) estimates that the growth rate in real aggregate total payouts broadly matched the real GDP growth rate of 3.3% between 1901 and 2014, with payouts lagging GDP growth until 1980 and outpacing thereafter. Also see the Online Appendix of AQR Portfolio Solutions Group (2017a).

[19]The term "dilution" is at times used narrowly for the per-share versus aggregate dividends (or earnings) growth gap, and at other times broadly for the DPS versus GDP growth gap. Interestingly, the latter gap in the US has flipped sign in recent decades given a benign corporate environment. Between 1997 and 2017, the real DPS has grown annually 3.8%, well ahead of the GDP-per-capita real growth rate of 1.4%, and this has happened despite the growing use of buybacks instead of dividends. Also the global broad-dilution gap has narrowed to near zero (2.2% DPSx versus 2.1% GDPpcx) over this period (compared to 0% versus 2.4% in the 20th century). The gap for China is in double-digits (−3% versus 8%), reflecting the dilutive IPOs of large state-owned enterprises.

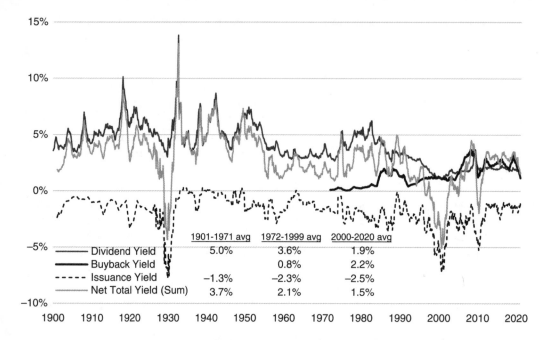

Figure 4.8 US Annual Dividend Yield and Other Parts of the Net Total Payout Yield, 1900–2020
Source: Data from Straehl-Ibbotson (2017), extended by the authors. Notes: Dividend yield is from Robert Shiller's website; buyback yield is estimated using the Treasury stock method with data from Compustat; issuance yield is the difference between the net total yield and the sum of dividend and buyback yields; and the net total yield is the sum of the dividend yield and the negative of the change in the number of shares among S&P500 constituents, using CRSP data.

The net dilution reflects (a) issuance of new shares and other corporate activities which raise the share count ("diluting" existing shareholders' stake) and (b) buybacks and M&A activities which reduce the share count. The index divisor is one way to track the net impact of all these effects over time. The index divisor is the index market capitalization divided by index level. Besides net buybacks, index additions and deletions also influence the index divisor.

Dilution effects vary a lot across countries – and tend to be larger in emerging markets. A 20-year study by Mee (2017) shows that annual GDP growth exceeded EPS growth by 3% in emerging markets, while the gap was -2% in developed markets. Moreover, the index divisor changed by 3.3% p.a. in emerging markets, compared to 0.5% in developed markets.

Dilution effects also vary over time. Net issuance and negative dilution dominated in Europe until ca. 2000 but weakened given increasing buybacks and M&A activities. Growing use of buybacks has even flipped the sign of (narrow) dilution in the US to net accretive since ca. 2006.

Refinement 3: One framework for decomposing growth/returns

L'Her et al. (2018) gives a useful framework and helps us better understand equity market returns. This study decomposes the total equity market return in several steps into more granular pieces. It first splits the nominal return into the real return and inflation/currency effects. The real return is further split into dividend yield (dy), DPS growth (dps), and valuation change (p/d), following the dividend discount model. The dps is then re-expressed as a DPS gap versus the real GDP per capita growth (gdp pc).[20] In the next stage, the DPS gap is further re-expressed as a sum

---

[20]The decomposition uses two convenient tricks. Log growth rates, expressed in small caps (e.g. dps instead of DPS), make the pieces additive. The gaps involve adding and subtracting an item to create a gap term, for example dps = (dps − gdp pc) + gdp pc = dps gap + gdp pc. At the next level, both eps and sps (sales per share) are added and deducted to give payout ratio (dps − eps) and profit margin (eps − sps) besides the sps gap (sps − gdp pc). And so on.

of sales-per-share gap (sps gap), payout ratio change (payout) and profit margin change (margin). Finally, the sps gap is split into two sources of slippage: the difference between per-share and total sales growth of the stock market (nbb, or net buybacks) and the difference between total sales growth of the stock market and the real economic growth (rd, or the relative dynamism of the listed equity index).

In the end, we have eight components whose historical contributions the authors then estimate for many countries. What is going on here? Why make something as simple as a total return more complicated through all these incremental steps?

The broad goal is to better understand the sources of historical returns and maybe to better predict future returns. In this study, the authors "only" present the historical average contribution of each component (see Table 4.2 for a taste). But this framework could be extended further if we believe that some components are unpredictable (which points to using the long-run average growth or the current level as the best prediction), while other components are subject to structural changes (which points to using a recent average as the best prediction), while yet others are mean-reverting (which points to expecting some normalization).

Overall, this seems like a useful area of future research. Yet a warning: There may be too little data to judge such issues statistically because we explore multiyear predictive ability, and we simply do not have enough independent observations.

As an empirical application, L'Her et al. (2018) decompose nominal and real equity market returns in 43 countries between 1997 and 2017. Table 4.2 picks three rows from their study – the global average, the US, and China. Globally, average dividend yield of 2.9% and DPS growth of 2.2% explain most of the 4.7% average real local-currency return. The broad dilution is near zero over this sample, as the global DPS growth matches the GDP per capita growth. Narrower dilution in net buybacks is negative but is just offset by benign profit margin growth, payout ratio rise, and relative dynamism. There are large cross-country differences, notably a massive dilution in China that more than explains the country's low realized equity market return.

For any forward-looking analysis, one could use historical averages from this table, but they are surely somewhat sample-specific over a relatively short history. Or one could shrink any estimated values toward multi-country averages or toward reasonable priors. In addition, one could study mean reversion tendency in each series and incorporate this feature if it is strong.

Refinement 4: What about mean-reversion and structural change arguments?

Many financial market series, including equity market valuations, exhibit some mean reversion tendencies. However, such tendencies are slow and empirically rather weak. Any contrarian strategies are vulnerable to structural changes. The choice not to include mean reverting valuations in the expected return estimate is a nod to the idea that some structural changes may move valuations sustainably higher. Many justifications have been made as to why the future CAPE of S&P500 may be near today's (mid-2021) 37 as a base case, or at least vary around its more recent-decades mean of 27 rather than its very long-run mean of 17. These include a global decline in cash and asset yields, a safer world, sustainably stronger earnings growth, and lower trading costs.

Moreover, when one uses a yield-based equity market expected return, one already assumes a below-average expected return because today's DY and CAEY are well below their past averages. Assuming that valuations will revert to their lower long-run mean over the next decade, as some capital market assumption providers (GMO, RAFI) do, would compound the bearishness.

Table 4.2 Empirically Decomposed Equity Market Return, 1997–2017

	Dividend Yield, dy	Price-to-Dividend Change, p/d	Real per Capita GDP Growth	Net Buybacks, nbb	Relative Dynamism, rd	Payout Ratio Change	Margin Growth	= Real Total LC Return, r	Inflation and Currency Return, inf+fx	= Nominal Total Return in USD
AllMktAvg	2.9%	−0.3%	2.1%	−2.2%	0.5%	0.5%	1.2%	4.7%	1.9%	6.6%
US	1.9	0.4	1.4	−1.8	2.4	0.7	1.2	6.1	1.9	8.0
China	2.6	1.0	8.2	−26.5	14.9	−0.9	1.3	0.7	2.8	3.5

Source: Data from L'Her-Masmoudi-Krishnamoorthy (2018). Notes: Selected evidence from a global study using MSCI data in 43 countries between 1997 and 2017. All series are log returns or growth rates for additivity. Dps is dividend per share, sps is sales per share. The difference between sps growth and gdp-per-capita growth is the sps gap, which in turn can be split into nbb (net buybacks) and rd (relative dynamism of listed index versus economy). nbb is calculated using the MSCI index divisor, which reflects the net of buybacks, issuance, M&A activity, and index additions/deletions. rd is a residual.

Box 4.2 Weak Empirical Relationship Between GDP Growth and Equity Returns[21]

Equity markets are often seen as *the* growth asset: a way of participating in economic growth and bearing the risk of poor performance during recessions. Yet, perhaps surprisingly, fast (GDP) growing economies have *not* delivered reliably higher equity market returns.

Dimson-Marsh-Staunton find *across countries* a negative correlation between long-term average GDP growth and equity market return over a century. Other studies find negative or zero correlation over shorter histories. However, long-term DPS growth and equity market returns are positively related.

- L'Her et al. find 0.0 correlation between average real market return and real GDP growth – but 0.15 correlation between average real DPS growth and real GDP growth, and 0.60 correlation between average real market return and net buybacks – across 43 countries between 1997 and 2017.
- Best-known example of the negative relation is China since the 1990s with its strong economic growth and low equity returns, caused by dilution (when state-owned enterprises were listed at relatively expensive levels). Meanwhile, Latin American equities provided high returns despite slower economic growth.

The empirical relation is also weak *over time*, say, for the US. Past economic growth tends to have negative correlation with equity market returns (over-extrapolation?), and contemporaneous growth has near-zero correlation (but growth surprises have positive correlation), while equity market returns predict positively next-year economic growth (asset prices are forward-looking).

Why does GDP growth not translate into EPS growth or stock returns?

- Many firms are global, earning much of their profits abroad (which GDP can miss).
- The corporate sector's share of the GDP pie versus consumers and the public sector varies over time (e.g. profit versus labor share). In competitive economies, consumers may benefit most from economic growth.
- The sectoral composition between the broad economy and equity markets may differ.
- The publicly listed sector may be less dynamic or profitable than the unlisted sector.
- Dilution effects related to buybacks/issuance/M&A/etc. are exogenous to economic growth but influence average stock market returns. Existing public equity shareholders only earn the EPS growth, not the earnings growth from the private side or new issuance of the corporate sector.
- Debatable time alignment with stock returns: Equities are forward-looking (the main empirical relation is lead-lag: equity returns predict future growth), and less rationally, equities may over-extrapolate fast growth prospects after periods of strong growth.

---

[21]Sources: Dimson-Marsh-Staunton (2002, 2005, 2010), Ritter (2005, 2012), Cornell (2010), Ilmanen (2011, pp.330–6), L'Her et al. (2018).

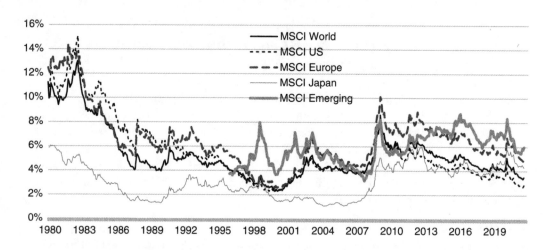

Figure 4.9 Forward-Looking Real Equity Return (Cyclically Adjusted Earnings Yield) in Different Markets, Jan 1980–Sep 2021
Sources: AQR, MSCI. Notes: Using the simplest measure, the inverse of Shiller CAPE.

A similar question of mean reversion or structural changes can be raised to any growth series. Academic research has found limited predictability in dividends/earnings/payout growth beyond the long-term average. Thus, I often assume 1.5% real growth rate for EPS, in line with more than a century of evidence in the US. In recent decades, with a corporate-friendly environment, this growth rate has been somewhat higher. It is debatable whether we should assume a structural change to a sustainably higher g_{EPS} (say, 2.0%) or mean reversion for the next decade(s) and thus a below-average g_{EPS} (say, 1.0%). I stick with the long-run g_{EPS} of 1.5% instead of using a shorter historical window or mean reversion, but one can argue both ways around it.

Current Outlook

Near mid-2021, the dividend discount model approach points to about 3.2% real return on US equities (say, 1.7% income, 1.5% real growth, 0% valuation change), while CAEY points a bit lower. Adding 2.3% for expected next-decade inflation gives a nominal total return estimate of 5.5%. This is also the (geometric) equity premium *if* cash is expected to earn zero over the horizon. The arithmetic expected equity return and premium would be 6.8% (assuming volatility of 16% and variance drain of 1.3%) and the SR 0.43 (6.8%/16%). Such a SR is above long-run average due to the low cash rate even while the expected real and nominal equity returns are well below their historical averages. Any estimates of future returns come with wide uncertainty bands, and this is also true for multiyear forecasts. Specifically, estimating even partial mean reversion in absolute valuations during the coming decade would darken the picture.

Outside the US, equity valuations tend to be lower and expected returns thus higher (see Figure 4.9). Indeed, the valuation gap between the US and the rest of the world is about as wide in 2021 as it has ever been.

The broad message is that global stocks are expensive in the absolute but look cheap relative to cash. That is, yield-based analysis currently points to below-average equity returns but above-average equity premia, thanks to the low cash rates.[22] Eventually these may morph into below-average equity premia and normal cash rates, with little change to expected equity returns.

I have stressed in the early chapters that while the low yields in cash and bonds are more visible, they make virtually all asset classes expensive and give them low starting yields. This is the broad low expected return challenge. I make this case so that investors prepare for the harsher future, not to propose aggressive market timing into the low/no/negative-yielding cash. Timing made more sense in 2000 when equity valuations were even higher than today and real bond yields were near 4% instead of -1%. There will be more on market timing in Chapter 16.

4.3. Bond Risk Premium

US Treasuries are sometimes called the most important market in the world, both because of the market size[23] and because their yields serve as anchors to so many other assets. Government bonds are safer than equities and often considered free of default risk[24], but they are subject to meaningful interest rate risk. Bonds' holding-period returns reflect the gradual yield income and the more volatile capital gains/losses, which are well approximated by the product of inverse yield change and bond duration.[25] The premium for the other main risk in non-government bonds, credit risk, will be covered in the next section.

The bond risk premium (BRP), or term premium, is the (realized or expected) excess return of a long-term government bond over cash. It is thus the reward for duration extension, for bearing interest rate risk. The simplest forward-looking measure of this premium is yield curve steepness or the term spread, for example, between 10-year Treasury bonds and 1-month Treasury bills. The yield curve reflects both the required BRP and market's interest rate expectations. Yield curve steepness is thus a noisy measure of either part. Better BRP proxies try to strip out the unobservable rate expectations from the curve.

---

[22]Historically, low bond yields, cash rates, and inflation rates have tended to coincide with lower equity earnings and dividend yields (i.e. higher equity valuations). The relation appears nonlinear in that low positive rates are the goldilocks environment for equity valuations, while both high inflation and deflation can hurt equities. I stress that even if low rates justify high equity valuations and support the assumption of no mean reversion in valuations, those high equity valuations still imply lower starting yields for equities and thus below-average expected returns.

[23]Bond markets are larger in nominal size than equity markets, though the higher volatility of the latter makes them more dominant drivers of most portfolios' risk and return. *The 2021 SIFMA Capital Markets Fact Book* quotes the end-2020 global equity market size at $106trn and global fixed income at $123trn (biggest markets US $47trn, China $19trn, EU27 $25trn, Japan $15trn). Government bonds are the largest segment. Numbers would be even higher if bonds held in government accounts or money market assets were included.

[24]More precisely, government bonds issued in their local currency are perceived riskless because the government has the ability to tax its citizens and the central bank has the option to print money (inflate instead of default). In practice, both ability and (political) willingness are needed. Even the credit rating of the US government was questioned in 2011 when the Congress debated the debt level ceiling. Perceived default risk is related to debt sustainability. A high debt/GDP ratio can be problematic but is more sustainable amid low rates or fast economic growth.

[25]I will presume some familiarity with bond market terminology here, or I direct readers to my book *Expected Returns* Chapter 9 or the longer series *Understanding the Yield Curve* I wrote, ah, more than a quarter century ago. Yield and duration are useful simple approximations of bonds' expected return and interest rate risk, respectively. They have their pitfalls, but these are beyond this book. I will thus ignore here concepts like rolldown and convexity, as well as yield curve steepening or flattening, and their second-order impact on bond returns. See Ilmanen (1995, 1996, 2011).

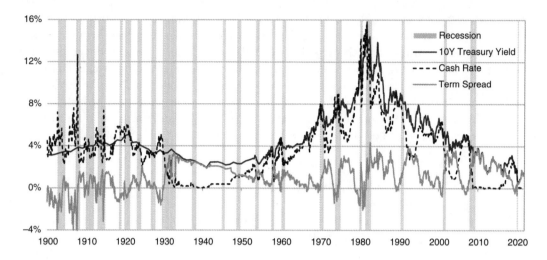

Figure 4.10   US Long- and Short-Term Treasury Yields and Their Spread, Jan 1900–Sep 2021
Sources: AQR, FRED (St. Louis Fed), NBER. Notes: 10-year Treasury yield and short-term Treasury bill yield, and their difference (the term spread). Recession periods are shaded.

Because yields are so visible, it is natural for bond investors to use them as proxies for expected returns. Still, it is worth studying the historical yields *and* returns of Treasuries.

Historical Bond Yields and Excess Returns

Figure 4.10 shows a history of the US 10-year yields and short-term bill yields as well as the term spread between them. The yield mountain stands out, as does the fact that both yield series are near all-time lows at the end of the sample.

This is a global phenomenon (see Figure 2.5). Indeed, many advanced countries even have negative short rates and bond yields, something we long thought should not happen due to paper money arbitrage.

The long-run excess return for bonds mainly reflects the positive carry over time (as seen in Figure 4.10, the yield curve tends to be upward-sloping), but is further accentuated during periods of falling yields, notably the decades since 1980. Conversely, Figure 4.11 shows that the cumulative excess return for global government bonds was especially negative during the 1970s, a decade of rising bond yields. Over the full century 1920–2020, the realized bond risk premium was 1.8% per annum, despite multiple-decades long drawdown. Thus, bonds outperformed cash ex-post by somewhat more than the ex-ante term spread indicated (average 1.4%). Given bonds' lower risk (volatility of 4–6%), it may be interesting to scale the bond performance if it had been levered up to have the same volatility as equities. Figure 4.11 shows that the century performance of the two asset classes would have been broadly similar but the best decades rarely coincided. The long-run SR was comparable to that of global equities, 0.3 for the 10-year Treasury, and 0.4 for a global government bond composite.[26]

---

[26]Historical results are broadly similar for other major economies (when Germany's 1923 hyperinflation is ignored). Within a country, long-run bond risk premia line up with duration, though Sharpe ratios tend to be higher for short-maturity bonds. There is little further reward beyond the 10-year maturity, perhaps reflecting pension funds' liability-driven demand for the longest bonds. For some institutions, the long bond is arguably the riskless (liability-matching) asset.

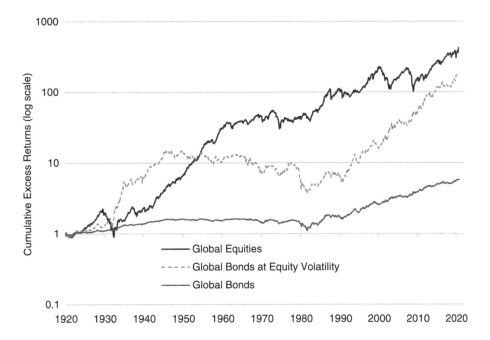

Figure 4.11   Cumulative Excess Return on Global Government Bonds Compared to Global Equities, Raw and Volatility-Adjusted, 1920–2020
Source: Data from AQR. Notes: GDP-weighted composites of multi-country equity and government bond portfolios. The last line scales bonds to the realized volatility of equities.

Bond yields tend to rise amid higher inflation, faster economic growth, and tighter monetary policy, thereby causing capital losses to bonds. Inflation history was discussed above in Box 4.1. The growth outlook is related to cyclical conditions, where business cycle troughs often coincide with low rates and steep yield curves, and business cycle peaks with high rates and inverted curves (see Figure 4.10 where negative term spreads often precede shaded recessions). These patterns partly reflect the Fed's attempt to act countercyclically, easing policy to cushion recessions and tightening policy amid overheating.

The old story of "the Fed taking away the punch bowl when the party gets going" sounds quaint in this century when the only question seems to be how much the Fed is spiking the bowl. The secular developments of disinflation, slowing economic growth partly due to demographics, and a lower natural rate of real interest rate have made central bank policies more accommodative every decade since the 1980s – through lower rates as well as quantitative easing. The Fed has also supported financial markets and risky assets whenever these show signs of trouble ("the Fed put").

Decomposing Forward-looking Treasury Yields

Since bond yields reflect both market expectations of future rates and required bond risk premia, the term spread is a noisy measure of the required term premium. The survey-based bond risk premium is a cleaner measure as it subtracts from long-term bond yield the consensus forecast

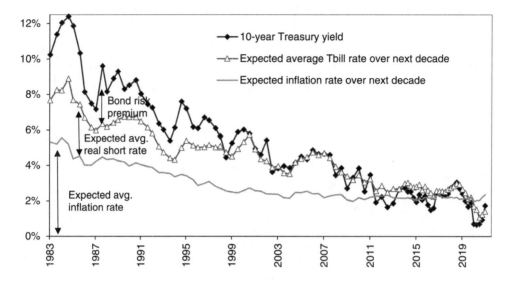

Figure 4.12   Decomposition of the 10-Year Treasury Yield Using Survey Data, Mar 1983–Mar 2021
Sources: Bloomberg, Blue Chip Economic Indicators, Consensus Economics.

of average future short rates over the life of the bond.[27] Such economist surveys exist in the US since 1983 and more recently in other countries.

Bond yields can be decomposed in many different ways. Subtract the short rate and get the term spread. Subtract expected inflation and get the real bond yield. Subtract expected future short rates and get the survey-based bond risk premium.

We gain the best understanding by decomposing the 10-year Treasury yield into three parts: expected average inflation rates and expected average real short rates over the next-decade as well as the required BRP. Figure 4.12 shows this decomposition. All three components contributed to the decline in Treasury yields: The expected inflation fell first (from 5% to 2%), the BRP next (from 3–4% to below zero), and the expected real short rates last (from 3% to below zero). All three were near historical lows in 2020.[28]

Such a yield decomposition can be based on survey-based expectations (as above) or on some term structure models. The historical patterns are broadly similar.[29]

---

[27]Logically, the survey-based BRP is a better predictor of future bond returns than the term spread (yield curve steepness) since it subtracts the expectations-related noise and should give a better risk premium measure. Yet, empirically the yield curve has been the better predictor of near-term returns. Apparently, expectational errors have contributed to yield curve's predictive ability, besides time-varying term premia. Ex-post predictability of forecast errors may not have been irrational or easy to identify in real time. They may reflect structural changes that investors could not foresee at the time. Cieslak (2018) shows how forecast errors in short rates contribute to bond return predictability; also see Box 9.3 in Ilmanen (2011).

[28]Figure 4.12 also suggests that macro-fundamentals explain the bulk of the decline in bond yields in recent decades – not a proactive central bank. Other studies show that the fall in the expected real short rate can be partly explained by expectations of slower real economic growth.

[29]See Best-Byrne-Ilmanen (1998), Ilmanen (2011), and Crumb-Eusepi-Moench (2018). Some of the decomposition histories with model-based bond risk premia by Fed researchers are updated regularly on Fed websites (Kim-Wright (2005), Adrian-Crumb-Moench (2012)).

Focus on the Drivers of Required Bond Risk Premia

I already discussed in section 4.1 why expected inflation and expected real short rates are so low. Now I address the BRP and argue that it turned negative for three reasons: a low inflation risk premium, a negative safe-haven premium, and exceptional demand effects offsetting rising bond supply.

Yields fell by more than 10% over the past four decades. Declining BRP explain a significant part of this – almost 4%.[30] Much of the early decline likely reflected the required inflation risk premium trending down from elevated levels.[31] Higher inflation level may be associated with a higher inflation uncertainty and thus a higher inflation risk premium. Several measures of inflation uncertainty were higher in the 1970s–80s than in later decades.

Treasuries became safe-haven assets when the stock-bond correlation turned negative near the turn of the century. Treasuries have since then had a negative equity market beta, which according to the CAPM would justify a lower expected return than cash. In practice it means that government bonds have hedged investors against the equity risk that dominates most portfolios.[32]

Supply-demand conditions include many aspects, during the past decade likely most importantly the quantitative easing (large-scale asset purchases) by central banks. For example, the Fed's assets on the balance sheet rose from $0.8 trn before the 2008 GFC to $4.5 trn by 2015. Assets fell somewhat before the Covid crisis but then doubled to $8 trn by mid-2021. However, the mechanical impact of quantitative easing was initially offset by fiscal policy and Treasury debt management. Growing Treasury issuance and extended Treasury durations brought more absolute interest rate risk to the market in the early 2010s than quantitative easing removed from it (see Greenwood et al. (2014)). That said, the signaling impact of easy Fed policy may have mattered more than any flow impact. Moreover, ECB and BoJ balance sheets have grown to broadly comparable size as the Fed's.

Other contributors include pension fund and insurer demand for liability-matching long-duration bonds and for "safe assets" (roughly, AAA rated bonds with low/no regulatory capital requirements). Bond markets for a long time ignored fiscal deficits and debt levels in major economies – witness Japan's high debt ratio and low yields, though the Greek experience shows

---

[30]Such a multi-decade downtrend in yields is a particular challenge for many term-structure and macro-finance models and empirical analyses. To allow changing expectations to explain much lower long-term yields, Cieslak-Povala (2015) includes an inflation trend (mainly pre-2000) and Bauer-Rudebusch (2020) also a real rate trend (mainly post-2000) into a shifting endpoints model. The empirical pattern of investors systematically overpredicting rates for many decades may be understood as surprises only recognizable with hindsight and not in real time, as rational learning about structural change, or as persistent expectational errors. For a recent overview on yield curve's drivers, see Brooks (2021).

[31]Both a level-dependent inflation uncertainty and a time-varying inflation-growth correlation likely contributed to the high inflation risk premium in the 1980s and the subsequent fall. High inflation tends to be unstable and could justify a large risk premium for bonds, as could the tendency of inflation coinciding with recessions. Both bad features occurred during the stagflations of the 1970s and the early 1980s. Many metrics of inflation uncertainty (time series of inflation volatility or of mean absolute inflation surprises, disagreement across forecasters, aggregated subjective uncertainty by each forecaster, some option-based evidence) have been used in the literature. See Wright (2011), D'Amico-Orphanides (2014), and Campbell-Sunderam-Viceira (2017).

[32]Ongoing research with my colleagues suggests that the sign change in stock-bond correlation 20 years ago reflects the relative decline of inflation uncertainty. Since growth news tend to move stocks and bonds to opposite directions and inflation news to the same direction, the sign of the correlation depends on the relative magnitude of these two macro uncertainties. As long as inflation uncertainty remains mild, stock-bond correlation is likely to remain negative. Incidentally, I am a little proud that I began to write in Salomon Brothers reports already near the 1998 LTCM episode about the possibility of stock-bond correlation flipping negative.

that markets can change their tune. Time will tell whether the post–Covid fiscal expansion especially in the US will yet trigger a positive relation between deficits and bond yields. For now,
real bond yields are surely lower than real growth expectations, and this improves fiscal space
(the sustainability of a given amount of government deficits and debts) and is clearly influencing
today's policymakers around the world.

Current Outlook

Low or negative bond yields sound bad for bond investors, let alone if one expects some mean
reversion to more normal yields or a meaningful uptick in inflation. However, yield curve steepness matters more than yield level for near-term excess bond returns or for currency-hedged
bond returns, and most countries' yield curves are likely to remain upward sloping. The diversification argument remains strong as long as one believes that government bond yields can
fall further in those crucial equity bear market scenarios when the safe-haven service is most
valuable. That said, a rising inflation scenario would certainly hurt bonds and if this were to
trigger rising real yields on bonds and riskier assets, the safe-haven service also would be in doubt.

Yields have long continued to surprise on the downside, and it is for a reason that shorting
Japanese government bonds was already 15 years ago called "the widowmaker trade." Many other
government bond markets have since joined Japan. One of the costliest mistakes of recent decades
for pension funds has been to assume that yields *must* rise from here. Consensus economist forecasts and the market forward rates have predicted rising Treasury yield for almost 30 years, presumably motivated by mean-reversion expectations. Yet, actual yields have kept moving lower.

Empirically, a steep yield curve has been a good predictor of strong excess bond returns, not
a very reliable market timing indicator but as good as it gets. Steep curves have been associated
with high required BRP or with market forecasts of rising yields which tended to be systematically wrong. Forecasting is hard, especially amid persistent structural changes.

Overall, today's low bond yields clearly point to low future returns.[33] This is widely known,
but many investors miss the same but less visible challenge for other assets. Bonds still have a
role in many portfolios given their services, ranging from liability hedging to economic hedging in most recessions. Return-wise, there are still two-sided risks to the yield direction; and the
upward-sloping yield curve gives bonds a cushion of positive expected returns over cash.

4.4. Credit Premium

The credit premium is commonly defined as the (expected or realized) excess return of corporate bonds over comparable (similar duration) government bonds. Credit premium is estimated
separately for investment-grade (IG) bonds and non-investment-grade, or high yield (HY) bonds.
It can be estimated more granularly for each credit rating and even for different countries, industries, and maturity subsectors. Since the US has the deepest credit markets and by far the longest
return histories, I will focus on them in the empirical analysis.

---

[33]Leibowitz-Bova-Kogelman (2014) and Lozada (2015) show that the starting yield is a surprisingly robust predictor of long-run returns for bond portfolios because any capital gains/losses due to yield changes are partly
offset by lower/higher reinvestment rates. For constant-maturity or duration-targeting portfolios, the yield's
prediction is most reliable for horizons near twice the portfolio duration. Rolling yield may be an even better
anchor than yield, if unchanged yield curve is the base-case expectation.

Credit Market Size in Perspective

Before turning to credit spreads and credit premia, I list the sizes of different fixed income markets in the US. SIFMA estimates mid-2021 AUMs to be $21.7trn Treasuries, $11.7trn Mortgages, $10.0trn Corporates, $4.0trn Municipals, $1.5trn Agencies, $1.5trn Asset-backed, $1.1trn Money markets.

In the more adventuresome corners of the FI market, leveraged loans have become the favored funding source of the private assets industry. IMF estimated in October 2020 that the global leveraged loan market size of $5trn clearly exceeded the global HY bond market size of $2.5trn. Private credit assets AUM had grown to almost $1trn and the CLO market AUM to $0.8trn. Emerging market bonds exceeded $1trn (much more if, say, Chinese local debt is counted).

The US corporate bond market, which I'll focus on, amounts to about a tenth of the global FI markets, yet it offers the best historical evidence outside government bonds (with lower liquidity). Moreover, credit returns in various parts of FI markets are positively correlated with each other and with the performance of equity markets.

For our purposes, it is important to study the excess return of corporate bonds over duration-matched government bonds, rather than their total returns or excess returns over cash. For IG corporates, the latter mainly reflect interest rate exposure and not credit exposure (while for HY bonds the credit risk tends to dominate). The two parts of the blend – rates and credit – tend to be negatively correlated, providing inbuilt diversification for corporate bonds.[34]

I first discuss historical returns, then turn to forward-looking estimates of credit premia.

Historical Average Excess Returns

My book *Expected Returns* gave a rather modest reading of the long-run excess return of US IG corporates over Treasuries, about 0.3–0.4%. Newer research comes up with a more positive message, reflecting both a revised reading on corporate bond performance many decades ago and strong performance during the 2010s. Related, I questioned whether credits really have added value over some blend of equities and Treasuries, whereas new research clearly answers in the affirmative.

The Bloomberg Barclays indices offer the excess return of corporate bonds over duration-matched government bonds since mid-1988. Before that we have index data since 1973 without clean duration matching.

The longest histories are commonly represented by the simple difference between the Ibbotson long-term corporate bond and government bond index returns. However, Hallerbach-Houweling (2013) noted that the corporate bond index has historically had a shorter duration than the government bond index and a higher credit quality than the full IG universe. Both features reduce the measured credit premium.

Asvanunt-Richardson (2017) remedied the former problem by estimating the empirical duration of the Ibbotson long-term corporate and government indices, and calculating the duration-adjusted credit excess return. Adding some credit-friendly years at the end of the sample helps further. Their estimate of the IG credit premium between 1936 and 2014 is near

---

[34]For example, the Bloomberg Barclays Global Aggregate (IG) index has 0.95 correlation with government bond returns and a −0.16 correlation with corporate-Treasury excess returns.

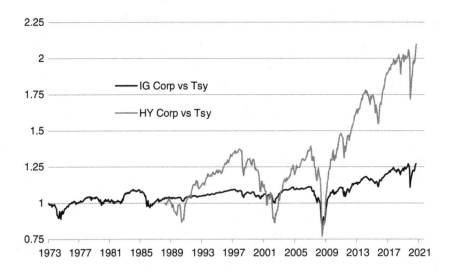

Figure 4.13 Cumulative Credit Excess Return over Matching Treasury for US Investment-Grade Corporates 1973–2020 and for Speculative-Grade (HY) Corporates 1988–2020
Sources: Barclays Capital, Bloomberg. Notes: To compute excess returns, US corporates are matched to similar-duration Treasuries since 1988 and earlier to similar-maturity Treasuries.

1.5%. Starting later, in 1973 or 1989, and ending in 2020 reduces the premium to 1.0% or 0.7%, respectively.[35]

Besides reporting a much higher credit premium than earlier research had, Asvanunt-Richardson (2017) directly addresses the marginal role of credits in a broader portfolio. When they regress the credit excess return on Treasury and S&P500 excess returns over their 1936–2014 sample period, they find a statistically significant regression intercept (alpha). And when they conduct a mean-variance optimization analysis across the three asset classes, credits were hardly a redundant asset. Instead, the weight of corporates in the ex-post optimal portfolio was 48% (compared to 35% for Treasuries and 17% for S&P500). Despite its positive (0.25) correlation with equities, the credit premium has been a useful contributor to investor portfolios.

Ben Dor et al. (2021, Chapter 1) confirm that a credit portfolio has significantly outperformed a comparable mix of equities and Treasuries (1.5% for IG, 3% for HY between 1993 and 2019) even when they carefully adjust for different company and sector compositions in equity and bond markets. They further explore the sources for this performance edge and trace it back to corporate bonds' exposure to positively rewarded variance risk premia and low-risk factors (to be discussed in Chapter 6 (6.3 and 6.4): Credits are effectively short volatility in equity and bond option markets, and they benefit from leverage aversion (investors prefer to go long corporate risk through equities than bonds, given the embedded leverage in the former). In contrast, the authors find that illiquidity cannot explain credits' performance edge.

HY corporate bonds have higher returns, higher volatilities, and higher equity correlations – as well as shorter histories – than IG bonds. Figure 4.13 plots the cumulative excess returns for

---

[35]Kizer-Grover-Hendershot (2019) and McQuarrie (2020) find, however, problems with corporate bond data in the early decades, which may have led to an overestimation of the credit premium. Thus, I will focus below on more recent evidence.

IG corporates since 1973 and HY corporates since 1988. Table 4.3 below shows a variety of performance statistics.

Forward-looking Estimates of Credit Premia

Apart from the better transparency and liquidity of corporate markets over time, our ability to measure the expected return advantage of corporates over comparable Treasuries has improved over time. Since mid-1988, we have "option-adjusted spreads" (OAS) which match corporate bonds to Treasuries with similar durations and adjust for any embedded options in these bonds.

- These spreads reflect some mixture of the expected default losses from corporates and the required excess returns of corporates over Treasuries due to credit risk as well as illiquidity, tax, or regulatory considerations.
- Given the expected default losses, spreads would be positive even if investors only expected the same long-run return from corporates as from Treasuries. Based on historical experience, the average break-even spread to offset expected default losses is modest (15–25 basis points) for the broad IG market, a small fraction of the typical OAS, but higher (200–250bp) and a larger fraction of the typical OAS for the HY market.[36] IG bonds have small default risk but the downgrading bias – tendency for a downgrade to be more likely and to have a larger spread impact than an upgrade – warrants some further OAS for them.

Turning to credit spreads and realized performance over recent decades, the first column in Table 4.3 shows that IG corporates earned 75bp (arithmetic) average excess return, more than half of the average OAS of 132bp. In my previous book when the sample period ended in 2009 with "unfriendly" above-average credit spreads, the "spread capture" was only 25%. Now thanks to more benign below-average credit spreads at end-2020, the spread capture is 56%.

A new reader may not be impressed with a 56% spread capture and rather wonder where the 44% (57bp) leakage comes from, when the break-even spreads from expected default losses and downgrading bias for IG bonds should be at most 30bp. I explained in my first book and will confirm later that the remaining leakage reflects index investors' bad selling practices, especially the fire sales of fallen angels. (I will explain soon in case you are not familiar with this colorful jargon.)

The second column shows that HY corporates earned about 2.8% excess return, compared to 5.2% average credit spread. The 54% spread capture is broadly in line with the long-run default losses and requires no further explanation.

The remaining columns show similar statistics across credit ratings. The average spreads rise monotonically with a lower credit rating, but the average excess return shows a bump for BB-rated bonds. This, too, can be explained by the fallen angels.

Credit spreads vary over time in intuitive ways. They are narrow in calm times and widen sharply during recessions and financial market crises (e.g. times of high equity market volatility and large market falls). Both expected default losses and higher required credit and liquidity premia likely contribute to such spread widening. All credit spreads, not just those for corporate bonds, tend to share these features.

---

[36]See Ilmanen (2011).

Table 4.3 Credit Performance Statistics, 1989–2020

	Bloomberg Barclays US Corporate Investment Grade	Bloomberg Barclays US Corporate High Yield	Bloomberg Barclays Aaa Corporate	Bloomberg Barclays Aa Corporate	Bloomberg Barclays A Corporate	Bloomberg Barclays Baa Corporate	ICE BofA BB US High Yield	ICE BofA B US High Yield	ICE BofA CCC and Lower US High Yield
Exc. Return GM	0.65%	2.39%	0.17%	0.45%	0.45%	0.84%	2.53%	2.09%	2.95%
Exc. Return AM	0.75%	2.83%	0.21%	0.49%	0.54%	0.99%	2.80%	2.55%	4.06%
Volatility	4.4%	9.5%	2.9%	3.0%	4.2%	5.4%	7.6%	9.7%	15.0%
Info Ratio	0.17	0.30	0.07	0.16	0.13	0.18	0.37	0.26	0.27
Avg Spread	1.32%	5.24%	0.75%	0.85%	1.17%	1.75%	3.48%	5.34%	10.98%
Spd Capture	56%	54%	29%	58%	46%	57%	80%	48%	37%
Skew	-2.1	-1.1	-4.3	-1.7	-2.5	-2.3	-1.6	-1.2	-0.8

Sources: Barclays Capital, Bloomberg. Notes: Returns are over duration-matched Treasuries and OAS spreads likewise. Last three series begin in 1994.

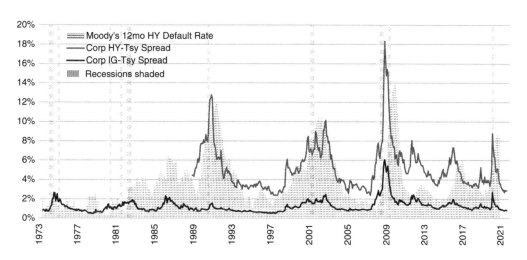

Figure 4.14   Corporate Yield Spreads and High-Yield Default Rates, Jun 1973–Sep 2021
Sources: Barclays Capital, Bloomberg, Moody's. Notes: Light-shaded areas highlight US recessions. Yield spreads are option-adjusted spreads (OAS) over matching Treasuries since 1988, earlier simpler maturity-matched yield-to-worst spreads.

The spread widenings during the 2000–2, 2007–9, and 2020 recessions and equity bear markets are visible in Figure 4.14. These often end by central bank help, and the role of central banks has increased over time, especially in response to the Covid-19 crisis. Meanwhile, the broad credit market characteristics have evolved over time – the IG index average credit quality declined and duration lengthened in a way that would justify somewhat wider spreads. The reach-for-yield or going-down-the-credit-curve pressures among many investors amid the low-rate world have offset those fundamental forces.

Figure 4.14 focuses on the relationship between HY spreads and actual default experiences among US (HY) corporates. There is a clear link, but the market spread anticipates rather than reacts to evolving defaults. The shaded recessions in the background emphasize the cyclicality of both credit spreads and default experiences. Again, aggressive central bank responses helped mitigate even worse outcomes.

Has the 2010s Changed My Storylines?

I review next whether two stories from my *Expected Returns* book have aged well.

1. **Fallen angels:** I highlighted the strong performance of "fallen angel" BB-rated bonds, which have just been downgraded from IG to HY. Many investors restricted or habituated to holding only IG bonds are forced to sell such bonds within a few weeks after the downgrade, despite the resulting fire-sale prices. Contrarian buying of such fallen angels has historically been a good strategy. The main question is whether widening investor knowledge of this opportunity[37] would weaken the selling pressure after downgrades below IG. It turns out that the profitable opportunity has persisted. Fallen-angel bonds earned double the

---

[37]Several Barclays research pieces, an article by Ng-Phelps (2011), and my book all described this opportunity a decade ago.

excess return of the all-HY bond index between 1997 and 2020 (4.6% versus 2.3%); the edge remained unchanged between 2010 and 2020 (6.5% versus 4.2%).[38]

2. **Front-end opportunity:** I emphasized the high risk-adjusted returns of conservative credit strategies at short maturities, which would require leverage to really matter. This pattern is consistent with common leverage aversion among investors. The risk-adjusted return (information ratio) has declined monotonically with maturity – e.g. 0.45 IR for one- to three-year corporates and 0.05 for over 25-year corporates between 1989 and 2020. The patterns are similar since 2010 (IRs of 0.74 and 0.12). Two qualifiers: First, front-end credits are most vulnerable to a sharp increase in actual default risk "where bonds trade on price, not yield" (a given amount of expected near-term default loss will widen short-dated credit spreads much more than long-dated spreads), such as fall 2008 and spring 2020. Second, the profitability of these strategies depends on money-market financing spreads. If these are not much narrower than the bond spreads, there is little opportunity to exploit.

What About Active Credit Managers?

It is more difficult to take passive exposure in credits than in government bonds or equities, due to the thousands of outstanding issues, many of them rather illiquid. Since credit mandates are still primarily active, it is important to mention active credit managers' practices even in this chapter on asset class premia.

My colleagues have written several articles demystifying the performance of active FI managers.[39]

- Most institutional FI funds with IG benchmarks take a persistent positive credit beta tilt in their active positioning, which explains much of their historical outperformance.[40] By doing this, they have made their products much worse diversifiers to an equity-oriented total portfolio than their benchmark indices, with meaningfully higher correlations with equity markets.
- The same pattern holds for credit hedge funds (with implicit cash benchmarks): systematically long credit. In contrast, mutual fund managers with a HY benchmark tend to take a little less credit risk than their already risky index.
- None of these groups show significant exposures to long/short style factor premia like value, momentum, and defensive.[41] Among these historically profitable FI styles, only carry (itself correlated with the credit premium) has seen clearly positive exposures.

---

[38]The quoted numbers are compound excess returns of credit portfolios (the ICE BofA US Fallen Angel Index and the All High Yield Index) over duration-matched Treasuries. The edge shows up also in risk-adjusted returns because fallen angels have only mildly higher volatility (11% versus 10%). See Ben Dor et al. (2021) for more detail.

[39]See Brooks-Gould-Richardson (2020) and Palhares-Richardson (2020).

[40]Simple active return over benchmark seems positive over the long run for most managers, unlike active returns for equity managers. There are three explanations: Most overweight credit beta (so the outperformance does not count even as one-factor alpha); the data set may reflect gross-of-fee performance; and returns may be overstated by survivorship bias.

[41]See Chapter 6 for evidence on style premia in equity and other markets. See Israel-Palhares-Richardson (2018) for FI applications and evidence.

Current Outlook

At the time of writing, credit spreads are well below historical averages. Yet, a bigger challenge for total returns is that cash rates and the riskless bond curve are so low that starting yields for all fixed income are historically low.

4.5. Commodity Premium

I include commodity futures as an asset class, mainly because it is that rare representative of an inflation hedge. Neither stocks nor bonds like rising inflation. Commodities share a positive growth sensitivity with stocks. With its growth and inflation exposures, commodities are opposite to bonds. Yet the correlations of commodities with either stock (+) or bond (-) markets are quite mild, so they are excellent diversifiers to balanced stock/bond portfolios. The investable market size is small (well under a trillion dollars), but the total value of many commodities (oil underground, outstanding gold, etc.) is much larger.

The two most important commodity indices are GSCI and BCOM composites of commodity futures. They mainly differ in how they weigh different commodities. GSCI uses world production weights and is energy-heavy, while BCOM uses a blend of liquidity and production weights, thus is more balanced. Both indices use front contracts and roll these to the next contract some time before expiry. Long-run futures returns (which are effectively excess returns over cash) are based on these chained series, and they can be naturally split into spot returns and roll returns.

Historical Average Excess Return

The disinflationary 2010s was a tough decade for commodities, reducing many investors' perception that commodity investing would be rewarded in the long run. Perhaps counterintuitively, as we'll see, new research during this decade strengthened the case for a positive long-run commodity premium. Most historical research had gone back only to 1970, but new studies go back a century further. Commodity futures have a long history, though admittedly until the late 1940s, these futures were mainly on grain products.

I extend data from my colleagues' study "Commodities for the Long Run" (Levine et al. (2018)) using the excess returns of up to 29 equal-weighted commodity futures between 1877 and 2020. Another study by Bhardwaj-Janardanan-Rouwenhorst (2019) collects an even broader commodity futures universe for the period 1871 to 2018. Both studies point to a long-run commodity premium of 3–5%.

Figure 4.15 plots over time the cumulative performance of a commodity futures composite and its two components. The chart starts in 1900 for consistency with other asset classes and reveals a positive long-run premium. Clearly, most of the long-run return came from spot return. The negative contribution of a negative roll is consistent in recent decades, reflecting the "contango" shape in the term structure of commodity futures prices.

For this 1900–2020 period, the compound average excess return (GM) is 4.9% and SR 0.37. Sample periods starting in 1877, 1950, or 1970 all give GMs of 3–4% and SRs near 0.3. The Bhardwaj et al. study finds GM of 4.3% in 1871–2018 for their equal-weighted composite, with a positive long-run premium for all sectors. The authors also report a long-run excess return of 3.7% for the DJCI, an actual index with real-time weights since 1933. Incidentally, non-surviving commodities are included in all these studies (they earned lower returns, which likely contributed to their non-survival).

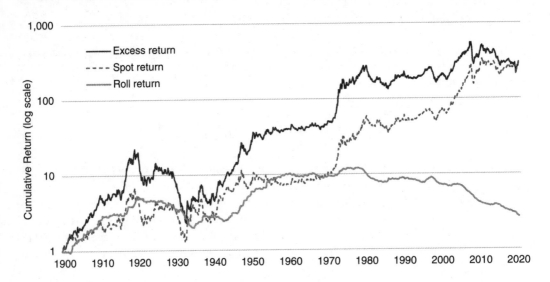

Figure 4.15   Cumulative Excess Return for Commodity Futures Composite, 1900–2020
Source: Data from AQR. Notes: Equal-weighted composite with up to 29 commodity futures. The composite futures return (excess over cash) is split into pot and roll return.

Diversification is especially important for the commodity asset class. Single commodities have high volatilities, typically almost 30%. The resulting volatility drag (or variance drain) brings the typical commodity's compound average (GM) return to zero, despite a 4% arithmetic mean (AM) return. Yet, a diversified portfolio of these commodities can earn over 3% compound average return because of its lower volatility (18%) and lesser variance drain. Table 4.4 shows that the full-sample statistics between 1877 and 2020 had these counterintuitive characteristics. Erb-Harvey (2006) dubbed this result "turning water into wine," while others call it merely a rebalancing bonus or diversification return.

Even if the average pattern for a broad set of commodities is that their performance stalls or trends sideways over a long history, their composite may still trend up by 3% annually over the same period. This indeed describes what happened over almost 150 years, which might explain why it is so commonly thought that commodities offer no long-run reward. Over this period, a typical single commodity's compound return line did not trend higher even if it had a positive arithmetic mean. (I will return to the rebalancing topic in Box 11.1 but already note that any rebalancing bonus is weaker in other asset classes where constituents have lower volatilities and higher pairwise correlations.)

Table 4.4   Turning Water into Wine, 1877–2020

	Equal-weighted Composite	Mean Statistics for Single Cmds
Exc. Ret GM	**3.4%**	**0.0%**
Exc. Ret AM	4.9%	4.0%
Volatility	18%	28%
Sharpe	0.27	0.12

Sources: AQR, Levine et al. (2018). Based on the (excess-of-cash) returns of up to 29 commodity futures. (If all series covered the full sample, the AMs would be the same for the two columns, but different sample lengths cause some wedge.)

Most commodity indices have shorter histories than the above studies, but the story is broadly similar. Table 4.5 shows best performance between 1970 and 2020 for an equal-weighted portfolio and worst performance for the energy-heavy GSCI index. The last five columns show performance statistics for five commodity subsectors – none has enjoyed a great performance and all have suffered from negative roll.

Forward-looking Estimates – Go for the Historical Average?

Commodity futures have historically exhibited some carry and momentum patterns that could be exploited by favoring commodities with the most positive roll and strongest recent performance. Even these cross-sectional patterns weakened in the 2010s. Similar patterns have been mildly evident for directional commodity index trading – next-quarter performance was better starting from typical backwardation (positive roll) or after strong recent performance. But the results were weak and only held at short horizons, not at multiyear horizons. There were also no useful mean-reversion or value indicators helping broad commodity index timing over, say, 5-year horizon. With no statistical evidence of time-varying expected return, the best forward-looking estimate for the long-term future is the historical average premium. Based on the evidence above, a constant premium of some 3% over cash seems appropriate for a diversified commodity portfolio – though not for single commodities!

Brief Focus on Gold

Few investment opportunities are as old as gold. And few have as new competitors as cryptocurrencies – as an alternative to fiat money. The value of all gold stocks above ground and proven reserves amounts to about $17 trn (with gold price at $1850/oz). Meanwhile, the market value of all cryptocurrencies reached $2 trn in 2021 quite fast.

The long-run return on gold is understandably modest, near zero real return (i.e. matching inflation) over centuries and millennia. This still makes gold a compelling store of value for those with a long horizon. The real price of gold rose sharply during the first decade after the Bretton Woods system (a quasi gold standard fixed at $35) ended in 1971, but for the 40 years since then there has been no net increase (see Figure 4.16).

Mechanically, gold's low return reflects its lack of interest or dividend income (hard to use the discounted cash flow pricing when there are no future cash flows), and fundamentally, its safe-haven services against a variety of ills. I will later show that gold has performed well in many equity market drawdowns and in many inflationary episodes – but not all. Still, gold remains the ultimate thing to carry with you or hide underground when you worry about ambiguous catastrophes, including cyber-terrorism.

The gold price is inversely related to the real interest rate. This makes sense since the opportunity cost of holding gold is lower when interest rates are low – as in recent years. Empirically this relation is not very strong (see Figure 4.16). Supply-demand conditions also matter. In the past, Asian jewelry demand was central, but more recently ETF demand may be a more important driver (see Erb-Harvey-Viskanta (2020) and Parikh (2019)).

Inflation Hedging Premium Angle

I highlighted earlier commodities' ability to hedge against inflation. It is not perfect but it is as good as it gets (or as bad as it gets, when a disinflationary decade arrives, as happened in the 2010s).

Table 4.5 Commodity Index Performance, 1970–2020

	AQR eq.wtd. Combo	Bloomberg Commodity Index	S&P GSCI Index	S&P GSCI Energy	S&P GSCI Precious Metals	S&P GSCI Industrial Metals	S&P GSCI Agriculture	S&P GSCI Livestock
Exc. Ret GM	3.9%	3.2%	1.2%	-0.6%	1.7%	1.5%	-1.8%	0.5%
Spot Ret GM	7.1%	6.3%	2.9%	1.8%	6.9%	3.1%	2.7%	2.1%
Roll Ret GM	-2.4%	-3.1%	-1.7%	-2.5%	-4.9%	-1.6%	-4.6%	-2.1%
Exc. Ret AM	5.0%	4.5%	3.3%	4.7%	4.0%	4.0%	0.2%	2.0%
Volatility	15.8%	16.7%	20.3%	32.2%	21.9%	23.0%	20.2%	17.4%
Sharpe	0.32	0.27	0.16	0.14	0.18	0.18	0.01	0.12

Sources: AQR, Bloomberg, Standard&Poor's. Notes: Three subsector indices begin after 1970: Energy in 1983, Precious Metals in 1973, and Industrial Metals in 1977.

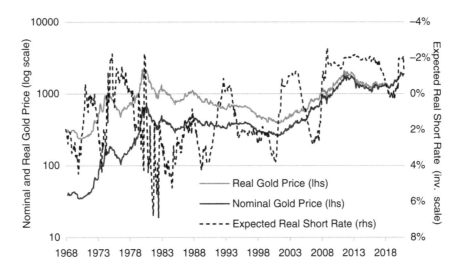

Figure 4.16 Gold Price History and Real Short Rates, 1968–2020
Sources: Bloomberg, Livingston survey (Fed Philadelphia).

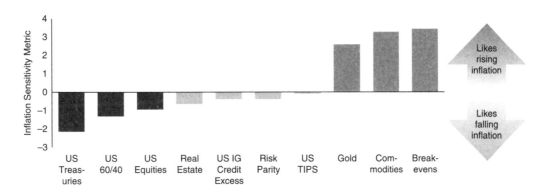

Figure 4.17 Inflation Sensitivities of Various Asset Classes, January 1972–June 2021
Sources: AQR Portfolio Solutions Group (2020a), Bloomberg, Survey of Professional Forecasters, US Bureau of Labor Statistics. Inflation sensitivity metric is a weighted average of contemporaneous risk-adjusted beta to inflation changes and surprises, each controlling for growth exposure, based on quarterly 12-month excess-of-cash returns and inflation data. Treasuries, TIPS, and Break-evens are for the 10-year maturity bonds. Equities are MSCI US. 60/40 contains 60% equities and 40% Treasuries. Real Estate is an average of the NCREIF NPI and FTSE NAREIT equity REITs. Credit Excess is the excess return of IG corporates over duration-matched Treasuries. Risk Parity is a hypothetical strategy that allocates equal volatility to three asset classes: global developed equities, global government bonds, and inflation-sensitive assets (commodities and TIPS). Gold is gold futures. Commodities are the S&P GSCI index. Before March 1997, TIPS and break-evens are synthetic series built using survey-based inflation expectations. Also see AQR Portfolio Solutions Group (2020a)

Broad commodity portfolios are especially useful because they can hedge against different types of inflation. Oil performs well amid energy-driven cost-push inflation. Industrial metals come through in demand-pull inflation, whether driven by domestic overheating or Chinese growth. Precious metals excel when central bank credibility is questioned.

Figure 4.17 estimates the inflation sensitivity of many asset classes based on a composite metric. Most assets that dominate investor portfolios – bonds, stocks, and real estate – tend to get hurt by inflation surprises. Commodities in general and gold specifically are among the few assets that benefit. The other one is break-even inflation trade (long TIPS, short Treasuries).

A common misperception sees equities and illiquid real assets as good *inflation hedges*. It is true that these assets may offer long-run *inflation protection* if they offer sufficiently high real premia. However, hedging ability is more about relatively short-term correlations. Historically, positive inflation surprises have tended to hurt the valuations of long-duration real assets. For example, real estate is a long-duration asset whose market capitalization was low in the inflationary 1970s and high in the disinflationary 2000s. Overall, illiquid real assets have inflation protection potential but less inflation hedging potential. This is why I say commodities (and break-even inflation) are as good as it gets when it comes to inflation hedging. I do not necessarily predict high inflation, but I can confidently say that most investor portfolios are not well-positioned if it arrives.

Commodities' rare inflation hedging ability raises the broader question on *why* commodities should theoretically offer a positive risk premium. Perhaps the inflation hedging ability points in the other direction. However, as noted in the context of bond risk premia, any inflation premium in bonds has been negligible since the turn of the century, so commodities' inflation hedging ability may be available for free. If inflation uncertainty rises meaningfully and inflation-related required premia increase, it should boost commodity prices and then lower their expected returns.

The historical long-run reward for commodities is better explained by positive growth sensitivities and equity market betas (many commodities are clearly cyclical). Idiosyncratic risks to commodities may also matter as highly volatile commodity returns could justify positive required premia in segmented markets. Or producers' hedging pressure could push futures prices lower and give rise to positive roll returns in commodity futures (an old theory of "normal backwardation"). The last explanation is, however, hard to reconcile with the persistent negative roll in commodity futures in recent decades.

Chapter 5

Illiquidity Premia

- Private illiquid asset classes are a small part of *investable* wealth, but a steadily growing share of institutional portfolios.
- Investor expectations of illiquidity premia and manager-specific alpha may be too optimistic. Growing popularity and investor liking of smooth returns may offset much of a fair illiquidity premium, and all managers cannot deliver positive alpha.
- Recent studies of equity-like long-run returns in housing have been challenged. It is debatable whether real estate earns positive or negative real growth besides net rental yields.
- Direct real estate has not earned any illiquidity premia over listed REITs, while long-run private-equity industry returns are fairly well matched by small-cap value stocks.
- Evidence on illiquidity premia within listed assets also looks underwhelming, but some liquidity provision strategies have been historically successful.

Liquidity is a nebulous, multi-faceted concept. Market liquidity refers to the owner's ability to trade an asset at low cost and minimal price impact. Three key facets of market liquidity can be listed as tightness, depth, and resilience.[1] High trading costs, inability to trade large amounts, and long lock-up periods during which an asset can only be sold at a punitive cost are distinct ways illiquidity can harm an investor.

---

[1] Apart from cost, volume, and time dimensions, there are also important aspects of funding liquidity and liquidity risk premia which I will ignore here. Acharya-Pedersen (2005) distinguishes rewards for illiquidity from rewards for liquidity risk (an asset's sensitivity to fluctuations in various liquidity conditions), both of which are relevant. See Ilmanen (2011, Chapter 18) and Amihud-Mendelson-Pedersen (2012) for overviews.

This multidimensionality means that it is hard to measure illiquidity well within one asset class and almost impossible across as different asset classes as government bonds, stocks, hedge funds, and private equity. By combining different metrics, it may be possible to come up with a reasonable liquidity ranking across assets. Generally, the liquidity order is cash, futures, bonds, stocks, hedge funds, private assets; and within these groups, government bonds before credits, large-cap stocks before small-cap stocks, developed markets before emerging markets, and so on. Larger trading volumes and shorter maturities help.

Measuring illiquidity is hard but measuring illiquidity premia is harder because these tend to be blended with other risk premia. Many investors appear to believe in illiquidity premia as a reliable fact of life, with only the equity premium being a more reliable source of long-run return. Yet, more careful empirical analysis reveals surprisingly modest illiquidity premia.

I next categorize illiquidity premia in three ways: illiquid alternative/private assets, less liquid public assets, and liquidity provision strategies. This chapter will mainly cover the first and only review the last two briefly.

5.1. Illiquid Alternative/Private Assets

Ignoring niche markets like art and other collectibles or music royalties and litigation financing, the three largest illiquid alternative asset classes are:

- Real estate (residential and commercial real estate, farmland, infrastructure, etc.)
- Private equity (buyouts, venture capital, etc.)
- Private credit (plus other illiquid debt)

I focus next on real estate and private equity (buyouts). I cover only briefly other private assets because the histories are too short, markets too small, and data too dubious for conclusive analysis. I will present some evidence on other illiquids but argue that we may learn more by extrapolating from larger illiquid markets.

This is quite a disparate group of assets. What are the common characteristics among most of them?

- Alternatives are naturally defined by *what they are not: Traditional assets* (stocks, bonds, cash). One catch is that real estate is an older asset class than stocks, and it used to dominate the wealth of many early individual and institutional investors.
- Alternatives are *often private* (not listed or publicly traded) and thus less regulated. There are exceptions. Commodity futures are often counted as important alternatives even though they are publicly traded and liquid. In contrast, most bonds are not traded in exchanges, but there is more active trading and more pricing transparency than for illiquid privates.
- *Illiquid alternatives* are a subset where you lock your investment for a longer period, or at least the cost of liquidating is significant. This is not a binary choice as secondary markets are enhancing liquidity for private equity, and trading costs in real estate have edged lower over time. Hedge funds are quite diverse in their liquidity profiles, but I do not include them among illiquid alternatives.
- Illiquid alternatives are in practice *long-only* investments, in contrast to hedge funds and liquid alternatives. Some illiquid assets embed leverage, but no shorting is involved (though levered private asset purchases may be financed with risky high-yield debt or leveraged loans).

- Lack of mark-to-market pricing implies *smoother returns*, which may result in *understated risk* (volatility, drawdowns, equity market betas, and correlations). Many investors like this feature and it may have asset pricing implications.
- There is often *less data* in length, frequency, and quality in illiquid assets. Performance metrics based on internal rates of return (IRR) can be particularly problematic (opaque and game-able), and investors learn more slowly from them.
- Lack of investable indices means that *investors must be active* in illiquid assets, and the performance dispersion among managers is much wider than in traditional assets. Perceived alpha potential allows much higher fees.
- Besides having (somewhat hidden) *equity beta*, many illiquid alternatives are viewed as inflation-protective *real assets*, even if the evidence is hardly clear.

Box 5.1   Share of Illiquid Assets in Global Wealth

Are illiquid assets a sideshow or a headline act? Clearly private asset markets are becoming increasingly popular among institutional investors, given their promise of superior returns without sometimes-painful mark-to-market valuations. Yet, the estimated size of all invest-able private markets (by Preqin in mid-2020) amounts to $7.3trn, out of which one third is "dry powder" (committed but not yet called or deployed capital). This is not a trivial size, nor are the fees earned on it, but it pales in comparison with global equity and bond markets, each of which exceeds $100trn size. See Chapter 3 (Box 3.1) on the global wealth portfolio.

The $7.3trn of investable private markets consists of a majority in broad private equity $4.5trn (split between buyouts or "narrow private equity" $2.3trn, venture capital $1.2trn, growth and other $1.0trn) and a minority in real estate $1.1trn, infrastructure & natural resources $0.9trn, and private debt $0.9trn.[2]

While the growth rates are impressive, these private markets are still at most 5% of the comparable public equity markets and 1% of the public debt market. The use of leverage may boost these shares a little but not meaningfully.

The picture is different, however, when we look at real estate. *The word "investable" makes a difference of one or two orders of magnitude.* The investable real estate market size estimated by Preqin is near $1trn. This is lower than the size of the Reits market – estimated at $1.4–3trn depending on definitions – or the MSCI estimate of professionally managed global real estate at $10trn. And it is nothing compared to some estimates of the total value of global real estate wealth! Tostevin (2017) (gu)estimated a value of $228trn for all global real estate, split between residential real estate $168trn, commercial real estate $32trn, and agricultural land and forest $27trn.

(continued)

---

[2]The $7.3trn estimate from Preqin is in McKinsey (2021). Also see Bain (2021) and PWC (2020). Incidentally, the $7.3trn is geographically split roughly 60% North America, 25% Europe, and 15% Asia and others. It only includes externally managed private capital. Private capital markets are expected to grow further in the 2020s. For example, US public pension plans' alternatives target allocations (private capital plus hedge funds) have risen from 12% in 2001 to 23% in 2010 and to 30% in 2019, and these plans signal interest in further increases.

Another recent study by Goetzmann-Spaenjers-Van Nieuwerburgh (2021) estimates that real and private-value assets – defined as the sum of real estate, infrastructure, collectibles, non-corporate business equity – is an investment class worth $85trn in the US alone.[3]

So taking a really big picture, and ignoring investability issues, total global wealth in 2021 may amount to $400–500trn, half of it in real estate, a quarter in debt, almost a quarter in public equity, and "the rest is change." Comfortingly, a very different method by the Credit Suisse global wealth report points to a 2019 total global wealth of $400trn. But Gadzinski-Schuller-Vacchino (2018) comes up with higher totals by including high estimates for private businesses and non-securitized loans. Finally, many natural resources and human capital are even less directly investable, and their total value can hardly be estimated. In this spirit, Carney (2021) contemplates about the respective values of two Amazons (the river and the company).

Table 5.1 presents performance and risk statistics for a variety of private markets (and a couple of public proxies), all in the US, with varying starting dates but most with 30- to 40-year histories. Importantly, the private market returns are IRR-based and given the lack of mark-to-market pricing and artificially smooth returns, their risks are understated.

The smoothed returns ensure that all private assets have attractive risk-adjusted returns. Yet, in most cases, also the long-run raw returns (note everything is in expressed in excess of cash) look striking.

Does Housing Beat Equities in the Long Run?

The Jorda-Knoll-Kuvshinov-Schularick-Taylor (2019) study has a proud title, "The Rate of Return on Everything, 1870–2015," and is arguably the past decade's most important new empirical study of long-run asset returns. This magisterial effort analyzes a long and broad data set: one and half centuries worth of returns in sixteen countries on equities, bonds, bills, and – as the novelty – on housing. This addition is so important because housing is the world's largest asset class *if* we omit the word "investable." Further, the authors make their data set publicly available in http://www.macrohistory.net/data/, and have already used it in many studies – to explore the impact of pandemics, banking crises, and monetary policy. Kudos.

---

[3]The components are commercial real estate ($33trn), residential real estate ($31trn), agricultural real estate ($3trn), infrastructure ($7trn), collectibles ($6trn), and noncorporate business equity ($6trn). The last item is especially interesting and perhaps underestimated, though its valuation remains debatable. Apart from uninvestable private equity, the unlisted private enterprises include a long tail of millions of uninvestable mom-and-pop stores. These are beyond what Mauboussin and Callahan (2020) remind us are 3,640 listed companies in the US employing 42 million people, 7,200 firms owned by buyout funds employing 5.4 million, and 18,400 companies backed by venture capital firms employing 1.1 million. Although the number of listed US firms has halved since the late 1990s, the firms "lost" to the private side are a small fraction of the listed equities' total market cap. Overall, fewer than 0.1% of all US firms are listed, and unlisted firms account for 69% of private-sector employment and 49% of aggregate pre-tax profits. Vissing-Jørgensen and Moskowitz (2002), Kartashova (2014), and Randl-Westerkamp-Zechner (2018) discuss the relative sizes and relative profitability of listed and unlisted sectors. Early research suggested that these unlisted firms are less profitable than the listed firms, but the new research challenges this finding. Unlisted private sector is likely as important outside the US, famously including the "Mittelstand" firms in Germany and huge family-owned private ventures in the Far East.

Table 5.1 Illiquid Asset Class Performance and Risk Statistics

Series	Buyout PE	Venture Capital	Commercial RE	Residential RE	Timber	Farmland	Infra-structure	Public PE proxy	Public REITs	Private Debt
	Cambridge US Buyout	Cambridge US VC	NCREIF PMI	US Housing Case-Shiller, DLM	NCREIF	NCREIF	Cambridge US Infra	Small Value Stocks	US NAREIT	Leveraged Loans CS
Start date	1986	1986	1978	1978	1988	1991	2003	1986	1978	1992
End date	2020	2020	2020	2020	2020	2020	2020	2020	2020	2020
AM excess/cash	10.45%	12.71%	4.20%	4.60%	7.53%	7.97%	10.54%	11.33%	8.59%	3.26%
GM excess/cash	10.38%	11.49%	4.19%	4.61%	7.50%	8.03%	10.62%	8.81%	7.15%	2.99%
Sharpe ratio (YoY)	0.81	0.28	0.59	0.77	0.79	1.11	1.56	0.57	0.46	0.41
Volatility YoY	13.0%	45.9%	7.1%	6.0%	9.5%	7.2%	6.8%	20.0%	18.6%	7.9%
Max drawdown	-34.4%	-72.6%	-24.7%	-20.0%	-11.2%	-2.2%	-9.5%	-57.8%	-67.4%	-32.8%
Equity mkt correl. YoY	0.75	0.31	0.15	0.24	0.08	0.04	0.22	0.63	0.57	0.62
Autocorrelation Q1	0.34	0.59	0.76	0.62	0.06	0.07	-0.03	-0.09	0.07	0.14

Sources: Bloomberg, Cambridge Associates LLC (with explicit approval by Cambridge Associates), Credit Suisse, NAREIT, and NCREIF. Residential RE returns combine Case-Shiller (1990) house price changes and Davis–Lehnert-Martin (2008) rental yields. Notes: All series end 2020Q4. All are *returns in excess of cash*. Most series are IRR–based except for the two public proxies. Though IRR estimates are based on quarterly data, volatilities and correlations are based on YoY returns to mitigate smoothing effects. Memo item: I quote average cash rate and inflation rate since 1978 (4.9% and 3.5%) and 1988 (3.3% and 2.6%) so that readers can convert above excess returns to total or real.

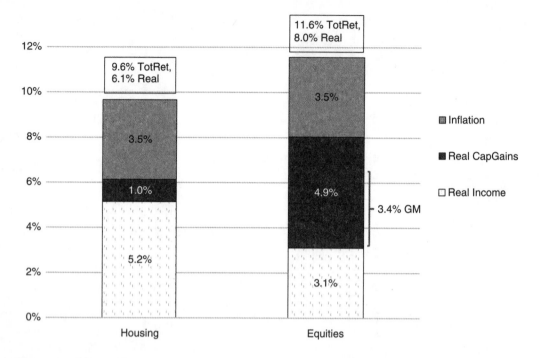

Figure 5.1 Decomposing Arithmetic Mean Returns of US Housing and Equities, 1960–2020
Sources: Jorda et al. (2019), AQR. Notes: I extended the Jorda et al. data with 2016–2020 data from NCREIF and AQR. For anyone wanting to convert these total returns into excess-of-cash returns, cash rates averaged 5%. Income is rental yield and dividend yield, respectively. The main difference if we used geometric means would be 3.4% real capital gains for equities (instead of 4.9% arithmetic), and correspondingly lower total/real returns. For less volatile housing, the geometric means would give only 0.2% lower real capital gains.

That said, the article's most headline-grabbing result is controversial. The authors claim that the long-run returns on housing, or residential real estate, have broadly matched those of equities, and with much lower volatility to boot. Across the 16 countries in the Jorda et al. study, the equal-weighted real return is higher for housing (7.26% versus 6.67%), though when countries are GDP-weighted, the edge goes to equities (6.69% versus 7.04%). Housing was ahead in 10 of 16 countries, though not in the large US and UK and only ahead in 5 of 16 countries since 1950. But housing offered better risk-adjusted returns everywhere, thanks to lacking mark-to-market returns.

Figure 5.1 picks one example. I use Jorda et al. data for US assets 1960–2015 and extend it with 2016–2020 data. I follow the authors in decomposing arithmetic real (and nominal) returns, but I select a more valuation-neutral period, 1960–2020, when neither equity nor housing valuations changed a lot (net).[4] Over this period, equities were ahead by 2.0% (arithmetic mean) or 0.7% (geometric mean).

This case is representative of most countries' long-run experience in that for equities the contributions of real income and real capital gains are roughly comparable, but for housing real capital gains are only a small fraction of real return. (Moreover, the excess-of-cash capital gains are somewhat negative for housing.) Housing earns its long-run returns mainly from income – an empirical

---

[4]The results are broadly similar if I use their longest common sample for housing and equities (1891–2015), though inflation was lower, and equity returns came about 1% more from income than capital gains.

fact that may be missed by people used to house price appreciation during recent decades of falling yields and windfall gains.

The Jorda et al.'s results vary across countries and periods on whether equities or housing outperformed, but the overall finding that housing earned close to equity-like returns with apparently lower risk was a real surprise compared to the earlier literature.

Understandably, this result has been challenged. There are two broad grounds for criticism: possibly overstated *net* rental yields and possibly overstated *quality-adjusted* house price appreciation.

- Total (real or nominal) returns on any asset reflect income and capital gains: in the case of housing, rental yield and house price appreciation. There are fair questions of data availability and quality on both return components (even more so than with stocks and bonds), and the questions have more bite the further back we look.
- Rental yields need to be adjusted for costs (capex, etc.), as only net rental yields are relevant for investment performance. But such costs are especially hard to measure, and the pre-WWII data on either rents or costs is scarce. A large part of these histories reflects the authors' assumptions instead of any real-time sources. Many studies agree with Jorda et al. that the long-run costs are 30–40% of gross rents.[5] However, the validity of the Jorda et al. choice to use recent net rental yields and extrapolate them back to the olden days can be questioned.
- House price appreciation trends should be adjusted for the evolving quality of housing over time, as only the quality-adjusted house price rises accrue to the holders of the existing housing stock. The Knoll-Schularick-Steger (2017) data set used by Jorda et al. includes some quality adjustments in parts of their data histories, but the authors acknowledge that "accurate measurement of quality-adjustments remains a challenge." If quality adjustments are insufficient, housing returns to their owners are overstated.
- A study by Chambers-Spaenjers-Steiner (2021) is a case in point. It uses actual returns on the housing holdings of several UK university endowments, and thus measures more cleanly net rental yields and quality-adjusted house price appreciation. For the most direct comparison, it finds 2.8% net real return for the UK residential real estate portfolio 1901–70, which is 1.6% lower than the Jorda et al. estimate for this period.
- For another example, Jorda et al. estimate that US housing achieved a long-run real total return of 6.0%, including 5.3% rental income and 0.7% real price appreciation between 1891 and 2015. In comparison, Dimson-Marsh-Staunton (2018) find a long-run annual raw real house price appreciation of 0.3% in the US. Worse, after adjusting the series for quality improvements and home expansions, they estimate a negative real growth rate of −2.1%.[6]
- To their credit, Jorda et al. try to preempt various critiques and offer defenses to them, but the inherent limitations in historical housing data may leave the debates unresolved. It is fair to say that their study raises the perceived long-run returns on housing compared to previous literature, even if we'd haircut their estimates by 1.5%. Apart from questions on the average returns for housing, there remain the issues of understated volatility and limited investability.

---

[5]See Demers-Eisfeldt (2021) on US housing, Chambers-Spanjers-Steiner (2021) on UK real estate, and Pagliari (2017) on US commercial real estate. These running costs should be distinguished from the (very high but one-off) transaction costs when buying or selling a house.

[6]In the same vein, Eichholtz et al. (2021) study long-run histories of housing returns in Paris and Amsterdam using direct historical sources, and they find 1.4–2.3% lower estimates than Jorda et al. for the overlapping periods. Evidence on rental income growth echoes these findings. Eichholtz-Korevaar-Lindenthal (2018) reports real growth of rent near zero in many cities over very long histories, and negative after quality adjustments. Pagliari (2017) finds that in the US commercial real estate (1978–2016), real income growth has even been negative.

Real Estate Returns in Recent Decades

So far the analysis focused on housing returns, and housing is not very investable. Let us now consider commercial real estate, often proxied in the US by the NCREIF index. Table 5.1 pointed to broadly similar returns for US commercial real estate as for housing for 1978–2020 (above 4% over cash, near 8% real, and above 9% total return). Francis-Ibbotson (2020) reports more recent evidence 1991–2018: real compound return for housing of 3.8%, commercial real estate of 1.5%, and farmland of 4.4%. In all cases, the net rental income yield exceeded the total return. Average net rental yields over this period were near 5% for housing but even 7% for commercial real estate and farmland. Such high yields make me wonder if cost adjustments have been sufficient; in any case, today's rental yields are much lower. And while all these return estimates must be taken with a grain of salt, any risk estimates require a heap of salt given the artificially smooth returns.[7]

In general, I argue that unlike equities, real estate may earn all (and more than all) of its long-run return from income (and nothing sustainable from real capital gains). Empirically, the long-run real price appreciation or real income growth have been modest, and there are opposite estimates on their sign after quality adjustment.[8] The real quality-adjusted growth rates may well be negative and offset the abundant net rental yield (recall the 5–7% estimates earlier).

My simple takeaway is more cautious than that from Jorda et al. (2019). A housing purchase involves land and structures. The real value of structures built on land decays over time (you spend money fixing it, and eventually many houses get replaced with a new one), while the real value of land could stay stable or even rise over time. If you rent out the house, some of the rental income goes to various costs and the rest (in excess of Treasury yield) is compensation for the various hassles and risks. (Even though house prices evolve smoothly, most generations get at least one reminder that real estate investing *is* risky.) The rental growth rate might match inflation over time, but it seems plausible that it lags inflation for a given house, reflecting its decaying quality. Finally, there may be valuation changes over time; these tend to wash out over the very long term but can matter for decades. Unfortunately, the current generation of real estate investors may extrapolate past decades' generous returns. (Some windfall gains reflect higher capitalization partly due to lower real yields, partly to improved investability and liquidity, and partly to the greater availability of mortgage credit.) Such investors will not easily believe that the net rental yield they earn from a house is likely the ceiling on its long-run expected return, not the floor (pun intended).

---

[7]The fact that most properties are traded infrequently makes the construction of property indices much harder than that of, say, equity indices. An index of property values may be constructed based on appraisals (which are smooth and often stale) or on actual transactions prices (which involve a smaller sample and may represent a biased version of the universe). To adjust for the evolving quality of properties, index providers use some mix of hedonic-price method and repeat-sales method. For total return calculations, the net rental income needs to be added. The net income is the gross income minus diverse estimated expenses, such as the maintenance costs, home insurance, property tax, and other administrative costs normally associated with property ownership, plus any lumpy capital expenditures. Many studies subtract either a proportional one-third of gross income or a fixed 2% annual cost.

[8]Studies with positive real quality-adjusted house price trend (ca. 1%) include Jorda et al. (2019), Case-Shiller (1990), and Demers-Eisfeldt (2021), while Dimson-Marsh-Staunton (2018), Chambers-Spanjers-Steiner (2021), and Eichholtz et al. (2021) point to negative trends in real prices or rents after quality adjustment. The experience of recent decades may have been more benign, thanks to the windfall gains likely related to the general fall in real yields. For commercial real estate (especially the NCREIF index since 1978 or 1991), Pagliari (2017) and Francis-Ibbotson (2020) imply negative real growth or price trends that offset some of the abundant net income. Ruff (2007) and Ilmanen-Chandra-McQuinn (2019) assume a zero real income growth trend.

Comparing Direct and Listed Real Estate

The positive rewards for many assets in Table 5.1 may be taken as evidence of illiquidity premia. Yet, arguably the cleanest comparison is between direct private real estate and listed REITs. The 43-year window 1978–2020 is also the longest history we have to estimate the illiquidity premium in private assets – and there is no sign of it. Rather the reverse, as the more liquid REITs trounced the illiquid NCREIF (7% versus 4% compound return over cash).

Now, to be fair, the NCREIF index is unlevered while REITs may involve leverage of nearly 50%; thus, NCREIF's lower volatility is not only due to its lack of mark-to-market pricing. However, Ang-Nabar-Wald (2013) adjusted the indices to be comparable in terms of leverage as well as sector composition – and still found mildly higher return for the more liquid REITs than NCREIF. So even if there may be some illiquidity premia in real estate, they have historically been no larger than what we find in some corners of listed equity markets (REITs). Some observers counter that even after adjustments, the two asset classes are simply too different to draw conclusions on illiquidity premia.

Private Equity (Buyout) Returns

Leveraged buyout funds are the largest segment of the PE market, and often the label PE is used narrowly for them. PE managers strive to create real value through active ownership and governance of firms, or what Kaplan-Stromberg (2009) call governance engineering, financial engineering, and operational engineering. Active PE managers may conceivably help transform companies ("grow the pie"), while active public equity managers arguably compete in a zero-sum game.

At first blush, the long-run performance of US buyouts has been extraordinary. Their funds outperformed the S&P500 index by 2–3% annually over 30+ years, and this is after 5–6% annual all-in fees,[9] and for all buyout funds – not just the top quartile.[10] Gross-of-fee returns or top-quartile

---

[9]It is not straightforward to translate into one all-in fee the typical diverse PE fund fees: 2% management fee, 20% performance fee ("carried interest"), a hurdle rate with waterfall provisions, and additional portfolio company fees. Phalippou-Gottschalg (2009) estimated all fees to amount to 6% per year. More recently, CEM Benchmarking surveyed large institutional investors, and found total fees to be 5.7% p.a. comprising 2.7% in management fees, 1.9% in carried interest (performance fee), and 1.2% for other fees, including net portfolio company fees (see Doskeland-Stromberg (2018)). Coinvestments and direct investments can have clearly lower fees, but the deals may suffer from selection bias (the "lemons" problem), and Ivashina-Lerner (2019) find no higher net returns to end-investors from such arrangements than from the more costly PE funds.

[10]See Ilmanen-Chandra-McQuinn (2020). This positive verdict has gone through various gyrations over time in the academic literature. Kaplan-Schoar (2005) and others showed that buyout firms did not outperform the S&P500 after fees in the long run, which I summarized as a PE-cautious consensus view in Ilmanen (2011). Then Stucke (2011) found an error in some PE databases, which had led to understated returns in the 1990s; after this correction, the long-run evidence again pointed to PE outperformance. But then Harris-Jenkinson-Kaplan (2014, 2016) reported that buyout fund vintages since 2006 no longer outperformed the S&P500, while Phalippou (2014) and L'Her et al. (2016) showed that even the long-run outperformance crumbled when more PE-relevant public equity benchmarks were used. I took these studies as the basis for another PE-cautious consensus view in Ilmanen-Chandra-McQuinn (2020). Brown-Kaplan (2019) brought a more positive reading of the evidence, partly based on new 2010s data, and Brown-Hu-Kuhn (2019) reported outperformance of PE and venture capital over 60/40 for 1987–2017. Beath-Flynn (2020) analyzed PE performance for large institutional investors in the CEM Benchmarking database for 1996–2018 and found mild underperformance against small-cap stocks. Phalippou's overviews (2019, 2020) presented the most critical view.

The only safe prediction may be that this seesawing of verdicts is not over yet. And this is the fluctuating reading on a relatively mature illiquid asset class, PE. Maybe readers can now appreciate why I believe it is premature to form judgments based on the historical performance of newer illiquid assets such as infrastructure and private debt.

manager returns are even more impressive. Combined with apparently lower risk than for public equities (lack of mark-to-market helps), and great stories to boot, the lure is understandable.

However, what is relevant for end-investors is the prospective net return, and the experience has been less compelling after David Swensen's Yale Model popularized private assets among institutional investors. The industry has been hard-pressed to deliver any net outperformance over public equities in fund vintages since 2006 (using better performance measures than internal rates of return, such as public-market equivalents); see Figure 5.2A.

Historical performance measures are not the only relevant evidence on prospective PE returns. Forward-looking indicators, such as the narrow valuation gap between private and public equity (see Figure 5.2B), as well as the tighter competitive environment (PE firms, cash-rich corporations, and large institutional funds have much capital arguably chasing too few deals), point to lower PE outperformance in the future. It does not seem like a coincidence that the growing institutional popularity of PE in the mid-2000s was followed by a much slimmer ex-ante valuation edge and ex-post return edge of PE over public equity. Continued investor inflows point to still-high return expectations, but unless the high PE fees fall, it may be hard for PE funds to keep beating the fees.[11]

So far, fee pressure on PE managers has been limited amid persistent institutional inflows. Some institutional investors have begun to ask if PE returns can be demystified or even replicated with public equities. One goal is to enhance understanding of the total portfolio (public and private assets) in a common framework. Another goal is to help push PE fees lower over time if PE performance could be even partially replicated at lower fees, thereby creating a viable challenger to the high-fee industry (as happened with hedge funds in the past 15 years).

The PE demystifying effort is at its early stages, with a few commercial providers and limited institutional uptake. Empirical analysis of PE fund holdings reveals plenty of market beta (though partly hidden by smooth returns), plenty of leverage (though less than in the olden days), factor tilts toward small-cap and value stocks, as well as persistent sector tilts that could be replicated in public markets. But with public markets comes mark-to-market volatility, and the manager-specific activism within portfolio companies can hardly be replicated. The long-run outperformance of PE looks slimmer if PE is compared to more relevant equity benchmarks such as levered equity or small-cap value stocks (see Figure 5.2A and Table 5.1).[12]

All these topics are discussed in more detail in Doskeland-Stromberg (2018) and Ilmanen-Chandra-McQuinn (2020), with extensive literature references. Asset owners should better understand the fundamental sources of the private equity return edge over public equity, instead

---

[11]Investors may still expect abundant illiquidity premia for the asset class, motivated by marketing materials, which tout high past returns based on potentially misleading and gameable performance metrics such as internal rates of return. Or investors may be overoptimistic about manager-specific alpha. Catching the top-quartile managers was long thought to be easier in private assets, but the early evidence on alpha persistence has later been overturned. It remains easier to be confident on your own investments when half of the funds claim to be top-quartile (Harris-Jenkinson-Stucke (2012)) and performance feedback arrives slowly. Overoptimism and overconfidence are generally found to be more prevalent in situations where learning and feedback opportunities are weak. Finally, investors like private assets for their smooth returns.

[12]On performance comparison versus more PE-relevant benchmarks, Ilmanen et al. (2020) reviews the literature, such as Phalippou (2014) and Stafford (2017); also see Figure 5.2A. While some replication/demystifying efforts have focused on the similarity of buyout targets with small-cap value stocks, others have focused on the sector choices by PE managers (see Kinlaw-Kritzman-Mao (2015)). The latter approach was surely more successful in the 2010s when small-cap value stocks lagged, while the tech sector overweight of buyout firms excelled. Re the levered equity as a benchmark (e.g. 1.3 × market index), Czasonis et al. (2020) challenge this idea because PE leverage may be mainly applied to lower-risk equities.

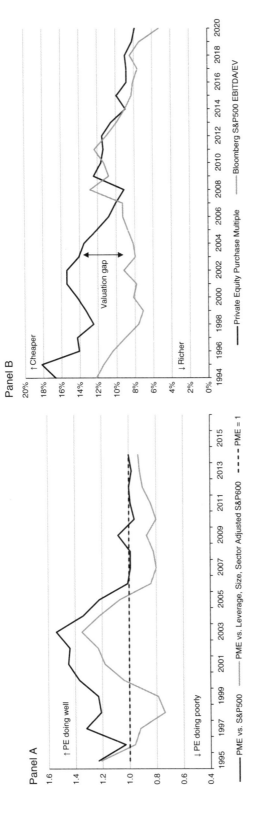

Panel A

Panel B

Figure 5.2 A–B Both Ex-Post and Ex-Ante Edge of Private Equity Are Weakening.

Sources: Public market equivalent returns (PMEs) are from L'Her et al. (2016). Vintage years are assigned based on the year of the first investment by a fund. EBITDA/EVs since 2008 are calendar-year averages of the median EBITDA/EV from Pitchbook and the average EBITDA/EV from Bain & Company. PE EBITDA/EV from 1998 to 2008 are a proprietary dataset from Dan Rasmussen, based on data from Cambridge Associates and Capital IQ. S&P500 EBITDA/EV is from Bloomberg. Notes: PME or public–market equivalent on the left chart is a performance metric which shows how much a PE fund, or here a vintage of PE funds launched in a given year, outperformed a public equity index (S&P500 or a better-matching index) over the fund's life. PME values above 1 signal PE outperformance. The typical long-run value of PME 1.2 signals 20% total outperformance and corresponds to roughly 3% annual outperformance, given funds' typical capital usage of six to seven years. The valuation chart on the right uses the most common valuation metric in private equity (after inverting it, as with E/P): EBITDA/EV or the earnings before interest, taxes, depreciation, and amortization over the enterprise value which includes both equity and debt.

of just relying on elusive illiquidity premia. Our study tried to decompose the PE edge to the growth, leverage, valuation, and yield advantages – and the fee disadvantage. Such efforts are hampered by data limitations, and the role of components may vary over time. Some observers say that 20 years ago the main edge came from the valuation gap, a decade ago from leverage, and now (2021) from growth advantage (which to me seems hardest to sustain, but the argument goes that the unlisted sector is more dynamic than the mature listed sector).

Smoothing Service Offsetting a Fair Illiquidity Premium

The long-run evidence of a scant illiquidity premium in real estate and private equity markets is surprising to many and raises a natural question: *Why?*

It is important to distinguish between normative and descriptive results. Many studies that estimate how large the illiquidity premia investors *should* require (due to high trading costs and inability to sell assets or rebalance portfolios)[13] do not stress enough that the empirical reality may be quite different. Investors perhaps should demand, say, 3–5% excess return as a fair reward for locking up their money for a decade;[14] yet I argue that both logically and based on historical evidence, receiving as much is not a realistic expectation.

My best explanation for the finding of scant illiquidity premia in real estate and private equity is their lack of mark-to-market pricing. This feature makes private assets' measured risk artificially low and flatters their diversification potential. Yet, we likely collectively pay for this comfort by accepting a lower return premium for private assets. A common investor preference for smooth returns may offset a large part of the fair illiquidity premium that would otherwise be required for locking the money away for a long period (Ilmanen 2020).[15] Asness (2019b) even raises the possibility that the sign gets flipped and PE funds may offer an illiquidity *discount* – that is, lower expected returns than public equity in exchange for their lack of mark-to-market volatility.

Figure 5.3 illustrates this point visually. The "bumpy ride" chart shows the cumulative return over 35 years of a small-cap value index, while the "smooth sailing" chart shows the Cambridge buyout index return. As seen in Table 5.1, both series earned broadly comparable long-run returns. Which experience would you prefer?

---

[13]See Ang-Papanikolaou-Westerfield (2014), Kinlaw-Kritzman-Turkington (2017), Baz et al. (2021), and Broeders-Jansen-Werker (2021). Liquidity needs and thus requires illiquidity premia to vary across investors, and the aggregate premium may depend on the share of long- and short-horizon investors in the economy.

[14]This is just an example, if broadly in line with the Ang-Papanikolaou-Westerfield (2014). Specific numbers depend on the model and its parameters.

[15]These points are so far underappreciated in the academic literature. It has of course been widely noted that the use of appraisal values and internal rates of return in private assets results in artificially smooth returns and understated risk measures. Symptoms of smoothness include high autocorrelation (see Table 5.1) or high lagged correlation with equity markets. Researchers have proposed various corrections that reveal the higher "true" risk in illiquid assets: statistical techniques (e.g. de-smoothing based on return autocorrelation patterns, including lagged betas using longer return sampling periods) and theoretical considerations (e.g. the much higher leverage in PE implies higher risk than in public equity). Any portfolio optimization exercises either try to modify the inputs to make public and private asset risks more comparable, or impose constraints or caps on illiquid allocation, so that illiquid assets with smooth returns don't dominate the optimal portfolio. But the impact of return smoothness on investor demand for private assets and on their expected returns has hardly been covered in the extant literature.

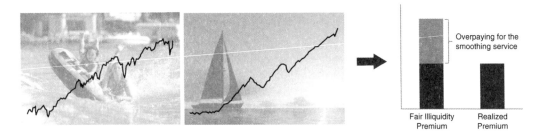

Figure 5.3 Smoothing Service May Offset the Fair Illiquidity Premium.
Sources: AQR, Cambridge Associates, Ken French Data Library, Getty Images, Adobe Stock.

Smoothness preference is nothing new. John Maynard Keynes wrote already in 1938: "Some Bursars will buy without a tremor unquoted and unmarketable investments in real estate which, if they had a selling quotation for immediate cash available at each Audit, would turn their hair grey. The fact that you do not [know] how much its ready money quotation fluctuates does not, as is commonly supposed, make an investment a safe one."[16]

Some purists argue that we should just ignore the raw private asset returns in any risk analysis. I don't. Even thoughtful investors who regard the reported private asset returns as misleadingly stable[17] may still care about them. Reported returns often have real-world consequences – for example, regulatory required cash flows may depend on these reported returns. As importantly, smoothness can improve organizational patience and enable institutions to make larger equity allocations and thus earn more equity premium. Just contrast the 25% drawdown by the Cambridge buyout index experienced during the GFC against a 60% drawdown by small-cap value stocks over the same period. This difference matters, as a larger drawdown is more likely to trigger ill-timed capitulations.

Smoothness confers perceived and actual benefits to investors. But investors should not think such benefits come without a cost.

Other Private Assets

I have less to say about other private assets, such as venture capital, farmland, timber, infrastructure, and private debt.[18] These smaller asset classes may have even better-looking historical performance than real estate and private equity, though over shorter histories and with the same possible biases in the databases (IRR-based returns are always problematic even if there were no

---

[16]Chambers-Dimson (2015) found this less famous quote in Keynes, *Post Mortem on Investment Policy,* p.108. King's College, Cambridge, Archive. For context, Keynes managed the King's College endowment and was ahead of his times in making the portfolio heavily equity-oriented. This worked out great in the long run, but it must have frustrated Keynes to listen to his smug non-marked-to-market peers during visible market downturns.
[17]For example, such investors might think that an economically realistic annual return volatility of PE is near 20% rather than the reported 9% (long-term volatility for the Cambridge Associates buyout index using quarterly returns), and a reasonable equity market beta is nearer 1.3 than the reported 0.5. In reality, reported PE returns have a large equity market beta for persistent market moves but a small beta for temporary fluctuations. The latter feature may have contributed to the (mis)perception that PE is a good diversifier to public equity. Smoothing helps private assets in fast, V-shaped bear markets, but not in protracted ones. These assets have "slow beta."
[18]See Ivashina-Lerner (2019), Nicholas (2019), Andonov-Kräussl-Rauh (2021), and Munday et al. (2018), as well as Bain and McKinsey private market yearbooks.

selection biases among funds) and/or in the sample period (a benign window of falling real yields and growing institutional demand).

The returns shown in Table 5.1 reflect varying degrees of (partly hidden) market beta, illiquidity, and other premia, and manager-specific alpha (which is not always positive). My message that fair illiquidity premia get partly offset by our collective preference for smooth returns applies to all private assets.

Private asset classes have become increasingly popular among institutional investors, and large amounts of "dry powder" are one symptom of related absorption challenges. Despite gradually improving transparency, private markets are so opaque that few clear metrics show how much valuations have increased and/or deal quality has fallen in recent years. Anecdotal evidence and expert comments suggest caution is warranted.

Current Outlook on Illiquid Alternatives

I focus here on real estate. Investors used to rising real house prices in recent decades may not recognize the one-off boost from falling real yields. Extrapolating this return experience when real yields on both bonds and real estate are low seems dangerous, just like with equities. After falling sharply around the 2007–9 GFC, house prices have again risen to record-high levels in many markets. As emphasized for bonds and stocks near Figure 2.1, "rearview-mirror expectations" miss the twin facts that although low real bond yields can *justify* higher real asset valuations, *past realized returns include windfall gains* from those yield falls, and current high valuations imply low starting yields and thus *below-average prospective real asset returns*.

The attribution exercise in Pagliari (2017) is helpful to better understand both historical performance and prospective returns in commercial real estate. I extend his sample period with some years to study the 1978–2020 performance of the NCREIF index (the broad results are unaffected). Figure 5.4 shows that the average gross income yield was 7.6% and the net income 5.1% (so various costs deduct one third from gross). The realized annual growth rate in real rents was –0.8%, reflecting what Pagliari calls "insufficient inflation passthrough" (nominal rental growth does not quite match the general inflation rate). However, this negative term was offset by the windfall gains due to the index cap rate falling from roughly 8% to 4% during the 43-year

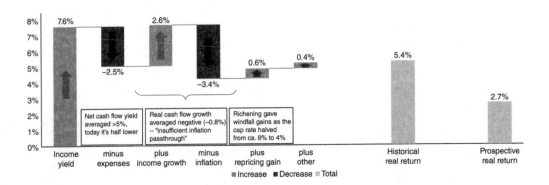

Figure 5.4 Decomposing the Real Return of the NCREIF Commercial Real Estate Index, 1978–2020
Sources: Pagliari (2017), NCREIF. Notes: I extend until 2020 the performance attribution analysis in Pagliari (2017) for 1978–2016.

sample period and to other effects missed by the attribution. Overall, the realized real return of the index was 5.4%, near the average net income.

For a forward-looking analysis, we can start from the recent gross income yield near 4% and deduct a third for costs to get a net income yield of 2.7%. If we then assume zero real cash flow growth rate (better than the historical experience of -0.8% but lower than commonly expected) and assume zero for valuation changes and "other," the expected real return is 2.7%. This prospective return could easily be lower if the real income growth remains negative and/or if real estate valuations mean revert. Still, any positive estimate would beat Treasuries whose expected real returns are negative or near zero.

Overall, it seems that much of the actual and expected returns on private assets may be explained by traditional risks (equity beta, interest rate risk), especially after adjusting for smooth returns. There may have been larger required illiquidity premia in the olden days and in distressed market conditions such as Fall 2008 and Spring 2020. In more complacent times, required illiquidity premia may vanish.

Valuation and expected return data are even harder to come by for private asset classes than historical return data. Figures 5.2B and 5.4, as well as Ilmanen-Chandra-McQuinn (2019, 2020), give some forward-looking estimates on private equity and real estate (which come with all the warnings of data limitations in private assets; they also miss the further richening of housing and other assets in 2021). They support one of my key messages: It is not just bonds — also private assets have expected returns near record-low levels. Their popularity among institutions makes it likely that even the relative expected returns are not what they used to be. That said, even a modest positive expected return over public assets is welcome. And those who really can identify superior private-asset managers in advance will fare much better.

5.2. Less Liquid Public Assets

Within stock and bond markets, some less liquid segments may offer illiquidity premia. However, illiquidity premia are almost never measured purely, or harvested alone. Instead, they come bundled with other premia. The most common examples are small-cap stocks and corporate bonds.

My colleagues' research indicates that small-cap stocks offer limited long-run premium beyond their higher beta exposures (see Chapter 6 (Box 6.1)). Whatever premium remains is in micro-caps and is best interpreted as an illiquidity premium. Academic literature includes numerous specific liquidity-related factors, such as the Amihud (2002) price impact measure and the Pastor-Stambaugh (2003) liquidity risk premium proxy.[19] These liquidity-related premia have not been a great success in the practitioner world (as factor tilts or alternative risk premia products), and the academic study "Replicating Anomalies" by Hou et al. (2020) found their replication success the worst.

Turning to debt, corporate bonds and convertible bonds may earn both a default premium and illiquidity premium, among other things. Again, these are not easy to disentangle. A sharper cross-sectional study of corporate bonds by Richardson-Palhares (2019) finds little evidence that, after controlling for credit quality, less liquid bonds earn higher returns. Lastly, inflation-indexed

---

[19]The Pastor-Stambaugh measure has on paper excellent in-sample and out-of-sample performance. However, the strategy is very trading intensive — it is correlated with short-term reversal strategies — and may not be profitable net of trading costs.

government bonds are often less liquid than nominal government bonds; they seem to offer some illiquidity premium, especially during flight-to-quality and flight-to-liquidity episodes. Indeed, illiquidity premia may be more clearly identified by asset performance during such episodes than by their long-run average returns.

Overall, evidence from this brief section concurs with the first section's message that, while many investors consider illiquidity premia to be among the more reliable long-run return sources, supportive empirical evidence is surprisingly limited.

5.3. Liquidity Provision Strategies

The last section of liquidity-related premia gives the most promising empirical evidence, at least on paper. Liquidity provision can be done at any horizon, from within-second to within-day to multi-month. The fastest variants have the best breadth but obviously involve high turnover. Only a small subset of market participants with either an intermediary position (crossing end-investor flows), or a niche specialist role, or a superior trading technology with low trading costs are likely to make net profits. Moreover, these strategies are capacity constrained: The percentage returns may be high, but available dollar returns are capped.

Liquidity provision implies taking the other side against investors who have particular liquidity needs and being rewarded for this (while hoping that the presumed "liquidity traders" are not actually "informed traders" who take advantage of you). Liquidity providers may try to anticipate further flows and position accordingly, but they can also exploit the temporary price pressure amid intensive buying or selling. The former approach involves extrapolation, the latter a contrarian style (i.e. buy cheap when an asset price is temporarily depressed by selling pressure, and enjoy the likely rebound).

Here is a list of diverse liquidity provision strategies:

- Short-term reversal and Pastor-Stambaugh factors in stock selection (these are related to market-making or high-frequency trading strategies); contrarian market timing strategies have the same spirit but a longer horizon.
- Arbitrage strategies such as merger arbitrage (buy the target and sell the acquirer upon a merger announcement when the natural investor flow goes the other way), convertible arbitrage (buy convertible bonds at issuance and hedge their key risks), and fixed-income arbitrage (e.g. buy the less liquid off-the-run bond against the popular liquid on-the-run bond). None of these involve truly *riskless* arbitrage.
- Other "event" regularities such as index rebalancing (S&P500/Russell/MSCI index additions and deletions), government bond auctions, price pressures with "fallen angels" in credits, or futures rolls (GSCI monthly roll to new contract).
- Long/short strategies favoring the back contracts in many futures where most market participants prefer to be long the most liquid front contact.
- Some calendar or seasonal regularities appear related to liquidity provision, but there are also other explanations (see Box 5.2).

Finally, this chapter said little about *hedge funds*. They do offer all three types of illiquidity premia, especially the last one, but no single metric will capture this well. Hedge funds are a poster boy for the notion that illiquidity premia cannot be harvested alone but are bundled with other premia. I return to hedge funds in Chapter 7, when after covering various systematic long/short premia I address manager-specific alpha.

Box 5.2   Calendar Strategies

Calendar or seasonal strategies come in many forms and frequencies. I only cover them briefly because trading costs often make them unimplementable for most investors.

My previous book (Chapter 25) discussed in some detail the January effect (seasonally strong performance for risky assets, such as volatile, low-quality, small-cap stocks) and the Halloween effect (strong overall equity market performance for six months starting from Halloween, followed by "sell in May and go away"). Here I will briefly discuss same-month seasonality across years, announcement day effects, turn-of-the-month effect, and within-day effects (mainly in equity markets).

Same-month seasonality refers to the tendency of observing high returns in the same calendar month each year. Heston-Sadka (2008) report this pattern for individual stocks, while Keloharju-Linnainmaa-Nyberg (2016) find it even stronger in systematic factors and also document it in other asset classes. There has been some debate to what extent this pattern can be explained by information events (say, earnings announcements) and related resolution of uncertainty, seasonal dividend payments, or varying risk tolerance tendencies across the year.

Risk taking has been better rewarded on announcement days than other days. This higher reward seems to go beyond just higher risk on such days. Single stocks tend to earn higher returns on the earnings announcement days, as do many style premia and anomalies. Beta risk tends to be rewarded on macroeconomic announcement days (the equity index future performs abnormally well and high-beta stocks outperform low-beta stocks). Resolution of uncertainty seems like a natural explanation, except that some recent studies suggest that the main rewards have already been earned in the hours before the announcement.[20]

Turn-of-the-month effect refers to the tendency for equity markets to underperform about a week before the month end, and outperform at the turn of the month. Etula et al. (2020) explain these patterns by systematic payment cycles that imply selling pressure ("dash for cash") before the month end and buying pressure when new cash has been received.

Within-day effects include many regularities. Lou-Polk-Skouros (2019) report that much of the equity premium and all the momentum strategy profits are earned in the overnight hours when the US equity markets are closed, while many defensive strategies perform better during the trading day. Overnight returns predict positively the next overnight returns but negatively the next intraday returns. Possible explanations include market-makers' inventory management where they want to be compensated for taking overnight risk; the tug of war between retail investors trading more in the morning and institutions more near the market close; and patterns of persistent execution flows.

[20]See Frazzini-Lamont (2007), Savor-Wilson (2014), Engelberg-McLean-Pontiff (2018), and Cieslak et al. (2019). Especially the FOMC days (US central bank meetings where major monetary policy decisions are made) and preceding periods have been bullish times for equities in recent decades – possibly reflecting some information leakage of generally equity-friendly policies.

Chapter 6

Style Premia

- Style investing through long-only smart-beta strategies and long/short alternative risk premia grew in popularity in the 2010s. However, disappointing performance especially by stock selection value strategies later cooled investor interest.
- Long-run evidence is still compelling for four broad styles, which have provided positive long-run rewards in multiple asset classes. Combining styles and diversifying across asset classes should smooth style premia performance.
- Value-based stock selection and other contrarian strategies have been profitable over a century or more within and across stock, bond, currency, and commodity markets. Yet they are vulnerable to structural changes, as seen again in the late 2010s. As a flipside, the terrible performance of value-based stock selection brought ex-ante value spreads to record levels.
- Momentum strategies across securities and directional trend-following strategies have, if anything, an even better – and longer – historical track record. The blemishes include the "momentum crash" in spring 2009 for stock selection momentum, and bland performance of trend following in the 2010s amid curtailed trends.
- Carry and other income strategies also combine a strong long-run record with at-best middling recent performance. Some carry strategies (currency, credit, volatility selling) are obviously risky, with large equity beta and tail exposures, yet other carry strategies have remained curiously benign.
- Defensive and quality strategies are especially powerful within equity markets, where they have performed well over multiple decades, including the 2010s. In short, risk taking has not been well rewarded *within* asset classes, likely due to a mix of leverage aversion and lottery preferences.

Style premia have together with asset class premia the most compelling empirical evidence on earning long-run rewards in many contexts. Style premia (also called alternative risk premia, alternative beta, liquid alternatives, exotic beta, etc.) are publicly known dynamic long/short strategies with expected positive rewards.

- I focus on long/short applications, which are a pure way of harvesting style premia. Another possibility is to harvest them through overweight and underweight tilts in a long-only portfolio. Long-only portfolios that blend asset class premia and style tilts are often called "smart beta" strategies.
- "Factor investing" or "style investing" are broad terms that encompass both long-only smart beta and long/short style premia. Long/short strategies enable much more aggressive use of diversification, through shorting and leverage, than long-only style tilts. In comparison to asset class premia, style premia have more dynamic portfolio contents. These strategies target certain portfolio characteristics and involve trading when asset characteristics change over time.
- In this chapter, I cover four style premia, broadly described as value, momentum, carry, and defensive. In Chapter 7, I turn to more proprietary "alpha" which is the manager-specific excess return unexplained by systematic factors.
- Apart from using factors/styles to improve our portfolios, we can use them to improve our understanding. Even if you only invest in discretionary active managers, factors/styles can help demystify their active returns and show how much they reflect simple market exposure, various alternative risk premia, and proprietary alpha.

For years, academics and practitioners have tried to identify persistent systematic sources of return. The list of potential rewarded styles is endless, and researchers are incentivized to find promising results. Concern for data mining or overfitting thus makes it reasonable to be skeptical about any empirical findings. However, most studies agree on a set of a few long/short styles backed by sound economic rationale, high requirements of consistent empirical performance, and realistic implementability. I highlight four: value, momentum, carry, and defensive. These styles pass the requirements that they have historically generated positive long-run returns in- and out-of-sample (persistent), across a variety of asset classes (pervasive), and using many specifications (robust).[1]

Which Factors Best Represent the Alternative Risk Premia?

Like some self-appointed arbiters of good taste, my senior colleagues at AQR and I feel that our collective contributions might justify a role in debating which factors deserve a place in the

---

[1]My sourcing will be quite AQR-centric in Chapter 6 because AQR has been so central in the style premia literature. There are the pioneering articles which cover individual styles value and momentum, trend, carry, low-risk, and quality: Asness-Moskowitz-Pedersen (2013), Moskowitz-Ooi-Pedersen (2012), Koijen-Moskowitz-Pedersen-Vrugt (2018), Frazzini-Pedersen (2014), and Asness-Frazzini-Pedersen (2019). We've also covered all styles together and emphasized multi-factor composites in Asness et al. (2015) and Ilmanen et al. (2021). There are also "fact versus fiction" overviews on momentum, value, size, and low risk – Asness-Israel-Moskowitz (2014, 2015), Alquist-Israel-Moskowitz (2018), Alquist-Frazzini-Ilmanen-Pedersen (2020) – and many other articles on more specific topics. Of course, there's a massive literature on style premia beyond AQR; for other overviews, see Berkin-Swedroe (2016) or Wes Gray's co-authored *Quantitative Value* and *Quantitative Momentum*. Most studies focus on experience since 1926, but a new study Baltussen-van Vliet-van Vliet (2021) shows that similar style premia performed well in US stock selection "out of sample" between 1866 and 1926.

canon. For example, Professors Fama and French describe a five-factor model to explain stock returns, but find value redundant within it, while Asness (2014b) resuscitates value by using a timelier variant and adding momentum as a sixth factor.[2] Furthermore, the Fama-French (2015) model excludes momentum, while AQR's research emphasizes the role of momentum but recommends dropping size.

As we'll see later, four major styles – value, momentum, carry, defensive – perform empirically well in several asset classes, and this book uses this quartet as umbrella concepts for ARP. There is a growing consensus on these four factors, though broadening to 6–10 factors is possible. One path involves splitting each factor into two parts: value and reversal, momentum and trend, carry and volatility selling, (statistical) low risk and (fundamental) quality. To split factors further, we could count separately the factor's application in each asset class.

These major styles are the evidence-based choices of *well-rewarded* systematic factors. The choices are admittedly subjective and may reflect some hindsight, even if we emphasize the robustness of the supporting evidence. There are other factors which might be considered well rewarded but which are not as well known. And then there are plenty of *unrewarded* risk factors, for example, those related to industry, country, and currency. In our opinion, the small size factor belongs to this list, unless it counts as one of the modestly rewarded illiquidity premia (see Box 6.1).

Any chosen factor should be distinct from other factors and show similarity within the group. There are intricate ways of creating empirical groupings, such as cluster analysis based on high correlations within clusters, low across clusters – but I simply display one correlation matrix of asset class premia and style premia in Table 6.1.

Box 6.1   The Size Premium

The size premium on small-cap stocks was the first major non-market premium identified (Banz (1981)) and widely applied in practice. It remains a staple in most academic and practitioner analyses since Fama-French (1992). Yet, research by my colleagues (Alquist-Israel-Moskowitz (2018) and Asness et al. (2018)) finds that there is no size premium in the long-run data. Any premium that is not explained by the higher betas is in nontradeable micro-caps.

There may be a positive alpha when multiple factors are controlled for. Specifically, excluding small low-quality (e.g. low profitability) stocks or small growth stocks can resurrect a positive long-run premium for a subset of small-cap stocks.

Any small-cap or microcap premium looks logically like an illiquidity premium. The underwhelming evidence on illiquidity premia in private assets as well as among listed stocks using other metrics is in line with at best modest small-size premia.

As a distinct matter, many other premia appear larger within the small-cap universe, at least on paper, so it might be a "better fishing pond" for factor investing. Higher trading costs and lower capacity offset much of this advantage, however.

Finally, there is limited evidence of a size premium in other asset classes.

---

[2]Among other academic multi-factor models, the four-factor models of Hou-Xue-Zhang (2015) and Stambaugh-Yuan (2017) stand out.

Table 6.1 Correlations Across 17 Premia, 1990—2020

	10Y Treasury	Blmbg Barc Global Agg	Blmb Barc US Corp IG vs Tsy	Blmb Barc US Corp HY vs Tsy	US S&P500	MSCI ACWI	MSCI EAFE	MSCI Emg	GSCI Cmdty	Gold	Hedge Funds	Value Broad	Momentum Broad	Carry Broad	Defensive Broad	Trend Broad	Vol Sell (Index Put)
10Y Treasury	1.00																
Blmbg Barc Global Agg	0.84	1.00															
BlmB US Corp IG vs Tsy	−0.34	0.05	1.00														
BlmB US Corp HY vs Tsy	−0.45	−0.13	0.82	1.00													
US S&P500	−0.14	0.10	0.56	0.61	1.00												
MSCI ACWI	−0.15	0.10	0.61	0.64	0.92	1.00											
MSCI EAFE	−0.13	0.10	0.56	0.58	0.77	0.95	1.00										
MSCI Emg	−0.18	0.04	0.57	0.63	0.70	0.80	0.74	1.00									
GSCI Cmdty	−0.16	−0.09	0.36	0.31	0.25	0.32	0.32	0.31	1.00								
Gold	0.22	0.17	0.08	0.03	−0.01	0.10	0.12	0.22	0.22	1.00							
Hedge Funds	−0.16	0.09	0.60	0.58	0.65	0.69	0.63	0.71	0.43	0.16	1.00						
Value Broad	−0.15	−0.05	0.20	0.24	0.12	0.10	0.08	0.16	0.02	−0.10	−0.03	1.00					
Momentum Broad	0.23	0.13	−0.25	−0.31	−0.20	−0.22	−0.21	−0.22	−0.04	0.10	0.07	−0.61	1.00				
Carry Broad	0.05	0.12	0.25	0.21	0.20	0.22	0.21	0.25	0.20	0.13	0.29	0.06	0.06	1.00			
Defensive Broad	−0.01	0.09	0.11	0.06	−0.13	−0.06	−0.01	−0.03	0.15	0.13	0.07	−0.08	0.16	0.05	1.00		
Trend Broad	0.32	0.34	−0.06	−0.17	−0.06	−0.05	−0.04	−0.04	−0.04	0.18	0.19	−0.35	0.67	0.16	0.14	1.00	
Vol Sell (Index Put)	−0.12	0.05	0.50	0.34	0.20	0.26	0.27	0.28	0.19	−0.03	0.36	−0.10	0.03	0.19	0.01	0.10	1.00

Sources: AQR, Bloomberg.

Generally, within-asset-class correlations across regions are high (0.6 and up), while correlations across asset classes and across styles tend to be low, some even negative. Equity market correlation is by far the most important commonality, and hedging market risk often gets correlations much closer to zero. I will dwell in Chapter 11 on the benefits of low correlations across styles.

6.1. Value and Other Contrarian Strategies

Value investing is the best-known investment style. The contrarian spirit of buying out-of-favor assets can be applied to security selection, broader asset allocation, and even market timing. It can be applied systematically with simple or complex rules, or with discretion. The idea of buying undervalued stocks and selling overvalued stocks dates back to at least Graham-Dodd's work in the 1930s, while the Fama-French research (1992, 1993) brought it to the academic mainstream.[3] Despite evidence of centuries of success, value investing may be as famous for its failures, with losses often coinciding with periods of perceived structural change.

Readers should distinguish value as a contrarian security selection strategy across stocks (which I cover here) from contrarian market timing (which I'll cover in Chapter 16). Chapter 10 will include a brief description of different predictive techniques, also highlighting the differences between cross-sectional and timing applications.

Flagship Strategy: Value-based Stock Selection

I will focus on value-based stock selection using systematic rules but will also briefly discuss other contrarian strategies. Value investing compares the current market price with some fundamental anchor to deem whether an asset is cheap or rich. In a typical academic implementation of the value style, we sort a set of stocks by some measure of fundamental value to price, and we go long or overweight the cheap ("value") stocks, while shorting or underweighting expensive ("growth") stocks.[4] A long/short portfolio may contain hundreds of stocks on each side to capture the value style exposure but hopefully little else, as the market exposures of longs and shorts broadly cancel out and the idiosyncratic security risk gets diversified away.

Academic research mainly uses a deliberately simple ratio of market price to a fundamental anchor, such as a firm's book value, and then favors stocks with a high book/price ratio (B/P).[5]

---

[3]I was lucky enough to be a Ph.D. student in Chicago when Professors Fama and French conducted their influential research and gave the first presentations on it. Although my own research was on bond market behavior, the two professors co-chaired my dissertation committee. I later managed to get myself to Stockholm to witness live when Professor Fama received the 2013 Nobel Prize in Economics. Among the highlights of my life!

[4]Labelling expensive stocks as growth stocks has become a common practice but has also been subject to fair criticism. These stocks tend to be both more expensive on some valuation metrics and have faster growth (of earnings, sales, and other fundamentals) than value stocks. Yet, nobody buys stocks because they are expensive; buyers believe that the better growth prospects justify the higher price. Instead of using a unidimensional value versus growth split of the universe by valuation metrics, some growth strategies and indices ignore valuations and instead favor stocks with high past and expected fundamental growth. I stick with the unidimensional language but acknowledge the caveats.

[5]It is possible to adjust the valuation ratio to "smuggle in" quality aspects such as intangible investments, or to use a more complex fair-value model such as a residual income model. The simplistic ratio approach can miss subtleties of equity valuation, including future earnings growth and any accounting distortions due to differences in how the conservative accounting system records transactions and allocates revenues and expenses across fiscal periods (see Israel-Laursen-Richardson (2021)).

Investors can also use other fundamental anchors besides book value, including earnings, cash flows, and sales.[6] Composite value measures may be more robust to evolving markets and accounting practices.

Another important decision is whether stocks are compared to a broad universe ("raw") or more narrowly to their within-sector peers, or even more granularly to within-industry peers. Within-industry comparisons subtract the industry mean or median value ratio from each stock before ranking stocks, resulting in industry-neutral positions. This approach ensures better breadth (hundreds of stock-specific exposures are not being dominated by fewer sector or industry exposures) and better comparability (Ford is compared to General Motors and not to Microsoft). Yet, many commercial factor indices and the Fama-French factor portfolios do not use sector- or industry-neutral positions.

Other design decisions include the universe (large caps, small caps, or all stocks), the mapping of value scores to portfolio weights (say, cap-weighting or equal-weighting stocks in the top and bottom tertile/quintile/decile, or rank-weighting all longs and shorts), and the choice between dollar-neutral or beta-neutral long/short portfolios.[7]

Economic Rationale

Academics still debate why the value premium should exist. I keep this section brief, not because it is unimportant but because we may never get a conclusive answer. There are explanations rooted in investor behavioral biases, such as excessive extrapolation of growth trends, delayed overreaction to information, and equating good companies with good investments irrespective of price.[8] There are also many risk-based explanations (e.g. value stocks have more default or distress risk), though these have been less well supported by empirical analyses.

Both sets of theories are grounded in economic intuition with ample theoretical foundation, and both sets have likely contributed to the existence of the observed value premium. Many investors may not care which set matters more, while some believe that risk-based explanations are less likely to be arbitraged away.

Bringing the value-growth debate back to the practical level, value investors believe in the stabilizing forces of supply/demand responses, competition, and even regulation. A company with excess profits is likely to attract more competition as well as regulators' interest. Growth investors believe that cheap companies are cheap for a reason, reflecting lower profit growth or a declining industry. Empirically, it is true that stocks with higher valuation multiples tend to grow faster, both retrospectively and prospectively. But the valuation gap between those richer stocks and value stocks discounts even wider profit growth differences than what tend to materialize later. Therefore, value (growth) stocks tend to experience positive (negative) profit surprises, and the related repricing has in the long run been enough to offset the value stocks' profit growth disadvantage and has given them a net performance advantage.

I will discuss economic rationales on style premia further in Chapter 8.

---

[6]Because sales and cash flows are generated by the entire operations of the firm, it is appropriate to compare these to the enterprise value, whereas book value and earnings are better compared to equity market capitalization. Enterprise value is computed as the sum of total equity market capitalization, preferred stock, minority interest, and total debt.

[7]Israel-Jiang-Ross (2017) and Kessler-Scherer-Harries (2020) explore the many design decisions and show that the indicator choice and sector neutrality matter most empirically. Asness et al. (2015) and Ilmanen et al. (2021a) use deliberately simple factor specifications to ease communication and to mitigate any concern of data mining.

[8]See Lakonishok-Shleifer-Vishny (1994), Barberis-Shleifer-Vishny (1998), and Daniel-Hirshleifer-Subrahmanyam (1998).

Historical Performance

The original Fama-French (1992, 1993) research focused on the performance of US long/short (L/S) portfolios based on book/price from 1963 to 1990.[9] They later broadened their analysis to other metrics and markets. Asness et al. (2013) concluded that value and momentum work everywhere. Baltussen-Swinkels-van Vliet (2019) and Ilmanen et al. (2021a) studied a century or two of return histories in multiple asset classes.

Mikhail Samonov (2020) has compiled into one cumulative return series two centuries of research on the performance of simple US stock selection value strategies; see the thick line in Figure 6.1. The lowest two lines show separately the return of the long leg (value stocks with high B/P) and the short leg (growth stocks with low B/P) in excess of the universe. Before the Fama-French dataset began in 1926, Samonov used so-called Cowles data value selection across industries 1872–1926 and Will Goetzmann's archive work on early US stock selection 1825–71 (with an admittedly narrow cross section of stocks among its data challenges). I further add into this graph a more recent strategy variant that shows that multi-metric and industry-neutral value strategies have fared somewhat better since 1968 (the very top line).

The 2010s were clearly a disappointing decade for value, but should this offset in our minds two centuries of positive evidence, or the evidence in other markets? I will return to this question many times in this book.

The returns here and throughout the book, unless otherwise stated, are before subtracting trading costs and fees. The long/short portfolio gives a pure exposure to value (though controlling

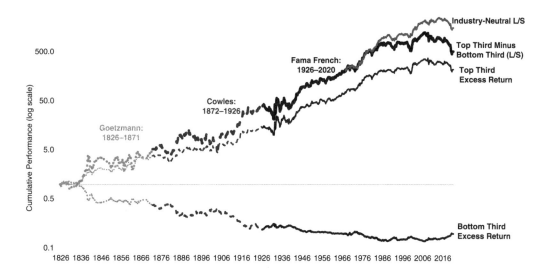

Figure 6.1 Cumulative Performance of US Value-Based Stock Selection Strategies, 1826–2020
Sources: Mikhail Samonov, Two Centuries Investments, using data from Goetzmann, Cowles, and Fama-French studies. AQR for the industry-neutral value strategy since 1968.

---

[9]The method Fama and French used for the HML series became an academic standard for many later studies. They use one signal, such as B/P, to rank all the stocks in the universe. They create a long/short portfolio between 30% of top-ranked and 30% of bottom-ranked stocks. They separate the whole equity market into large-cap and small-cap universes and present average performance of the two. They include no sector- or beta-neutrality adjustments. They rebalance once a year, conservatively adjusting both book and market values midyear to allow for publication lags. The Asness-Frazzini (2013) "Devil" variant agrees in lagging the book values to ensure data availability but uses the most recent market values.

for industry and beta exposures would arguably be even purer). Figure 6.1 indicates that the market-adjusted excess return has been reasonably symmetric for the long and short sides.

Consistency and Extensions

Many studies report consistently positive long-run value returns for a variety of value metrics, countries, and strategy designs – and consistently poor performance for the 2018–2020 period. For one example, Table 6.2 shows SRs between 1984 and mid-2021, all positive.

Two patterns hold in all four universes (US and non-US developed market large caps and small caps): The multi-metric composite (which combines book, earnings, forward earnings, cash flow, and sales multiples) outpaced the book/price ratio, and the industry-neutral design outpaced raw. The first finding might be sample-specific as there have been other historical periods where the book/price ratio is among the better value metrics, while here it's the worst of the lot. The composite approach is attractive mainly for its better consistency, not because any single metric is expected to be reliably worse or better than the others. The second finding should be more robust. Given the better breadth and better comparability, picking stocks within an industry is likely the most useful extension to original value strategies of Fama-French that rank stocks across the whole universe.

Looking across columns, value strategy has fared better outside the US than within the US and mostly better in small caps than large caps. These patterns might be somewhat sample-specific. The raw US B/P strategies have been in a long drawdown since near the GFC, while all strategies in the last row (multi-metric industry-neutral specifications) began their drawdown only in 2017/2018.

More detailed cross-country analysis shows that value investing with a multi-metric industry-neutral approach earned long-run SRs ranging from 0.1 to 0.7 in large caps and from -0.05 to 1.0 in small caps across 14 countries, all suffering in the late 2010s. Moreover, emerging markets would have given even higher SRs.

One recently popular idea is to correct the book/price ratio for intangibles. There has been a multi-decade-long structural change where intangible investments have become more important than tangible investments for US firms. Some argue this development makes the book/price

Table 6.2   Long-Run Sharpe Ratios for Value-Based Stock Selection Strategies, 1984–Jun 2021

	US LargeCap	US SmallCap	Ex-US LargeCap	Ex-US SmallCap
BP Raw	0.15	0.16	0.35	0.30
Multi Raw	0.31	0.39	0.42	0.64
BP IndAdj.	0.28	0.32	0.65	0.43
Multi IndAdj.	0.50	0.79	0.73	0.99

Sources: AQR and Israel-Laursen-Richardson (2021), starting in 1984 or when available, extended by the authors to June 2021. Notes: The multi-indicator approach combines strategies based on book/price, earnings/price, forward earnings/price, sales/enterprise value, and cash flow/enterprise value. The industry-adjusted value strategy compares stocks within the same industry and thus neutralizes industry exposures.

ratio obsolete.[10] Yet, even studies that argue for the intangibles-adjusted book/price ratio report only mildly better long-run performance and somewhat lower recent losses.[11]

Applications in Other Contexts

Value can be applied beyond the original context of stock selection to equity indices and other asset classes, using simple and consistent measures of value as a ratio of fundamentals to price.[12] Across countries (using equity indices), an aggregate measure of B/P or CAEY for the entire market can be used to implement value investing. For bonds, value can be measured by real bond yields. For currencies, it can be anchored on purchasing power parity. For commodities, in the absence of a consistent fundamentals-to-price measure, long-run mean reversion may be used, for example by comparing the spot price five years ago with the most recent spot price. In all cases, a systematic process can sort assets by these measures, going long the cheap (relative to fundamentals) assets and short the expensive ones.

Figure 6.2 presents evidence from Ilmanen et al. (2021a), almost a century of value premia in several asset classes, split by decade. The idea is not to focus on the trees (single bars) but on the

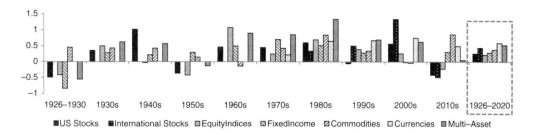

Figure 6.2   Per-decade and Century-long SRs of Value Style Premia in Several Asset Classes
Source: Ilmanen-Israel-Lee-Moskowitz-Thapar (2021), with explanations of each series. Data available and regularly updated in the AQR Data Library. Notes: Decades are from 1 to 0 (e.g. 2011–2020), except that the 1920s begins in 1926.

---

[10]For example, Mauboussin-Callahan (2020) writes that tangible assets, such as factories, are on the decline, while intangible spending, such as research and development, is on the rise. Intangible investments are treated as an expense on the income statement. Tangible investments are recorded as assets on the balance sheet. Thus, a company that invests in intangible assets will have lower earnings and book value than one that invests an equivalent amount in tangible assets. All this suggests that earnings and book value are losing their ability to represent economic value. While this is true, intangibles are subjective and sometimes gamed. R&D and marketing can also be wasteful or used for empire building, so spending on them is not guaranteed to be productive. In any case, intangibles-adjusted B/P would not have saved the value strategy in 2018–20. This adjustment does improve long-run backtests somewhat, but similar gains may be achieved by including intangibles within the defensive style, as is often done.

[11]The following studies on the impact of intangibles offer a range from strong to weak effects: Lev-Srivastava (2019), Eisfeldt-Kim-Papanikolaou (2020), Amenc-Goltz-Luyten (2020), Israel-Laursen-Richardson (2021), and Rizova-Saito (2020). Ignoring intangibles is a bigger problem in raw value since industry-neutral value strategies already mitigate the challenge of different levels of intangibles across industries.

[12]See Asness-Moskowitz-Pedersen (2013), Asness et al. (2015), and Ilmanen et al. (2021a).

forest (broad impression). The bars are reasonably consistently positive, though the 1920s, 1950s, and 2010s saw negative value performance in several asset classes. Over the full sample, all bars (boxed on the right) were positive.

Beyond the above examples, I list briefly a few other contrarian strategies:

- In stock selection, a simpler contrarian strategy than the use of valuations involves mean reversion: favoring stocks that have underperformed in the past. It is well known that stocks tend to exhibit cross-sectional momentum over the past year, but that this pattern has been sandwiched between a short-term reversal pattern over the past month or week and a long-term reversal pattern over multiple years. Ken French's data library contains long-run return histories for the US STREV and LTREV factors (one-month and five-year reversals). The former has a high paper SR since the 1930s (0.77) but was arbitraged away by the mid-2000s. LTREV has a lower SR than B/P (0.27 versus 0.34) and 0.6 correlation with it.
- Value-based issuer selection in corporate bond markets has an especially good track record, though typically it does not use just a simple valuation ratio but a more complex fair value model (see Israel-Palhares-Richardson (2018)).
- Contrarian strategies are famously used in global asset allocation between asset classes or between regions, as well as in market timing of equities, government bonds, and credits. While the main approach to contrarian market timing is based on market valuations (see Chapter 16), other related indicators can help. Signals based on the premise that persistent good times cause complacency, overheating, excessive credit activity, and leverage have been used to predict future recessions and bear markets. Yet, as with valuations, such contrarian signals often flash too early.
- Finally, portfolio rebalancing strategies (see Box 11.1) have a contrarian flavor. They involve buying recent losers and selling recent winners to return portfolio weights to long-run targets.

Risks and Pitfalls

The market beta exposures largely wash out between the long and short legs, but a long/short value strategy need not be market-neutral. The Fama-French HML (high-minus-low, the prototypical stock selection strategy of buying high B/P stocks and selling low B/P stocks) has had periods of positive market correlation (e.g. losing money during the 2008 and 2020 bear markets) but generally exhibited negative market correlation in the 20th century (e.g. lagging during the bull market in the late 1990s and making money during the 2000-3 bear market). Cheap stocks also underperformed in the deflationary recessions in the 1930s but fared better amid the 1970s stagflations. Looking ahead, it is thus hard to know whether value will tilt toward a positive or negative market correlation. Zero beta may be a decent base case, but unless the strategy's beta is actively managed, it can differ from zero for long periods.

For standalone risk, the worst drawdowns of the US B/P-based value strategies in Figure 6.1 in terms of both depth and length were the recent period – a fall of 63% between the 2007 peak and 2020 trough[13] – and a more distant 59% fall between the 1890 peak and 1904 trough (a period of great monopoly power, whose ending was influenced by antitrust legislation – suggesting potential parallels to today's FAMAG firms). Beyond these two, the depression-era

---

[13]Using more thoughtful value specifications (multiple indicators, industry neutrality), the recent drawdown is much shorter (starting in 2017 instead of 2007) and somewhat shallower.

1926–32 value drawdown of -53% and more recently the tech bubble 1998–2000 drawdown of -35% stand out.

What characterizes these periods of value losses? There are many warning clichés on value investing: Beware value traps; don't catch a falling piano (or knife); cheap for a reason; cheap things can get cheaper. These clichés reinforce the case for combining value with other styles, especially momentum and quality. Another key observation is that *contrarian strategies are inherently short a structural change*. Thus, it is not surprising that many major value strategy drawdowns coincided with technological revolutions. Amara's Law says, "We tend to overestimate the impact of new technology in the short term and underestimate it in the long run," perhaps justifying the more sustainable second leg of the internet-based bull market after the first dot-com bubble ended in a bust in 2000.

Structural changes can break historical regularities or imply a change in a long-run mean, thus weakening the usefulness of trusted fundamental anchors. However, financial markets seem to succumb to "new age" or "this time is different" beliefs more often than is warranted, which has been a source of long-run gains for the value strategy. Indeed, as Figure 6.1 shows, the value strategy has survived two centuries of successive technological revolutions (as well as other revolutions, pandemics, and world wars). That said, major structural changes can be a headwind to value strategies, and this is certainly true amid the persistent shift from the physical to digital world and the increasing role of disruptive firms in a "winner takes all" environment.

Current Outlook

Stock selection value strategies performed very poorly between 2018 and 2020, raising investor doubts about these strategies' long-run viability. My colleagues and other researchers have written extensive post-mortems trying to explain how and why this happened and what this means for the future.[14]

- While the best broad story of what happened is related to disruptive tech-oriented platform firms, the outperformance of FAMAG is only a small part of value losses.
- Value losses were not US-only. They occurred in all regions and most industries.
- Value losses were not specific to the much-maligned book/price ratio. Other value indicators suffered almost as much, some more.
- The dislocation created by value losses was as exceptional even if the tech-media-telecoms sectors were excluded, the mega-caps were excluded, or the priciest stocks were excluded. If anything, more of the dislocation seemed to arise from the cheap side than from the rich side.
- Value losses cannot be explained well by low or falling bond yields. Despite a plausible theoretical link, serious studies show a weak long-run empirical link, and at best yield curve moves could explain a small fraction of the 2018–20 value losses.
- Value losses were not caused by crowding or excessive popularity. Analysis of institutional portfolio holdings shows no sign of large or increasing value overweights in the 2010s. It is hard to argue that after its meager performance since 2007, the value style would have been popular in 2018.

The list does not stop here. Many other explanations were offered and found wanting.

---

[14]See Asness (2020), Israel-Laursen-Richardson (2021), Maloney-Moskowitz (2021), and Arnott et al. (2021).

My best reading of the situation is that there may have been some fundamental underpinning to the value-growth relative performance, but during 2018–2020 markets took things too far, as often happens at such times. All the outperformance seems to have come from the market pricing the disruptive growth stocks more richly. There was little change in measured fundamentals to justify such richening, except for the benefit virtual firms derived from the 2020 lockdowns.

Of course, growth stock proponents argue that fundamentals are mismeasured. And they have some logical case. The most popular way to improve fundamental anchors involves the role of intangibles. But, as previously discussed, broader value measures would not have made much difference in the recent drawdown.

I hesitate to use these words, but overall it seems like another case of bubble and irrational exuberance, echoing the dot-com times in the late 1990s.

The flipside of the poor recent realized returns for the value strategy is that the ex-ante opportunity has become record-high – or at least competing for that honor with the 1999 dot-com era. Value spreads show the relative pricing of value stocks versus growth stocks. Figure 6.3 tracks these relative valuations over time, averaging multiple value metrics within industries. I show here only US data, but the latest value spreads are even more extreme outside the US, especially in emerging markets.

Value stocks are always cheaper than growth stocks, by construction. The two lower lines show that value stocks tend to be 1.3 times cheaper than the median, while growth stocks are richer (the average ratio of fundamentals/price is about 0.7 of the median). The top line focuses on the ratio between those two lines and is called the value spread (sometimes expressed as "raw" as opposed to a normalized Z-score). As always, there are different ways to measure cheapness or to neutralize unwanted exposures, but most tell a similar story.

Figure 6.3 reminds us that 2020 began with a historically wide value spread, before the Covid-19 pandemic led to widespread lockdowns and work-from-home arrangements, speeding

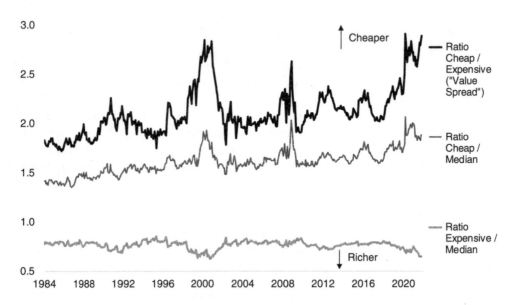

Figure 6.3 Value Spread History in the US: Valuation for Long and Short Sides and the Ratio Between Them, Jan 1984–Oct 2021
Source: Data from AQR. Notes: The series evaluate large- and mid-cap US stocks on an industry-neutral basis, sorting them by an average of book/price, earnings/price, forward earnings / price, sales / enterprise value, and cash flow / enterprise value. The top line shows the composite ratio ("value spread") between cheap versus expensive valuations; the lower lines show each side separately versus the median valuation.

up the shift from bricks-and-mortar to the digital economy. As one consequence, the value strategy lost more and its ex-ante value spread widened further during the lockdown period.

The latest value style drawdown troughed, finally, in late 2020, coincidentally with the US presidential election and the Covid vaccine news. Some observers tie the value style's recovery to prospective changes in interest rates or the ending of lockdowns, while others argue that rising corporate taxes, antitrust regulation, and good old competition may soon challenge the recent winners-who-took-all. Just as it was difficult to explain the value's losses beyond storytelling, it was always difficult to identify one catalyst for its recovery, let alone the timing, and this remains true now. One contributor is surely the valuations, which became so extreme that growth stock outperformance was likely to fall by its own weight or by any excuse (a rubber-band effect).

Many investors have lost faith in value investing after the deep and persistent drawdown, but historically such capitulations may make a long recovery even more likely. I hope this chapter, besides the recent signs of improvement, helps convince readers that value investing is by no means dead. In a low expected return world where so many assets are expensive, the case for any cheap opportunities is even stronger.

6.2. Momentum and Other Extrapolative Strategies

Extrapolative strategies buy recent winners and sell recent losers. This approach can be applied on single assets using only their own past history – directional trend following – or on a cross-section of assets by creating long/short momentum portfolios based on relative recent performance. These variations are also called absolute (or time series) and relative (or cross-sectional) momentum. Two simple examples: (i) A trend-following strategy could involve buying equity index futures if their recent performance is positive and selling if it is negative; the position sign could be based on the past year's returns or on some other metric. (ii) A cross-sectional momentum strategy among a thousand stocks could involve buying each month the 300 stocks with the best recent return while selling short the 300 with the worst recent return, regardless of market direction.

Extrapolative strategies are interesting because so many assets exhibit performance persistence, or positively autocorrelated returns. Therefore, strategies which favor assets with high recent returns (over the past few months, up to a year) have been historically successful in almost any asset class researchers have looked into. Such strategies may also be excellent diversifiers to risky portfolios, but they require relatively high turnover and thus trading costs.

There is at first blush a visible tension between sections 6.1 and 6.2. While contrarian strategies (such as value) buy into weakness, extrapolative strategies (such as momentum) buy into strength. How can both approaches be profitable in the long run?

- The key is that value and momentum work well at different horizons. Many assets exhibit trending tendencies up to one year but mean-reverting tendencies at multiyear horizons.
- The sweet spot for any asset comes when value and momentum signals agree: Buy a (multiyear) cheap and (recently) improving asset, or sell a rich and declining asset.
- Single stocks exhibit also a short-term reversal tendency besides the long-term reversal tendency. Short-term reversal over the past week or month seems related to liquidity provision and price pressure effects. In more liquid futures markets, assets exhibit momentum also at short horizons.
- The negative correlation between value and momentum strategies (often near -0.5) makes them great complements. Such a negative correlation implies that the optimal blend of value and momentum is not far from 50/50, unless their standalone SRs are very different.

Flagship Strategies: Momentum-based Stock Selection and Multi-asset Trend Following

I cover two distinct strategies: relative momentum across US stocks and a broad trend-following strategy in four liquid asset classes. Both strategies only use an asset's own past returns as input.

For cross-sectional momentum, I use the common measure of the past 12-month cumulative raw return for individual stocks, skipping the recent month's return to avoid one-month reversal in stock returns.[15]

For trend following, I likewise use a deliberately simple variant, 12-month lookback window with a one-month execution delay. It is more common to blend a slow 12-month trend with faster one- to three-month trends, and not include a lag, but my conservative variant could be viewed as a poor man's trading cost adjustment. I use volatility targeting (equal-volatility weighting across assets and over time) but no correlation information when combining assets.

As noted, momentum is close to market neutral, whereas trend following can be highly market directional at any point in time, though in the long run it averages near zero market beta.

Economic Rationale

As with value, academics have asked whether the long-run gains of momentum and trend strategies can be better explained by behavioral or risk-based theories.

Behavioral theories offer two main explanations for momentum. The first is initial underreaction to new public information, especially less salient news – whether company-specific, sector-relevant, or macroeconomic – due to anchoring or inattention. The second is extrapolative expectations on fundamentals or eventual overreaction to price moves due to positive-feedback trading (e.g. investors becoming more confident in their positions and beliefs when they are supported; becoming more risk averse or forced to delever after market declines; herding and social contagion). In addition, the disposition effect, which is the tendency for investors to sell winners too soon and hold on to losers too long, may contribute to momentum.[16]

Risk-based theories posit that high-momentum stocks are somehow riskier, for example, because they contain more growth options in earnings which makes them more sensitive to aggregate shocks.

Behavioral explanations ring truer, and they fit better the evidence that similar patterns are found in many different asset classes and that trend following has been an empirically successful safe-haven strategy.

Historical Performance

I first focus on the two flagship strategies. The evidence for them is at least as compelling as for contrarian strategies and for the major asset class premia in previous chapters. As before, all returns are shown before trading costs, but this matters more here because momentum strategies involve higher turnover. (To balance this, I use simple variants with one-month execution delay.)

Figure 6.4 shows that momentum-based stock selection has earned visually impressive (and, it turns out, statistically highly significant) gains for two centuries. The lower two lines display the

---

[15]See Jegadeesh-Titman (1993) and Asness (1994).
[16]See DeLong et al. (1990), Barberis-Shleifer-Vishny (1998), Daniel- Hirshleifer-Subrahmanyam (1998), and Frazzini (2006).

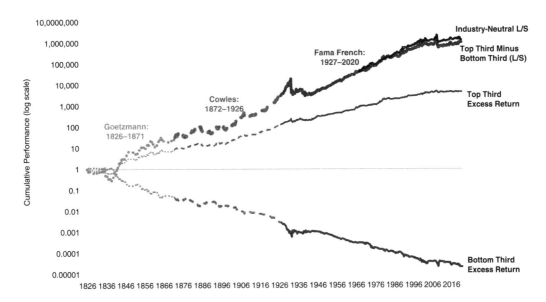

Figure 6.4 Cumulative Performance of US Momentum-based Stock Selection Strategies, 1826–2020

Sources: Mikhail Samonov, Two Centuries Investments, using data from Goetzmann, Cowles and Fama-French studies. Industry-neutral return series since 1968 from AQR. Notes: Momentum uses the last-year return with a skip-month.

performance of the long leg (last-year winners) and the short leg (last-year losers). The market-adjusted excess return for the cross-sectional momentum has been broadly symmetric for longs and shorts, just like with value.

The top line shows the performance of the long/short strategy – including an industry-neutral variant since 1968. I will later discuss the appealing consistency but can already note that when we use a magnifying glass, what now looks like some dips in momentum returns turn out to be "momentum crashes."

Trend following has even more compelling-looking history in Figure 6.5, despite its deliberately conservative strategy design (12-month lookback window and one-month execution lag).[17] The strategy has been profitable in all four asset classes and of course as a composite ("Trend"). I plot cumulative gains since 1880 but provide performance statistics since 1926.[18] Last-decade performance has been relatively flat, as commodity trend losses offset fixed income trend gains.

---

[17]Moskowitz-Ooi-Pedersen (2012), the first major academic study on trend following, uses just 12-month lookback window with data starting in the 1980s. Hurst-Ooi-Pedersen (2017) uses a blend of 1-, 3-, and 12-month windows with data starting over a century ago. Other authors have gone even further back with extrapolative strategies since they require only price and return data. Geczy-Samonov (2016, 2017) and Baltussen-Swinkels-vanVliet (2019) present two centuries of gains for multi-asset momentum, while Greyserman-Kaminski (2014) beats all others by documenting trend following profits all the way back to 1300s (understandably with a narrower set of assets). None of these studies include a one-month execution lag.

[18]The long-run SRs are broadly similar before and after 1926. For the composite, it may be interesting to contrast the 0.89 SR of my conservative specification to an almost twice higher SR (1.67) in Hurst-Ooi-Pedersen (2017) which does three things better: multiple lookback windows, immediate execution, incorporating correlations. Using correlation information in asset weighting would boost the 1926–2020 SR from 0.89 to 0.96, using no lag would cause a leap to 1.27, and averaging three windows (1mo/3mo/12mo) another leap to 1.67. The raw SRs for 1mo/3mo/12mo lookback windows are 1.45/1.24/1.27, respectively. After including a one-month execution lag or estimated trading costs, the fast one-month trend following strategy would have the lowest SR.

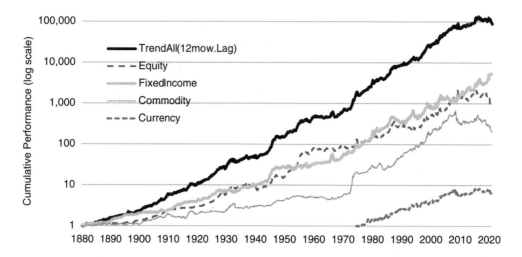

Figure 6.5 Trend Following Strategy (Simple Specification) Cumulative Performance, 1880–2020
Source: Data from AQR. Notes: Trend-following strategy excess returns for up to 29 assets in four asset classes, using a
12-month lookback window, but with a one-month lag. Currency returns begin in 1974. Assets are volatility-scaled but no
correlations are used in weighting returns; the sizing is however scaled down by √N to invest less when the universe
is narrower.

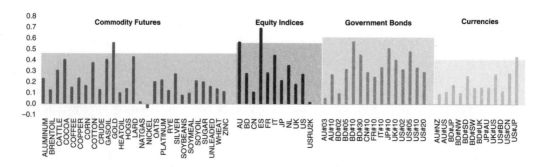

Figure 6.6 Sharpe Ratios of Trend Following Strategies for 60+ Assets, 1926–2020
Source: Data from AQR. Notes: SRs shown for the longest histories available per asset between Jan 1926 and Dec 2020,
using the simple design in Figure 6.5. (12-mo window and 1-mo lag). Shaded areas show SRs for diversified asset class
composites.

Consistency and Extensions

Research by my colleagues in Asness-Moskowitz-Pedersen (2013) and Moskowitz-Ooi-Pedersen
(2012) highlighted the compelling consistency of momentum and trend following gains over
time as well as across markets and specifications.

Using the longest available histories for each asset, Figure 6.6 shows that trend following
earned positive rewards in virtually all assets and all four asset classes studied. Diversification
boosted the asset class SRs (ranging from 0.44 in currencies to 0.62 in bonds). The results benefit
from volatility targeting across assets and over time. (Also cross-sectional momentum has performed in stock selection as well outside the US as within it. Most SRs are lower in the 2000s
due to the 2009 momentum crash, though.)

Academics and practitioners have tried to overlay many novel design features to momentum
and trend strategies. The relative weight of fast and slow signals may be allowed to vary across

assets and over time, or perhaps based on the volatility environment. Momentum signals may be more informative when associated with news events. Risk estimates can be made more accurate and smoother with the help of high-frequency data. Positions may be reduced based on an off-setting medium-term reversal or overextension signal or when frequent market turns indicate a whipsawing environment. Very short-term momentum (or reversal) patterns based on daily data may be exploited (and if they raise trading costs too much, they may at least be used as filters to sometimes delay trading). Beyond the constant volatility targeting, inverse volatility weighting may be considered, as may directional beta hedging or chasing idiosyncratic momentum (as these features may help reduce drawdowns after sharp market turns).[19]

Any such tinkering clearly raises overfitting risks (as well as estimation risk and complexity), so the benefits on paper should be compelling before such overlays are added to core strategies.

Extrapolation does not need to be confined to the single measure of own-price momentum. Cross-sectional stock selection strategies have long applied earnings momentum (see Chan-Jegadeesh-Lakonishok (1996)) and other fundamental momentum strategies, which rely on market underreactions to public fundamental news (e.g. changes in profit margins, analysts' growth forecasts, or management actions).

The same idea has been applied to macro strategies. For example, a macro momentum strategy would favor an equity market with a benign backdrop – recently strong growth surprises, soft inflation news, easy central bank policies, and improving terms of trade. The idea of markets underreacting to relevant macro news can be further extended to bond, currency, and commodity asset classes. Backtest performance has been comparable to trend following and sufficiently lowly (0.4) correlated to be an interesting complement (see Brooks (2017)).

Macro momentum can be applied to both cross-country allocation and to market timing. It is worth noting the parallel to section 6.1, where I noted that contrarian equity market timing can be based on more than valuations and include "level" concerns of excessive leverage and market complacency during bull markets. The other school of thought is not to anticipate turns but to react to changes: Then tightening credit conditions and rising risk aversion are bearish signals to follow, in the spirit of trend following and macro momentum. The two approaches can be combined.

Academic studies have also explored lead-lag relations between connected companies and peers (e.g. Cohen-Frazzini (2008) and Misirli-Scida-Velikov (2020)) as well as flow momentum in other asset classes. Lazy thinking about flow momentum may ignore the fact that net flows add up to zero (for every buyer there's a seller; see Chapter 8). Thus, flow momentum can only be useful if we can identify a subset of investors worth following. Academic studies have identified short sellers and hedge funds as such "smart money" (e.g. Drechsler-Drechsler (2016)). Following them has worked on average, but they too are fallible and are especially subject to deleveraging risks.

Applications in Other Contexts

Cross-sectional momentum has worked well also in other asset classes, though generally not quite as well as trend following. Figure 6.7 presents evidence from our longest/broadest study (Ilmanen et al. 2021a): a century of long/short momentum premia in several asset contexts, split by decade. The cross-sections involve hundreds of stocks, 23 equity markets, 13 government bond markets, 10 currencies, and 40 commodities. Each asset class had a positive SR for the century and for most decades. The composite was mildly down only in one decade (1930s).

---

[19]See Daniel-Moskowitz (2016), Barroso-Santa-Clara (2015), and Garg-Goulding-Harvey-Mazzoleni (2020).

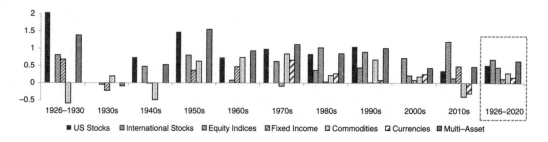

Figure 6.7   Per-decade and Century-long SRs of Momentum Style Premia in Several Asset Classes, 1926–2020
Source: Ilmanen-Israel-Lee-Moskowitz-Thapar (2021), with explanations of each series. Data available and regularly updated in the AQR Data Library. Notes: Decades are from 1 to 0 (e.g. 2011–2020), except that the 1920s begins in 1926.

Similar analysis would show that trend following was profitable every decade for the composite and almost without exception for each asset class. Trend following has also worked well in markets with less liquidity and capacity. Babu et al. (2018) shows positive rewards when trend following has been applied to emerging market equities and currencies, interest rate swaps, credit default swap indices, exotic commodity futures, volatility futures, and equity long/short factors ("factor momentum"). Gupta-Kelly (2018) and Ehsani-Linnainmaa (2019) report evidence of time-series and cross-sectional factor momentum among stock selection factors.

Private asset returns exhibit even stronger positive autocorrelation, due to artificially smooth returns, but such apparent return persistence is hardly exploitable in practice.

Risks and Pitfalls

The risks for extrapolative strategies are in sharp market turns and in whipsawing trendless markets. The former risk materialized for cross-sectional stock momentum in spring 2009 (risk of a bang), while the latter more gradual risk materialized for trend following through the 2010s (risk of a whimper). Trend exhibits a "smile" pattern (U-shape) when its performance is plotted on equity market returns. Akin to a long option straddle's gamma payoff, the trend strategy benefits from large market moves to either direction and does less well in choppy, unchanged markets. Related to the risk of whipsawing markets, cost-effective trading execution is especially important to these relatively high-turnover strategies.

Trend has performed very well in the worst equity market drawdowns, especially if they are protracted (see Figure 6.8; Table 13.1 gives numerical details). If the drawdown is not too sudden and sharp, the trend strategy has time to turn from "risk-on" to "risk-off" positions in four asset classes – short equities, long duration, anti-carry in currencies, long gold, and short growth commodities – and ride the bear market. All these directional channels have helped trend in most of the history's largest market drawdowns, and it may not be just a matter of luck. The forces that make trend profitable in the long run may also make most bear markets gradual; they tend to involve initial underreaction to bad economic news and later positive-feedback trading once the market is falling.[20]

---

[20]Fast drawdowns are then the potential Achilles' heel for trend. Yet, trend has performed surprisingly well also in many of the worst equity months. Those worst months tend to come later in bear markets rather than at the turning point (as if a major plunge requires the bear market to mature). Even when the equity market turns suddenly, the other asset classes may be suitably positioned for risk-off news, as happened with the Covid crash in March 2020. See Ilmanen et al. (2021b) and Kaminski (2011) which calls this safe-haven service "crisis alpha." I return to this topic in Chapter 13.

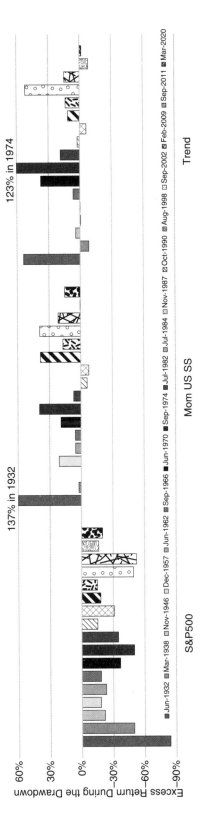

Figure 6.8 Equity Market Tail Performance of Momentum (Stock Selection) and Trend Strategies, 1926–2020

Source: Data from AQR. Notes: The worst drawdowns of S&P500 excess return over cash, listed by the trough month. Table 13.1 describes these drawdown events in a table, including peak, trough, length, and depth for each.

The stock selection momentum strategy also tended to perform well during these major bear markets. Yet there have been some infamous "momentum crashes" just after the market turn. This happened in the junk rally of summer 1932 amid the Great Depression as well as in spring 2009 after the Great Recession (and in November 2020 after Covid vaccine news).[21] Interestingly, trend following (which is explicitly directional and thus would seem more vulnerable to sharp market turns) has never experienced crashes as large as the cross-sectional stock selection momentum strategy.

Current Outlook

Stock selection momentum had relatively good 2010s, while trend following disappointed after its excellent 2008 performance. The latter result reflects trends that were relatively short compared to history (Babu et al. (2020)). Curtailed trends seem best explained by central bankers' desire to steady market moves after the extreme volatility during the GFC. Central banks worried about too large falls but also about too large rises in risky asset prices. Such smoothing attempts seem plausible also in the future, but we may reach a point where central banks have to make hard choices and allow larger market moves. In particular, if we do see larger changes in inflation than in the past decade, such changes tend to be gradual and may thus well suit trend-following strategies.

I will not display the valuations of momentum or trend strategies because their high portfolio turnover makes value spreads less relevant. Overall, there is little evidence to suggest momentum and trend can be profitably timed. Both are good strategic exposures, even more so due to their low or even negative correlation with the equity market and with value/contrarian strategies. But they are not conducive to tactical timing, either based on their own valuation or recent performance.

6.3. Carry and Other Income Strategies

This section covers a broad set of strategies that earn positive income or carry over time, typically by buying high-yielding assets against selling low-yielding assets. An asset's yield (or its spread over the funding rate) is a good proxy for carry, but a broader definition of carry includes *an asset's return in unchanged capital market conditions* (see Koijen et al. (2018)).[22]

While positive carry does not ensure positive future returns, it does empirically predict them. The shortcomings of yield or carry as expected return proxies must be understood, and these vary across assets. For risky bonds, yield overstates expected returns, in some cases by a lot (for high-yield bonds, historically by about a half). For equities, dividend yield understates expected

---

[21]Momentum crashes are discussed in Daniel-Moskowitz (2016) and Barroso-SantaClara (2015). Beta hedging or chasing idiosyncratic returns may help mitigate these crashes and the resulting negative skew. Anyway, if stand-alone momentum is dangerous, combined with value it is much safer and has a higher SR.

[22]For currencies, the yield income of short-term deposits is the only thing counted as carry. For bonds and commodity futures, unchanged term structure means that an asset may also earn a predictable rolldown return over time as it ages; such expected capital gain in unchanged capital market conditions counts as part of carry. For equities, I use dividend yield, though I should ideally include other payout yields related to net buybacks, cash acquisitions, and so on, and for currency-hedged foreign investments I should subtract the foreign cash rate. For index option selling, carry reflects the time decay of the option cost as well as the rolldown along the implied volatility surface. Koijen et al. (2018) provides a more technical discussion.

return because it misses growth. Naïve yield-seeking could push investors to a foreign market suffering from hyperinflation, or to the debt of a company at the brink of default, or to a structured bond which embeds short positions in myriad options and such high risks and high costs that a realistic expected return is negative.

Yield-seeking strategies can be applied in every asset class but the best-known carry strategy is currency carry, favoring high-yield currencies over low-yielding ones. Credit risk strategies are even more prevalent (covered in Chapter 4.4). These carry strategies are obviously risky given the asymmetric return profile (negative skew) and poor performance in equity bear markets. Yet it turns out that many other long-run profitable carry strategies within other asset classes have better tail risk characteristics. A well-diversified carry strategy looks therefore much better behaved than the flagship currency carry strategy: a higher SR, less negative skew, and better performance in equity bear markets.

It is perhaps surprising that naïve yield-seeking strategies have fared as well as they have. Their historical profitability suggests that there have not been enough yield seekers to bid a required risk premium down to zero. However, the low-rate environment (which brought out more reach-for-yield investors in the 2010s) may have done the job, at least temporarily.

Flagship Strategy: Currency Carry

A classic application in currency markets ranks countries by their short-term interest rate, going long the currencies of countries with the highest rates and short the currencies of countries with the lowest rates. Among the G-10 currencies, this traditionally involved buying currencies like the New Zealand, Australian, and Canadian dollars, while selling the Japanese Yen, the Swiss Franc, and the Deutsche Mark or the Euro. In early 2021, short-term interest rates in all developed countries are tightly packed near 0%, raising fair questions about the usefulness of this strategy in the current environment.

Economic Rationale

It is easy to give a rational explanation for certain carry strategies – currency carry, credit premium, volatility selling – but much harder for some more benign (lower beta) carry strategies as well as for the diversified combination.

Let's start with the easy part. I already used in my 2011 book several colorful expressions on currency carry, characterizing it as "picking up pennies in front of a steamroller" to capture the negative skew angle or "selling financial catastrophe insurance" to go beyond the rare large losses and to focus on their poor timing.

- In practice, the riskiest currencies – emerging markets, or the AUD and NZD within G-10 – have a positive equity market beta, while the safe-haven "funding" currencies JPY and CHF have a negative equity market beta.
- The exposure for currency carry goes beyond simple market beta. Carry positions can experience sharp periodic unwinds when capital flees for low-yielding safe havens. Empirically, currency carry is significantly exposed to equity market risk as well as to volatility risks in both equity and currency markets. These nonlinear exposures may also be modeled as crash risk or jump risk.
- Credit strategies and volatility selling strategies share many of these characteristics that certainly warrant a long-run risk premium.

Risk-based explanations are not the only possibility. Currency carry strategies had less beta risk in the olden days when they were more consistently profitable. And it is harder to justify why other carry strategies, with more benign characteristics, have earned high historical risk-adjusted returns. What other explanations do we have for the long-run rewards for carry strategies?

- Overconfident expectations of market moves and capital losses may offset the carry edge. As discussed later, the empirical fact that carry strategies have been profitable could be explained by systematic expectational errors (violations of the uncovered interest parity, the pure expectations hypothesis, etc.).
- Currency carry gains may reflect the process of balancing out supply and demand for capital across markets. High interest rates can signal an excess demand for capital not met by local savings, while low interest rates suggest an excess supply of capital. Attracting home-biased foreign investors requires some compensation.
- The presence of non-profit-seeking market participants, such as central banks, may sustain market inefficiencies.
- Generic risk premium ("1/price effect"). Like value, even if we do not understand the source of the risk premium, any required premium will tend to push the current market price low compared to some fundamental anchor, and thereby boost prospective returns.

Historical Performance

Many carry strategies have limited historical length, but however far we can go, we find positive long-run rewards. For the flagship currency carry strategy it makes most sense to start in the 1970s after the quasi-fixed exchange rate Bretton Woods system ended.[23] Figure 6.9 reveals

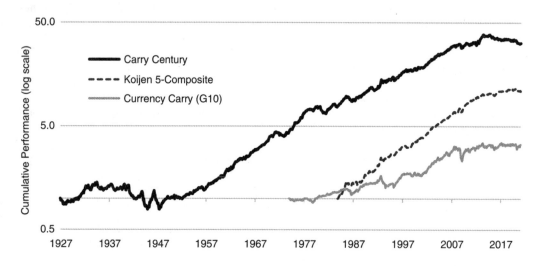

Figure 6.9 Cumulative Performance of Carry Strategies, 1927–2020

Sources: AQR Data Library and Ralph Koijen website. The Carry Century is a composite of equity, bond, currency, and commodity allocation strategies since 1927. The Currency Carry is a strategy trading G-10 currencies based on carry since 1974. The Koijen 5-Composite is a composite of equity, bond, slope trade, currency, and commodity strategies since 1983. The series are described in detail in Ilmanen-Israel-Lee-Moskowitz-Thapar (2021) and Koijen et al. (2018).

---

[23] Accominotti et al. (2019) studies the pre-Bretton Woods regime performance of the currency carry trade in the 1920s–30s and finds positive rewards there as well, while Chen (2019) reports currency carry trade gains over even longer histories.

positive cumulative rewards for multi-asset carry composites in Ilmanen et al. (2021a) and Koijen et al. (2018), as well as for currency carry. The longest strategy has a SR of 0.8, double that of currency carry, largely thanks to better diversification. The Koijen composite begins in 1983 and is even broader, thus earning an even higher SR.[24]

Carry positions tend to be persistent. In extreme, BBB credits always have higher yields than AAA credits (and more than expected default losses imply), and selling index puts always earns positive income (and most of the time the implied volatility exceeds the recent realized volatility). Across currencies there is more variability. AUD short-term rates have exceeded JPY short-term rates virtually always, whereas the USD was ranked the highest-yielding G-10 currency in 2000 but the lowest-yielding one in 1993. We can study average carry and average return across countries over long histories. The positive relation between these persistent parts captures some of the carry story, but empirically the time-varying part is a much more important share of the cumulative return than the persistent part (Koijen et al. (2018)).

Consistency and Extensions

Besides the nominal short-term rate, countries can be ranked based on real short-term rates, long-term rates, carry per volatility, and so on – they all have worked. Carry strategies may be based on a combination of pairwise carry trades (which could emphasize the role of the anchor currency, say, dollar) instead of more neutrally ranking, say, the G-10 markets. The weighting can involve simple inverse rank weights, equal-weighted first three versus last three, or may reflect the signal strength (interest rate dispersion) – and there are many ways to incorporate volatilities, correlations, or other risk metrics. The currency universe may be broad or narrow, and position sizes may reflect some liquidity weighting. It has long been common to trade developed market and emerging market currencies in separate universes, but this distinction is weakening.[25]

How much of positive carry advantage filters through to realized returns in different asset classes? Before I answer empirically, it is worth putting this question into a broader context. It is closely related to the other one, which asks to what extent positive carry reflects required risk premia. There is a massive literature on this, mainly regarding bond yields and exchange rates. Does an upward-sloping yield curve indicate that the market expects rising yields or is it a sign of a positive required term premium? Do higher money market rates in Australia than Japan reflect expectations of AUDJPY depreciation or a required risk premium?

Recall that carry reflects an asset's return in an unchanged capital market environment. This statement does not reveal whether market participants expect the income advantage to be fully offset by capital market developments or whether they expect an unchanged environment (random walk) – or something between these two extremes. So, carry reflects an unknown blend of market expectations of a changing environment as well as required risk premia.

This is true for the dividend yield differential between equities, curve steepness, or credit spread in bonds; short-rate differential between currencies; or roll return differential between commodities. The expectations refer to relevant changes in market environment for each asset

---

[24]I only include in the Koijen 5-Composite carry strategies in five asset class contexts that are updated in Koijen's website (equal-volatility weighting them). The original Koijen et al. (2018) article also includes carry strategies across Treasury maturities, across US credit markets, and across index Puts and Calls. The broadest variant in that article achieved a SR well above 1 (before trading costs) between 1971 and 2012.

[25]My first book covered the early literature. Relevant studies after that book – besides Koijen et al. (2018) – include Lustig-Roussanov-Verdelhan (2011), Christiansen-Ranaldo-Söderlind (2011), Menkhoff, et al. (2012), Jurek (2014), Lettau-Maggiori-Weber (2014), Daniel-Hodrick-Lu (2017), and Bekaert-Panayotov (2020).

(faster growth in equities, higher yields in government bonds, widening credit spreads or defaults in corporate bonds, spot price depreciation in currencies and commodities). Some theories (e.g. pure expectations hypothesis for bond yields and uncovered interest parity for exchange rates) assume zero risk premia. Then the relevant market expectations would imply just enough future capital losses to offset the carry's income advantage and thus reduce the future excess return to zero.

It is ultimately an empirical question how much positive carry predicts either relevant changes in market environment or realized excess returns. Figure 6.10 offers a great visual answer inspired by Koijen et al. (2018, with data extended to end-2020). It compares the cumulative ex-ante carry and ex-post return for yield-seeking strategies in each asset class.

For cross-country strategies among equity, bond, and currency markets, the two lines align reasonably well, suggesting that in the long run the whole carry advantage is earned, on average (presumably reflecting a required risk premium). In contrast, for commodities, cumulative carry clearly exceeds cumulative return, suggesting that much of the carry advantage reflected market expectations of carry-offsetting capital market developments (perhaps mean-reverting prices after scarcity-induced spikes).

Koijen et al. (2018) shows further that the carry strategy results (up to 2012) for Treasuries, credits, and index options are somewhere in between; capital market losses "give back" part of the carry advantage, but not as much as for commodities.[26]

The long-run profitability of carry strategies is evidence against the so-called risk-neutral hypotheses, which assumed zero profits from carry seeking. Under the presumption of rational expectations, this is evidence of (mainly time-varying) required risk premia. However, another interpretation explains the same data by systematic expectational errors. Survey evidence on investor expectations tends to point to the latter interpretation.[27] The last hope for the rational camp is that such errors are not necessarily a sign of irrational expectations. They could partly reflect investor learning or the so-called peso problem, where the in-sample outcome was not fully representative of investor expectations.

Applications in Other Contexts

Koijen et al. (2018) and Ilmanen et al. (2021a) present evidence of profitable carry strategies within many asset classes.

Volatility selling is arguably the ultimate yield-seeking strategy, and one whose reward is clearly compensation for risk. For references on its long-run performance in different asset classes, see Ilmanen (2011, Chapter 15) and Fallon-Park-Yu (2015).

Risks and Pitfalls

It is worth looking beyond SRs to gauge performance, especially since carry strategies are notorious for their asymmetric outcomes ("going up the stairs, down the elevator") and ill-timed

---

[26]I covered this topic in *Expected Returns* (Chapters 13 and 21). When it comes to the split of income (carry) and capital gains as long-run return sources, I noted above that real estate may resemble credits or index options as an asset class whose long-run return is more than fully earned from the income part and whose long-run capital gains may well be negative or at least lower than cash return.

[27]I encouraged in *Expected Returns* greater use of survey data in empirical research, despite some academic qualms. I have in turn been encouraged by research such as Bacchetta et al. (2009), Greenwood-Shleifer (2014), and Giglio et al. (2021). Shleifer (2019) concurs.

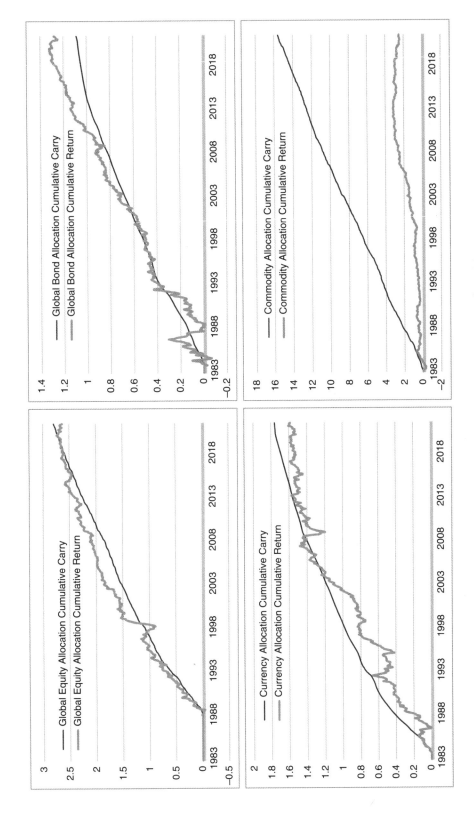

Figure 6.10 Cumulative Return and Cumulative Carry in Selected Strategies, Jan 1983–July 2021
Source: Data from Ralph Koijen, with similar carry strategy designs as in Koijen et al. (2018). The cumulative series are summed across months.

losses ("selling lottery tickets that pay off in bad times"). I already emphasized that this bad reputation is not warranted for all carry strategies. Credit and currency carry as well as volatility selling have negative skew and negative performance in equity market drawdowns, while the fixed income carry (country allocation strategy favoring countries with steep yield curves) looks more benign, and a dividend yield-based stock selection strategy looks even risk-reducing. The real puzzle is why also the latter strategies would be positively rewarded.

The currency carry strategy experienced its worst drawdowns in 2008 and 1992, while broader carry strategies suffered more in 1974 and 1981 (as well as in the 1930s–40s). The left-tail risk tends to be asset-class specific and much of it can be diversified away in a broad carry portfolio. Thus, positive carry returns may be captured while mitigating much of the occasional carry crashes that occur in one asset class.

The beta risks of carry strategies also vary over time. In the 1990s, currency carry was not yet widely known and could be considered an alpha strategy. Even though academics had written about the forward rate puzzle since the 1970s, carry strategies were spelled out for practitioners only later. Over time this alpha morphed into an alternative risk premium or even market beta exposure. Figure 6.11 supports this claim, as we see currency carry's equity market correlation rising over time.

One interesting question is *why* different carry strategies exhibit different degrees of beta risk. Is the currency carry strategy riskier because it has become more popular and this "commoditization" made it more systematic? Or are there some simpler, more native differences between carry strategies in varying asset classes. My answer is the latter. Carry is not earned in isolation but reflects the underlying assets' beta risks.

The simplest contrast is between a credit carry strategy based on corporate credit spreads and a stock selection carry strategy based on dividend yields. Wider credit spreads are inevitably associated with bonds of higher risk (lower credit ratings), whereas higher dividend yields are often offered by more mature and conservative companies, thus less risky stocks. Figure 6.11 confirms that long/short credit and stock selection carry strategies have had positive and negative equity market correlation, respectively.

As noted, currency carry's equity market correlation has risen from near zero to above 0.5. The correlations for equity country allocation (based on the spread between dividend yield and

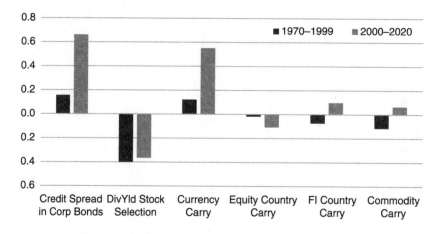

Figure 6.11 Evolving Equity Market Correlations of Various Carry Strategies, 1970–2020
Sources: Ken French Data Library for dividend yield strategy, AQR Data Library for credit returns based on Asvanunt-Richardson (2016), and factor century returns based on Ilmanen et al. (2021a).

cash rate), bond country allocation (based on curve steepness), and commodity allocation (based on backwardation/contango) have hovered near zero.

Current Outlook

Many carry strategies suffered during the 2008 GFC and again, if less, during the March 2020 Covid crash. Few carry strategies had an inspired performance even between these events. Straightforward credit strategies and volatility selling at least earned positive rewards amid the widespread investor reach for yield. Currency carry strategy benefited less as the slim cross-country yield differentials in the zero-rate world weakened its profit potential.

Since the basic strategy has been well known for over 20 years, many investors have tried to enhance it through tactical timing. It turns out to be no easier than equity market timing.

The most popular carry timing strategies involve cutting or reversing carry positions in response to an incipient rise in market risk aversion (using a variety of proxies including simply momentum in carry strategy performance). Such tactical carry timing would have positioned investors correctly (anti-carry) by late 2008. But these strategies worked less well in the whipsaw environment of the 2010s where central banks curtailed trends (too many false alarms).

Another timing approach is based on carry dispersion across markets. Narrower opportunity implies smaller profit potential and warrants smaller positions. Global policy rates are closely anchored near zero, limiting the prospects for currency carry, but even a small divergence may create opportunities.

6.4. Defensive and Other Low-Risk/Quality Strategies

Defensive, or low-risk, strategies take advantage of the empirical fact that, within most asset classes, "boring" assets have earned better risk-adjusted returns than their speculative peers.[28] Within stock markets, there is evidence that defensive stocks have earned at least as high long-term (raw) returns as riskier stocks, maybe even higher. At first blush, such evidence goes against the notion of a positive risk-reward trade-off.

Low-risk investing is best known within stock markets. As far back as in 1972, Fischer Black pointed out that the empirical security market line in US equities (the line linking average returns to market betas) was too flat relative to what the CAPM theory predicts. This point was almost forgotten until the 2000s, when new research on strong performance made many variants of low-risk investing better known (e.g. Ang et al. (2006), Clarke et al. (2006a)). Frazzini-Pedersen (2014) expanded the theory explaining the low-beta phenomenon and showed empirically that it applies to many different markets beyond the US and to asset classes beyond stocks.

The scatter plot of five beta-sorted portfolios in Figure 6.12 gives strong evidence of a flat security market line. This is true even if we use arithmetic means over 90 years. If we use geometric means, the reward/risk relation is actually inverted, and low-beta stocks have outperformed high-beta stocks. Moreover, subperiod analysis would show that this inversion has become more pronounced over time.

The defensive concept may be extended beyond statistical measures (low beta, low volatility) to include more fundamental measures of risk — or of high *quality*. Quality for stocks could be

---

[28]Recent overviews on defensive strategies include Van Vliet-de Koning (2016), Blitz-van Vliet-Baltussen (2020), Alquist-Frazzini-Ilmanen-Pedersen (2020). This section borrows liberally from the last paper.

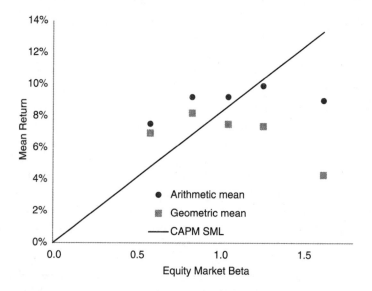

Figure 6.12 The Flat Security Market Line Among US Stocks, 1931–2020
Source: Data from AQR. Notes: Arithmetic and geometric mean excess-of-cash returns of five beta-sorted portfolios over the full sample period, January 1931–December 2020. The red line is the CAPM-based security market line (SML), where the slope is the full-sample market risk premium.

proxied by high profitability, low leverage, stable and high-quality earnings, good credit rating, as well as other metrics.

There are different ways to take advantage of the low-risk stocks' higher risk-adjusted returns. One is to overweight low-risk stocks in a long-only portfolio, thereby earning the same equity premium as the cap-weighted portfolio but at lower risk.[29] Another is to earn excess returns by creating a market-neutral long/short portfolio, such as the bet-against-beta (BAB) factor of Frazzini-Pedersen.

Regarding terminology, it remains open whether "Defensive" (or "Low Risk") is a better umbrella concept which includes statistical risk measures like beta and fundamental risk measures like quality, or whether "Quality" is the preferred umbrella concept which can include both fundamental and statistical metrics. Asness-Frazzini-Pedersen (2019) took the latter approach with their QMJ (quality-minus-junk) composite factor.

Flagship Strategy: Defensive Stock Selection Based on Low Beta and Quality

I present core evidence on two long/short strategies or factors applied to US stock selection: a market-neutral strategy BAB based on a statistical risk measure, and a dollar-neutral strategy QMJ based on mainly fundamental risk measures. Both are widely used in the literature and their returns are regularly updated in the public AQR Data Library.

---

[29]This statement is true if the low-risk stocks and high-risk stocks (and the market) have the same average returns, which still implies better risk-adjusted returns for low-risk stocks. If these low-risk stocks even have superior raw returns – as has been the case, for example, with some quality factors – they can offer a mix of higher return and lower risk.

The BAB, or "bet-against-beta" factor, by Frazzini-Pedersen (2014) involves buying stocks with low beta and selling stocks with high beta every month, rank-weighting stocks by their betas and targeting market neutrality. That is, the long side of low-beta stocks is levered up and the short side of high-beta stocks is levered down to ensure an ex-ante beta of zero for the long/short portfolio. Being long $2 worth of a 0.5-beta portfolio against shorting $0.67 of a 1.5-beta portfolio achieves this goal. The beta is estimated by using daily returns over the past year for volatility and three-day returns over the past five years for correlations, and applying shrinkage to these estimates. Strategies like low volatility or minimum volatility are related to BAB.

The QMJ, or "quality minus junk" factor, by Asness-Frazzini-Pedersen (2019) is a broad composite based on 16 single metrics within three subgroups (profitability, growth, and safety). Using a composite is apt because the literature on quality has come up with a large number of relevant metrics. QMJ is constructed using no leverage, resulting in a net negative beta.[30]

Economic Rationale

The evidence that lower-beta assets offer higher risk-adjusted returns contradicts the standard CAPM, which predicts that expected excess returns are proportional to betas. Nevertheless, low-risk investing is consistent with other economic theories, notably the theory of leverage constraints (Black (1972) and Frazzini-Pedersen (2014)) and the theory of lottery preferences (Barberis-Huang (2008)). In brief, high-risk stocks offer embedded leverage and lottery characteristics ("high bang for the (unlevered) buck"). Many investors like and pay for these characteristics, thereby accepting a lower long-run SR for high-risk stocks. Leverage-constrained investors cannot take advantage of the boring stocks' superior SRs by levering them up. This explains the too-flat security line. The same ideas of leverage aversion and lottery preferences may apply to other asset classes.

Asness et al. (2020) seek to disentangle these theories and find separate evidence for both, but the article documents stronger evidence for leverage constraints. Also, the theory of leverage constraints is supported by direct evidence on the underlying mechanism, not just evidence on returns. In contrast, Bali et al. (2017) find stronger evidence for the lottery preferences channel. In practice, investors may not care which of these explanations drives the low-risk premium or how much each contributes. The bottom line is that there are at least two good theories on why the low-risk premium exists and is likely to persist.

Historical Performance

Low-risk stock selection strategies have a compelling performance history. BAB has offered a higher SR and better out-of-sample performance (whether after the first discovery or the rediscovery) than other core factors like Value and Momentum, as seen in Figure 6.13. The QMJ strategy has also performed well since accounting data became available in the 1950s; QMJ looks even better when the alpha series credits it for its negative market beta.

---

[30]QMJ follows the Fama-French (1993) procedure used in many academic papers: double-sort stocks by their market capitalization and some characteristic; then buy a cap-weighted portfolio of the 30% of most attractive stocks and sell a cap-weighted portfolio of the 30% of least attractive stocks; do this separately for the large- and small-cap universes, and then average the returns of these portfolios.

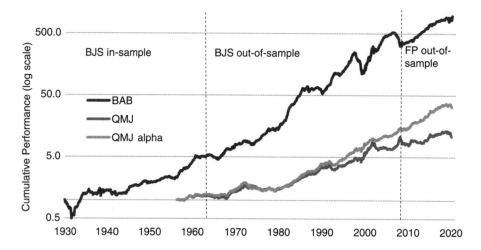

Figure 6.13   BAB and QMJ Performance in US Stocks, 1931–2021
Source: Data from AQR. Notes: This figure depicts the cumulative return of the BAB factor for three subperiods: the Black, Jensen, and Scholes (BJS, 1972) original sample, 1931–1965; an out-of-sample period for BJS, 1966–2009; and an out-of-sample period for Frazzini and Pedersen (FP, 2014), 2010–2021. The lower lines show the cumulative return and CAPM alpha of the QMJ factor since 1957.

Consistency and Extensions

The low-risk phenomenon is highly robust to using different strategies to capture the phenomenon as well as to different performance metrics.

Table 6.3 provides various long-run performance measures for four statistical low-risk strategies and one fundamental low-risk strategy. The designs of BAB and QMJ were described earlier; here is a brief description of the designs of the other statistical low-risk strategies:

- The SMR (stable-minus-risky) factor ranks stocks using betas estimated in the same way as BAB, but it weights them in a dollar-neutral rather than a market-neutral way, resulting in a net negative beta. Like QMJ, SMR follows the Fama-French (1993) procedure in stock weighting: It buys a value-weighted portfolio of the 30% of stocks with lowest betas and sells a value-weighted portfolio of the 30% of stocks with highest betas separately for the large- and small-cap universes and then averages the resulting portfolio returns.
- The SMRMN is the market-neutral version of SMR. SMRMN resembles the BAB strategy design in the market-neutrality target, but it resembles SMR in the stock weighting design within the long and short legs. SMRMN thus helps us see the separate impact of design decisions used in BAB and SMR.
- The IVOL or idiosyncratic volatility factor estimates (beta-adjusted) volatility using daily returns over the past year, and then follows QMJ and SMR in creating dollar-neutral Fama-French portfolios.

Over a 90-year history (64 years for QMJ given limited availability of some accounting data), all the low-risk strategies have earned large CAPM alphas, 9% for BAB, and 6% for QMJ. SRs for these two are compelling 0.73 and 0.54, but this metric understates the benefits of QMJ with its negative beta. The information ratio, or alpha over tracking error, for QMJ is 0.91, even beating BAB's 0.80. When we raise the bar and ask if these factors add value beyond a broad set of other factors, both BAB and QMJ earned a statistically significant marginal alpha of 3–4%.

Table 6.3 Performance of Defensive US Equity Strategies over a Long History, 1931/57–2020

	Annual Return	Sharpe Ratio	CAPM Beta	Annual Alpha vs. CAPM	Alpha T-Stat vs. CAPM	IR vs. CAPM	Annual Alpha vs. FF5 + MOM	Alpha T-Stat vs. FF5 + MOM	IR vs. FF5 + MOM
BAB	8.2%	0.73	−0.08	8.9%	5.5	0.80	4.0%	2.5	0.44
SMR	−0.5%	−0.03	−0.84	6.4%	4.8	0.58	2.9%	2.2	0.35
SMRMN	7.6%	0.69	−0.04	7.9%	5.3	0.72	2.8%	1.9	0.3
IVOL	−0.4%	−0.02	−0.54	4.1%	2.8	0.32	1.4%	1.2	0.19
QMJ	4.1%	0.54	−0.26	5.9%	6.1	0.91	3.2%	5.4	0.84

Sources: AQR, Alquist–Frazzini–Ilmanen–Pedersen (2020) (extended to end-2020). Exhibit A1 in this article details how each strategy was constructed. Notes: This table shows performance statistics for six statistical low-risk strategies and four fundamental low-risk strategies. The first two columns are about simple long/short returns, the next four control these returns for market exposure (CAPM), and the final columns controls returns for the five Fama-French (2015) factors (market, size, value, profitability, investment) as well as momentum ("FF5+MOM"). The sample period is 1931–2020 for the four statistical measures and 1957–2020 for the fundamental measure (QMJ), while the multi-factor regression results in the final columns are for 1952–2020 due to data availability. IR is information ratio.

While the columns show robustness across performance metrics, the rows show robustness across different specifications of defensive strategies. The one nuance is that dollar-neutral strategies SMR and IVOL, with significantly negative betas, earn their outperformance through risk reduction and thus in alpha. Their raw returns are near zero, but that fact understates – nay, conceals – their diversification benefits.

We can also ask how robust the low-risk phenomenon is in different parts of the equity market. The long-run SRs for BAB are 0.38 in large-caps and 0.85 in small-caps, and for QMJ 0.39 in large-caps and 0.63 in small-caps.

One important question is how well low-risk strategies work within sectors or industries (earlier we show results for the raw approach, ranking all US stocks together). Asness-Frazzini-Pedersen (2014) addressed this question and showed that the BAB strategy earned a positive SR between 1926 and 2012 within *each* of the 49 US industries studied. And looking at global data since the 1980s, BAB earned a positive SR within most global industries. If anything, industry neutralization, which we do not apply here, gives even stronger results.

Turning to stock selection performance outside the US, using data available in the AQR Data Library, I find positive SRs between 1990 and 2020 for both BAB and QMJ strategies in *all* countries studied. The global composite SRs are 0.98 and 0.70, and both information ratios are near 1.

Applications in Other Contexts

The Ilmanen et al. (2021a) century study shows that BAB-like strategies worked especially well in stock selection strategies but also in equity country allocation. Within bond markets, the SR was near zero for country allocation, but earlier studies show that the BAB strategy had a long-run SR of 0.8–1.0 for both US Treasuries and US Credits across maturities. Figure 8.4 later in the book will confirm that short-maturity bonds have higher risk-adjusted returns than long-maturity bonds both within Treasury and Credit markets. Taking advantage of this opportunity would require levering up the short-maturity bonds, something leverage-constrained investors cannot do.

The notion that lower-risk assets have higher SRs than their riskier peers extends well beyond financial markets; see Falkenstein (2012) and Ilmanen (2012) for surveys and references. For instance, in sports betting, the "long-shot bias" is a clear example of the low-risk effect. Betting on a favorite is a relatively low-risk bet (a high chance of a small gain) compared to betting on a long shot (a small chance of a large gain but a large probability of losing the bet). The latter bet offers much worse odds and thus seems systematically overvalued, likely more due to lottery preferences than leverage aversion (see Moskowitz-Vasudevan (2021)).

Risks and Pitfalls

The riskiness of defensive strategies depends crucially on whether they are designed to be dollar-neutral or market-neutral. Table 6.3 shows that the market betas of dollar-neutral SMR, IVOL, and QMJ were -0.3 to -0.8, while those of the market-neutral BAB and SMRMN were near zero. The market tail performances of all strategies are in line with their market betas. The dollar-neutral long/short strategies are truly defensive and quite reliably earn positive returns in large equity market drawdowns. The BAB and SMRMN strategies are as likely to gain or lose in such drawdowns. Finally, long-only defensive strategies with beta 0.5–0.8 will reliably lose money in large market falls but outperform beta-1 equity indices.[31]

Some defensive equity strategies have a reputation for being "bond-like." This is empirically true for dollar-neutral defensive strategies across industries. Intuitively, many utility and consumer staples companies are conservative and provide a relatively stable dividend stream, thus resembling bonds. Beta neutralization and industry neutralization together have tended to remove most of the bond sensitivity in defensive equity strategies.

Current Outlook

Defensive equity strategies have performed extremely well in the 2010s but also over much longer histories. Their outperformance cannot be explained merely by the bond market tailwinds or by richening valuations. Until recently, they tended to be rich according to value spreads, but this was the case for over a decade, and historically this valuation signal was not a very helpful factor timing indicator.[32]

Overall, any relative richness of defensive stocks is something to consider but this concern has often been overstated. At the very least, the defensive style deserves its place in the diversified menu of long-run rewarded factors we should stick with. Leverage aversion and lottery preferences are common investor characteristics which are unlikely to disappear, thus sustaining the style's theoretical underpinnings.

---

[31]See Exhibit 12 in Alquist et al. (2020). It is worth stressing that the term "defensive strategy" is arguably a misnomer for market-neutral applications, like the BAB factor. The BAB strategy buys low-beta stocks and sells high-beta stocks; it is defensively-oriented in that sense. However, since it uses leverage to buy more of the former than the latter, to target beta-neutrality, it is not a defensive strategy in the sense that it should reliably outperform when the equity market falls. Long/short strategies with a clearly negative net beta are also defensive in the latter sense, as are long-only strategies with a clearly below-one beta. (The BAB factor's odds are near 50/50, maybe even slightly tilted toward losses due to so-called beta compression effect whereby large market falls tend to result in indiscriminate stock price falls.)

[32]The value spread was broadly unchanged during the 2010s and yet the BAB factor performed extremely well, despite being persistently on the rich side. Ilmanen-Chandra-Nielsen (2015) and Asness (2021) show how various "wedges" weaken the link between valuation changes and contemporaneous returns of l/s factors, more so for BAB than for asset class premia or the value factor, given its high turnover and beta mismatch. Separately, Asness et al. (2017) and Ilmanen et al. (2021a) document the limited usefulness of contrarian factor timing.

Chapter 7

Alpha and Its Cousins

- Many investors seek manager-specific alpha beyond the systematic market and alternative risk premia. Alpha is the holy grail, but also elusive and costly.
- Boundaries are fuzzy for semantic and empirical reasons. Practitioners often equate alpha with active return, the simple difference between manager and benchmark returns. Academics want to risk-adjust this difference, but with what?
- Growing fee consciousness has prompted outflows from traditional active funds into cheaper index funds, ETFs, and factor funds. Yet, investors have also been willing to pay up for hedge funds and private-asset funds.
- Reality is more nuanced than the common view of passive managers dominating, active managers underperforming, and hedge funds disappointing.
- Even investors who do not wish to invest directly in systematic factors are often interested in using such factors to demystify their active managers' performance.

7.1. Alpha and Active Returns

I have so far covered major systematic return sources from asset class premia, illiquidity premia, and alternative risk premia (ARP, mainly style premia). Many investors who pay high fees to their active managers expect to earn *something more*: manager-specific active return or proprietary alpha.

In theory, alpha is the extra uncorrelated return achieved beyond any common systematic factors. Alpha is often taken as a measure of unique managerial skill. Unfortunately, alpha is elusive and its definition is often confusing and misused. Even if we could agree on a definition, alpha is often blended inside a broader portfolio that contains simple market exposures (betas). Because a single fee is charged for the portfolio, investors may end up "paying alpha fees for beta performance."

This section first covers some definitional issues, then turns to active versus passive management, including the evidence on and impact of the growth of passive, as well as empirical evidence on active managers' outperformance. Finally, some demystifying analyses help us assess how much the performance of hedge funds and other active managers, including superstar investors, reflects pure alpha (as opposed to the systematic return sources covered previously).

Are Active Return and Alpha Different?

Active return is defined as excess return over a specified benchmark or some factor model. Factor models try to adjust this return for risks, but that leaves us with many choices. We can measure one-factor (CAPM) alphas or any number of multi-factor alphas (where alpha is the average return left unexplained by the chosen factor model).

- Most practitioners associate the term "active return," and even alpha, with a simple difference: excess return to benchmark without any beta adjustment.
- For academics, alpha is the part of return achieved beyond the known risks in the CAPM or other factor model (the regression intercept). Unlike the simple difference, the CAPM alpha penalizes (or credits) each fund for any above-market (or below-market) beta.
- Academics increasingly study multi-factor models beyond the CAPM, such as the Fama-French 3- or 5-factor model. The difference between CAPM alpha and multi-factor alpha can be attributed to other market risk premia or ARP. However, there is little consensus on which factors to include, on how to treat trading costs (these are rarely subtracted from factors), or on other design decisions.

The bottom line is that there is no unique measure of alpha for any fund/strategy. Any judgment of active return or alpha estimates should also consider the impact of fees as well as any reporting/selection biases. Finally, let's remember that sample-specific luck can trump skill even over long evaluation periods. That is, ex-post randomness often overwhelms ex-ante edges.

I will soon return to the fuzzy boundaries between proprietary alpha and widely-known ARP, but here is some foretaste. If you are an investor with limited allocations to ARP, they are "alpha to you" and may improve your portfolio as much as any alpha. And some observers use the "alpha" term quite broadly to include any return offered by hedge funds (however much it contains equity market beta), while others save the "alpha" term only for proprietary strategies (whether discretionary or systematic). Such proprietary alpha can morph over time into more widely-known ARP. This has happened long ago to many value, momentum, and carry strategies, and it may eventually happen to others, including fundamental momentum and quality signals.

Active Versus Passive

The best definition of active investing is anything that deviates from market-cap weighted investments. Conversely, passive investing involves market-cap weights and is inactive in many ways. (It implies low turnover, no deviations from the average investor, and little discretion.)[1]

---

[1]Even this definition can get fuzzy across asset classes when we debate how much of market capitalization is investable (see Box 3.1.). There is long history of academic research on the unobservability of the market portfolio ("Roll's critique").

Overall, the active/passive distinction is not binary but involves many shades of grey.[2] The distinction is not even a continuum in one dimension (say, the tracking error to measure the magnitude of active risk). Other relevant dimensions include strategic versus tactical, diversified versus concentrated, low versus high turnover, and transparent versus proprietary.

Investors have increasingly shifted from active to passive investing. The market share of passive investing is somewhere between 20% and 50% in the late 2010s, depending on the asset class, region, and manager universe, as well as on definitional questions (e.g. how to treat increasingly popular and increasingly active ETFs or the large group of non-delegated active investors). Taking a broad view gives a surprisingly low market share for passive equity investing, as low as 18%.[3] For delegated managers, the passive market share is near 40% for equities but remains much lower for fixed income. For example, Morningstar estimates that the passive share of mutual fund assets has risen from 19% to 50% for US equities between 2007 and 2021, and from 7% to 31% for US fixed income.[4]

There has been much debate about the market impact of the shift to passive investing. Here are my favorite insights:

- Investors have benefited from lower fees (even on the active side, thanks to competitive pressures).
- We are likely far away from passive levels which would hurt price discovery in the market. If we ever get to such levels, less competition among fewer delegated active managers may help them find better opportunities, earn better returns, and then recover market share from passive managers. It thus looks like passive indexers can continue to "free-ride" on the price discovery service of active investors.
- Whether the shift to passive has made markets more or less efficient depends on whether passive inflows mainly replace the activity of inexperienced retail investors or their more skillful delegated active managers.
- A shift from active stock picking to passive investing will influence market pricing mainly if the active assets sold come from certain corners of the market (e.g. from disappointed value

---

[2]Examples of borderline debates include: (1) Cap-weighted ETFs on market segments (if such index ETFs are used actively, do they still count as passive?); (2) Home-biased index portfolios (is anything other than global market portfolio active?); (3) Funds with very low tracking error (how low a tracking error qualifies as passive?).

[3]A BlackRock study by Novick et al. (2017) estimated that out of (then) $68 trn of global equities, only $12 trn, or 18%, was passively managed. More than half of all global equities ($40trn out of $68trn) was managed directly (internally) by institutions and retail, and BlackRock classified most of it as active. If we focus on the more commonly cited universe of external or delegated equity management, 38% ($10.5trn out of $28trn) was passive. The share was somewhat higher (42%) for institutional investing than for mutual funds (and is only 22% for mutual funds if ETFs were excluded). Note that the active/passive choice is distinct from the external/internal management choice. Many large institutional investors have brought assets in-house, to save costs, and either invest them actively or passively. Retail investors were increasingly delegating their asset management to external managers, until the appearance of free trading apps encouraged more active and direct market participation in 2020–1.

[4]The passive share is clearly higher in the US and Asia than in Europe and emerging markets. For European mutual funds, the passive share has risen to 39% for equities and to 24% for fixed income. For US *institutional* investors, the share of passive mandates is about 30% of public assets and below 20% if (inherently active) alternative allocations are included. For example, Ennis (2020) quotes US public DB pension plan allocations: active public 52%, passive public 20%, active alternative 28%. For large US endowments, the respective numbers are 28%, 14%, 58%.

investors) or if the main passive indices differ from the broad market (e.g. the popular S&P500 index has a clear large-cap tilt).

- The shift to passive, as well as to ETFs and factor investing, could lead to higher correlations between single stocks and thus higher systematic risk. The greater use of basket trading may open opportunities for active single-stock traders. Finally, the shift may contribute to increasing market concentration.

Box 7.1 Systematic Versus Discretionary Investing[5]

Apart from the active versus passive distinction, two main approaches have evolved in active management: systematic and discretionary investing. Systematic (or "quant") generally applies a more repeatable and data-driven approach, relying on computers to identify investment opportunities across many securities. In contrast, a discretionary approach involves in-depth analysis across a smaller number of securities and relies more on information that is not always easily codified. Systematic investing requires longer data histories and liquid markets, but the best opportunities may arise just when new markets are maturing.

Systematic and discretionary managers can overlap in what characteristics they like in assets. A fundamental stock picker or equity analyst often looks for cheap stocks with a catalyst and a quality filter. This is not so different from a systematic stock selection strategy which relies on value, momentum, and quality signals. Thus, systematic and fundamental are not mutually exclusive in the same way systematic and discretionary are. That said, discretionary managers tend to hold more concentrated positions, desiring high stock-specific risk, while at least factor-oriented quants target well-rewarded factor exposures while diversifying away stock-specific risk. Systematic managers are long on breadth and short on stories. They are often described as "black boxes," yet they can offer much more transparency on the investment process. Discretionary stock pickers do deeper bottom-up analysis − "kicking the tires" − which also allows them to motivate better their individual investments with compelling stories.

Active investing is still dominated by discretionary managers, with systematic approaches remaining a minority − albeit a growing one. For example, Morgan Stanley estimates that the market share of active systematic equity managers remains under 10% even after doubling during the 2010s.

Looking at past performance, neither approach seems to consistently outpace the other in raw returns, but the diversification applied by systematic managers may give an edge in risk-adjusted returns. Unless an investor has a strong prior belief in either approach, they may be excellent complements: We observe equally low correlations within both systematic and discretionary manager universes (average pairwise correlation of active returns ca. 0.15, incidentally contradicting the myth that all quants are alike), and even lower between managers across the two groups (ca. 0.05). Finally, some try to combine the best of both approaches through "quantamental" investing or thematic investing.

---

[5]See AQR Portfolio Solutions Group (2017b) for more analysis on systematic versus discretionary investing.

Active Manager Performance

Sharpe (1991) has famously argued that even as a matter of arithmetic, active managers' higher costs mean that these managers must collectively underperform passive managers (since each group collectively holds the market). Active management is a zero-sum game before fees, a negative-sum game after fees.

This argument can be challenged by recognizing that (i) passive investing also involves turnover and costs,[6] and (ii) active investors do not only include (delegated) active managers but also retail and institutional direct investing. Direct investors are collectively large (they hold more than half of global equities), their performance is rarely measured, and they are a plausible negative alpha source (since they may not be as well-incentivized or as well-resourced as delegated managers). Taken together, it is thus *conceivable* that delegated active managers tend to outperform as a group at the expense of other investors. That said, these active managers must earn sufficient gross alpha from other investors to cover their costs and fees if they are to offer any positive net alpha.

The conventional wisdom is that while markets are not perfectly efficient in the sense that market prices are always right, beating the market is really hard. Pedersen (2015) calls such markets "efficiently inefficient" in his eponymous book, in the spirit of Grossman-Stiglitz (1980). Rationally, there needs to be some degree of inefficiency to incentivize market participants to try active management, but the quest may keep getting harder over time.[7] However, the best argument for overtrading and widespread active management is overconfidence. Many investors believe that "my managers" will provide positive alpha even if most won't. The gradually rising passive share suggests that realism is increasing.

Turning to empirics, numerous studies over more than half a century have documented negative net alpha for active mutual funds, in line with Sharpe's arithmetic. Other delegated managers have a more positive track record (possibly in line with Sharpe's challengers above): collectively positive active returns over 20+ years for manager universes among institutional funds, hedge funds, and private equity. In all cases, measured alpha has tended to decay over time. Moreover, the positive alphas can be questioned given the possibility of survivorship and other selection biases in manager databases. Likewise, the outperformance of institutional funds over mutual funds might reflect greater reporting biases, but other studies seem to support this outperformance.[8]

---

[6] See Pedersen (2018) which quantifies some of these costs.

[7] The theoretical literature on active manager net alpha has at least three strands. First, the Berk-Green (2004) model assumes positive manager skill but also perfect competition across asset owners for superior managers, which ensures that any positive net alpha gets competed down to zero. Berk-van Binsbergen (2015) provides empirical evidence of mutual fund manager skill, but in the context of this somewhat depressing model where all gains from skill accrue to the managers. Second, Garleanu-Pedersen (2018) is more optimistic on the possibility of asset owners earning positive net alpha. The competitive balance between asset owners and asset managers does matter and may result in fairer fee levels. Intuitively, while asset owners are seeking superior managers, asset managers are seeking investor capital in a world where both sides are uncertain about the manager's future alpha. Third, Pastor-Stambaugh-Taylor (2014) emphasizes the role of decreasing returns to scale; growing asset size at manager and industry level tends to reduce prospective alpha.

[8] See Swedroe-Berkin (2015), Sullivan (2021), and Bollen-Joenvaara-Kauppila (2021) on hedge funds, Fama-French (2010) and Cremers-Fulkerson-Riley (2019) on mutual funds, Gerakos-Linnainmaa-Morse (2016) on institutional funds, Harris-Jenkinson-Kaplan (2014, 2016) on private equity funds, and AQR Portfolio Solutions Group (2018) on all. Chapter 11 (11.4.2) in Ilmanen (2011) covered extensively the selection/survivorship/other biases which may overstate measured active manager returns. New research includes Aggarwal-Jorion (2010), Ibbotson-Chen-Zhu (2010), and Dimensional (2020).

Figure 7.1   Hedge Fund Index Cumulative Excess Return over Cash, 1994–2020
Sources: DJCS, HFR, MSCI. Hedge fund industry is proxied by an average of the asset-weighted DJCS index, the
equal-weighted HFR index, and the HFR fund of funds index. Equities are proxied by the MSCI ACWI (all-countries)
Index. I use 36-month rolling beta for hedging the equity exposure.

Figure 7.1 illustrates alpha decay in hedge fund industry performance over time. Raw hedge fund returns have persisted in the 2010s, but the CAPM alpha has been modest. Performance may, however, be better for funds not reporting to hedge fund databases.[9]

Underlying Figure 7.1 is the finding that hedge funds tend to have meaningful equity market exposure. Hedge funds are often viewed as absolute return managers (implying zero market beta) but they are also compared to equity markets (implying beta of one). The industry has converged to a compromise where its equity market beta is near 0.3 and correlation near 0.8 (though lower for single managers). Investor recognition of this fact has contributed to the fee pressures which have pushed management and performance fees down from the classic "2+20%."

Do some active manager characteristics indicate more likely outperformance? Although there is only debatable evidence of performance persistence across single managers, a fund's past performance may have mild predictive ability.[10] Other results may reflect reporting biases, such as the edge of smaller and younger funds. There are few uncontested patterns in the literature, and manager selectors tend to rely more on subjective proprietary analyses than on systematic rules.

Are there pockets of markets where active managers tend to fare better? Conventional wisdom says that the "dusty corners" of financial markets, characterized by few active managers and fewer fundamental analysts, are less efficiently priced.[11] Candidates include small/micro-caps, emerging/frontier markets, less-liquid fixed income markets, and private assets.

---

[9]See Barth et al. (2021) which includes all hedge funds from regulatory reports. Many best-performing funds are closed to new investors and choose not to report to common hedge fund databases, but their results are included in regulatory reports. This new finding challenges the traditional assumption that hedge fund databases show overstated results due to various selection biases. The study also finds that the industry size may be closer to $5trn than oft-quoted $3trn.

[10]See Fama-French (2010), Jones-Wermers (2011), and Elton-Gruber-Blake (2012) on performance persistence. Empirical results on persistence vary depending on the sample, horizon length, and performance metric used. Overall, it is safest to say that the results are mixed and any evidence of either persistence or mean reversion is relatively modest or context-specific. There may also be less persistence in purely manager-specific alpha than in total returns, and less among top performers than laggards. Finally, the conventional wisdom used to be that private asset returns exhibit alpha persistence, but this has no longer been true for private equity after the late 1990s, though still holds for venture capital in the 2000s (see Harris-Jenkinson-Kaplan-Stucke (2020)).

[11]Beyond dusty corners, it may be worth seeking markets with a large pool of plausible negative-alpha players. Using a poker analogy: You'd rather play with patsies than with sharks. Thus, investors should look for markets with many unsophisticated investors (say, retail) and/or non-economically motivated participants.

For some supportive evidence, Dyck-Lins-Pomorski (2013) document higher active returns among emerging market and non-US equity managers than among US equity managers. One counterargument is that these dusty corners have higher fees, and they, too, have active losers.

One thing for certain is that dusty corners have more alpha dispersion across managers. The benefits of identifying superior managers are greatest in private assets.[12] Investors should recall, however, that this opportunity comes with risks. Wide alpha dispersion implies that private-asset alpha can also be deeply negative. Overconfidence about picking winners may be even more prevalent in private markets.

"Samuelson's dictum" refers to the conjecture that financial markets may be micro efficient but macro inefficient. This conjecture rings true since fair relative pricing of assets is easier to enforce by arbitrage than the absolute level of asset prices. However, it is debatable whether the world of low expected returns implies an irrational bubble, while the relative pricing of value and growth stocks in 2021 seems far from efficient markets (let alone the pricing of meme stocks).[13]

Are some end-investors more likely to be skilled or to identify skilled/successful active managers? Overconfidence is such a prevalent trait that humility is warranted, Yet, better-resourced organizations with better compensation and better incentives presumably have some edge. As noted, institutional funds have tended to outperform mutual funds, and some institutions have a compelling long-run track record – reflecting some mixture of lower costs and asset allocation or manager selection choices. My own investment beliefs may admittedly make me give too short shrift to discretionary active managers.

Are there environments or times where active managers generally fare better? The evidence of alpha decay over time suggests markets were less competitive in the olden days. There is also some evidence that active stock pickers tend to outperform during recessions, at times of high dispersion between stock-specific returns, and especially during "differentiated declines" – when weak markets and wide dispersion coincide.[14] Finally, it helps when active managers' common structural tilts are working well.

The most obvious examples of common structural tilts are active fixed income managers' tendency to load up on credit risk (and thus equity markets) and hedge funds' typically positive equity market betas. Figure 7.2 shows that the pairwise correlation across fixed income managers and their typical correlation with the equity market are 0.6–0.7. Correlations are almost as high for hedge fund subsectors, but close to zero for active equity managers. These differences matter both for manager diversification and for fair fees.[15]

---

[12]Mauboussin-Callahan (2020) estimates with almost four decades of Pitchbook and Morningstar data that the interquartile range ("middle fifty" between 25th to 75th percentiles) of US venture capital and buyout funds was near +/−10% (internal rate of return compared to median manager), while that of long/short equity funds was near +/−3% (5-year annualized return compared to median), that of US equity mutual funds near +/−2%, and that of US bond funds near +/−1%.

[13]For a more serious treatment of Samuelson's dictum, see Garleanu-Pedersen (2021).

[14]See Parikh-McQuiston-Zhi (2018).

[15]The positive credit and equity market sensitivities explain why active fixed income managers tended to outperform their benchmarks during the bullish 2010s (see Brooks-Gould-Richardson (2020)). At the same time, active equity managers tended to lag, leading some observers to claim that active fixed income is "easier" than active equity. There is a simpler explanation. The typical tilts of a large-cap US equity manager are out-of-benchmark exposures in cash, small-caps, and non-US markets. In some decades they help or wash out, but all three tilts hurt in the 2010s, a bull market led by US large-caps. Lucky or unlucky periods to common structural tilts can cause lengthy periods of out-/underperformance, but we should not expect them to persist going ahead. The hopeful takeaway is that the recent bad times for active US equity managers are at least partly environmental, making them more likely reversible than secular. Conversely, we have little reason to expect active fixed-income managers to keep producing as high active returns as they did during the bullish 2010s.

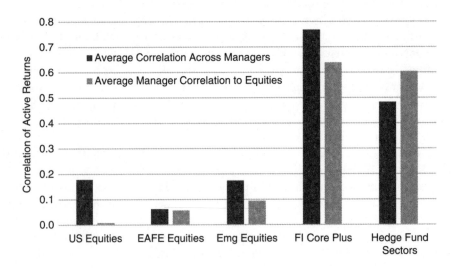

Figure 7.2 Common Directional Factors Among Hedge Funds and Active FI Managers, 2010–2019

Sources: AQR, eVestment, Credit Suisse. Equity and fixed income managers used in this graph are the ten largest funds by assets with at least ten years of data. Active returns are all calculated against the managers' stated benchmarks. For hedge funds, eight Credit Suisse hedge fund sector indices are used and their entire return is viewed as an active return. AQR Portfolio Solutions Group (2020b) provides further details.

To sum up, true alpha is valuable but elusive. It is also increasingly scarce if competition is heating and the pool of negative alpha players is shrinking. Any evidence of individual manager alpha persistence is modest at best. You should thus not assume lightly that your active managers (or your own active investing) can achieve significant positive alpha. And you should try to better understand your active managers' performance, so as not to pay alpha fees for beta performance.

7.2. Reviewing the Classification of Portfolio Return Sources

The pyramid shown earlier in Figure 4.1 summarizes the return sources described in the last few chapters: riskless rate, market risk premia (MRP), illiquidity premia, alternative risk premia (ARP), and alpha. Unfortunately, there are many debatable choices within the classification used in this pyramid. I already asked in Chapter 6 whether the four umbrella concepts I use for ARP are sufficient. Here I review the blurred line between ARP and alpha. Finally, most real-world investors and investments *blend* different parts of the pyramid. To illustrate, section 7.3 will decompose and demystify the long-run returns of the hedge fund industry as well as of some superstar investors.

The boundary between ARP and alpha is fuzzy. As already noted, practitioners and academics often have different ideas of "alpha." If we count ARP as part of a given multi-factor model, then by definition their reward cannot be multi-factor alpha. But they can be one-factor (CAPM) alpha or simple active return versus some naïve benchmark.

A practitioner perspective on the pyramid highlights two key dimensions: market directionality and uniqueness. The alpha and ARP layers are market-neutral, while the MRP and ARP layers are publicly known. ARP is thus alpha-like in being near market-neutral but beta-like in being widely known.

Not being widely known is a fair distinction that makes proprietary signals more alpha-like. It is more questionable to argue that being complex (contextual, conditional, interactive, non-linear), or discretionary or tactical, makes any strategy inherently more alpha-like. Lastly, better implementation skills or trading cost efficiency are one source of alpha for even widely known investment strategies.

The ARP versus alpha debate is related to two broad schools of thought among quant managers: one favoring publicly known factors, another seeing proprietary (often new and complex) signals as the holy grail. How much should one rely on classic "tried-and-true" factors – while still refining and expanding signals and implementation capabilities – versus the alternative which in extreme requires continuously coming up with new signals and discarding old ones? ARP has the benefits of higher capacity, simpler rules, greater transparency, and academic backing – but may be too widely used or insufficiently adaptive in an evolving world. Novel proprietary signals are more exciting and adaptive, and they almost inevitably look better in recent backtests (since they have shorter histories and complexity that opens more degrees of freedom for overfitting). The key trade-off is between the *overfitting* risk in proprietary alpha and the *overcrowding* and obsolescence risks in ARP.

It remains open whether the widely-known ARP or the proprietary alpha will provide better future performance, but the former are more likely to have the capacity to help a large group of investors. That said, neither approach can help *all* investors earn more than low expected returns if that is what markets currently offer.

Understandably, I cannot write about the proprietary research done at my employer, and even my comments on ARP emphasize the best-known strategies.

7.3. Demystifying Hedge Funds, Superstars, and Other Active Managers

Most real-world investments or investors include a blend of several distinct exposures in the pyramid in Figure 4.1. A value-oriented long-only manager (or a systematic "fundamental index") is a blend of long-only equity premia and long/short value premia, and just possibly, some alpha. Most managers and asset owners have exposure to at least one market risk premium, some styles, maybe illiquids, and hopefully some alpha.

These exposures can be estimated through returns-based regressions or holdings-based analysis. This analysis can be conducted on a single manager, on an asset owner's total portfolio, or on a large group of active managers. Regression results will be inevitably model-specific and sample-specific.[16]

Table 7.1 illustrates demystifying the whole hedge fund industry, based on a "kitchen-sink" 12-factor regression of a composite of broad hedge fund indices. In the context of a regression model, each factor's contribution reflects its beta coefficient multiplied by the full-sample factor premium. Between 1994 and 2020, when hedge funds collectively outperformed cash by 4.3% p.a., almost half (2.0%) reflected market risk premia, mainly these funds' equity market exposure

---

[16]Chapter 7.1 and Chapter 10 (Equation 2) discuss the sensitivity of alpha estimates on the chosen factor model. Chapter 12 covers model errors and estimation errors in the context of optimizations, but similar issues arise with regression estimates. We assume stable linear relationships, unbiased sample periods, and so on. Illiquid assets with smoothed returns pose their own problems; holdings-based analysis may be needed.

Table 7.1 Hedge Fund Industry Excess-of-Cash Return Decomposed, 1994–2020

RSQ = 77%	Coefficient (A)	T-Statistic	Realized Premium (B)	Return Contribution (C = A*B)	EqMkt correl	HF correl	
Intercept	0.001	1.0		0.7%			Alpha 0.7%
Equities	0.261	14.2	6.0%	1.6%	1.00	0.77	MRP 2.0%
Equities Lagged	0.054	4.8	6.0%	0.3%	0.09	0.25	
Bonds	0.061	1.2	2.8%	0.2%	0.03	0.08	
Commodities	0.048	3.8	–1.6%	–0.1%	0.46	0.49	
Value SS	0.002	0.1	1.7%	0.0%	0.19	–0.05	ARP 1.6%
Momentum SS	0.163	3.9	4.4%	0.7%	–0.39	–0.07	
Quality SS	–0.062	–1.5	5.3%	–0.3%	–0.74	–0.65	
Carry	0.039	1.5	4.3%	0.2%	0.28	0.34	
Trend	0.131	4.0	3.6%	0.5%	–0.05	0.17	
Index Put Sell	0.052	2.6	5.4%	0.3%	0.30	0.37	
Tech Sector	0.035	2.6	7.5%	0.3%	0.22	0.28	
Small Size	0.201	6.3	–0.1%	0.0%	0.14	0.41	

Sources: AQR, Bloomberg, DJCS, HFR, MSCI. Notes: Hedge fund industry is proxied by an average of the asset-weighted DJCS index, the equal-weighted HFR index, and the HFR fund of funds index. Equities are proxied by the MSCI ACWI (all-countries) Index; Bonds by the Bloomberg Barclays Aggregate Index; Commodities by the Bloomberg Commodity Index; value, momentum, quality, small size global stock selection strategies and carry and trend macro trading strategies by style premia available in the AQR Data Library; index put sell by a strategy of selling one-month out-of-the-money puts on the S&P500 index; and tech sector by the excess return of the NASDAQ index over the market. A factor's return contribution of is the product of its regression coefficient and its realized in-sample premium. The regression's explanatory power (R-squared) is 77%.

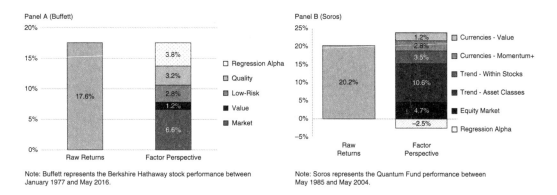

Figure 7.3   Superstars Demystified: Warren Buffett and George Soros
Source: Brooks-Tsuji-Villalon (2018). Notes: Regression alpha is the annualized regression intercept.

(embarrassingly high simple market correlation of 0.77 and further correlation to last-month equities, likely due to smoothed/stale pricing in some hedge fund strategies). Another 1.6% came from various ARP (mainly chasing returns through momentum stock selection and trend following in futures, but also further risks from put selling, tech sector, small caps), leaving 0.7% (the annualized regression intercept) as unexplained alpha beyond these systematic premia. Most style premia I tried had insignificant positive coefficients. Only defensive stock selection (Quality SS) has a negative loading, which cost hedge funds about 0.3% annually.

Even investors who do not like to use systematic factors for improving their portfolios may use them for return and risk attribution. Demystifying regressions – even with simpler variants which only estimate the CAPM beta and alpha – can help investors better understand their portfolios and assess whether they pay fair fees to their active managers or "alpha fees for beta performance."

It is particularly fun to apply such demystifying regressions to superstar investors such as Warren Buffett and George Soros.[17] My colleagues' work has shown that the world's most famous value investor actually earned more of his long-run returns from the market exposure and from quality and low-beta tilts than from a value tilt. The decomposition in Figure 7.3 still attributed some positive alpha to Buffett on top of these systematic exposures. The results were harsher to another giant, macro manager Soros. His Quantum fund's performance over two apparently golden decades could be more than fully explained by a handful of systematic factors mainly reflecting his self-professed macro trend chasing style. To be clear, any investor would have been grateful for the market-beating returns these superstars delivered, whether we attribute them to alpha or some factor premia.

---

[17]See Frazzini-Kabiller-Pedersen (2018) and Brooks-Tsuji-Villalon (2018). Caveats: Any results will be sample-specific and can be misleading if estimated over short samples, if manager positions vary a lot over time (holdings-based analysis may be more useful), or if the manager returns are net of trading costs and fees, while the explanatory factor returns are gross of trading costs and possibly overfitted.

Chapter 8

Theories Explaining Long-run Return Sources

- Academics have long debated whether each rewarded factor reflects a rational risk premium or irrational mispricing. In many cases, the answer may be both.
- Risk-based explanations require bad returns in bad times, whereas trend and quality strategies tend to provide good returns in bad times.
- Some believe that mispricings will be arbitraged away once they are known. Yet, limits of arbitrage sustain them, and even strategies with behavioral origins can suffer such persistent losses that they are risky.
- Simple empirical analyses explore if rewarded factors can be explained rationally by tail risk, skewness, illiquidity, or leverage – or by behavioral forces.
- Investor conviction on any long-run premium is reinforced if we have an economic rationale for its existence.
- It further helps if we can identify some investor groups "on the other side" of the opportunity based on theoretical considerations and empirical evidence. However, there is *always* someone on the other side; the implications of this adding-up constraint are often forgotten.

The market risk premia and alternative risk premia have provided significant positive average returns over the long run in many markets. Skeptics may argue that the selected premia were chosen based on the historical success, so we need more.

Apart from requiring persistence, pervasiveness, and robustness in empirical evidence, some economic intuition is also needed to convince us of positive rewards going forward. Any long-run return source should be backed by logic of what caused the opportunity in the first place – and why it doesn't get arbitraged away.

I listed in Chapters 4 and 6 specific explanations for each premium. Here I discuss some broad issues.

8.1. Rational Reward for Risk or Irrational Mispricing?

The main dueling explanations are risk-based (rational) and behavioral (irrational). There are many candidate theories from each camp for any premium (the key ones were referenced earlier), and data does not easily allow us to determine which theories matter more. Academic debates have been going on for decades. As a testimony to the importance of these debates, Eugene Fama, the father of the efficient market hypothesis, and Robert Shiller, arguably its most ardent critic, shared the 2013 Nobel Prize in Economics.[1]

Some observers consider only risk-based explanations sustainable, claiming that arbitrage forces and investor learning will quickly eliminate any behavioral anomalies. The counterargument is that limits of arbitrage and slow learning can sustain behavioral anomalies for long periods after the opportunity has been identified.

Limits of arbitrage are explanations that help especially behavioral anomalies stick. The classic case is noise trader risk for contrarian strategies: Rich things can get richer.[2] Other limits include trading costs, short-selling constraints, and leverage constraints. The last one is a crucial force limiting arbitrage. Even the "unconstrained" arbitrageur is limited from fully exploiting the available opportunities, especially assets/strategies with low natural volatility or highly diversified composites.

Sometimes, these limits are even viewed as the original reason for certain regularities. Market frictions, such as prevalent investor constraints, can both cause a regularity (recall leverage constraints causing the low-beta factor) and prevent its undoing by arbitrage (the latter aspect applies to all long/short factors).[3]

Overall, for most premia it seems likely that *both* risk-based and behavioral explanations matter, and we can just debate their relative roles. Some premia, like the equity premium and asymmetric strategies that effectively sell financial catastrophe insurance, are most obviously about risk. In contrast, trend following and quality factor premia seem more likely behaviorally based, given their benign safe-haven characteristics.

It is also worth noting that most of the proposed risk-based explanations are specific to one asset class, while behavioral explanations often apply to many asset classes, in line with the empirical evidence. This pervasiveness makes me lean more toward behavioral explanations for the style premia strategies described in Chapter 6.

In any case, the boundary between risk-based and behavioral explanations is another blurred line. For example, it is debatable whether leverage aversion and leverage constraints (which

---

[1] The third winner in 2013, Lars Hansen, is closer to the rational camp, as are most other finance professors who have won the economics Nobel prize (Markowitz, Miller, and Sharpe in 1990; Merton and Scholes in 1997, Engle in 2003). The behavioral camp has been gaining ground, however, with the Nobel prizes of Professors Kahneman (2002) and Thaler (2017). Chapters 5 and 6 in Ilmanen (2011) cover both sides in detail.

[2] See DeLong et al. (1990) and Shleifer-Vishny (1997), and recall the possibly apocryphal Keynes quote, "Markets can stay irrational longer than you can stay solvent."

[3] Leverage aversion or constraints seem especially relevant for explaining the performance of diversified ARP portfolios. Combining many lowly correlated return sources can elevate the portfolio SR meaningfully, but diversification reduces portfolio volatility. Investors would have to accept a meaningful rise in portfolio leverage to achieve, say, 10% volatility target. Few investors want to have 5–10 × leverage applied (even through unlevered investments in delegated funds) to their total portfolio.

underlie the defensive factor) are rational or irrational – more likely a mix. Even long/short factor premia with behavioral origins are subject to risks related to crowding and deleveraging, especially if they are widely known. Most importantly, the fact that so many investors capitulate from almost any factor after a few years of underperformance justifies the word "risk" in alternative risk premia strategies. Wise men have said "no pain, no premium" – it is precisely the painful times that will sustain the premium and prevent it from being arbitraged away.

Beyond the two main explanations, any historical premium may be explained by data mining and other selection biases. Another critical interpretation is that some premia may truly have existed in the past but the world has changed. I will discuss both ideas in Chapter 9.

8.2. "Bad Returns in Bad Times" at the Heart of Risk Premia

According to the CAPM, investors should care about covariances and not about an asset's stand-alone volatility. When an asset loses matters more than how much it loses. An asset's equity market beta determines its contribution to portfolio volatility and thus its required return. Systematic beta risk matters, while an asset's idiosyncratic volatility can be diversified away, and thus does not drive required returns. An asset that performs poorly when the equity market fares poorly is risky and warrants a high premium.

The CAPM is a too simple model, but its central insight can be generalized to many other asset pricing models. Assets that perform poorly in "bad times" – think of recessions and financial crises – are especially risky and warrant high required returns. Conversely, we call safe-haven assets those that tend to perform well just when it is most needed. Such investments smooth overall portfolio returns and could justify required returns even lower than cash. Government bonds have offered this service between 2000 and 2020 (though their returns have been bolstered by falling yields).

In reality, we live in a multi-factor world. Even then, the sign of any factor's long-run reward should follow the above logic. Factors or strategies that tend to earn "bad returns in bad times" should offer a large long-run reward. Conversely, investors should be happy to hold some safe-haven strategies in their portfolio even if these offer much lower long-run returns.

Bad times are hard to define but as Justice Potter Stewart said in another context, "I know it when I see it." In that spirit, Figure 8.1 characterizes bad times loosely as periods of major equity

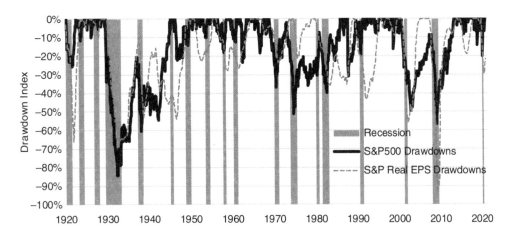

Figure 8.1 What Are Bad Times?, 1920–2020
Sources: Standard&Poor's, NBER.

market drawdowns and economic contraction. Clearly, the length of bad times, and between bad times, has varied over time, making it dangerous to expect historical patterns to repeat precisely.

Broad macro series like GDP growth and unemployment rate tend to be lagging indicators. Some financial market series (e.g. yield spreads across bonds) and economic confidence series may be leading indicators, though not too reliable. More contemporaneous common features of bad times are high volatility, deteriorating liquidity, and forced deleveraging. Some bad times are prompted by rising inflation and Fed tightening, and bad times in turn may prompt disinflation and Fed easing.

Economic recessions and equity market declines seem like obvious measures of bad times, but it was not always thus. In the olden world, when economies grew at a snail's pace and equities hardly existed, the main risks may have been interest rates (or idiosyncratic – as countries and even regions were quite segmented). William Bernstein (2013) replaces the classic four horsemen of apocalypse (war, famine, pestilence, death) with inflation, deflation, confiscation, devastation, while Walter Scheidel (2017) lists major wars, revolutions, plagues, and state collapses as the great levelers (which have resulted in the destruction of riches and thereby improved equality). Once economic growth accelerated two centuries ago, it changed everything; growth became the biggest driver of progress but also the biggest risk factor. The post-WWII era has been aided by the absence of major depressions, wars, hyperinflations, and violent revolutions in the developed economies.

Turning to empirical analysis, it is clear that equities have been the riskier asset class and bonds the safer asset class – whether we study volatilities, betas, or bad-times performance. I now ask whether we can find robust relationships between the performance of a broader set of main long-run return sources highlighted in this book and a variety of plausible risk measures. I can already reveal that the visual patterns are rather weak – which may imply opportunities for investors to improve risk-adjusted returns.

The 20 factor premia I study in Figures 8.2–8.4 include: liquid asset class premia in equities (S&P500, non-US "EAFE," emerging market, and global), fixed income (US Treasuries, investment-grade credits, high-yield credits, and global government bonds), commodities (diversified index, gold), hedge funds, illiquid asset classes (real estate, private equity, venture

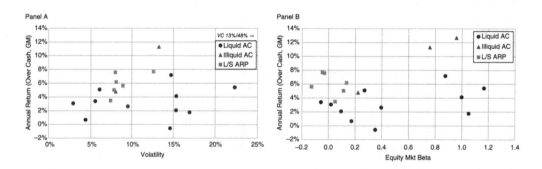

Figure 8.2 A-B Scatterplot multi-asset average return on (A) volatility, (B) equity market beta, 1990–2020

Sources and Notes: Volatility and equity market beta are full-sample statistics for 1990–2020. The 20 premia are: liquid asset premia in equities (S&P500, non-US "EAFE," emerging market, and global – using MSCI data), fixed income (US Treasuries, investment-grade credits, high-yield credits, and global government bonds – using Barclays Bloomberg data), commodities (diversified BCOM index and gold), hedge funds (HFR indices), illiquid asset class premia (real estate, private equity, venture capital – using NCREIF and Cambridge indices); and long/short premia multi-asset value, momentum, carry, defensive, and trend styles, as well as S&P500 index put selling – using AQR data). Cash is implicitly in the origin. I use annual returns for illiquid assets when calculating SR, volatility and beta (which partly corrects for the smoothness in quarterly returns).

capital); and long/short premia (broad value, momentum, carry, defensive, trend, and index put selling).

I first scatterplot their compound average returns or SRs over different risk metrics using the 1990–2020 sample period. Panels A and B in Figure 8.2 reveal only modestly positive relations between the average premia and volatility or equity beta. Even more puzzling: When I drilled deeper, I found a *negative* correlation (-0.3) between SRs and equity correlations. Apparently, you did not have to trade off higher SR against lower equity exposure.

The weak relations could reflect the multi-factor world (where any pairwise relations are clouded by the other factors) or sample-specific effects and biases in any empirical analysis. The 1990–2020 sample period is known to be disinflationary and generally friendly for risk taking, which partly explains the negative commodity return and high bond and risky-asset returns. Illiquid assets (measured by internal rates of returns) and long/short premia may have their own sources of biases.

8.3. Other Core Ideas for Rational Risk Premia and Behavioral Premia

It's really a multi-factor world, but which other factors matter beyond the equity market? The sign of other factors' long-run premium should in theory depend on their equity correlation (though there was no evidence of this) as well as on investors' risk preferences beyond portfolio variance. I could add other return factors like the bond risk premium or the value premium, but instead I explore more generic candidates for explanatory factors – tail risk, skewness preference, liquidity preference, leverage aversion.

- Tail risk is part of portfolio risk, but it's a nonlinear variant that matters especially for investors with highly asymmetric risk preferences. Some risk preferences are purely symmetric (mean-variance preferences), others are mildly asymmetric (e.g. power utility with constant relative risk aversion), and yet others require strict downside protection (e.g. portfolio insurance preferences).[4] I try to capture the main tail risk, "bad-times average return," by studying an investment's performance in the ten worst global equity drawdowns.
- Skewness preferences are related to downside risk above if they pertain to the total *portfolio*. For each asset *standalone*, investors may like both downside protection and lottery characteristics – and positive skewness helps both, so it is no wonder if investors like it. Negative skewness may earn a premium due to asymmetric risk preferences and/or asymmetric return distributions.[5]

---

[4]There are many downside risk metrics and asset pricing models modified for downside risk, for example, Bawa-Lindenberg (1977), Ang-Chen-Xing (2006), and Lettau-Maggiori-Weber (2014). Apart from preferences, tail risk matters if return distributions are significantly non-normal (skewed and fat-tailed). If returns were normally distributed, upside potential and downside risk would be proportional and volatility would be a sufficient risk measure. I simply study performance in the ten worst equity market drawdowns.

[5]Harvey-Siddique (2000) studies coskewness, which matters for the total portfolio, while Barberis-Huang (2008) studies standalone skewness, motivated by the prospect theory or lottery preferences. Dahlquist-Farago-Tedongap (2017) discusses the relative roles of asymmetric preferences and asymmetric return distributions. Ilmanen (2012) provides an overview.

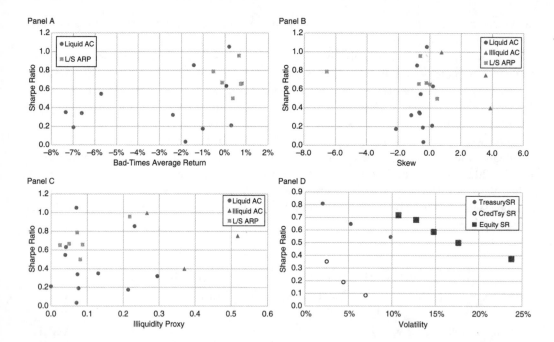

Figures 8.3   A–D Scatterplot multi-asset Sharpe Ratio on (A) bad-times average return, (B) skew, (C) illiquidity proxy, (D) volatility, 1990–2020

Sources and Notes: Bad-times average return is the average monthly return in ten worst equity drawdowns. Illiquidity proxy is average correlation of current return with last-month (for illiquid assets last-quarter) own return and equity market return. Panels A–C use the same assets as in Figure 8.2 (see sources). Panel D uses five beta-sorted portfolios for US equities and three maturity-sorted portfolios of both US Treasuries and corporate credits (over TSY). I use annual returns for illiquid assets when calculating SR or any risk metrics (which partly corrects for the smoothness in quarterly returns), but do not include illiquids with bad-times performance since they lack monthly data.

- Preference for liquid assets and lower trading costs should make investors require positive illiquidity premia. Fair illiquidity premia may be partly offset by the smoothing feature in private assets, which may explain historically limited realized illiquidity premia (see Chapter 5 (5.1)).
- Leverage aversion and lottery preferences can give rise to higher risk-adjusted returns to less risky assets if investors pay for the embedded leverage and lottery characteristics in riskier stocks (see Chapter 6 (6.4)). Leverage constraints on financial intermediaries are especially important for arbitrage strategies, which imply low risk and low return without leverage; this book hardly covers them.

Figure 8.3 scatterplots the SRs of diverse liquid asset class premia, illiquid asset premia, and long/short ARP on tail risk, skewness, illiquidity, and volatility measures. Panel A shows the counterintuitive pattern that some less-risky premia earned higher SRs than equity premia which had worse bad-times performance, at least during the 1990–2020 sample. Panel B shows no relationship between SRs and skewness, in contrast to some earlier literature. Panel C shows a very mild positive relationship between SRs and my illiquidity proxy (average of correlation with own lagged return and equity market's lagged return).

Panel D includes a different set of assets because volatility comparisons are misleading for private assets with artificially smooth returns, whereas long/short premia may be levered to any target volatility level. The panel shows that within each of three asset classes – US Treasuries, credits (excess over matching Treasury), and equities – SRs are inversely related to asset volatility. This pattern is consistent with leverage aversion and lottery preferences.[6]

The evidence in Figure 8.3 and broader literature is at best mixed on the ability of tail risk, skewness, and illiquidity metrics to explain SR variations across rewarded factors.[7] The inverse relation between the SR and volatility is more robust.

Turning to behavioral premia, the behavioral finance literature has been criticized for offering too many distinct "just-so" stories instead of one comprehensive theory (e.g. Fama (1998)). The closest to meeting this challenge is the prospect theory by Kahneman-Tversky (1979), which encompasses many features: preferences on gains and losses – thus implying narrow framing; loss aversion (moderated by diminishing sensitivity to gains or losses); and overweighting low-probability events. These features have been studied separately in many papers, while the broadest empirical study of its investment implications is in Barberis-Jin-Wang (2020).

Several excellent surveys have given structure to the behavioral finance literature.[8] I briefly state three key areas:

- *Biased beliefs* (related to extrapolation, overconfidence, availability heuristic, anchoring, conservatism, confirmation bias, hindsight, etc.)
- *Non-standard preferences* (within the prospect theory: loss aversion (part of narrow framing) and simultaneous insurance and lottery preferences (part of probability weighting); elsewhere leverage aversion, regret aversion, ambiguity aversion, home bias, impact of moods/sentiment, etc.)
- *Cognitive limits* (bounded rationality)

In addition, there are the *limits of arbitrage* sustaining all anomalies caused by these forces.

Major style premia can be traced back to many of these forces. I have already mentioned leverage aversion and lottery preferences behind the defensive style. Value and momentum styles have many candidate explanations in this list (and they often ring truer than the risk-based candidates). While there may be many complementary forces, if I'd have to pick one storyline, it would be this: Momentum and trend styles exploit both initial underreactions to public news (anchoring, conservatism) and later overreactions to past returns (extrapolation). Eventually, such over-extrapolation should correct and give profits to patient contrarian investors (rubber-band effect).[9]

We can check how strong momentum and reversal patterns that we observe affect each of the various premia studied in the previous figures. Figure 8.4 documents relatively consistent

---

[6]Using the same premia universe for panel D as for panels A–C would also give an inverse relation (overall correlation −0.4 and negative correlation within each subgroup). Even a flat relation would point to major diversification benefits when harvesting several equally volatile premia with comparable SRs and low correlations. For investors able to use leverage, any inverse relation is just an icing on the cake.

[7]For some datasets, sample periods, and specifications, researchers find stronger relations than I document here (for example, Lettau-Maggiori-Weber (2014) downside risk versus Sharpe, and Lemperiere et al. (2014) skewness versus Sharpe). Others find as weak or inconsistent patterns as I do, for example Koijen et al. (2018), Baltas-Scherer (2019), and Vatanen-Suhonen (2021). Baltas-Scherer (2019) also combines multiple factors in one regression, beyond my simple pairwise analysis, and again finds weak patterns.

[8]See Barberis surveys (2013, 2017), Barberis-Thaler (2003), Hirshleifer (2015), and Chapter 6 in Ilmanen (2011). Barberis emphasizes the importance of three features: overextrapolation, overconfidence, and gain/loss utility (in prospect theory). I would add underreaction, especially to mundane public news.

[9]One challenge to this literature has been its reliance to both overreactions and underreactions. When should we expect either? Underreaction is more typical and causes momentum, and is stronger in more mundane, non-salient news ("frog in the pan" as in Da-Gurun-Warachka 2014), while overreactions can become more likely in salient news events (or with lotterylike assets and glamour stocks) (Bordalo-Gennaioli-Shleifer 2013).

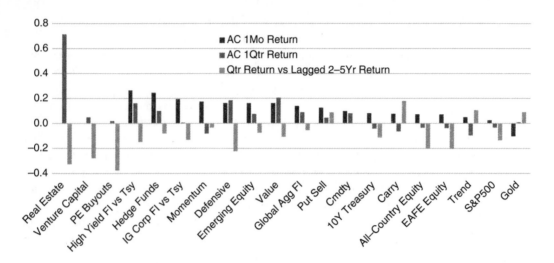

Figure 8.4   Monthly and Quarterly Momentum and Long-Term Reversal Patterns for Various Premia, 1990–2020

Sources and Notes: The first two bars are monthly and quarterly return autocorrelations for the twenty series listed below Figure 8.2 (see sources). There are no monthly returns for illiquid assets. The last bar is the correlation between quarterly return and the average returns 5–20 quarters earlier (i.e. lagged second- to fifth-year return). The sample period is 1990–2020.

monthly and quarterly autocorrelation (momentum) for liquid assets and much higher auto-correlation for the smooth real estate returns between 1990 and 2020. The last bars tend to be negative, indicating moderate multiyear reversal patterns.

Figure 17.2 will complement this time series analysis with a cross-sectional counterpart, by showing the average returns of portfolios of US stocks sorted by their past-year and earlier multi-year returns. The one-year momentum and multiyear reversal patterns are evident.

The market ecology encourages a self-sustaining balance between momentum-oriented and reversal-oriented investors. If one side becomes too dominant, we get too much extrapolation or too much stabilizing, and this imbalance sows the seeds of future underperformance of the majority approach. Examples of the extrapolative players include trend-followers, stop-loss sellers, and some volatility targeters, while stabilizing market participants are exemplified by contrarian investors, central banks, and rebalancers – including the fast-growing target-date fund industry.

8.4. Who Is on the Other Side? – and Related Crowding Concerns

If a factor makes money in the long run, it is worth asking: *Who is on the other side losing money and why?*[10] One way to answer is to consider what various theories imply as the natural "other side."

---

[10]Only the cap-weighted market portfolio is *macro-consistent* in the sense that all investors can hold the same port-folio of risky assets in equilibrium (see Perold-Sharpe (1988), Sharpe (2005)). Any active strategy (deviation from market-cap weights) needs other investors as counterparties, and arguably growing popularity (smaller other side) of any strategy should reduce its long-run reward. Said differently, non-market factors are zero sum in their returns. If someone profits, someone else must lose. However, all exchanges need not be zero sum *in utility*; both sides can benefit for example in risk transfer trades or trading off expected return for liquidity.

Table 8.1   A List of Selected Explanations for Four Style Premia as Umbrella Concepts

Style Group	Behavioral and Risk-based Rationales	Who Is On The Other Side?
Value Contrarian Timing Reversals	Over-extrapolation of past growth Delayed overreaction to price trends Discomfort with "dogs" Distress risk, dynamic betas Generic risk premium (1/P)	Over-extrapolators of multiyear growth Multiyear return-chasers Investors attracted to glamor stocks Investors averse to some risks in value stocks
Momentum Trend Following Fundam. Momentum	Underreaction to public news Overreaction to price trends Procyclical risk tolerance or risk management Disposition effect	Inattentive, conservative or overconfident investors Contrarians resisting the herd Investors without stop-loss rules Investors realizing gains or hanging on to losers
Carry Volatility Premia	Premium for skew / jump risk / bad times losses Overconfident expectations of capital losses to offset carry Non-profit-driven flows and capital supply/demand imbalances	Tail insurance buyers, positive skewness lovers Overconfident holders of salient macro views Non-profit-driven actors
Defensive Low Risk Quality	Leverage aversion / constraints Lottery-seeking preferences Relative risk preferences, conventionality Under-appreciation of "boring" quality characteristics	Leverage-constrained investors Investors who prefer lottery-like upside Managers minimizing tracking error, not total risk Overconfident-and-constrained active managers, and inattentive, "story-oriented" analysts

Sources: Asness et al. (2015), Asness-Moskowitz-Pedersen (2013), Ilmanen (2011), Koijen et al. (2018), Frazzini-Pedersen (2014), Ilmanen et al. (2021), and references therein.

In the case of risk, it is investors who are willing to pay a premium to avoid bearing that risk. In the case of behavioral explanations, it is investors who are willing to pay because they dislike characteristics of these assets, perhaps because of a behavioral bias.

I have discussed diverse rationales for style premia in Chapter 6 as well as in my earlier writings. Table 8.1 lists one possible menu of candidate rationales for value, momentum, carry, and defensive – as well as the implicit other side for each candidate. This list is only partial, and I will not go through it in detail here. It makes me think that while it is useful to demand an economic rationale for an empirical regularity, when it comes to these major style premia, we face an abundance of rather than a shortage of theories to choose from. Maybe the concept of data mining has its pair in *theory mining*.

A more data-driven approach is to study investor flows and holdings. Can such data identify a well-defined large investor group that takes the other side of a known rewarded factor and loses money as a result? Academic research has in recent years drilled into 13F reports on US stocks[11] and other sources of investor flows and holdings, as well as into indirect positioning inferred from return-based regressions.

---

[11]See Lewellen (2011), Edelen-Ince-Kadlec (2016), Calluzzo-Moneta-Topaloglu (2019), Lettau-Ludvigson-Manoel (2019), and McLean-Pontiff-Reilly (2020). Only large investors with more than $100 million of assets need to file the 13F report, and it only covers their long equity positions. Non-13F reporting investors are often viewed as small or retail investors. Return-based regression analysis is a useful complement to 13F analysis of hedge funds because returns reflect all positions, including shorts and derivatives.

In Asness et al. (2022), we try to improve on earlier analyses and present our main empirical evidence. In some cases we find a persistent "other side" even at a broad investor group level. Small (non-13F-reporting) investors provide the other side to the momentum strategy, while hedge funds are one of the other sides for the defensive strategy.[12] We do not find that any broad investor group takes a strong tilt for or against the value strategy; the other side is apparent *within* main investor groups (e.g. concentrated growth managers).

We document some time variation in various investor groups' factor tilts but importantly find that these tilts tend to be directionally persistent over time. Such evidence is even stronger when we study tilt persistence at single-manager level. Overall, we observe that those who are on the other side today are more likely to be on that side also going forward. Evidence of a persistent other side should lessen any worries that the factor premia are not sustainable.

An Important Qualifier: There Is Always Someone on the Other Side

Analysis of net flows or holdings turns out to be less interesting when we remember the adding-up constraint (net flows must add to zero except for net issuance). The qualifier "for every buyer there is a seller" is both obvious and yet frequently forgotten. It means that if all investors' aggregate preferences for a factor change over time, their net portfolio holdings remain unaffected. Instead, the factor's valuation should change (see Box 8.1).

This is well understood for equity markets – if risk aversion spikes, we cannot all rush to the exit at the same time, but market prices must fall. It is less well appreciated for long/short strategies. My first answer to anyone concerned with crowding in style premia (factor investing) is that growing popularity should show up in persistently richer factor valuations. Interestingly, there was no sign of a richening trend in the 2010s at the aggregate factor level (only in pockets like defensive stocks). In sum, if you worry about crowding, I suggest checking valuations as the best crowding indicator.

When it comes to concerns about capacity and crowding, I have sympathy for the argument that more dollars chasing an asset class or strategy reduces its expected return. Yet, the adding-up constraint complicates any interpretation of crowding.

Dan di Bartolomeo summarized the situation well for *Investment & Pensions Europe* a few years ago: "Every security is owned by someone. So, if a certain set of securities, say, those representing a factor, is concentrated in a few people's hands, by definition that set is not concentrated in other people's hands. What we should be concerned about is not how many people own a particular security or factor, it's whether those owners share other common properties, such as margin leverage or higher-than-usual liquidity needs. A factor doesn't become crowded – what may become crowded is the type of investor holding that particular factor."

---

[12]Baltzer et al. (2015) and Luo et al. (2020) confirm that both German and US retail investors tend to be anti-momentum, perhaps a surprising result, while Blitz (2018) confirms that hedge funds tend to be the other side for the low-risk strategy. Our Asness et al. (2022) "Who is on the other side?" paper still waits to be finished. So far only Ilmanen (2016) Q-group presentation is in public space. This project has been in the works for a decade but has so far lost to other priorities.

Box 8.1   How to Make Sense of Flow Data When Every Buyer Has a Seller

The adding-up constraint is an accounting identity, which is hardly novel but yet remains underappreciated. Whenever we see historical flow data, we need to ask how to reconcile any apparent net flows with accounting identities "for every buyer there is a seller," "the average investor must hold the global market portfolio," and "all active tilts against it must add up to zero."

In sum, we must ask, "Who is on the other side (to this reported flow)?" For example, for the 13F reports, the non-reported other side includes the small investors who do not need to file 13F reports, while for some custodial flow reports, it includes everyone else than the custodian's clients.

Let's think this through carefully. First, it is reasonable to study flows of some investor subgroups, such as mutual funds, hedge funds, or retail investors; such flows need not add up to zero. However, then we should consider which investor groups are worth tracking. Some flow series are contemporaneously related to returns (sign of demand pressure), and flows often follow past returns (sign of return chasing), but if flows predict returns at all, it is crucial to ask whose flows are profitable to track?[13]

Investments were long considered so close substitutes that demand for them was deemed perfectly elastic, making flow data uninteresting for asset prices. Research has identified numerous counterexamples to this traditional view, from index inclusion effects to recent claims that flows have a large and persistent impact on asset prices. Gabaix and Koijen (2021) lead this challenge with their "inelastic markets hypothesis." They try to measure how much prices need to move to entice the other side for any flows to appear (though it is hard to estimate whether a given trade is initiated by a buyer or a seller). Relatedly, Maggiori et al. (2021) uses survey data to show that even large changes in expected returns imply modest investor flows.

The adding-up constraint bites when we think about aggregate holdings and net flows. One implication is that *any changes in aggregate investor preferences should show up in valuations and not in net flows* (which must amount to zero, unless there is new net issuance). For example, in October 1987 or March 2020, if all investors became more risk averse at the same time, they could not simultaneously sell their stocks (who would be the buyer?). Instead, stock market valuations needed to fall. Likewise, if investors became less interested in, say, value stocks in 1999 or 2020, they could not all replace their value stocks with growth stocks, but relative valuations needed to change.

(continued)

---

[13]The main empirical answer has been that hedge funds and short sellers are examples of informed traders, or "smart money," which have had some ability to predict future returns (while retail investor inflows have more often predicted low future returns). Interestingly, the same smart-money investors are considered sources of crowding risk, as leveraged hedge funds and short sellers may be especially vulnerable to sudden deleveraging pressures. This means that attempts to hedge against crowding risk can be very costly, as they require going against historically profitable "follow the smart money" strategies.

Another valve to the accounting identity besides valuation changes is net issuance. Some definitions of net flows do not amount to zero but to new net issuance by public entities (including central banks) and private companies.

Public flows have been exceptionally important since 2008. Through their quantitative easing, major central banks have absorbed vast amounts of government bond issuance as well as some corporate bonds and even equity in Japan. So even if private investor preferences did not change, large asset purchases by public institutions may have richened assets, starting from government bonds and extending to other assets through direct purchases or the so-called portfolio balance effect.

The private sector was also active in net issuance. After the large IPOs by Facebook and Alibaba, there was a multiyear slowdown, but IPO and SPAC activity picked up dramatically in recent years. Securitization of existing assets also involved new issuance, notably when the Saudi oil company Aramco became for a while the world's largest listed company. Conversely, many listed firms releveraged their balance sheets amid low yields by issuing debt and buying back their shares.

Chapter 9

Sustaining Conviction and Patience on Long-run Return Sources

---

- Patience is a virtue also in investing – and one that is hard to sustain. Investors tend to demand more performance consistency than is feasible in competitive markets, often resulting in ill-timed capitulations.
- This chapter covers behavioral causes of impatience, financial consequences of impatience, as well as ideas on how to cultivate patience.
- Conviction and patience are boosted by having solid economic rationale and empirical evidence. We also need to address natural concerns that the world has changed, undermining the rationale – or that overfitting or selection biases distorted the results, undermining the evidence.
- Each concern can justify discounting historical performance, apart from the need to adjust gross returns for trading costs and fees. Such discounting makes sense but is more art than science.

Sustaining conviction and patience is rarely hard when a given strategy performs well. The real challenge arises when investors face adversity.

Let's make it tangible: *How would you balance disappointing performance over the past three years against positive evidence over the past century?* For statisticians, there would be no question. Indeed, they say that we might need decades of data to learn and to modify our statistical judgment on a factor's reward or a manager's efficacy.[1] Yet, real-world investors tend to care about what happened to *their* investments, *recently*. They will discount any performance data before their own allocation, especially if the evidence is contradictory. A bad draw eats up faith. They can reasonably ask whether the world has changed and the opportunity has been arbitraged away, or whether the long evidence was overstated by data mining.

I will first discuss the prevalence and costs of investor impatience and propose some methods for cultivating patience. I then expand on some challenges to economic rationale and empirical evidence that can undermine patience. Conviction is enhanced by having an economic rationale for why a premium exists and by addressing concerns that the world has changed. Empirical evidence needs to be compelling enough to overcome doubts after inevitable bad phases as well as any data mining concerns. Both types of concerns may warrant discounting historical performance.

9.1. Patience: Sustaining Conviction When Faced with Adversity[2]

The virtue of patience is widely known, reinforced by economists' studies of hyperbolic discounting and psychologists' marshmallow tests. Yet, many investors, both individuals and institutions, demand more performance consistency than is realistically available in financial markets. Many also believe that past performance contains more predictive information than it does. Too-easily disappointed investors may "misbehave," impatiently churning their portfolios and hurting their long-run performance prospects. This section diagnoses the problem – discussing both the causes and consequences of impatience – and then suggests some practical remedies against impatience.

Causes of Impatience

Many investors are aware of the academic argument that we may need decades of data to statistically distinguish luck from skill. And yet, and yet, it seems humanly impossible to wait for evidence to accrue. Guided by what Nobel Prize winner Daniel Kahneman has mischievously called "the law of small numbers," investors tend to expect any long-run edge to manifest itself within a short period. When outcomes fail to live up to the anticipated (but unrealistic) consistency, investors too often assume that the edge has vanished, and may then impatiently deallocate.

---

[1] Such requirements can plausibly be satisfied for asset class or factor backtests, but less often for live track records of systematic strategies or of discretionary managers. And even in the rare cases where we have long track records, the successful ones might reflect luck as much as skill. When Warren Buffett's name inevitably comes up, efficient-markets-oriented academics argue that *some* managers will beat the market over long periods even by chance, but we only recognize such winners ex post (Fama-French (2010)).

[2] This section warrants special thanks to Thomas Maloney, even more than the rest of the book. It summarizes a draft paper we wrote a couple of years ago. It never felt right to publish it because in the midst of a challenging period performance-wise, covering this evergreen topic could seem too self-serving for an asset manager. That said, we published articles on the need for realistic expectations and the benefits of investor patience also during periods of strong performance (see e.g. Asness (2014a) and Goyal-Ilmanen-Kabiller (2015)).

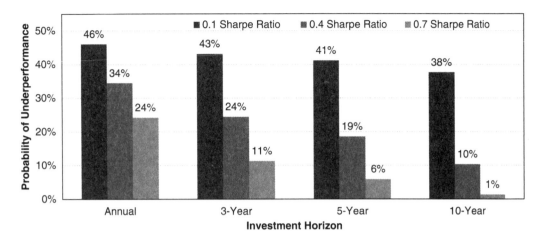

Figure 9.1   Frequency of Underperformance, for a Given Horizon and Sharpe Ratio
Source: AQR. Notes: Hypothetical portfolio modeled assuming a normal distribution, no autocorrelation, and independent portfolios. For details, see AQR Portfolio Solutions Group (2013).

The stereotypical three- to five-year performance evaluation period is too short according to academics, but uncomfortably long for many real-world investors.

This tendency to underestimate the role of chance is not the only behavioral bias investors must address.[3] There is also the powerful combination of myopia (focus on the short term) and loss aversion (losses loom larger than gains) that has been proposed as one explanation for the "equity premium puzzle"[4] and also applies more broadly to investor responses to recent performance.

Investors may better recognize impatience in their responses to past performance if they are familiar with *realistic* expectations on performance consistency as well as with tangible anecdotes where even the most successful investors suffer surprisingly long losing periods.

Figure 9.1 shows a pure statistical approach: the probabilities of underperforming cash simply due to random variation, highlighting the impact of horizon and Sharpe ratio (or information ratio if underperforming a benchmark). These probabilities give a sense of how frequently investors may draw wrong inferences and prematurely deallocate from a good investment by impatiently judging performance based on too-short sample periods. For example, an investment with a SR of 0.4 (or an active manager with IR of 0.4) can be *expected to* underperform its benchmark

---

[3]I emphasize throughout the book how luck (randomness) can trump skill (long-run edge) over surprisingly long periods. Investors often underestimate regression to the mean, which says that unexpectedly high or low returns are likely due to good or bad luck, and the best forecast after them may still be the long-run average. Regression to the mean should be distinguished from mean reversion which says that an above-average outcome is likely to be followed by a below-average outcome. Any mean reversion tendencies in performance should promote even more patience.

[4]Benartzi-Thaler (1995) shows that if investors review performance too frequently and suffer twice as much discomfort from interim losses as much as they enjoy interim gains, they will tend to allocate less to equities, to reduce the utility loss from interim fluctuations.

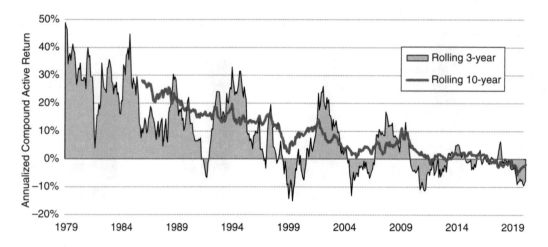

Figure 9.2   Rolling Relative Return of Berkshire Hathaway vs. S&P500, Jan 1977– Mar 2021
Source: Bloomberg, CRSP, and AQR.

in 24% of three-year evaluations and in 10% of ten-year evaluations.[5] A higher SR of 0.7 would reduce these probabilities to 11% and 1%.[6]

For those who prefer tangible narratives to abstract statistics, Figure 9.2 tracks the performance of Warren Buffett – the world's most admired and arguably best investor – over 40+ years. The chart shows the rolling 3-year and 10-year active return of Berkshire Hathaway stock over the S&P500. Clearly, Buffett experienced several deep and long periods of underperformance versus the market, yet many believers stuck with him. While he ended up outperforming the S&P500 by 9.5% p.a. over 44 years, the 3-year relative performance was negative for 30% of the time, and by double digits (annualized!) during three episodes. If the world's most admired investor has faced such challenging episodes, how hard is it to be patient with others?

Consequences of Impatience

There are three main ways impatience can hurt an investor's bottom-line: missing out on long-run expected returns; costs and frictions from excessive strategy or manager turnover; and any mean reversion in strategy or manager performance.

Loss averse investors may miss out on long-term rewarded exposures if they disinvest after a bad experience, or never gain exposure for fear of such experiences. By forgoing rewarded risks,

---

[5]For more analysis, see AQR Portfolio Solutions Group (2013). Incorporating non-normality or autocorrelation would change these probabilities somewhat. Fat tails would make underperformance more likely than standard assumptions imply (but fat tails tend to be less prevalent at longer horizons). Positive autocorrelation (momentum bias) also tends to make underperformance more likely, while mean reversion has the opposite impact (but these impacts are small for most investments).

[6]Another approach asks how many years of evidence is needed for statistical significance. Under standard assumptions (no non-normality or selection bias), statistical significance at the 95% confidence level requires a t-statistic near 2.0. Since the t-statistic is a product of realized Sharpe ratio and time period (the square root of years), a performance history with a Sharpe ratio of 0.4 will be significantly different from zero (with 95% confidence) after about 25 years ($0.4 \star \sqrt{25} = 2$), while a Sharpe ratio of 0.7 will be significantly different from zero after roughly 8 years ($0.7 \star \sqrt{8} \approx 2$).

loss averse investors actually *increase* the risk of not earning enough to achieve long-term goals. But realized losses tend to be felt more keenly than opportunity losses.

The costs of excessive turnover include transaction costs, operational costs, and redemption fees. For strategies with performance fees, there is an additional cost to investors: forfeiting a high-water-mark option by disinvesting after a drawdown. (Investors typically do not have to pay performance fees until the fund has reached the high-water mark, whereas other funds will be charging performance fees from initial investments.)

Goyal-Ilmanen-Kabiller (2015) emphasizes the tension between multiyear procyclic investor flows and multiyear mean-reverting returns. Unfortunately, investors too often "act like momentum investors at reversal horizons." This bad habit, including empirical evidence on it, is discussed further in Chapter 17.

Detour: Perils of Too Much Patience

To be clear, patience is not always a virtue. Sometimes it is right to capitulate. Most obviously, multi-month momentum strategies are often profitable. The "disposition effect" implies that investors may hold on to losing investments for too long, contrary to our main narrative, perhaps because selling would involve realizing losses and admitting that the original decision was wrong. Even multiyear momentum does sometimes hurt inertial investors – say, when the highest-fee managers have persistently poor net performance, or when structural changes hurt both contrarian and patient investors who wait for performance normalization.[7]

Which problem is worse? Well, recall the statistical fact that one needs at least a decade of performance data to statistically judge between manager luck and skill (or whether a factor's bad performance is likely to reflect more than a random bad draw). Yet, many investors make their own judgments after a year, the patient ones after three to five years. Such evidence suggests that impatience is by far the more common problem than excessive patience.

How Can We Enhance Investor Patience?

If investors agree that patience usually is a virtue, how can they cultivate it?

Smooth returns: One obvious answer is that a smoother ride makes patient investing easier. For a given expected return, this implies a higher SR. This can be achieved in many ways, such as skillful investing and aggressive diversification. Grinold's (1989) fundamental law of active management says that higher risk-adjusted returns can be achieved through some combination of skill and breadth.

There are more questionable ways to achieve smooth returns. Avoiding mark-to-market pricing in illiquid assets has been a popular approach. Others include strategies that tend to incur severe but very infrequent losses, which may not be present in any evaluation period ("peso problem"), or those resorting to outright crime (Bernie Madoff's returns were famously smooth). For

---

[7]There are other entirely good reasons for changing allocations after losses. Investors don't have the same transparency as managers into the drivers of performance. The nature of an episode of poor performance could tell investors something about the investment that they didn't know before. The losses may be due to unintended exposures, errors, or poor controls. Investors tend to ask tough questions of managers during drawdowns, and may learn something they don't like about the manager or their investment process. Finally, investment objectives can change. Nevertheless, much research suggests that investors tend to add a dose of irrational impatience to their rational decisions.

a given SR, the simplest way to reduce potential losses is to take less risk. In the extreme, cash investments give very smooth but low returns. This approach shifts risks from failing fast to failing slowly (by being too conservative and not earning enough to achieve long-term financial goals). We may be too patient with all these questionable approaches, as their shortcomings emerge only at a later date.

It is more interesting to ask how investors can enhance patience *for a given risk-adjusted return*. Below are some suggestions:

- **Education:** To avoid the above bad habits and their adverse consequences, an organization needs to have realistic expectations on how frequently merely random bad outcomes can occur even for good investments. Separately, it is important to understand the strategic case for any investment strategy, such as the equity premium or the value premium, and the likely long-term implications of capitulation during tough periods. As noted, such conviction is best enhanced through a mix of empirical evidence and economic rationale.
- **Review the portfolio broadly and infrequently:** Reviewing performance *broadly* helps guard against "line-item thinking," which undermines the power of diversification. Typical casualties of line-item thinking include the most capital-efficient investments (those with a high standalone volatility but a small allocation) and the most diversifying investments. Such investments are likely to sometimes stand out and invite proposals for deallocation – leaving the portfolio worse off.[8] Separately, as noted, myopic loss aversion undermines a long invest-ment horizon. Thus, reviewing performance *less frequently* helps reduce impatience. Boards that can take a long-term view are better able to harvest the equity premium and other risk premia than boards with a short-term focus.
- **Greater organizational commitment:** If the initial allocation is made after thorough due diligence and education, this sets a higher bar for capitulation. If a strategy's inclusion is based on criteria beyond its past performance, patience during a bad patch is more likely.[9] ESG strat-egies that align well with the investor's values may inspire more patience amid lagging perfor-mance. Further, if a strategy or a factor is included as part of the benchmark or reference portfolio, such senior-level long-term commitment enhances patience. Other commitment devices include writing down your (own or institution's) investment beliefs or adopting action plans for bad times, such as rebalancing as a default option. These can mitigate career risk con-siderations ("either I replace this losing investment, or I may be replaced") in cases where decision-makers still believe in a strategy's long-term prospects.
- **Conventionality:** Only the equity premium is easily forgiven a losing decade. (Few investors deallocated fully from equities after the 2000–09 losses.) Equity market exposure is the com-mon and conventional way to lose money, and this helps beyond the well-founded conviction investors have in the long-term equity premium. One could even argue that any active risk taking requires multiyear patience, and without it, investors should prefer to stay passive.[10]

---

[8]Thoughtful boards should thus welcome seeing portfolio performance with less granularity, and any line items presented in terms of portfolio contribution (return attribution) rather than standalone performance. Reporting diversification characteristics as well as returns would mitigate line-item thinking. Reviews should also focus on as long performance window as possible, even if also more recent periods need to be covered.

[9]For ideas on selection criteria beyond past performance, see Goyal-Ilmanen-Kabiller (2015) and Cornell-Hsu-Nanigian (2017). Swedroe (2018) reviews related ideas of enhancing patience.

[10]Over time, other factor exposures have begun to acquire some of these conventionality advantages, as they are increasingly used by peers and supported by academia and consultants. They might therefore enjoy more patience after a bad patch than would a single active manager.

- **Gradualism:** Many investors are especially concerned about the performance of a new strategy "out of the gate." Investors often wonder how they can be sure of a good first year. Unless a strategy can be timed tactically (which is hard), a high long-run SR gives the best reassurance. But since a bad draw is always possible over a year, and investors' deallocation decisions often reflect their own performance experience (rather than the strategy's since-inception performance),[11] investors may consider incremental allocations into new strategies. Such gradualism can help reduce regret if a bad patch occurs in the first year, and may thereby help avoid a knee-jerk response.

9.2. Economic Rationale – and Has the World Changed?

Conviction and patience are boosted by having an economic rationale of why a premium is earned in the first place and does not get arbitraged away even when more investors learn about it. It also helps to have an answer to a common follow-up question during any premium's bad patch: *"Could it be that the world has changed?"* Since I covered economic rationale in Chapters 4–6 for single factors and more generally in Chapter 8, I focus here on the follow-up question.

Even if there is long-run empirical evidence of robust factor performance and an economic story explaining it, a skeptic can still worry that the world has changed and the forward-looking opportunity has been arbitraged away or otherwise removed.

Certain "the world has changed" arguments are endogenous to the factor – as more people have learned about it and more arbitrage capital has been allocated to it, it follows that alpha may morph into beta or even that the opportunity will fully disappear. I have already mentioned some counterarguments; there are many limits of arbitrage, including costs, risks, and constraints. Still, in this scenario, the growing popularity of a given factor (or broader factor investing) should show up in strong performance and rising valuations. Clearly then, this type of crowding and arbitraging-away logic cannot explain the recent performance of the value stock selection factor, as a somewhat disappointing decade was followed by exceptionally bad years 2018–20 together with widening value spreads.

Other "the world has changed" arguments are more exogenous. One idea is that the Regulation Fair Disclosure in 2000 made subtle management signaling illegal and reduced gradual dissemination of company information and thus momentum strategy profits in stock selection. Another idea is that central bank policies are curtailing directional trends and that this will hurt macro-oriented trend following.

It is common to argue that structural changes hurt contrarian strategies. Some believe that the shift from brick-and-mortar to a digital world has killed the stock selection value strategy – another case of "the more things change, the more they stay the same," as Figure 6.1 displays persistent value strategy gains through two centuries of technological revolutions. Some concerns about structural changes are valid, but financial markets too often say, "This time is different." Exuberant markets can take these ideas too far or forget that some structural changes can revert – say, thanks to competition (disruptors get disrupted), regulation, or policy shifts.

---

[11]This claim is anecdotal: My colleagues have observed it in practice, and my dialogues with asset managers and asset owners support it. The claim is consistent with research by Malmendier and Nagel (2011, 2021), which shows how sensitive investor-specific expectations are to lifetime experience (article title "Depression Babies" is memorable). It also fits well with Hertwig-Erev's (2009) work on so-called description-experience gap in risky choice where people overweigh their own experience over an objective description of risky prospects. This topic seems worthy of further research.

9.3. Empirical Evidence – and Data Mining Concern

Evidence-based investing relies on historical analysis in the belief that history at least rhymes. The "gold standard" evidence is a live track record, and ideally one you have invested in. Such histories are often too short, so we supplement them with more generic evidence. We have performance data from multiple markets over decades, in some cases over centuries. Even for market risk premia, there are fair questions of selection biases. Say, are we focusing on the most successful capital markets and excluding countries whose stock markets disappeared after a revolution or whose bonds lost their real value in a hyperinflation?

The concerns on selection biases are elevated when we turn to style premia or alpha strategies. It is reasonable to question how much the performance of any successful historical factor premium – or a successful manager – has been overstated by data mining and other selection biases.[12]

The fear that data-mined factors inhabit a factor zoo justly raises the bar on empirical evidence. Pure out-of-sample evidence on the same factor/manager is best but may take years or decades to emerge. The previous footnote refers to some academics' statistical answers to this challenge,[13] while my preferred answer is summarized in the triplet persistent/pervasive/robust. To prospectively believe in a factor, the historical positive rewards need to be persistent over long histories (both in in-sample and out-of-sample periods), pervasive across countries and asset classes, and robust across design specifications. Some market risk premia and style premia easily overcome this higher bar, as evident from material in this book and in the many references. I especially like the fact that style premia have positive long-run rewards in so many distinct asset classes, with low correlations between them. That said, we cannot be too greedy on consistency requirements. In competitive financial markets, even well-rewarded factors will sometimes experience unpleasantly long periods of underperformance.

I argue that any data mining or overfitting concerns should be targeted more to novel, proprietary, and complex strategies (including nonlinearity, context-dependence, interaction effects, possible use of "big data," and machine learning) rather than to the simpler, "tried-and-true" ARP strategies. As a flipside, these well-known ARP strategies are more subject to overcrowding risks. Thus, I often say, "Pick your poison!" – which of these dangers to systematic investing do you find worse? The answer is almost a matter of taste, or prior beliefs, and determines which types of systematic strategies the respondent prefers. I worry more about overfitting than overcrowding.

Both concerns may warrant *discounting* the historical performance, but for quite different reasons. The overfitting argument implies that the opportunity identified in backtests (or selections among many live strategies) was never as strong ex ante as was reported ex post.

---

[12]The literature on selection biases, such as survivorship bias and incubation bias, has focused on hedge funds but applies to any manager or strategy universes. See Black (1993) on data mining concerns, Cochrane (2011) on factor zoo, Bailey-Lopes de Prado (2014) on deflating performance metrics, Harvey-Liu-Zhu (2016) on diagnostics and remedies, and Hou-Xue-Zhang (2020) on replicating anomalies. Yet, Jensen-Kelly-Pedersen (2021) presents compelling evidence that the case for a replication crisis in finance has been overstated.

[13]There is a problem with statistical answers which adjust the significance of a single result for the broad set of trials and errors made. Such adjustments often require quantifying how many strategies/models/specifications were tried. Since our understanding on various factor premia reflects the gradual collective effort of generations of researchers, this quantification may be infeasible. We cannot become virgins again with data, as my senior partners taught me. That said, I am not suggesting making perfection the enemy of good. Such statistical adjustments are worth doing, especially whenever a researcher analyzes a broad number of strategy specifications, but one should recognize the limits of this approach.

The overcrowding argument implies that the opportunity really was there, but the world has changed, and the greater awareness and greater popularity of a strategy implies lower rewards going ahead.

Choosing how much to discount historical backtests – to subtract the impact of trading costs and either of the overfitting or "the world has changed" effects – inevitably involves judgment. A common practice of halving the gross SR is crude but not a bad starting place.[14] More nuanced approaches may try to separately estimate trading costs and then overlay a smaller dose of discounting after it. It seems reasonable to apply larger discounts to more distant returns (with more "the world has changed" potential) and to more complex strategies (with more overfitting potential). Discounting based on trading costs is especially complex because these costs vary over time and across investors (depending on their size and trading efficiency), and because costs can be reduced by netting across strategies and by modifying strategies to focus on net expected returns (more on these in Chapter 15). Discounting is an art, not a science.[15]

---

[14]McLean-Pontiff (2016) finds performance decay (though still positive rewards) for a large set of academic factors in the US after the research was published. They interpret the out-of-sample performance decay as evidence of learning or arbitraging away activity. However, Jacobs-Muller (2020) finds no evidence outside the US of such performance decay. Ilmanen et al. (2021a) finds for a broad range of factors about one-third lower returns outside the in-sample period. Interestingly, performance decay was stronger before than after the in-sample period of the original research, thus more consistent with overfitting than learning effect. Suhonen et al. (2017) finds larger performance decay for various bank premia products.

[15]Jensen-Kelly-Pedersen (2021) presents a more theoretically robust way of forecasting any factor's out-of-sample performance in a Bayesian fashion. This involves blending the in-sample performance with a prior (which could involve just shrinking the in-sample estimate toward zero or toward a theoretically motivated prior).

Chapter 10

Four Equations and Predictive Techniques

- Two equations and their extensions help understand *how asset returns are generated* and *what returns investors require*.
- The next two equations introduce *mean-variance optimization* and the *fundamental law of active management*.
- We can use various predictive techniques to estimate expected returns. We may assume constant or time-varying expected returns, take a short or long horizon, use time-series (directional) or cross-sectional (relative value) approaches and regression or sorting methods.

To bridge Part II describing various return sources and Part III discussing how to put them all together, I want to introduce the four arguably most important equations for investment management. Then I provide a brief overview of techniques to predict investment returns, contrasting those based on time-varying and constant expected returns, long and short horizons, time-series and cross-sectional analyses, as well as regression and sorting methods.

10.1. Four Key Equations and Some Extensions

While some readers dislike my way of communicating through words and graphs instead of equations, I suspect the majority thanks me. That said, I offer now this book's four key equations, and even those mainly in prose. If you want to go through these equations in more detail, you can refer to other books and articles. Here I try to explain intuitively why these four equations are such helpful starting places for our understanding of asset returns and investment management.

How Are Returns Generated? Income Plus Capital Gains and Beyond

The first two equations are on asset returns (both expected and realized), looking at the generation (supply) of returns and required (demanded) returns.

We can learn much about asset returns even from a one-period equity example where the total return is split into "income and capital gains" parts, and then more expressively into the dividend yield, growth, and valuation change components.[1]

Equation 1:

$(1+)$ **Return = Income & Capital Gain = Dividend Yield & (Div.) Growth & Valuation Change**

$$1 + Return_{t+1} \quad = \quad \overbrace{\frac{D_{t+1}}{P_t} \quad + \quad \frac{P_{t+1}}{P_t}} \quad = \quad \overbrace{\frac{D_{t+1}}{P_t} \quad + \quad \frac{D_{t+1}}{D_t} \quad \star \quad \frac{P_{t+1}/D_{t+1}}{P_t/D_t}}$$

Now, let's start to broaden our view of this equation. It shows total nominal returns, but we could also subtract inflation to study real returns or subtract cash to study excess returns. The relationship applies to a single stock, to the equity market, and beyond.

Equation 1 is an accounting identity on *realized* returns. We can take *expectations* of both sides, effectively splitting the realized return into expected and unexpected parts. This presumes consistency of expectations though not necessarily rationality.[2]

In a rational setting, an investor's expected return equals her required return which equals the equity issuer's discount rate or cost of equity financing. Chapter 4 discussed a special case, the famous dividend discount model ("DDM"). The Gordon growth model variant, which assumes constant growth and constant valuations, can be expressed as "Expected return equals dividend yield plus growth," or succinctly, $E(R) = DY + g$.

With some tweaks, we could convert the right-hand side of Equation 1 from dividend yield, dividend growth, and dividend multiple into another payout measure, another payout or earnings growth, and another valuation multiple.

For example, we can start from the dividends-based Gordon model and get to an earnings-based model. If we assume a fixed payout ratio $k = D/E$, we could rewrite dividend yield = $k \star$ earnings yield, and $g = (1 - k) \star$ return on equity. In a steady state, a firm's return on equity converges to its cost of equity (expected return). Under these assumptions, a firm's expected real return equals its return on equity and its earnings yield, broadly justifying the use of the CAEY (inverted Shiller CAPE) as an expected return proxy.

---

[1] The second equality uses the trick of multiplying and dividing the capital gain part by D_{t+1}/D_t and rearranging. These relations would be even additive as log returns, but I use here simple returns. Cf. the discussion on L'Her et al. (2018) in Chapter 4 (4.2).

[2] Academics further distinguish between unconditional (roughly, long-term) and conditional (roughly, near-term) expectations. This distinction matters if we want to model time-varying expected returns and study market-timing strategies.

We could also shift from a one-period world to a multi-period world by expressing P_{t+1} in the Equation 1 as the expected value of future cash flows beyond ($t + 1$), divided by the relevant discount rates. The discount rate equals the required return (a sum of the riskless return and required risk premia, as we'll soon see).[3]

In models with time-varying expected returns, the last term of valuation multiple changes could become quite important. Recall that a fall in expected/required future returns implies a contemporaneous rise in realized returns and thus higher valuations, all else equal.[4] Some analysts assume that market valuations tend to mean-revert over time and thus influence expected asset class returns in a contrarian way.

More generally, the "income plus capital gains" split can be applied to other asset classes besides equities. For government bonds with no default risk or expected cash flow growth, we can view coupons as dividends in Equation 1, while capital gains can be approximated by duration multiplied by yield decline. The simplest case involves a flat yield curve and a par bond: Its coupon equals its yield and its expected return.[5]

There is no reason for the expected capital gain to be structurally positive. It is positive for equities, but it clearly is negative for some assets and strategies where carry gives an optimistic expected return and is likely combined with some capital losses. The most obvious example is volatility selling (where the option seller's price premium is the maximum the seller can gain). Other examples include credit strategies (where default losses and downgrades tend to offset some of the initial spread advantage) and emerging currency carry strategies (where currency depreciation tends to offset some of the carry advantage). As noted in Chapter 5, real estate may belong to the same category. The abundant net rental yield gives a big income advantage, but some studies suggest this has historically been combined with nominal rental growth below inflation.

What Returns Should Investors Demand? The CAPM and Beyond

The core idea in modern portfolio theory is that investors require some compensation for time (riskless return from, say, Treasury bills) and some compensation for risk. The classic Capital Asset Pricing Model (CAPM) by William Sharpe (1964) states that investors only care about (equity) market risk, and that the market risk premium is their fair reward for bearing this systematic risk. Security-specific and diversifiable risks do not warrant a risk premium. The CAPM is a one-factor model, with a simple expected return equation, under some restrictive assumptions:

---

[3]Likewise, if you take expectations over the first equation, the expected return $E(1 + R)$ equals the expected future cash flows divided by the current price. from starting point t. Or conversely, flipping the left-hand side $E(1 + R)$ with P in the denominator of the right-hand-side, we see the current price equals expected cash flows discounted to present value with $E(1 + R)$. (To geeks, I ignore Jensen's inequality effects.) In more complex multi-period models, the dividend growth rate may vary over time, unlike in the Gordon model.

[4]This contemporaneous negative relation is sometimes called the discount rate effect. A lower discount rate, that is, required return, pushes today's prices and valuations higher. We have experienced plenty of this in recent decades as most assets have seen falling discount rates and thus rising valuations since the 1980s. As noted near Figure 2.1, we should recognize that past realized returns include some windfall gains beyond what investors expected, and furthermore, expected returns today are lower than expected returns in the past.

[5]In other cases, predictable changes add an expected capital gain component to the bond return – say, through a "rolldown effect" if the yield curve is expected to remain unchanged and the bond's yield would roll down the curve as it ages, or a "pull-to-par" effect when some of the predictable return for non-par bonds accrues through predictable price changes as the bond ages.

Equation 2:

Expected return on an asset = Riskless rate + Beta of this asset * Market risk premium

According to the CAPM, then, expected returns vary across assets only because of their beta. Beta is an asset's sensitivity to the market return.[6] High-beta stocks are riskier and should offer above-market returns to compensate for it. Investors can increase their expected portfolio returns by accepting a riskier portfolio. However, within the CAPM this is more efficiently done by raising the portfolio weight of the market portfolio vis-a-vis the riskless asset, not by taking more security-specific risk by overweighting high-beta stocks. In the CAPM equilibrium, homogeneous investor expectations and market clearing requirement imply that all investors hold an efficient mix of the riskless asset and the same risky market-cap portfolio (see Box 12.1 below).

A key insight is that an asset's standalone risk (volatility) is not crucial for expected returns because this risk can be largely diversified away. Only the systematic risk matters, and this is what beta captures. Not only does beta measure an asset's sensitivity to the market return; it also determines the asset's contribution to portfolio volatility. Intuitively, the asset's correlation with the other assets (and thus with the total portfolio) is more important than its volatility. In sum, the risk that investors care about is their portfolio volatility,[7] and in a one-factor world an asset's beta tells how much it contributes to portfolio volatility.

Now, the real world is more complicated than the CAPM assumes. I could cover extensions based on relaxing any number of the CAPM assumptions (normally distributed returns or mean-variance preferences, one-period model, homogeneous expectations, unlimited leverage, frictionless markets). I will only comment on extensions beyond a one-factor model.

Already in the 1970s, research in Merton's (1973) Intertemporal CAPM and Ross's (1975) Arbitrage Pricing Theory pointed to multi-factor models. Later, empirical models dominated the literature and practice. Chen-Roll-Ross (1986) considered interest rate risk and other macro factors as relevant risks to investors beyond equity markets. The Fama-French 3-factor model (1992, 1993, with market, size, and value factors; later extended to 4- or 5-factor models) was a real turning point. The Fama-French models were motivated less by which risks need hedging and more by which risks have been rewarded in the long run. As factor investing grew in popularity, the list of empirically motivated factors continued to grow.

Equation 2 has been modified to include multiple sources of risk, all with their own premium and factor sensitivities. Such models have been used for performance attribution, estimating multi-factor alpha, and demystifying active managers' realized performance (see Chapter 7). Even with multi-factor models, each factor's long-run premium should be consistent with the idea that a factor which gives bad realized returns in bad times (in academic jargon: covaries with the marginal utility) should offer a high expected return as compensation. And the intercept

---

[6]Beta is the ratio of the relative volatility between an asset and the market as well as the correlation between the two. It is also the covariance of the asset with the market divided by the market portfolio's variance (i.e. volatility squared). The market portfolio has, by construction, beta of one. I assume readers are familiar with basic portfolio statistics. I use terms beta, exposure, and sensitivity interchangeably. In a single-factor context, an asset's equity market beta measures its return sensitivity to market returns (to be pedantic, *excess* returns over cash for both).

[7]To those who say they don't care about volatility but about losses, I counter that higher volatility implies higher potential losses. (Some adjustments need to be made for strategies with highly asymmetric return distributions or artificially smooth returns.) This mapping made value-at-risk models so popular. VaR gives largely the same statistical information as volatility, but in a language of losses, which resonates better with many investors' perception of what risk means. The CAPM can also be modified to focus on downside risk measures.

in a factor model regression is the estimated alpha or average extra return beyond the chosen systematic factors.

Finally, the literature focuses largely on an equities-only world. A multi-asset context would warrant further factors: bond market factors, maybe an illiquidity factor, and so on.

How Should Investors Construct a Portfolio? Mean–variance Optimization and Beyond

The next two equations go beyond the supply and demand of returns and consider combining different return sources. One key equation we must include is the mean-variance optimization (MVO) in the expected utility framework, despite its many criticisms. It gives us essential insights which make it a natural starting place, while its many practical pitfalls have inspired various extensions to it.

The expected utility maximization problem involves an investor who selects an optimal portfolio from an available investment opportunity set based on the investor's beliefs and preferences. The preferences (goals and constraints) are represented in a utility function, in Equation 3 a simple one where the investor prefers more return to less and is averse to risk in a way that is fully captured by portfolio variance.[8]

Equation 3:

Max Expected Utility = Maximize Expected Portfolio Return – Risk Aversion * Pf.Variance

In short, the investor maximizes the expected return subject to a penalty for portfolio risk.[9] For an unconstrained investor, the solution amounts to identifying the portfolio with the highest SR.

The optimal portfolio weight of each asset is, unsurprisingly, positively related to its expected return and negatively to its contribution to portfolio volatility. For the special CAPM case (and more broadly for investors whose portfolio risk is dominated by equities), the latter means that assets with a higher market beta (higher volatility and/or correlation with the market), will have lower optimal weights for a given expected return.

Rearranging terms, the optimal weight depends positively on an asset's SR and negatively on its equity market correlation. The general optimality condition for the unconstrained case is that

---

[8]This formulation does not specify the investment horizon or for what future expenditures the money is meant. It allows comparison between different portfolios that maximize returns for a given variance. Other constraints are ignored. Mean-variance optimization can be motivated, say, by assuming either normally distributed asset returns or mean-variance preferences. Neither assumption is precisely right but both seem sufficiently close to the right ballpark that this can be a good starting point for major asset classes. I will not dwell here on the links between mean-variance efficiency, the CAPM, and the multi-factor models.

More broadly, the expected utility framework is the academic workhorse for saving and investment decisions under uncertainty. The core idea is that we derive utility from consuming our wealth, and the diminishing marginal utility explains both our risk aversion in investment choices and our preference to smooth consumption through time. The many applications, extensions, and criticisms are beyond this practitioner book.

[9]The risk aversion coefficient determines how volatile portfolio the investor selects. Risk aversion may vary across investors. Some empirical evidence indicates that risk aversion rises with age and falls with wealth. Note that a risk-neutral investor would not penalize volatility but would just maximize the (arithmetic mean) return . . . and would almost surely go broke. Another investor might maximize the geometric mean (which is lower than the arithmetic mean, due to so-called variance drain) or, equivalently, the compound wealth growth. Related to this, there is a whole subgenre of literature on growth-optimal investing, partly tied to concepts like the Kelly criterion and ergodicity economics – beyond this book.

in the optimal (maximum SR) portfolio, the ratio of marginal contribution of return to marginal contribution of risk is the same for all assets. This condition ensures that we cannot improve the portfolio by marginal reallocations between constituent assets.

As an aside, the last term in equation 3 gives some insights to the determinants of the market risk premium in the CAPM equation 2. The CAPM is a one-period model and thus not well-suited to studying a time-varying investment opportunity set and especially time-varying risk premia. Yet, logically, the required market risk premium should fall if the aggregate risk aversion falls or the expected market risk falls (e.g. as proxied by the VIX index, though the VIX focuses on very short-term risk).

So far, we discussed an unconstrained portfolio problem. It is very common to add constraints such as no-shorting and no-leverage, that is, each asset's portfolio weight is between 0% and 100%. Some users impose so many constraints that they effectively force the optimizer to give results they want to see. They set targets or tight limits on asset class, country, and sector weights, as well as on portfolio volatility, beta, leverage, illiquidity, turnover, and so on. Finding the right balance requires experience.

Although MVO is the premier tool for portfolio construction, many real-world investors eschew using it, partly because of problems related to model errors and estimation errors. Others stick with MVO and try to deal with these problems by some modifications or by imposing ad-hoc constraints on portfolio weights (see Chapter 12).

How Can Investors Add Value? Fundamental Law of Active Management and Beyond

The final equation I chose shares the spirit of the apple harvesting picture in Figure 1.3. So-called fundamental law of active management (FLAM) emphasizes the benefits of portfolio diversification as well as careful management of constraints and costs. As with the previous equations, FLAM's beauty is in the broad strategic insights it gives, not in being precisely right (as it too involves simplifying assumptions).

The history of FLAM is worth sharing. The main portfolio algebra relations had been mapped in the 1960s and 1970s by the pioneers in academic finance (such as Eugene Fama and Richard Roll). Yet they were not widely used among investment practitioners until Richard Grinold made many key insights lucid and applicable for active investment managers. Grinold (1989) introduced the concept of FLAM in an eponymous article, together with "information ratio" (IR, the risk-adjusted active return).[10] Grinold and Kahn's (1999) great book *Active Portfolio Management* developed both concepts further.

IR and SR are the most common measures of relative and absolute risk-adjusted returns in investment practice. For a manager whose benchmark is cash, IR is equivalent to SR. FLAM states that, as a good approximation, *the IR is a product of skill and (the square root of) breadth*, where skill is the correlation between a predictive signal and a stock's return and breadth is the number

---

[10]IR is the ratio of the average beta-adjusted active return over active risk (an active manager's alpha to its benchmark divided by its tracking error). To be clear, the Grinold-Kahn IR focuses on beta-adjusted active return (which they call residual return, also called the CAPM alpha) and not on what some others call the active return (raw difference between a manager's return and the benchmark, without beta-adjustment). Both return measures have their corresponding risk measures (residual risk or tracking error versus simple active risk without beta-adjustment).

of independent return forecasts over a year. Intuitively, you must play well and play often to consistently succeed in the investment management game. For example, if you can diversify better and apply your forecasting skill in four times as many independent opportunities in a year (without diluting it), you double your IR.

Among later extensions of FLAM, the work of Clarke-de Silva-Thorley (2002, 2006b) stands out.[11] They add a third term, implementation efficiency, to reflect the impact of real-world constraints and trading costs. This term, dubbed the transfer coefficient, is the correlation between the unconstrained optimal portfolio and the actual portfolio with constraints and costs. Equation 4 gives this extended version of FLAM.

Equation 4:

$$\text{Risk-adjusted active return} = \left(\text{Forecasting}\right)\text{Skill} \star \sqrt{\text{Breadth}} \star \text{Implementation efficiency}$$

$$\text{Information Ratio}\left(\text{IR}\right) = \text{Information Coefficient}\left(\text{IC}\right) \star \sqrt{\text{N}} \star \text{Transfer Coefficient}\left(\text{TC}\right)$$

FLAM was originally written for an active stock-picker, but it works as well for asset allocation and factor allocation even in terms of absolute risk-adjusted returns (SRs). When we assess diversification across market risk premia or long/short premia which have nearly uncorrelated returns, the breadth math of halving the volatility and doubling the risk-adjusted returns with four independent return sources is more realistic than it is for diversification within a stock portfolio whose constituents are highly correlated.

Specifically, risk parity investing may involve taking equal risk in three or four nearly uncorrelated asset classes with similar SRs and thereby boost the portfolio SR to be 1.5–2 times the typical asset class SR. Long/short premia diversification can do even better if (perhaps a big if) four on-average uncorrelated styles can be applied in four or five asset classes in lowly correlated ways. The portfolio SR could plausibly be doubled by style diversification and doubled again by multi-asset applications.

This math explains why I like long/short styles so much. Not only do the historically pervasive gains of certain styles make me more confident that they will also work individually in the future; the diversification benefit makes me even more confident about the combined portfolio's long-run prospects.

I repeat that the square root math only works for uncorrelated investments. The breadth boost is much more modest for correlated opportunities. Some observers emphasize that correlations often rise in bad times. Moreover, any SR boost happens in the denominator, as better diversification reduces portfolio volatility. If investors want to convert the higher SR into higher expected return, they need to apply corresponding leverage. The next chapters pursue these themes further.

There has been some debate on whether *factor allocation* allows in some ways superior diversification compared to *asset allocation*. Simple math shows that given the same universe and same constraints, there is no difference. However, in Ilmanen-Kizer (2012) we note that most practical asset allocation is applied with shorting and leverage constraints. Relaxing those constraints with long/short factor investing is the key to improving portfolio SR because it enables combining

---

[11]For a review of the FLAM literature and extensions, see Ding-Martin (2017) and Grinold-Kahn (2020).

lowly correlated opportunities with comparable risk weights, instead of letting the market-directional risk dominate.

Finally, FLAM can also be adopted to the time-series dimension where it gives good insights on the limits of market timing. It is hard to achieve a high SR on a slow-moving market timing strategy because it involves no breadth. Forecasting skill would need to be commensurately better to offset this handicap compared to strategies that involve more breadth.

10.2. Overview of Predictive Techniques

I provide here a very brief overview of the main techniques to predict investment returns that are used in the literature and also in this book. I contrast techniques based on constant and time-varying expected returns (roughly, historical average returns versus starting yields), their use at long and short horizons, in time-series and cross-sectional analyses, as well as the application of regression and sorting methods.

These techniques can be applied to all kinds of return sources, including various asset class premia and long/short style premia.

Constant Versus Time-varying Expected Returns

The traditional approach to estimating any long-run risk premium is to take a historical average. The underlying assumption is that expected returns are constant over time. If there are no structural changes, the longer the history, the more precise the estimate.

- Data availability or quality, and some concern of structural changes (distant data is less relevant), may warrant the use of shorter histories.
- If the sample period is very biased, in that the historical average return is overstated or understated due to sample-specific net richening or cheapening, it is useful to debias it. This is especially relevant if the sample period starts or ends at extreme valuations – for example, we know that equity markets are today historically rich and the value strategy historically cheap. Figure 2.1 showed how we can adjust historical average returns for the richening of equities or bonds over the past 40 years. Regressing past returns on contemporaneous valuation changes absorbs the impact of the net valuation change in the regression slope, and the (annualized) regression intercept gives the average return in the absence of the sample-specific valuation change.[12]
- This adjustment purges windfall gains (or losses) from realized average returns. The intercept indicates what returns investors were expecting, on average, during the sample period, and it

---

[12]Avdis-Wachter (2017) presents a related method to estimate the historical equity premium controlling for the valuation change, showing that the inclusion of contemporaneous valuation changes gives not just a less biased but also a less noisy estimate of the equity premium. Asness (2021) re-estimates the historical premium of equities, Treasuries, US versus EAFE markets, and value versus growth, controlling for the valuation change. In all cases, the discount rate effect (windfall gains or losses) was meaningful even over 40- to 70-year long sample periods. One might also use other measures than valuation changes to debias a sample period; for example, using a history of contemporaneous growth and inflation surprises as control variables.

should be a better measure of prospective expected return than the raw historical return. However, it does not recognize that conditional expected returns may be even lower now, if today's starting yields are below the sample-average yields.

The common approach to estimate asset class premia has shifted away from assuming constant expected returns to assuming time-varying expected returns. Typical capital market assumptions for equity markets rely on starting yields (such as the cyclically adjusted earnings yield as a proxy for expected real return) or on some version of the dividend discount model.

- As discussed, the three components of a dividend discount model are payout (income) yield, payout growth, and expected valuation change. Many observers, myself included, turn off the last component and assume no mean-reverting valuations (effectively assuming a persistent structural change has occurred). Even without assuming mean reversion, high valuations drive expected return estimates lower through low starting yields.
- More generally, one could make the expected equity market returns more granular and decide for each component whether to predict it based on the historical average (e.g. growth), the current value (e.g. yield), or assume mean reversion (e.g. valuation ratio); see discussion in Chapter 4 near Table 4.2.
- I did not distinguish above between the constancy of total returns and excess returns. One possibility is to use current riskless rates and constant risk premia.

For style premia, it remains common to anchor expected return estimates on historical average returns, though possibly discounting historical performance and adjusting for the impact of sample-specific valuation changes. For style premia with a low turnover, such as value-versus-growth, it is possible to incorporate starting yields and mean-reverting valuations. Mean reversion mainly matters when valuations are near extremes (as they recently have been for value-versus-growth). Valuations may also be combined with, say, factor momentum as timing indicators (see Chapter 16).

Long Versus Short Horizons

For expected returns based on historical averages, the horizon should not matter if we assume constant expected returns. The qualifier is if we are currently in an exceptional environment. Notably, the last decade has seen negative real cash returns while longer historical evidence points to positive real cash returns. It is common to assume the negative real cash rates to persist over the next few years, but for a multi-decade horizon it seems more reasonable to assume normalization to positive real cash rates.

If we assume time-varying expected returns, the horizon does influence our chosen predictors. For the 5- to 10-year horizon typical for capital market assumptions, starting yields and valuations are the most important predictors. Over shorter horizons (say, from one month to one year), predictors like momentum, cyclical macro conditions, or company-specific news tend to matter more than value, but their impact washes out (or even reverts) over a decade. And over multi-decade horizons, even value and yield effects get diluted.

For 5- to 10-year horizons, the weights of the components are often assumed based on strong priors – for example, 1 for current yield, 1 for historical growth, 0 for valuation change. They could also be estimated in a regression, but there are limited long-horizon observations ("small data") and various econometric problems with long-horizon predictability. For short horizons, predictor weights are more often estimated in a regression or based on the optimal weight in a "view portfolio."

Time-series Versus Cross-sectional Approaches

Near-term return forecasts or allocation decisions are either made for each investment individually (e.g. taking an *absolute* view on the equity market) or comparing many investments and assessing their *relative* performance for a given period (e.g. taking long/short views across different equity markets). The former is about time-series predictability, the latter about cross-sectional predictability.

- The best-known example is trend following (time series momentum) versus relative performance (cross-sectional momentum). If we study 20 equity markets and all were up last year, the trend-following strategy goes long all of them, thus embracing a market-directional view. In contrast, the cross-sectional momentum goes long the markets that went up the most but shorts the markets that went up the least, so as to take a market-neutral view on relative performance.
- Likewise, a contrarian market timing approach can involve overweighting several cheap markets and go directionally long, whereas a cross-sectional country selection (or stock selection) strategy tries to be market-neutral or at least dollar-neutral. Contrarian market timing strategy is the most vulnerable to structural changes because it requires estimating a "neutral" long-run valuation from data.

Regression Versus Sorting Methods

Academics like to run regressions for statistical evidence, while practitioners like to evaluate strategies based on their economic performance. Conveniently, one can bridge the two approaches (under some simplifying assumptions, such as normally distributed returns).

- The risk-adjusted expected return in a time-series strategy is a product of predictive correlation and signal strength.[13] And I already noted that the risk-adjusted return of a premium is related to the t-statistic of the predictive regression slope (adjusted by the sample size).
- Later in Chapter 16, I will illustrate predicting equity market returns with valuation ratios using both visuals related to regressions (time series, scatter plots, sorted quintile buckets) and the cumulative performance of a timing strategy whose market weights vary with the valuation ratio.
- For cross-sectional analysis, so-called Fama-MacBeth (1973) regressions estimate the rewards for different factors or characteristics by regressing each period various assets' returns on a set of factors or characteristics. The regression coefficients can be interpreted as returns on long/short portfolios that have a unit exposure on the corresponding factor and zero exposures to other factors. These factor coefficients can then be averaged over time to estimate the long-run average rewards for each factor (after controlling for its correlation with other factors) and to study their statistical significance.

---

[13]If we normalize time-series regression predictors (to zero mean, unit volatility), the expected return is a product of predictive correlation, signal strength, and volatility. ("IC ★ Z ★ Vol" in Grinold terminology). Multi-factor regression coefficients correspond to partial correlations (showing the independent impact of each predictor).

- In reality, these Fama-MacBeth factor-mimicking portfolios are so complex that it is more common to use simpler characteristic-sorted long/short portfolios, as in Fama-French (1992).[14] Style premia are typically defined through such sorts, then perhaps hedging away any undesired factor exposures.

Pedersen (2015) emphasizes the near-equivalence of the regression approach and sorting securities into portfolios. Any predictive regression can be expressed as a portfolio sort and vice versa. A time-series regression maps to a market timing strategy, and a cross-sectional regression maps to a security selection (relative value) strategy. Simple regressions correspond to sorting assets by one factor. Bivariate regressions correspond to a double sort (e.g. controlling the value factor for beta or size). Multiple regressions correspond to sorting by several factors and identifying the independent impact of each factor.

Finally, recall how in Chapter 7, the performance evaluation of a manager or a strategy could focus on a range of metrics from raw (measuring total returns or simple excess returns over a benchmark) to sophisticated (measuring the CAPM one-factor alpha or in extreme a multi-factor alpha). The parallels should be clear. We may try to predict and trade total returns (very crude, often dominated by market exposure) or something purer (hedging the directional beta risk, maybe also the industry risk and some macro sensitivities, and even the exposure to all other factors). A warning: The purest positions may sound great but require quite complex long/short positions and are subject to so much estimation error that they might not be worth the trouble.

This quick overview did not go into topics like discounting factor returns for trading costs and overfitting, in-sample versus out-of-sample results, combining empirical evidence with Bayesian priors, characteristics versus covariances, or econometric problems with some of the methods mentioned earlier. I touch upon these issues elsewhere in the book, albeit briefly.

Box 10.1 Machine Learning

The classic forecasting approaches rely on stable linear relationships between predictors and future returns. Many statistical techniques allow incorporation of various complexities and nonlinearities – tailoring contextual models for different markets or sectors, conditional models for different environments, interaction effects between predictors, and more. Newer techniques, called machine learning or artificial intelligence, do not specify

(continued)

---

[14]Fama-French (2020) and Jacobs-Levy (2021) discuss the relative merits between time-series and cross-sectional methods and strategies as well as between regression and sorting approaches. Also note that Fama-French (1992) asks how useful value characteristics are for sorting stocks into portfolios with high different average returns, while Fama-French (1993) asks how well value factor sensitivities explain cross-sectional stock returns. Academics have debated whether it is more useful to use characteristics or covariances in stock selection – say, whether to favor stocks with cheap valuation ratios or stocks that load up on the value factor in regressions (e.g. Daniel-Titman (1998)). Characteristics seem to perform better as return predictors (in part because they give more timely information), but covariances (value factor sensitivities in regressions) are needed for explanatory factor models or for hedging and demystifying purposes.

these relationships but let a machine learn any complex relationships between predictors and future returns. The main departure of machine learning from its statistical roots is in the massively increased computing power. Machine learning also allows the use of much larger data sets ("big data"), including unstructured data such as text or images. Downsides include heightened overfitting risks and black-box nature.

Machine learning is already having a huge impact in many fields. In finance too, it shows great promise but may also be overhyped. Machine learning is an evolutionary, not revolutionary, extension of statistical methods long used in quantitative investing. When it comes to forecasting multi-month or multiyear returns (not high-frequency returns), machine learning still faces limitations of small data. Worse, the signal-to-noise ratio is inevitably low in financial markets when competition ensures that predicting returns cannot be too easy.

Combined with some innovative alternative data sources, machine learning may help predict the next macroeconomic or firm-specific announcements ("nowcasting") which would give some edge in short-term trading, but this would do nothing to help us collectively in the low expected return challenge. Machine learning may improve stock selection and market timing strategies, but should be aided by theoretical models to limit overfitting. It has more potential to add value in the less sexy areas of portfolio implementation, such as risk management and trading cost control, where we have more data and where relatively efficient markets are not as constraining.[15]

---

[15]See Israel-Kelly-Moskowitz (2020) and Lopez de Prado (2018) on broader discussions. For applications, Gu-Kelly-Xiu (2020) shows how equity return prediction can be improved in a machine learning framework, while Engle et al. (2020) uses textual analysis among other tools to hedge climate change news.

Part III

Putting It all Together

Chapter 11

Diversification – Its Power and Its Dark Sides

- The magic of diversification is frequently underutilized. Most investors have home-biased portfolios dominated by equity-directional risk.
- Few investors take full advantage of multiple rewarded factors as this would require shorting and leverage. What other approach could feasibly boost single-strategy Sharpe ratios fourfold?
- Aggressive diversification does have its downsides, besides high leverage. Diversified portfolios often lack conventionality and easy narratives (stories).

11.1. Outline of the Remainder of This Book

The rest of the book deals with assembling the building blocks described so far. Recall Figure 1.3 which illustrated how wasteful the apple harvesters were on the unexciting, yet invaluable, parts of the investment process.

This brief chapter takes a bird's eye view on the topic of diversification. (If you think your portfolio is well diversified, you may be challenged soon.) Later chapters drill into the three key themes identified in Figure 1.3 – portfolio construction, risk management, and cost control – as well as ESG investing, tactical market timing, and bad habits.[1]

Diversification deserves its own chapter, given the huge benefits it can give to investors. This brief chapter is a testimony to its power but also acknowledges its dark sides.

---

[1]The Part III heading "Putting It All Together" overpromises. I am still just giving a cookbook of ideas and best practices on many important parts of the investment process. Their use will differ across investors. For examples which try to integrate lessons of academic investing and saving models into real-world solutions, see Campbell (2019) and Haghani-White (2021), both of which build on Robert Merton's pioneering work.

11.2. Ode to Diversification

The benefits of diversification are hardly news. The Talmud said perhaps 2000 years ago: "Let every man divide his money into three parts, and invest a third in land, a third in business, and a third let him keep by him in reserve." (The interpretation today is one-third real assets, one-third equities, and one-third cash/bonds. We do not know if these refer to nominal or risk weights) And Shakespeare wrote in his play *The Merchant of Venice*: "My ventures are not in one bottom trusted / Nor to one place; nor is my whole estate / Upon the fortune of this present year: / Therefore my merchandise makes me not sad."

We've all heard that diversification is the only free lunch in investing. But did you know that well-executed diversification is indistinguishable from magic?[2]

Diversification's ability to reduce portfolio volatility and to improve risk-adjusted returns is perhaps best captured by the role of breadth in the fundamental law of active management (FLAM) in the previous chapter. Improving breadth seems an easier way to double risk-adjusted returns than improving skill.

I cover below a few practical examples.

Global equity diversification versus home bias. The FLAM has less bite in this case because equity markets are highly correlated across markets, so the effective increase in breadth is limited. This is particularly true for the US whose market cap is close to half of global equities and whose flagship companies have a large footprint outside the US. For investors in smaller countries, home bias is more damaging.

That said, I find it puzzling that giants John Bogle and Warren Buffett agreed in endorsing highly US-centric portfolios (motivated by some mix of greater familiarity and belief in US entrepreneurship, property rights, etc.). Well, they got it right in the 2010s. At least theirs are better arguments for home bias than hindsighted medium-term return chasing: The US focus is often more popular after a strong decade. Yet, both logic and empirics suggest that globally diversified portfolios should provide better risk-adjusted returns in the long run.

Risk parity versus 60/40. Decent notional diversification can hide poor risk diversification.[3] Famously, the 60/40 stock/bond portfolio implies roughly 90/10 risk concentration for equities, given their higher volatility. Investors with a risk-balanced portfolio are likely to achieve a higher SR in the long run. Since stocks often have an order of magnitude larger risk share than other asset classes in many portfolios, their SR should be an order of magnitude higher (for these stock allocations to be mean-variance optimal). It is not.

If investors assume that stocks, bonds, and commodities have similar SRs and near-zero correlations (broadly in line with a century of evidence), then a risk parity portfolio with equal risk in all three asset classes will have a SR 1.7 ($\sqrt{3}$) times higher than the asset classes (e.g. 0.3 SRs per asset class diversify into 0.5 SR for a risk parity portfolio). Even if stocks are assumed to have a higher future SR than the two other asset classes, this edge needs to overcome risk parity's diversification advantage.

---

[2]Credit for this Arthur C. Clarke-inspired pearl goes to Butler et al. (2018). One example of such magic is covered in Table 4.4. about the long-run commodity premium being a case of "turning water into wine" through diversification, originally due to Erb-Harvey (2006).

[3]While I suspect that notional asset class allocations will be with us forever (they are the natural allocation decisions we make, after all), I strongly suggest that investors also track their *risk allocations* across asset classes (or other classification units). I am not proposing a revolution but *complementary* perspectives, shining light on the portfolio from different angles. Indeed, investors are increasingly measuring also their risk diversification. And whether the risk allocations are mere volatility allocations or risk contributions (which also incorporate correlation information); that's a luxury question (latter is better, former is OK).

To convert the higher SR to a higher expected return than a 60/40 portfolio, some leverage is needed.[4] Common leverage aversion and unconventionality slow down the adoption of risk parity strategies.

Alternative risk premia diversification. The potential benefits of breadth are the greatest with lowly-correlated long/short strategies discussed in Chapter 6. Uncorrelated, market-neutral return sources are very valuable portfolio enhancers in a multi-factor world (while the majority of observers couched in a single-factor world or with leverage constraints will miss this point).[5] Using four styles to predict relative returns in one asset class could double the per-style SR from 0.2 to 0.4, and applying the same idea in four distinct asset classes could double the SR again to 0.8. Yet, to make these strategies have a full impact on the total portfolio, much leverage is needed.

Let's first look at the math of diversification benefits in Figure 11.1. Portfolio volatility declines when more assets are added, but the decline is much steeper when lowly correlated investments are combined. So international equity market diversification across long-only assets with a common market risk corresponds to the top lines in this chart, while ARP diversification corresponds to the lower lines where four-item diversification can halve portfolio volatility (and thus double the SR).

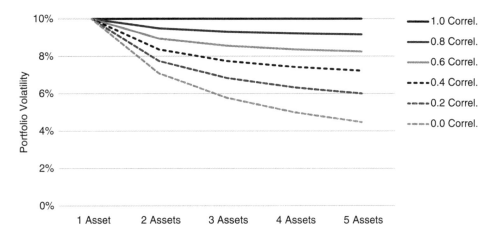

Figure 11.1   Volatility as a Function of the Number of Assets and the Correlation Between Them
Notes: The estimates assume equal volatility and correlation across assets, for simplicity.

[4]The 60/40 portfolio has a long-run volatility near 10%. The risk parity portfolio would typically need to be levered 2–2.5 times to target the same 10% volatility and to fully "monetize" the SR edge. Or risk parity investors could use less leverage and mix a somewhat lower portfolio volatility and a somewhat higher expected return than 60/40. Many investors may find it helpful that the leverage can be outsourced to external managers and that the leverage involves high futures notionals while supporting large cash balances.

Dhillon-Ilmanen-Liew (2016) quantifies empirically the manifold diversification benefits of risk parity approach. One of them is balanced risk allocations in many asset classes. Another is volatility targeting. Besides ensuring that portfolio risk is reasonably stable over time (unlike that of a 60/40 portfolio), this feature may enhance portfolio SR through embedding an indirect trend-following characteristic. Volatility targeting is discussed in Box 13.1.

[5]When shorting and leverage are not allowed, the diversification potential is limited by the large common market exposure all stocks share. Long/only "smart beta" portfolios, which blend market premia and style premia, are thus dominated by market risk. In contrast, ARP are ideally all about style premia, with no market risk. The intermediate solution is to relax the shorting and leverage constraints moderately, as is done in so-called 130/30 or relaxed-constraint strategies. Such strategies can exploit style premia much better than long-only portfolios, but the market risk still dominates.

Panel A

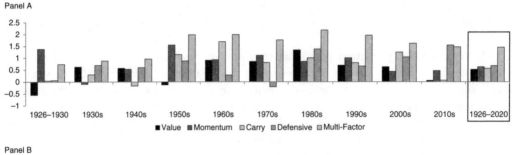

Panel B

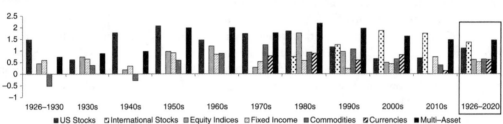

Figure 11.2 A–B Value of Diversification Across Asset Classes and Across Styles, 1926–2020
Sources: AQR, Ilmanen-Israel-Lee-Moskowitz-Thapar (2021), with more details on strategies. Data available in the AQR
Data Library.

Turning to empirics and our study of a century of long/short style premia (Ilmanen et al. (2021a)), Figure 11.2 combines per-decade SRs (A) across multi-asset applications of single styles and (B) across multi-style composites in several asset classes. Eyeballing either panel shows significant diversification benefits since almost every decade the last bar exceeded most other bars. The negative correlation between value and momentum styles makes style diversification particularly potent.

Diversification has given a large and consistent boost to the SR, broadly in line with the FLAM. For a single style in one asset class, the average SR was 0.4 using the full 19262020 sample period. After combining three to four styles per asset class, the average multi-style SR was 0.8. Then after also diversifying across the asset classes, the all-in composite SR was 1.5, an almost fourfold increase to the granular style premia's 0.4.

Importantly, the paper performance here is before subtracting trading costs and fees. Moreover, the decade-long perspective conceals the very disappointing 2018–20 real-world performance even for the all-in composite. The main culprit was value-based stock selection, but the other style premia did not do well enough to offset its losses.

Figure 11.3 tracks rolling 10-year SR series over time at the most granular level, after style diversification, and after style-and-asset diversification. While the SR levels have varied over time, the SR *boost* between the three lines looks pretty stable. Indeed, the range of the SR boost of style diversification (the ratio between the lower two lines) has been 1.9–2.3, and that of asset diversification a bit wider. Overall, the rolling SR boost from average single style per asset to the total multi-style, multi-asset portfolio (the ratio between top and bottom lines) has varied between 3 and 5 over time.

The key behind all that SR boosting is of course low correlations among long/short style premia. Table 6.1 shows that most style pairs have near-zero correlations with each other – and the value-momentum correlation is a very helpful -0.6. Correlations of multi-style composites across asset classes are also low, though mainly positive, and the all-in style premia composite has a -0.1 correlation with equities.

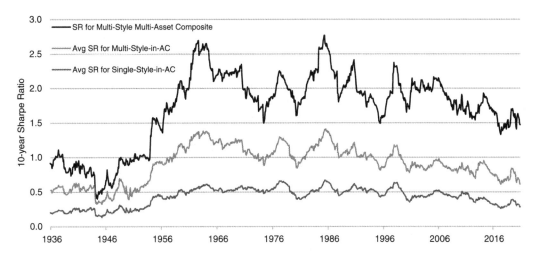

Figure 11.3   Sharpe Ratio Boosting Through Diversification, 1926–2020
Sources: AQR, Ilmanen-Israel-Lee-Moskowitz-Thapar (2021).

Such low correlations are not available when diversifying within a long-only asset class. Within equity markets, pairwise correlations tend to exceed 0.5, given the common systematic risk. Within bond markets, typical pairwise correlations are even higher. Between asset classes there can of course be good diversification opportunities.

Going into the weeds for a moment, diversification can be improved at many levels in systematic strategies. Design and implementation decisions can help at every stage of the investment process, and many intelligent features can be traced back to their ability to improve diversification. In the spirit of diversifying across diversifiers, I list several features for systematic factor investing strategies which seem to provide a small long-run edge:[6]

- Focus on strategic risk diversification rather than on tactical timing.
- Favor long/short strategies to have more diversified risk exposures and less market risk; or at least mildly relax the no-shorting, no-leverage constraints, if possible.
- Apply your edge in many different markets.
- Diversify across several signals per factor, instead of cherry-picking just one.
- Map signals to positions in a continuous fashion, for example, rank-weighted, instead of holding extreme decile positions which create unnecessarily lumpy trading.
- Combine factor signals through "integrating" their net wisdom into a multi-factor view before trading, so as to favor all-around good factors (cf. triathletes in sport), instead of "mixing" separate factor portfolios (which favors winners in a given event without caring how poorly they perform in weaker events).
- Hedge industry or sector exposures to achieve better breadth and comparability in stock selection.
- Target equal volatilities rather than equal nominals across strategies and over time, so as to reduce the impact of the most volatile investments or periods.
- Diversify model rebalancing over time to reduce arbitrary "rebalancing timing luck" (as Corey Hoffstein calls it; for more on rebalancing, see Box 11.1).
- Diversify trade execution over time to reduce the market impact of lumpier trades.

---

[6]Israel-Jiang-Ross (2017) covers some of these ideas as "craftsmanship alpha." These edges are not big individually, so it is no wonder that some researchers disagree (and just as well). But every little bit counts in the long run.

Box 11.1   Rebalancing

Rebalancing refers to adjusting portfolio allocations back to target weights. This can be done at a regular calendar schedule, triggered by large moves away from target weights or at the investor's discretion.

The main goal of rebalancing is to stay near risk targets and to maintain portfolio diversification. Without rebalancing, portfolios would tend to drift to a concentrated position in the highest-returning and presumably riskiest asset class. As an icing on the cake, systematic rebalancing might help enhance long-run returns, either through a lower variance drain (better diversification reduces portfolio volatility and boosts the geometric mean) or by synchronization with reversal patterns in market returns. At least, a systematic rule may give investors discipline to act when it feels difficult (e.g. to buy equities after October 2008 or March 2020).

Rebalancing can be done *within* any asset class but is most useful for allocating *across* liquid asset classes. Ilmanen-Maloney (2016) presents a typical five-asset-class case (unlevered domestic and international equities and bonds, plus commodities as an alts proxy) and assesses the empirical impact of various rebalancing methods over four decades. All rebalancing methods seem to improve performance compared to a buy-and-hold portfolio. Some trade-offs are evident: Fast rebalancing, say monthly full rebalancing, would ensure tight adherence to allocation targets, but at meaningful trading costs. More patient rebalancing, say yearly, would let the portfolio weights drift further away from the target, but this would improve historical performance somewhat by allowing momentum to play out.

There has been a multi-angled debate in the literature on whether rebalancing boosts expected returns.[7] Under narrow circumstances, the answer is yes even in a random-walk world, but the prospects are better if rebalancing frequency is well aligned with markets' typical momentum and reversal patterns. As noted, patient rebalancing may benefit from both multi-month momentum and multiyear reversal patterns. Rebalancing is not proactively contrarian by, say, overweighting past multiyear laggards, but it is defensively contrarian by selling past gainers and buying past laggards to get back to target weights. Like any contrarian strategy, rebalancing is short structural changes.

As a further nuance, I like "often-but-little" rebalancing approaches, such as quarterly rebalancing one-quarter toward the target. This is roughly equivalent to a full annual rebalancing, but it mitigates the "rebalancing timing luck" by averaging the execution days over the calendar year, and it saves trading costs by implying smaller trading sizes, while still letting momentum play out.

I will not discuss here the further challenges illiquid assets pose to rebalancing, or the additional complications from leveraged positions or risk-based rebalancing (which might require selling past losers). Interested readers may consult Huss-Maloney (2017), Qian (2018), and Rattray et al. (2020).

---

[7]For example, it is easy to imagine a case where it would help to let weights drift and eventually the highest-return asset would dominate – but you would then hold 100% equity and not a 60/40 portfolio. Huss and Maloney (2017) stresses that rebalancing dampens compounding effects and forgoes the very best buy-and-hold outcomes where winners keep on winning; in doing so it reduces the difference between mean and median expected outcomes for the portfolio. In other contexts than this macro example, rebalanced portfolios have also outperformed. Table 4.4 above showed how a diversified commodity portfolio has historically offered 3% higher geometric mean return than its average constituent (which had much higher volatility and thus more variance drain eating up the geometric mean); this is sometimes called diversification return or rebalancing bonus.

Rising from the weeds back up to the bird's eye view and beyond, recall the major market risk premia and ARP in Figure 1.2 in the Introduction, the long-run return sources with the most compelling historical evidence. If a truly unconstrained investor believed that these nine long-run return sources have broadly comparable SRs and modest correlations between them, then allocating equal risk to each should give a high portfolio SR and a very high bar to beat. This truly unconstrained investor should be able to lever this high-SR portfolio up to the volatility level that suits its risk tolerance.

As a segue to the caveats and criticisms, I acknowledge that in practice, few Earthlings act like this truly unconstrained investor. The proposed approach may involve too much leverage and unconventionality for real-world investors to apply it to their total portfolio.[8]

11.3. Critics' Laments

I start with criticisms on which I disagree, before turning to some fair criticisms.

We sometimes hear about the dangers of *overdiversifying* or *diworsification*. The message is that one should hold concentrated positions, avoid diluting the best ideas with middling ones, and more generally not accept the mediocrity of indexing or, worse, closet indexing.[9]

One way to address this question is through FLAM – is it easier to double the skill applied to one trade or to increase breadth by applying similar skill in four places? Mostly I view concentrated positions as a sign of overconfidence.[10]

The diworsification criticism is sometimes extended from stock picking to broader decisions, such as diversifying from US equities to global equities or from a 60/40 stock/bond portfolio to various alternative assets or strategies. Such criticism becomes more vocal with hindsight after diversification fares poorly for an extended period, as happened in the 2010s.

It is often said that *diversification fails when it is most needed*. Indeed, it is true that correlations within equity markets (across stocks, sectors, countries) are higher during sharp market falls (e.g. Chua-Kritzman-Page (2009) and Leibowitz-Bova-Hammond (2010)).[11] However,

---

[8]A case in point: To achieve total portfolio volatility near 10% after diversification, all the nine constituent subportfolios would need to be targeted at 25–30% volatility standalone, which would require levering even equities, and levering bonds and ARP even more, perhaps requiring overall gross positions up to ten times larger than assets under management. Even true believers would not use that much leverage with more than a part of their total portfolio. As a result, this unconstrained ideal is not realistic, and most real-world investors hold portfolios with much more equity concentration risk than leverage risk. If your beliefs are close to mine, you may still want to try to move to the direction of this unconstrained ideal as far as you can. For most investors, both beliefs and constraints differ from mine, which explains their larger weights on equity and illiquid assets, and smaller weights on diversified style premia.

[9]It is fair to argue that closet indexing involves too high fees. But the claim that a low active risk (tracking error or active share) predicts lower active return is hardly supported by empirical data. Taking more active risk increases the chance of both positive and negative outcomes.

[10]The misunderstanding that picking winners is easy or essential for good investing has been reinforced by a misreading of a recent Bessembinder (2018) article. This study found that the majority (58%) of US common stocks since 1926 have lifetime buy-and-hold returns less than one-month T-bills. In terms of lifetime dollar wealth creation, the best-performing 4% of listed companies explain the net gain for the entire US stock market since 1926, since other stocks collectively matched T-bills. Some readers interpret that these results validate concentrated picking of lottery-like winners (good luck trying!). A better reading of the evidence is that the article endorses broad diversification to ensure those winners are in your portfolio.

[11]To properly measure correlation asymmetry, we must adjust for mechanically lower correlations when part of a sample is excluded. Kinlaw et al. (2021) stress that the empirical asymmetry is often of the undesirable variety, characterized by downside unification and upside diversification. Investors would prefer precisely the opposite pattern, diversification working only on the downside.

Asness-Israelov-Liew (2011) shows that international diversification still works when evaluating more persistent market declines. Major economies have sufficiently different business cycles, and even the main bubbles (e.g. Japan 1990, US 2000, China 2007) occurred at different times. Arguably, multiyear diversifying ability is more important for long-horizon investors than smoothing out the worst months.

To guard against the pitfalls of diversification, it makes sense to protect portfolios against left-tail events through tail hedging strategies, constraints on liquidity and leverage, as well as drawdown control rules. These risk control approaches – which complement diversification – will be covered in Chapter 13.

It is more reasonable to criticize diversification for the following dark sides:

- As noted, its full use requires more *leverage* than many investors accept, and deleveraging episodes could pose material risks.
- Aggressive risk diversification can present a major *conventionality* challenge. Most peer portfolios are dominated by equity market risk. If you diversify better, you look different, and this "maverick risk" or peer risk leaves you open to losing alone.
- It lacks *stories* and intuition, which may slow the adoption and speed up deallocations in bad times. Humans are storytellers, and abstract statistical evidence loses out time and again to intuitive stories.[12]

Leverage constraints may be prominent reasons why the high SR of a diversified style premia portfolio has been sustained for decades, at least on paper. The unconventionality and abstraction may be further contributors.

It is easy to see why leverage and unconventionality may help long-run performance. And perhaps even being short (on) stories is a strength of diversification, not a weakness. We should remember that stories make us prone to base rate neglect (ignoring useful statistical information, while focusing on a salient case) and to hindsight bias (stories tell what happened and ignore what else might have happened, making the world appear more predictable than it really is). Captivating stories arouse human biases instead of containing them.

In conclusion, many investors talk diversification but walk concentration. Their portfolios are dominated by one key source of risk, the equity market. Those who truly believe in the benefits of diversification and in a multi-factor world will want to harvest multiple return sources in a more balanced way – even at the cost of leverage, unconventionality, and lacking cocktail-party stories. I acknowledge above that the ideal hyper-diversified levered portfolios are not realistic, but thoughtful investors should try to move in the direction of better risk diversification as far as they sustainably can.

---

[12]Whatever their impact on long-run success is, the excitement aspect declines from expected returns to volatilities to correlations. You can try this at a cocktail party. Asness (2019a) shows how diversification weakens our ability to offer intuitive narratives. Factor portfolios are already much more abstract than single-stock investments, then moving from a value portfolio (pretty easy to describe) to a diversified value+momentum portfolio is another step away from stories toward abstract statistics. The related SR boost should be easily worth the lost intuition.

Chapter 12

Portfolio Construction

- Constrained mean-variance optimization (MVO) is the main workhorse for construct-ing portfolios, whether formally or informally used.
- Important top-down decisions are often made before MVO can be applied, for example, the share of illiquid assets in the portfolio.
- The key insight in unconstrained MVO is that we like high SRs and good diversifiers, thus we trade off these features. In practice, constraints on leverage and illiquidity may matter more.
- MVO's pitfalls include model errors and estimation errors. Mitigating them requires adding constraints, shrinking inputs, or using robust optimization.

12.1. Top-down Decisions on the Portfolio

Mean-variance optimizers are tools designed to solve for portfolio weights based on the inputs given – expected return, volatility, correlation estimates, and risk aversion coefficient. These tools are excellent for dealing with the risk/reward trade-off and incorporating information about correlations (which does not come easily for humans). But we still need to provide these inputs – and hope we use a broadly correct model.

Many important ("top-down") decisions need to be made prior to using formal optimizers. Our beliefs determine the return and risk estimates. While our preferences on mean versus var-iance determine the risk aversion coefficient, our other preferences and constraints determine whether we need to go beyond the mean-variance framework.

The answers to the following key questions cannot be given by purely quantitative tech-niques, and ultimately they depend on investor judgment:

Q1: *How risk averse are you?* Anyone who has asked this question seriously – either for one-self or for one's institution – knows it is so hard to answer. But we must try and estimate what level of portfolio volatility or likely worst losses we can tolerate. Financial advisors have a set of questions to elicit a client's risk tolerance, and the method also applies for institutions. One method is to ask the investor, or an investment committee, to choose between numerical pairs of wealth outcomes or between visual examples of performance and drawdowns.[1] Actual experiences may teach us more about our risk tolerance than hypothetical comparisons. Even if most of us feel heightened risk aversion during times like Fall 2008 or March 2020, if we cannot stick with our portfolio through such experiences, we should learn for the future that we held a too risky portfolio.[2]

Q2: *Does the mean-variance framework miss crucially relevant considerations, such as ESG preferences, liquidity needs, or leverage constraints – or even your liabilities?* The answer may be "of course" and it is just a matter of how important those missed elements are. The maximization problem could be modified or constraints added to the framework to capture ESG, liquidity, leverage, or other missing considerations. Or the assets-only optimization perspective could be changed into an asset-liability surplus optimization to make it relevant for liability-oriented pension funds, or into a benchmark-relative optimization to make it relevant for active managers.

Q3: *What is the acceptable investment universe for your portfolio?* This is effectively a hard version of Q2 which implied penalizing certain assets or practices based on liquidity, ESG, and so on. Q3 is about fully excluding less liquid small-cap, emerging-market, or private investments – or perceived ESG-sinners.

The answers to these questions drive key portfolio choices such as the split between stocks and bonds or between public and private assets. And the answers inevitably vary across investors. No one size fits all.

A Case in Point: Illiquids' Share in the Total Portfolio

Mean-variance optimization can be especially misleading when we combine traditional and alternative investments. Given the artificially smooth returns and any illiquidity premia, unconstrained optimizers love private alternatives.[3] Investors often respond to apparently unreasonable optimization results by constraining private assets' share in the total portfolio. Leibowitz-Bova-Hammond (2010) proposes *starting* portfolio construction with a decision on the acceptable allocation to alternative asset classes, which are subject to unknown "dragon risk."

---

[1] Preferences revealed by such questioning may be our best way forward but they have many problems. For example, context matters: Most investors accept a given percentage or dollar loss more easily if it comes in conventional equities than if it is due to some unconventional investment. Similar answers can be explained by different utility functions. Risk aversion may also vary over time, perhaps rising after large losses. Finally, academics reveal inconsistent risk preferences between bets that are made on small or large part of the investor's wealth (Rabin-Thaler (2001)).

[2] Another way to address Q1 is to ask whether you consider yourself more risk averse or risk tolerant than the *average investor*. Cochrane (1999) suggests that since the average investor holds the market, we could ask ourselves how we differ from the average investor and let that guide our deviations from the market portfolio. This is a useful exercise, and I too recommend that every investor does some introspection about its distinctive characteristics (risk aversion, liabilities, liquidity needs, asset size and resources, etc.). Know thyself. Yet, there are major practical limitations: The answer really requires knowing what the investable multi-asset market portfolio and the wealth-weighted average investor look like.

[3] Given typical inputs, unconstrained optimizers also love liquid alternative risk premia, proposing very large weights, because diversification across lowly correlated long/short strategies can imply a much higher portfolio SR than diversification across market risk premia. Typical investor constraints then limit the use of leverage and shorting, and thereby cap the weight of ARP in the total portfolio.

The share of illiquids has generally crept up in recent decades and is especially high for large US endowments and Canadian pension plans. The merits of copying this approach are hotly debated.[4]

What would generally warrant a higher share of illiquid alternatives in portfolios? Here is one list of considerations I prepared for a Canadian pension fund:

- Younger workforce and more distant liabilities (long horizon argument)
- Lesser need of imminent liquidity for regulatory, collateral, or other reasons (ditto)
- Greater belief in illiquidity premia and/or belief in one's manager selection skill or internal ability to harvest alpha in illiquid assets (expected return argument)
- Preference for smooth reported returns (risk perception)
- Higher peer holdings of illiquid alternatives (conventionality argument)

Similar lists could be written for ESG, leverage, or other topics. A systematic use of such lists would require well-thought-out quantification and weighting of each item.

Macroeconomic Exposures

Another set of top-down decisions that is not well captured by the mean-variance framework pertains to factor allocations and macro exposures.

In my earlier book I used a cube to highlight how portfolios could, and should, be viewed from three complementary perspectives. The front side of the cube in Figure 12.1 focuses on traditional asset class allocations, the top side on strategy styles, and the last side on macro exposures. When the term "factor investing" became popular in the 2010s, any one of the three sides was sometimes described as factors, though the term was most often associated with styles. The terminology should not matter too much as long as discussants understand each other. Importantly, the front and top sides are about investable factors – largely long-only asset class premia

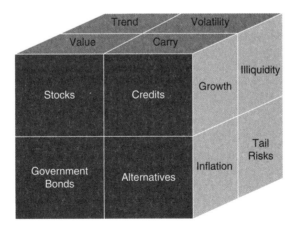

Figure 12.1 The Cube: Asset Class, Strategy Style, and Macro Factor Perspectives to a Portfolio

[4]See Ennis (2020), Hammond (2020), Beath-Flynn (2020), though also see Beath et al. (2021). Even David Swensen (2009) warned that Yale's success may not be replicable.

and long/short style premia – while the third side is about non-investable factors.[5] You cannot simply buy a portfolio of economic growth, for example.[6]

All three complementary perspectives are useful for understanding portfolios. For aggressively harvesting many investable return sources from the first two sides, you could choose a risk parity portfolio of liquid long-only asset class premia and a diversified portfolio of long/short style premia (cf. Chapters 4 and 6). While you cannot make direct allocations to macro risks, you can still estimate what kind of macro exposures your asset class and style premia allocations have historically implied.

At AQR, my coauthors and I have explored the macro sensitivities of various premia from different angles (economic growth, inflation, real yield, volatility and liquidity environments; later also monetary policy and tail risk environments). Since economic growth and inflation are often viewed as the two primary macro risks, Figure 12.2 shows our estimates of contemporaneous growth and inflation exposures for the major asset class and style premia. I only outline here the major design decisions and results; for details see Ilmanen-Maloney-Ross (2014).

- We assign quarterly 12-month periods over almost 50 years into four environments, growth and inflation up or down, based on US macroeconomic data such as growth and inflation surprises. We then report for every investment the SR separately for each of the four environments (and for the full sample).[7]
- The top panel shows that global equities performed best in the growth-up, inflation-down environment and worst in the opposite (stagflationary) environment. Global government bonds performed best in the growth-down, inflation-down environment and poorly in the opposite environment. Commodities had precisely the contrary pattern to bonds. These patterns make sense.
- The middle panel shows clearly milder SR variations across macro environments for five style premia applied in several asset classes.[8] The intuition is that these style premia are designed to be both beta-neutral and duration-neutral, and removing the directional market sensitivities also removes most of the macro sensitivities observed in the top panel.

---

[5]Admittedly, only growth and inflation in the last side are purely macro exposures; liquidity and tail risk exposures are other broadly understood investment exposures and yet not directly investable. My most careful readers may also notice that in this new book, I switch the last style "volatility" to mean defensive investing. In my first book, "volatility" style referred to option-based volatility selling, while the defensive style was covered elsewhere.

[6]Equity markets are often seen to give exposure to long-run economic growth and to business cycle risk, so I stick with this practice. Yet, Box 4.2 argues that the empirical links between economic growth and equity market returns are surprisingly tenuous.

[7]One challenge is the time alignment between financial market returns and macroeconomic series. Should we align returns contemporaneously (before the macro news are known), or use previous quarter's macro news (to capture the market reaction to the published macro announcements), or use future macro developments (since asset prices tend to be forward-looking)? Since there is no correct answer, we map to each quarter the year-on-year asset returns and macro news (so as to reduce any time alignment problems). Another issue is whether to focus on levels or changes/surprises? For example, is "inflation up" about high or rising inflation? We choose a blend of both.

[8]These style premia are closely related to those discussed in Chapter 6, but design details are in Ilmanen-Maloney-Ross (2014). Importantly, they include both stock selection and asset allocation strategies, while trying to hedge away market directional exposures. Unlike in the original paper, we have recently discounted heavily these style premia SRs for costs and other reasons discussed in Chapter 9 (9.3), so that they are more realistic in a forward-looking sense. In any case, the main point is not the level of SRs but their variation across environments – which is quite mild. I would not read much into the regime differences in SRs, which could be sample-specific. To me the main takeaway is that long/short style premia have more modest macro sensitivities than directional asset class premia.

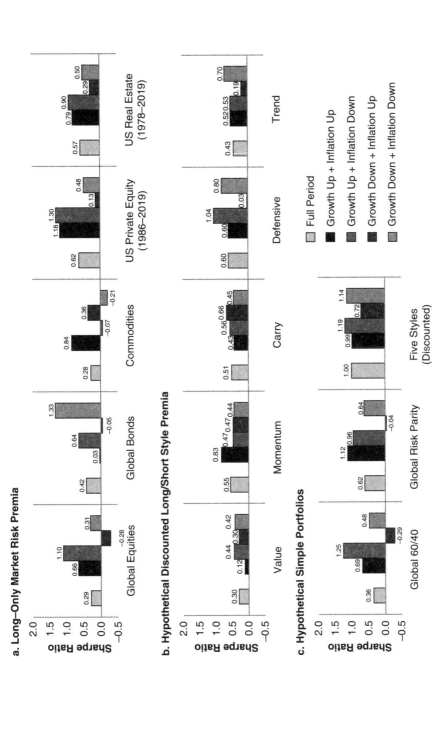

Figure 12.2 Macroeconomic Sensitivities of Major Asset Premia and Style Premia, 1972–2020

Sources: AQR, Bloomberg, Cambridge Associates, NCREIF Global Equities is MSCI World Index. Global Bonds is GDP weighted composite of Australian, European, Canadian, Japanese, UK and US 10-year government bonds. Commodities is equal dollar-weighted index of 24 commodities. Private Equity is an average of the Cambridge US Buyout Index and 1.2-times levered Russell 2000 index. Real Estate is an average of the NCREIF NPI and FTSE NAREIT equity REITs. Long-Short Style Premia are heavily discounted backtests of multi-asset style premia from AQR. Global 60/40 takes 60% Global Equities, 40% Global Bonds. Global Risk Parity is a hypothetical strategy that allocates equal volatility to three asset classes: developed equities (GDP-weighted), government bonds (GDP-weighted), and commodities (equal-weighted), with allocations based on 12-month volatility. Five Styles is an equal dollar-weighted composite of the five discounted long/short style premia.

- The bottom panel studies composite portfolios, with three key results. First, a 60/40 portfolio largely inherits the macro exposures of global equities in the top-left panel (consistent with the notion that from risk perspective, 60/40 is almost all-equities). Second, simple risk parity (an equal-volatility-weighted portfolio of the three liquid asset class premia in the top row) earned a higher SR than 60/40 overall and in three of four environments, as well as a more stable performance across environments – thanks to its better risk diversification.[9] Third, the style composite (averaging the five style premia in the middle row) had a high SR and relatively stable performance across environments – thanks to its best risk diversification.

Note that any information on contemporaneous macro sensitivities is not directly tradeable. Only investors who believe they can forecast well the next quarter's or year's macro regime can translate information in Figure 12.2 into profitable tactical trading strategies. Few investors have such a clear crystal ball. Thus, I'd rather try to construct portfolios that are robust across all these macro scenarios. Good risk diversification is the recipe for this.

Finally, investors who try the tactical macro forecasting game should recognize that the macro sensitivities are more reliable in the top row, so investors are better off applying their skill in timing major asset classes than in style timing.[10] Asness (2015) notes that successful macro traders need to be "twice right," just as racetrack bettors need to be in an exacta bet when wagering on the first two positions. Investors could get the macro forecast right, hard enough, and then see the contemporaneous mapping between investment return and the macro regime differ from that seen in Figure 12.2. Such a frustrating outcome is much more likely in style timing than in directional timing, given the less reliable macro sensitivities for market-neutral style premia.

12.2. Mean-variance Optimization Basics and Beyond

Let's remind ourselves of the MVO basics in Chapter 10. We all like returns, we dislike risk, and we have constraints. The inputs to the basic optimization problem are a set of expected returns on assets in the available investment universe, a set of related risk measures (volatilities and correlations between assets), and an investor-specific risk aversion coefficient.

Maximizing the expected return subject to a penalty for portfolio risk (with no other constraints) amounts to identifying the portfolio with the highest SR. The optimal portfolio weight of each asset is positively related to its expected return and negatively to its volatility and correlation with the rest of the portfolio. Said differently, an asset's optimal weight depends on its

---

[9]It is comforting that two quite different approaches to creating risk-balanced asset class portfolio end up in so similar places. Whether one uses standard portfolio theoretical approach and seeks well-diversified portfolios using volatility and correlation information (our approach) or one starts by seeking a portfolio with comparable performance in different macro regimes (Bridgewater's All-Weather approach), the result is a risk parity portfolio with roughly equal risk allocations from the three lowly-correlated asset classes and with partly offsetting macro exposures. Better risk diversification shows up in both a lower portfolio volatility (higher SR) and a better performance balance across macro scenarios. Also see Roncalli (2013) and Amato-Lohre (2020).

[10]While I do not report here the results from our related studies – for example, exposure to monetary policy environments – I note that the broad picture is similar. Market-directional asset class premia have more robust macro exposures than do market-neutral style premia. Any studies that report significant macro exposures for style premia tend to involve cases where market beta and duration risks have not been hedged. Well-designed style premia have had modest macro sensitivities, especially in diversified style composites. Even among individual style premia, we find few with clear market exposures or macro exposures. Two well-known exceptions are currency carry style (equity-like with its positive beta and growth exposures) and defensive industry selection (bond-like with its interest rate exposure).

SR and its equity market correlation. Intuitively, the optimizer gives a recipe for an unconstrained investor: Start with an equal-volatility allocation to various investments (to boost diversification) and then tilt toward those with higher SRs or better diversification abilities.

Portfolio-level MVO in Action

To give flavor of MVO analysis, I first present the simple two-asset case of equities (EQ) and fixed income (FI). I later discuss verbally a broader case with illiquid alternatives (such as private equity,

Table 12.1   A Set of Return and Risk Assumptions

	Exp. Ret.	Volatility	Net SR
Equities	5.0%	15%	0.33
Fixed Income	1.0%	5%	0.2
Illiquid Alts	7.0%	10%	0.7
Alt Risk Premia	7.0%	10%	0.7

Correlations

	EQ	FI	Illiqs	ARP
Equities	1			
Fixed Income	0.0	1		
Illiquid Alts	0.7	0.2	1	
Alt Risk Premia	0.1	0.1	0.1	1

Source: AQR Portfolio Solutions Group (2015).

	Constrained 6% vol	Constrained 10% vol	Unconstrained 10% vol
Exp.ExR	2.3%	3.6%	3.9%
Volatility	6.0%	10.0%	10.0%
SR	0.39	0.36	0.39

Source: AQR Portfolio Solutions Group (2015). Notes: See input assumptions in the first two rows of Table 12.1.

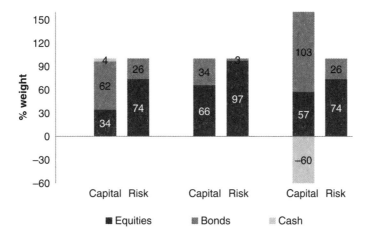

Figure 12.3   Optimizing the Equity-Bond Allocation

private debt, real estate) and liquid alternative risk premia (ARP). The results, of course, reflect our inputs. Table 12.1 shows one set of expected excess return, volatility, and correlation assumptions. These are plausible forward-looking estimates, guided by long-run historical experience, adjusted for the low expected return world.

Investors reveal their subjective risk tolerance by selecting an acceptable target level of portfolio volatility. This is often proxied by the target equity weight in the EQ/FI allocation. I first show the optimal weights at low (6%) and high (10%) volatility levels when no shorting or leverage is allowed. Figure 12.3 shows that the optimal EQ/FI capital weights are 34/62% and 66/34%, respectively, at these volatility levels. These nominal capital allocations are complemented with more relevant, but less often quoted, risk allocations. Recall the claim that a 60/40 asset allocation implies at least 90/10 risk allocation. Figure 12.3 shows both capital and risk allocations for each portfolio.[11]

The low-risk portfolio has a higher SR while the high-risk portfolio has a higher expected excess return. However, if we allow leverage and shorting (third column), the optimal portfolio is the tangency portfolio (see Box 12.1) levered up to the target volatility level — this offers somewhat higher expected return than the leverage-constrained version.

Box 12.1 Modern Portfolio Theory and Two-Fund Separation

If cash is not available for borrowing and investing, the best investors can do is to choose from the efficient frontier of risky assets a portfolio that best suits their risk tolerance. The availability of cash allows investors to do better (see Figure 12.4 with only two risky assets, equity and fixed income). The pioneers of Modern Portfolio Theory showed that the selection of an optimal portfolio involves two separate decisions: First, what is the most efficient or maximum SR portfolio among risky assets, and second, how much risk to take? Investors who agree on the opportunity set should all agree on the first portfolio. It is called the tangency portfolio because it is at the tangent of the (capital market) line between cash and the efficient frontier; thus it has the highest SR among all portfolios on the efficient frontier. With cash available for leverage or lending, the second decision is how to mix cash and the tangency portfolio: deleveraging or leveraging the optimal risky-asset portfolio along the capital market line to reach a volatility level that reflects investor risk tolerance. Cash is at the origin since Figure 12.4 depicts excess-of-cash returns. Given the inputs, the tangency portfolio has 36/64% EQ/FI weights (cf. last column in Figure 12.3. where this portfolio is levered with 60% of cash to 57/103%). Including good diversifiers – such as commodities, illiquid alternatives, or ARP – into the available investment universe would expand the efficient frontier toward the top-left.

---

[11]Risk allocations measure each investment's contribution to the portfolio's variance. They account for both variances and correlations. Variance is the square of volatility (standard deviation), so variance contributions tend be more heavily weighted towards riskier assets than vol-adjusted weights. (A simpler way to proxy risk allocations ignores correlations and just counts each asset's volatility as a share of all constituents summed volatilities.)

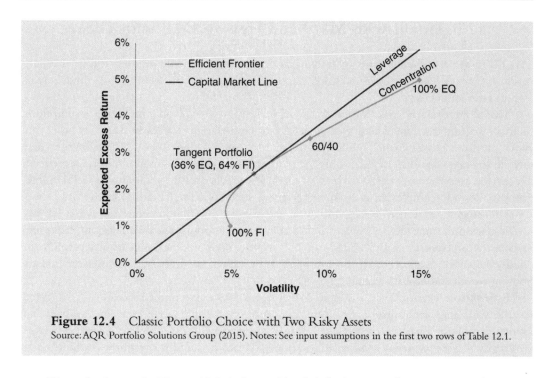

Figure 12.4 Classic Portfolio Choice with Two Risky Assets
Source: AQR Portfolio Solutions Group (2015). Notes: See input assumptions in the first two rows of Table 12.1.

Given the inputs in Figure 12.3, let's consider briefly how much investors can boost the portfolio's expected return and/or SR by any of the three paths: more equities, more illiquid alternatives, and more alternative risk premia.

- A 60/40 portfolio has an expected excess-of-cash return of 3.4%. Moving to a 66/34 portfolio (with 10% volatility), this rises to 3.6%. Moving to 100% equity, this rises to 5% (but volatility rises to 15% and the SR drops due to worse diversification).
- Allowing either illiquid alternatives or ARP (but no ability to lever them up beyond 10% volatility), expected excess return could be raised to 7%, and no traditional assets would be held. A mix of the two alternatives would boost the portfolio SR above 0.7.
- If shorting and leverage constraints are removed, the expected excess return of the optimal portfolio at 10% volatility target would be 9.8% (thus SR 0.98). This would require going long 159% of net assets in illiquid alts and ARP, while funding the 59% leverage by cash (25%) and by selling short public stocks and bonds (34%).[12]
- Few investors would consider such an extreme portfolio even if they had 10% return aspirations. In real-world solutions, the illiquid and ARP allocations would inevitably be capped.

If the optimizer results are deemed unacceptable, what caused this? I interpret this below as a model error: The unconstrained MVO setup does not capture investors' typical aversion to illiquidity, leverage, and shorting – and thus loads up on them. While it is possible to express such aversion by using constraints, MVO does not help in deciding how tight these constraints should be.

[12]For details, see AQR Portfolio Solutions Group (2015). I repeat that the results reflect the input assumptions; you may not agree with mine!

12.3. Pitfalls with MVO and How to Deal with Them

MVO is most useful when (i) its underlying assumptions are broadly satisfied and (ii) we have reasonable inputs. The two corresponding classes of problems for the MVO are (i) model errors and (ii) estimation errors.

Model errors: The risk/reward trade-off in MVO is based on simplifying assumptions, such as normally distributed returns or mean-variance preferences. Clearly, many investors care about portfolio characteristics beyond mean and variance. Other important preferences may include leverage, liquidity, ESG, and higher moments (e.g. skewness and tail risk). Moreover, a one-period, one-factor model in frictionless markets is hardly realistic; yet multi-period or multi-factor models add complexity, as do market frictions such as trading costs and taxes.[13]

The biggest error may be to deal with the wrong question or consider a too narrow investment opportunity set. Instead of doing an assets-only optimization, a pension plan could broaden its problem to include pension liabilities and optimize the asset-liability surplus. Or a retirement saver could broaden her optimization problem beyond financial assets to include housing wealth and human capital.

Estimation errors: Even a simple MVO needs reasonable input estimates for expected returns, volatilities, and correlations. Estimation error is the difference between the true and estimated value of a parameter. Expected returns are especially susceptible to estimation errors (returns are harder to predict than volatilities and correlations) and the optimizer's output (portfolio weights) can be quite sensitive to expected return inputs. If an optimizer sees two highly correlated assets with different SRs, it may seek to create a large leveraged long/short position between them to exploit this apparent opportunity.

Model errors and estimation errors also interact. Extending MVO to capture some missing element (e.g. ESG, illiquidity, or leverage) results in a more complex model where more parameters need to be estimated, increasing the potential for estimation errors. In practice, we cannot extend the model to too many dimensions for tractability reasons, so some constraints must be imposed.

Thus, care is needed when choosing the inputs. Using historical volatilities and correlations may be reasonable, but naive use of historical average returns is a recipe for trouble. Shrinking historical risk and return estimates toward some reasonable priors (such as zero or the group average) is often advisable.[14]

Since expected return estimates are the least reliable, many portfolio construction approaches (e.g. equal-weighted portfolio, minimum variance portfolio, risk parity portfolio) avoid using them. Implicitly, these approaches assume that risk-adjusted returns are similar across assets (or that the estimates are highly uncertain). Full MVO would be superior to such approaches if expected return or risk-adjusted return differences between assets were so large that we could

---

[13]Examples of more complex models with other preferences include leverage aversion (Frazzini-Pedersen (2014)), liquidity preferences (Acharya-Pedersen (2005)), ESG (Pedersen-Fitzgibbons-Pomorski (2020)), coskewness (Harvey-Siddique (2000)), and downside risk (Ang-Chen-Xing (2006)). On tastes more generally, see Fama-French (2007). Multi-factor and multi-period models are discussed in Cochrane (2005) and Campbell (2019).

[14]See Black-Litterman (1992), Pedersen-Babu-Levine (2021), and Jensen-Kelly-Pedersen (2021) who emphasize the role of thoughtful Bayesian shrinking of inputs (first paper shrinks active views toward CAPM-based equilibrium expected returns, second paper shrinks correlations toward zero, third paper shrinks historical average returns toward a theoretically motivated prior). Kolm-Ritter-Simonian (2021) provides an overview.

Table 12.2   Optimal Portfolios with Different Available Information

Optimal Portfolio Advice	Weighting Formula	Means	Volatilities	Correlations	Optimality Condition
Equal weighting	$w = \dfrac{1}{n}\mathbf{1}$	No	No	No	$\mu_i = \mu,\ \sigma_i = \sigma,\ \rho_{ij} = \rho$
Equal volatility scaling	$w = \dfrac{\sigma^{-1}}{\mathbf{1}'\sigma^{-1}}$	No	σ_i	No	$SR_i = SR_j,\ \rho_{ij} = \rho$
Minimum variance	$w = \dfrac{\Omega^{-1}\mathbf{1}}{\mathbf{1}'\Omega^{-1}\mathbf{1}}$	No	σ_i	ρ_{ij}	$\mu_i = \mu$
Equal risk contribution (risk parity)	$w = \dfrac{\beta^{-1}}{\mathbf{1}'\beta^{-1}}$	No	σ_i	ρ_{ij}	$SR_i = SR_j,\ \rho_{ij} = \rho$
Max Sharpe ratio	$w = \dfrac{\Omega^{-1}\mu}{\mathbf{1}'\Omega^{-1}\mu}$	μ_i	σ_i	ρ_{ij}	None
Cap weighted portfolio	$w = w_{mcap}$	No	No	No	Theory meets facts?

Source: A subset of Scherer (2015) Table 3.1. The table relates the decision maker's understanding of the world to justify his (mean variance optimal) portfolio weighting scheme. We use $\mathbf{w}$ to represent the $N \times 1$ vector of optimal portfolio weights, σ and μ to denote the $N \times 1$ vector of asset volatilities (σ_i) and mean returns (μ_i), Ω to summarize the $n \times n$ matrix of covariances, β to describe the $n \times 1$ vector of asset betas with respect to the risk parity portfolio. Further we use ρ_{ij} for the correlation between two assets (where ρ stands for constant correlation) and SR to describe a constant Sharpe-ratio across all assets.

reliably estimate them.[15] Table 12.2 (copied from Scherer (2015) with permission) illustrates the information needs of different portfolio construction approaches nested within MVO – as well as the conditions under which each would be optimal.

Instead of giving up on expected return information, one can try to make the optimization better behaved by adding constraints, shrinking inputs, or using robust optimization (a formal technique that tries to tame estimation errors in raw data).

The most common, "lazy" solution is to impose constraints, such as no shorting and no leverage (i.e. each asset's portfolio weight is constrained between 0% and 100%), and further to set targets or tight limits on asset class, country, and sector weights, as well as on portfolio volatility, beta, leverage, illiquidity, turnover, and so on.

To use an optimization approach, investors must *ask what problem they are really solving*. As discussed, the optimizer may need to incorporate important considerations beyond mean and variance, such as ESG, illiquidity, or leverage. Just as importantly, the investors must ask if the total (asset) portfolio is what they care about.

---

[15]See DeMiguel-Garlappi-Uppal (2009) and Kritzman-Page-Turkington (2010) on the 1/N debate. There is surprising robustness in equally weighting assets (or among predictors in a multiple regression forecasting model) if a limited sample size demands too much of the estimation. On the other hand, an equally-weighted (1/N) approach makes the binary "in or out" decision for assets' inclusion all-important, and even modest information on expected returns or correlations may be enough to justify going beyond equal weights.

- Perhaps the optimization problem is narrower (active risk budgeting or benchmark-relative optimization uses MVO on the active risk/return trade-off across strategies) or broader (surplus optimization uses MVO on the asset-liability surplus risk/return trade-off).
- One branch of literature considers the merits and pitfalls of two-stage optimization in delegated or decentralized asset management (see Sharpe (1981), Blake et al. (2013)). The asset owner makes asset class allocations and then gives mandates to active managers within each asset class (or within an even more granular regional or style box). The resulting portfolios may well be suboptimal from a total portfolio perspective. Yet the two-stage approach is very common because it simplifies the investment process and communication.[16]
- A similar question arises with asset-liability management. A pension plan in surplus can separate its asset portfolio into two parts, a liability-matching (or "safe") portfolio and a return-seeking (or "growth") portfolio. Again there is potential suboptimality (if the correlation between the return-seeking portfolio and liabilities is ignored), but the simplicity and communication benefits of the two-part approach may overweigh this.
- In reality, many institutions care about total portfolio risk as well as risk against their liabilities, their peers, and their benchmark.

Instead of using formal optimizers, investors may informally compare different portfolios and make heuristic choices between them. For example, we may consider the performance impact of shifting from 60/40 portfolios to a number of potential alternatives.

Staying with heuristics, I conclude by reviewing some core ideas for portfolio construction. Recall the fundamental law of active management: *Investment success is driven by forecasting skill, breadth, and implementation efficiency.* These insights are based on constrained MVO, so they are relevant for any kind of portfolio construction challenge – whether MVO is applied formally or informally, whether strategically or tactically, and whether for asset allocation, security selection, or active risk budgeting.

- While traditional active managers try to exhibit skill by case-by-case view-taking, active factor investors do this by identifying systematically rewarded risk premia.
- Breadth is especially important for factor investors: Multi-factor harvesters try to diversify across many rewarded premia, while diversifying (or hedging) away uncompensated risks.
- Implementation efficiency matters for every investor. Common constraints prevent bold diversification and leverage, while trading costs can preclude promising strategies with high turnover.

I am not sure which is worse, naïve use or no use of optimizers. Their thoughtful use can be a major help. This chapter only scratches the surface. Grinold-Kahn (1999, 2020) and Scherer (2015) give a deeper treatment on portfolio construction.[17]

---

[16]To the extent active risk is much smaller than asset class risk, any suboptimality should be modest. Moreover, if the asset owner can track the holdings of main risk exposure of its active managers, it can in principle manage the total portfolio risk. One key benefit of benchmarks is the clear accountability. The benchmark portfolio is both an ex-ante compass for the manager (a viewless neutral portfolio which presumably reflects the asset owner's strategic risk preferences) and an ex-post yardstick (since the manager's performance is evaluated against the benchmark). In practice, strict benchmarks and limited performance incentives may lead to benchmark hugging, but the absence of benchmarks all too often results in misunderstandings and miscommunication (e.g. unreasonable performance expectations that inevitably lead to disappointments).

[17]For other good practitioner-oriented books on aspects of portfolio construction, see Litterman (2003), Qian-Hua-Sorensen (2007), Lussier (2013), Roncalli (2013), Ang (2014), Faber (2015), and Kinlaw-Kritzman-Turkington (2017).

Chapter 13

Risk Management

- Risk is ultimately more about survival than volatility.
- Diversification, hedging, insurance, and dynamic risk control are the main techniques to manage investment risk.
- Risk management should focus on portfolio risk, which for most investors is dominated by equity market direction. Equity tail hedges, such as index puts and trend following, are potentially useful risk mitigators *if* their cost is not excessive.
- Volatility is often criticized as a risk measure, but it is a good starting point for most portfolios. However, it needs to be supplemented by other measures that capture tail risks, illiquidity, leverage, operational, and ESG risks.

R isk is a big word, with many definitions. Risk is the possibility of loss (or harm, or injury, or something bad happening). Risk is about failing to achieve your mission. Risk means that more things can happen than will happen.[1] Risk is a deviation from an expected outcome.

A statistical definition like standard deviation is unsatisfying to many, either because it is abstract or because it includes upside risks.[2]

---

[1] This Elroy Dimson quote highlights the unknowability of the future as a key feature of risk.
[2] Some like to say that risk can be an opportunity, while others only want to consider loss potential. This can be a matter of semantics since if the distribution of outcomes is roughly symmetric, downside risk is proportional to volatility.

13.1. Broad Lens and Big Risks

Risk can be found in the small and large. I will focus on the large because the big risks matter the most for financial "survival," and bearing them is more likely to be rewarded.

I remind readers that any investment's risk should not be mainly viewed standalone ("narrow framing" or "line-item thinking") but by its impact on the investor portfolio. Since equities are the most volatile major asset class and a large part in many investor portfolios, equity-directional risk tends to be the dominant portfolio risk. Correlation, covariance, or beta versus the equity market matters more for an asset's contribution to portfolio risk than its asset-specific volatility.

This broad lens on a financial portfolio could be applied even more generally to total wealth. Your ability to take financial risk is greater if you have large housing wealth, or abundant human capital, or rich relatives, or a generous social safety net to draw on if needed.

The broad lens also applies to risk taking over time. Some critics say that while diversification works cross-sectionally in that a single asset losing all its value has limited impact for a diversified portfolio, diversification does not work over time because losing everything in one period implies losing everything forever. Well, this is true *if* there are no other sources of income. The previous paragraph identifies many safety valves that may help if risk taking ends up badly. Some countries like the US are famously supportive of entrepreneurial risk taking and tolerant of business failure.

The broad lens should also be applied to the borrowing/leveraging aspect of risk taking. Unlimited liabilities (selling short a stock, selling naked calls) are particularly dangerous because they can bankrupt you beyond a particular investment or even beyond your financial wealth. Using leverage through buying options, or investing through limited-liability entities like common stocks or investment funds, is safer than direct borrowing for a risky investment (levered or not) whose value may fall and where you are personally liable beyond the secured assets' value.

So *survival* comes first; you must be around to fight another day. What then are the big, existential risks which threaten survival (of your wealth, if not life)? I already highlighted equity market directional risks, and I will soon list the 1930s Great Depression, the 1970s Great Inflation, and the 2008–9 Global Financial Crisis as the three worst equity market drawdowns and the most memorable financial events of the past century for the Western economies. More modest 10–20% bear markets can be considered "dodged bullets" where central banks may have saved the market from deeper declines. Fast "V-shaped" recessions or bear markets may have been only a scare with no real wealth implications if investors managed to stick with their risky portfolios. The few big and protracted drawdowns were more serious (Japan since 1990 is the poster boy). Taking an even broader view, I alluded in Chapter 8 to Bill Bernstein's four horsemen of financial disaster which have in history served as efficient wealth destroyers: Inflation, Deflation, Confiscation, and Devastation. Spelling them out: severe hyperinflations (poster boy: Weimar Germany 1923); severe economic depressions with deflation (US 1930s); communist revolutions (Russia 1917, China 1949); and major wars (World Wars I and II for the main combatant countries).

When we think about existential risks, the link to equity markets may be tenuous. Certain events that have a huge impact on human lives and on the broad economy can have limited impact on equity markets. Recall the conundrum of strong equities amid lockdowns and high unemployment in mid-2020, or how US equities fared well during the two world wars (perhaps because they were fought overseas). Some other existential threats – of climate change, bioterrorism, pandemics, nuclear war[3] – before Covid-19 only had a limited impact on financial markets.

---

[3] An old story about existential risks tells how a novice investor asked an older colleague during the 1962 Cuban crisis (when a nuclear war within days was a real possibility) whether they should buy or sell stocks. The experienced investor answered: "Buy, of course. If the war doesn't come, it's the right call. If it comes, well, who cares about our investments?"

One underrated aspect of risk, apart from the depth of losses, is the *risk of failing fast versus failing slow*.[4] The risk of failing fast is more visible and thus often the focus of regulators, sometimes increasing the risk of failing slowly. For example, they may limit institutional risk taking in a low return world, thereby virtually ensuring that institutions will fail to reach their long-term goals (while maybe protecting them against even worse failures).

13.2. Techniques for Managing Investment Risk

Risk management is not the same as risk minimization. Given any risk/return trade-off, risks need to be embraced at least to some extent. Yet, investors should try to measure and manage the key risks they face, and especially aspire to protect against risks that threaten survival or an organization's ability to achieve its key long-run goals.

The classic techniques for managing investment risk are diversification, hedging, and insurance. All these techniques transfer risks between investors. They may also reduce net risks for both sides and improve the system's risk-taking capacity if risk transfers result in a better balance among final asset holders. That said, there exists a certain amount of fundamental risk – e.g. on equity market direction related to economic growth and business cycle prospects – which someone always has to bear. Beyond that unavoidable net risk, a large part of trading activity and diverging investor portfolios seems to reflect different views among (overconfident) investors who are each deliberately seeking risk exposures to match their views.

Diversification is used to reduce or even eliminate some risks by spreading allocations into multiple assets (e.g. through position limits), while retaining some rewarded systematic exposures. Hedging tries to eliminate some risks by taking an offsetting position to assets investor holds (e.g. asset-liability matching, beta hedging, currency hedging), often with derivatives like futures or swaps, thereby perhaps also offsetting a positive long-run premium. Roughly speaking, diversifying involves correlation less than one, while hedging involves negative correlation to existing holdings.

Insurance typically requires paying an upfront cost to limit a specific downside risk. Insuring is an example of making the shape of probability distribution of outcomes asymmetric (or reshaping the payoff profile as a function of the market level), whereas hedging and diversification mainly aspire to narrow the distribution. Option markets provide many ways to reshape the probability distribution (and the payoff profile). Risk-mitigating strategies that focus on tail outcomes have the same goal, whether implemented directly through options or indirectly through other strategies which tend to perform well amid equity market declines.[5]

Diversification, hedging, and insurance are forward-looking risk management strategies which may be complemented by more reactive *dynamic risk control strategies*, such as stop-loss rules, drawdown control rules, and portfolio insurance strategies. All of these react to portfolio losses by selling risky assets. The main goal is survival, to keep losses tolerable, to be able to fight another day. It is merely icing on the cake if these strategies also enhance medium-term returns. This might happen if their extrapolative flavor (sell into weakness) benefits from persistent market

---

[4]Corey Hoffstein and Aaron Brown have emphasized this in their blogs.

[5]If terms like "tail hedging" (or, equivalently, "tail insurance" or "tail protection") are not qualified, they often refer to equity market tail events because most investor portfolios are dominated by equity-directional risk. To be clear, one can also study each asset's own tail events (or the skewness and kurtosis of its return distribution) or explore other kinds of tail risks, such as those related to extreme inflation outcomes.

trends, as happened in 2008–9. More generally, some pre-planned course of action helps when the truly unexpected happens. A plan beats no plan, even if it isn't binding.

Since this book emphasizes the benefits of diversifying return sources, such as ARP, which require meaningful use of leverage to really matter, I must comment more on *leverage risk management*. Excessive risk taking by certain investors and some infamous deleveraging episodes (fire sales during the August 1998 Russia/LTCM event, August 2007 quant crisis, and September 2008 Lehman bankruptcy) have given leverage a bad name. Yet, leverage also has the potential to improve risk diversification and boost returns. It involves serious risks but these risks can and must be carefully managed. It is safer to lever up low-risk assets or to offset diversification gains than to scale up concentrated positions in already-risky assets. It is safer to use futures than short-term borrowing. It is safer to lever liquid assets because the combination of leverage and illiquidity can be especially toxic. Lastly, to prevent full loss of capital, leverage may be supplemented with option protection or dynamic risk control rules.

13.3. Managing Tail Risks: Contrasting Put and Trend Strategies

In a world with many long-run rewarded factors and even more potential risk sources, investors should start with diversification, followed by the costlier hedging and insurance approaches. So, first diversify across the well-rewarded factors and try to diversify away the unrewarded risk. If you then estimate that a certain risk (often equity market direction) dominates your portfolio or that some other risks threaten your financial survival *and* that these risks could be managed through hedging or insurance, then pay up, or explore dynamic risk control strategies.[6]

Scenario analyses may help but not much without probabilities. The problem is that there are always worst-case scenarios where you lose everything.[7] Some such scenarios are predictable or imaginable from studying history, while others may go beyond our history and imagination. It is also important not to take the one experienced history for granted but to consider alternative paths. Ultimately we must take some risks, and the best we can do is to estimate which plausible outcomes are existential threats or severe enough that we want to mitigate them through some mixture of diversifying, hedging, insurance, and dynamic risk control.

Nassim Taleb has discussed these topics extensively[8] and often insightfully. I have learned much from his writing but also disagree on some matters, notably on the long-run cost of option-based tail hedging. We debated publicly in an exchange of letters in the *Financial Analysts Journal* in 2013. I argued that both economic logic and empirical evidence strongly suggest that

---

[6]Diversification and survival intersect in the idea that we should fail often, in a survivable way, and learn from such failures. However, any learning needs to be balanced with maintaining convictions. How much patience we give to underperforming strategies is among the hardest real-world decisions.

[7]Moreover, losing all your wealth is hardly the worst case: You can also lose your life, and not alone but with your family and your planet, and you may have made a different wager than Pascal about afterlife and find out you will face an eternity in hell.

[8]See Taleb (2001, 2020). Brown (2011) covers similar broad issues but, unlike Taleb, tries to integrate his analysis with standard statistics and risk management methods. Bhansali (2014) provides a great overview on tail risk hedging, including various ways put buying strategies may be enhanced.

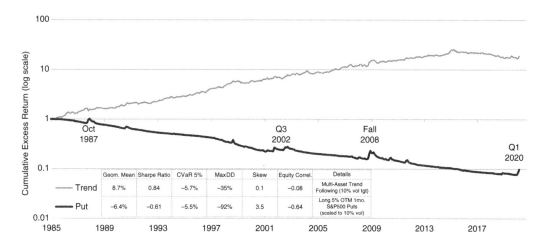

Figure 13.1 S&P500 Index Puts vs. Trend Cumulative Performance, Jan 1985–Mar 2020
Source: Data from AQR. The hypothetical Put strategy is a backtest which involves buying a 5% out-of-the-money one-month put on the S&P500 index (pre-1996 on the S&P100) at mid-month and rebalancing into a new put at expiry. Put returns are expressed as a percentage of the underlying index NAV, gross of trading costs and fees. For comparability, the series is scaled to 10% volatility based on the 6% volatility of the unlevered return over the full sample, implying a leverage of 1.67. The hypothetical Trend return is a backtest, gross of fees, net of estimated transaction costs. The strategy applies trend following at 1-, 3- and 12-month windows in four asset classes and targets overall portfolio volatility of 10%. Both Put and Trend returns are in excess of cash.

index put buying (or option-based tail insurance) has low or even negative expected returns in the long run, precisely because the insurance strategy provides valuable gains in bad times, when most needed. Taleb argued that we do not have nearly enough empirical evidence to study the expected return of an asymmetric strategy with rare winning outcomes.[9]

Besides the empirical debate, we also argued about the economic rationale. Against my point that investors should pay a premium for the valuable service of financial catastrophe insurance, Taleb suggested that put buying strategies may offer positive long-run returns because investors tend to underweight rare events (opposite to the prospect theory claim that investors overweight rare events). Taleb also saw investor aversion to long-run bleeding as a reason for keeping puts cheap. I agree that long bleeding periods – such as the 2010s when tail insurance strategies may have lost more than 90% of capital allocated to them – challenge investor patience. Yet, the empirical market pricing and long-term returns suggest to me that puts are expensive, not cheap, and this is best understood on insurance grounds.

My favorite empirical chart on this topic is Figure 13.1 which contrasts the long-run performance of representative "Put" and "Trend" strategies. A truck could drive between these two lines. The data start in the mid-1980s with the inception of index option markets, which

---

[9]I cannot do justice here to either side´s arguments. See Ilmanen (2012, 2013) and Taleb (2013) and judge for yourself. Not surprisingly, and with an obvious bias, I think I won the debate on merits. There was a postscript to this debate in 2020 in a twitter exchange between Taleb and Cliff Asness. Twitter is not my debating ground, but I later followed up in Ilmanen-Thapar-Tummala-Villalon (2021).

might not give enough data for statistical judgments,[10] but the picture is visually compelling. The Put strategy involves buying 5% out-of-the-money (OTM) index puts each month (as this specification allowed me to include the 1987 Crash). Ilmanen et al. (2021b) shows that also other regular put buying strategies, using 10–20% OTM puts and longer maturities than one month, share the broad pattern of negative long-run returns caused by persistent bleeding, interspersed by well-timed sharp gains.

While the Put strategy has lost money on a standalone basis, the multi-asset Trend strategy has been profitable (though less so in the 2010s). Trend has also performed surprisingly well in equity tail events. The best explanation is that these tail events have tended to be protracted affairs, which has given trend-followers time to turn from "risk-on" positions to "risk-off" and then ride much of the bear market. This logic also suggests that Trend's vulnerability is in sudden, gapping market falls. In general, Trend is better suited to slow long bear markets and Put to fast short ones.[11] Even if the long-run return advantage of Trend over Put has narrowed, it seems easier for investors to stick with a Trend strategy for which a bad decade has been flat, instead of Put for which a bad decade may involve major losses.

Any strategy should of course be evaluated in a portfolio context, and the Put strategy could be an exceptional complement to long equity portfolios, even with moderate negative standalone returns. If the inclusion of Put enables investors to take more risk (say, 70/30 instead of 60/40), the long-run cost may be offset. Yet, few investors will patiently take such an integrated view if Put standalone keeps losing money. More generally, I fear that few investors can hold on to *either* regular volatility buying or regular volatility selling strategies (or their close relatives). In the former case, most investors leave after some years of gradual bleeding, while in the latter case, investors capitulate after a blow-out. For either approach to have a sustainable role, it can only be a small part of a broad portfolio.

While my public debate with Taleb focused on the high cost of put-based insurance against large equity market drawdowns, his writing on major tail events is important. I agree that survival is crucial, and we should construct portfolios that are resilient in the most plausible bad scenarios (even if we cannot cover everything under the sun, including survival). Yet, when Taleb goes

---

[10]In any case, according to Taleb (2020), any standard or even modified statistical inference is misleading and useless for fat-tailed series. I will not debate that matter but just note that the strawman of normally distributed returns is not relevant when we study the return history of an option strategy. Option prices clearly discount non-normalities. Option market participants know that market returns are fat-tailed (implied Black-Scholes volatilities exceed realized volatilities most of the time), and either investors´ crash expectations or asymmetric preferences cause a pronounced skew or smirk where implied volatilities are especially high for deep-OTM index puts. Both patterns in option prices are prima facie evidence of index puts being expensive. The profitability over a given sample period depends not on the mere presence of non-normality but on whether the realized market returns were *even more non-normal* (fat-tailed or skewed) than index option prices discounted. Over the past 35 years, the clear answer is no; options markets had on average discounted even more extreme outcomes than what occurred. A remaining question is whether this too-short history is an unrepresentatively benign sample period, which would show tail insurance in unfavorable light. However, given the many financial crises and two 50% bear markets, I would argue that this was not a particularly uneventful or benign period. See Ilmanen et al. (2021b).

[11]For more on whether fast or slow market falls matter more, and which investments suit to each, see McQuinn-Thapar-Villalon (2021) and Ilmanen et al. (2021b). Separately, I acknowledge the "too good to be true" aspect of Trend strategy's positive SR and good tail-hedging abilities. The history is what it is, with hindsight a too-good deal. For the future, it seems fair to expect something less compelling – a more modest SR and less reliable tail hedging services – which is indeed what we have seen after the 2008–9 period when Trend excelled. Still, Trend looks like one of the more interesting complements to investors with equity-concentrated portfolios.

Table 13.1 Risk-Mitigating Strategies' Performance in the 18 Largest Drawdowns of the US Equity Market (S&P500 excess return over cash) over a Century

Peak	Trough	Length P-T	Depth P-T	Index Put	Trend	Treasury	Gold	QMJ US SS
Mar-1920	Aug-1921	17 (mo.)	-26%		10%	-4%		
Aug-1929	Jun-1932	34	-84%		54%	-1%		
Jan-1937	Mar-1938	13	-50%		-8%	6%		
May-1946	Nov-1946	6	-22%		4%	-1%		
Jul-1956	Dec-1957	17	-18%		-1%	-1%		1%
Nov-1961	Jun-1962	7	-23%		0%	0%		0%
Jan-1966	Sep-1966	8	-18%		6%	-2%		2%
Nov-1968	Jun-1970	19	-37%		37%	-13%		34%
Dec-1972	Sep-1974	21	-50%		123%	-11%	129%	5%
Nov-1980	Jul-1982	20	-35%		18%	-6%	-59%	13%
Jun-1983	Jul-1984	12	-15%		2%	-6%	-28%	17%
Aug-1987	Nov-1987	3	-31%	23%	-6%	0%	7%	4%
Aug-1989	Oct-1990	14	-18%	-6%	11%	-1%	-4%	29%
Apr-1998	Aug-1998	4	-15%	11%	13%	4%	-12%	12%
Mar-2000	Sep-2002	30	-49%	11%	52%	23%	5%	96%
Oct-2007	Feb-2009	16	-52%	31%	15%	14%	14%	53%
Apr-2011	Sep-2011	5	-16%	9%	-8%	10%	4%	20%
Dec-2019	Mar-2020	3	-20%	27%	-2%	10%	4%	4%

Source: Data from AQR. Notes: Index Put and Trend strategies were described after Figure 13.1. The 10-year Treasury, Gold, and QMJ (quality-minus-junk) strategies were described in Chapters 4.3, 4.5, and 6.4, respectively. The list of drawdown episodes for the S&P500 index (excess return over cash) includes a few cases where equity markets had not yet quite reached the past peak but had recovered most of the way before losing half of their value (1937–38, 1972–74, 2007–9 bear markets are such famous second legs). Figure 8.1 graphs the history of these drawdowns.

beyond creating resilience to creating "antifragile" portfolios which not only survive but flourish in bad times, it seems to me overly ambitious and an unnecessary luxury. Surviving such times is enough. Understanding that insurance is costly for important tail events reinforces my view.

Finally, it's hard to identify which of the many possible rare events we should insure against. We must pick our battles, and still acknowledge we may get them wrong. We may roll short-dated deep-OTM index puts to insure against sharp fast equity market falls – and then see the market lose half of its value but so slowly that the put strikes are rarely hit, implying unreliable protection (as happened in 2000–3). We may focus on insuring against the climate risk – and get hit by a pandemic. We may prepare our portfolio for inflation tail risk after the 2008–9 GFC – and look like a sucker when inflation does not materialize. With rare events, even more than with standard risks, luck matters more than skill. And given the rarity, hindsight will be even more powerful than with more typical events, whether you bought "unnecessary" insurance (and get criticized for being wasteful) or you left yourself uninsured before a terrible accident.

I will not go into topics like climate change or pandemics but stay a little longer on major equity market tail events. Table 13.1 documents pretty appealing performance by five candidate tail hedges (or "risk-mitigating strategies") during the 18 largest equity market drawdowns over a century. Put, Trend, and quality-minus-junk long/short stock strategy had the most consistent performance, faring even better than Treasuries or gold. But all of these candidates can be very valuable tail hedges – Put just happens to be by far the costliest when it comes to long-run returns.

13.4. Managing Market Risks: Portfolio Volatility and Beyond

Traditional analysis of investment risks focuses on portfolio volatility and its drivers. (Recall: Portfolio volatility depends less on the constituents' standalone risks and more on correlations between them.) Sometimes this perspective is translated to the more intuitive value-at-risk language. Volatilities are quite abstract, whereas "the dollar amount we could lose" (maximum likely loss, over a given horizon, at a given probability) hits home.[12]

I discussed earlier portfolio risk in the context of mean-variance optimization. In some cases, the explicit goal is to minimize portfolio risk, but more often risk limits serve as constraints to a return-maximizing goal. Table 12.2 nests minimum variance, risk parity, and other approaches within the mean-variance optimization. Many approaches, including risk parity, rely on the principle of diversification and our ability to more reliably estimate risk than expected return (which is more plagued by estimation errors). Other risks, say related to illiquidity or leverage, can be incorporated through constraints or by broadening preferences beyond mean and variance.

A risk framework which presumes normally distributed returns has well-known pitfalls, but I argue that we get surprisingly far with it. This framework can be a good starting point as long as those pitfalls are recognized and the simple single risk measures (portfolio volatility, equity beta on the market, bond duration, etc.) are complemented with further risk analyses. These include, among others, maximum drawdown and other downside risk measures, performance in equity tail events, and liquidity estimates.

Volatility has a bad name, and yet many other standalone risk metrics tend to be roughly proportional to volatility. If you worry about losses more than gains, volatility can map well to downside risk measures like value-at-risk or expected shortfall (also called cVaR), as long as the presumption of normally distributed returns is not too badly violated. The best-known violation is fat tails. If all investments have comparably fat tails, then we underestimate portfolio risk but we can still measure *relative* risks across assets quite well. (And it is quite hard to reliably estimate which assets have fatter tails than others.) Another key violation is asymmetry. For most traditional assets (not options!), return distributions are reasonably symmetric. Thus, the assumption of normally distributed returns is not a terrible approximation of reality, and it gets better when we move from single assets to diversified portfolios and from daily returns to monthly or quarterly returns.

Some argue that investors should not care about short-term volatility but about long-term loss potential.[13] We can counter that volatility also scales well over time – scaling by the square root of time – if returns are not serially correlated. That is, an asset with 1% monthly volatility has roughly 3.46% ($\sqrt{12}$) annual volatility. Momentum or mean-reversion tendencies in returns augment or reduce realized volatilities at longer horizons compared to the square-root rule. This

---

[12]Assuming normally distributed returns, there is a simple mapping between volatility and value-at-risk estimates of risk. Even when we use historical experience or Monte Carlo simulations for value-at-risk, the approximate mapping tends to work well for most investments.

[13]An extreme version of the last argument is purist value investors' refrain that patient investors should only care about permanent loss of capital. This often goes with the *margin of safety* argument: A cheap investment is not risky, only realized losses count, mark-to-market losses can be ignored. Even if it contains a sliver of truth, this argument has so many holes (cf. Asness (2014a)). Long-term loss potential is related to volatility. The notion that your valuation-based view must turn out right reeks of overconfidence. Cheap things can get cheaper, and you or your capital source may not be as patient as you wish. Everyone has a breaking point and investment horizons shorten when investors face tough times. You may ignore mark-to-market volatility, but your overseers or capital allocators may not. It is better to count any margin of safety (value cushion) as a source of expected return, not as risk mitigation.

issue matters most for illiquid assets where artificially smooth quarterly returns understate true risk, and annual returns tend to provide more realistic risk estimates, albeit at the cost of having fewer observations.

This book unfortunately gives short shrift to statistical risk models and methods of estimating risk. Typically risk estimates are backward-looking, based on historical volatilities and correlations.[14] Risks are more predictable than returns, partly due to volatility clustering. Whether to use simple rolling risks or exponentially weighted measures or any of the numerous GARCH models, and how to weigh recent versus more distant data, are issues beyond this book. Bollerslev et al. (2018) highlight the benefits of high-frequency data (giving rise to more accurate, more timely, and smoother risk estimates). Page (2021) documents the greater persistence of volatilities and correlations than returns or higher moments, as well as the better performance of daily returns than weekly or monthly returns and of short data windows than long data windows even when risk is forecasted over a relatively long horizon.

Beyond volatility: I may invite too-easy criticism by touting how far we get with a simple portfolio volatility measure, at least with traditional liquid assets. Yes, there are pitfalls, and this starting point for risk analysis needs to be complemented with analysis of tail risks, multi-factor exposures, leverage and liquidity exposures. As a final line of defense, dynamic risk control strategies (stop-loss rules or drawdown control rules which reduce positions after losses) can be used to prevent large losses from turning into existential losses.

Let's discuss some of these extensions:

- I already covered equity market tail risks. There are also other tail risks that could matter – say, an environmental catastrophe or a sharp rise in inflation – but unless they damage equity markets, their investment impact may be limited. Higher moment risks (skewness, kurtosis) are likewise less important to investors unless they are empirically related to equity market direction and financial crises.

- Many asset pricing and risk models extend the CAPM's one-factor world into various multi-factor models. The list of other factors includes interest rate risk, liquidity risk, volatility risk, or more recently, ESG-related risk, value style risk, crowding risk, and so on. There is little agreement on which of these other risk factors matter most.

- Investor preferences beyond disliking portfolio variance include pronounced aversion to downside risk, many types of liquidity preferences and leverage aversion, as well as ESG preferences. These preferences can be expressed by restricting the acceptable investment universe (full exclusion of non-listed equities, any use of direct leverage, certain sinful industries) or by capping the acceptable share in the portfolio. In some cases, the measures are not binary but continuous (e.g. requiring a certain average credit rating for the portfolio instead of excluding all speculative-grade bonds).

- If investors *also* care about other risks than the financial asset portfolio risk, the weight of these other perspectives is rarely spelled out. Institutions differ on how much they care about absolute asset portfolio risk relative to their active risk (versus the benchmark), surplus risk (versus liabilities), and maverick risk (versus peers). As noted, I recommend that thoughtful institutions debate in-house the question, "Which mix of these perspectives should drive our decisions?"

---

[14]Historical volatilities may be complemented with forward-looking implied volatilities from option prices or with subjective estimates around anticipated major event days (e.g. elections, referenda, big economic announcements) when we can expect a major resolution of uncertainty but also potentially dramatic market moves.

- Beyond market risks, there are important operational risks to consider, including the "bad apple" human risks (Madoff, Leeson).
- Then there is the contrast between measurable risk and unmeasurable "Knightian" uncertainty. The best recent treatment is in Kay-King (2020) *Radical Uncertainty*.
- Most analyses focus on short-horizon risk (e.g. based on weekly or monthly returns). Many investors care more about long-horizon risk, but we inevitably have limited data on it. There is even a debate on the question of whether equity market's riskiness rises or falls with horizon. Studying US data over the past century or so, annualized volatilities are lower using multiyear horizons, reflecting slowly mean-reverting return). However, Pastor-Stambaugh (2009) argues that estimation risk on the mean equity premium rises with horizon and that this aspect makes equities riskier over longer horizons.
- One branch of literature addresses appropriate risk sizing, extended from gambling bets to investment. The so-called Kelly criterion shows, based on the probability of gains and losses, how much to bet at each round to maximize long-term capital growth. This criterion has an uncomfortably high risk of big drawdowns. The positive expected return arises from a few lucky win streaks, while unacceptable losses are too common. Thus, most investors prefer "half Kelly" sizing which implies a higher probability of winning.

The best books in this field cover risks related to both portfolio volatility and beyond; see Brown (2011, 2015), Osband (2011), Scherer (2015), Harvey-Rattray-van Hemert (2021), and Page (2021).

Box 13.1   Can Risk Management Enhance Returns? Volatility Targeting

Although the word risk has negative connotations, successful risk management can go beyond risk reduction and also enhance long-run returns. I have stressed that better risk diversification is an attractive way of improving a portfolio's risk-adjusted returns. Mitigating the worst tail events can enhance long-run compounding of wealth, especially if it enables investors to buy bargains after large market falls. And proactive volatility targeting of asset class or style exposures may improve risk-adjusted returns. I conclude this section with some words on volatility targeting (volatility-managed portfolios or constant-volatility strategies).

Volatility targeting involves keeping larger nominal position sizes when estimated volatility is low and smaller nominal position sizes when estimated volatility is high. The primary benefit of volatility targeting is to offer investors a steadier level of risk. For example, the long-run volatility of a 60/40 stock/bond portfolio is a little under 10%, but the short-term volatility spiked over 30% in 2008. Investors with tolerance for 10% portfolio volatility may take much less risk in normal times because they fear such volatility spikes, thereby forfeiting some of the long-run risk premium. While volatility targeting cannot achieve its precise target ex post, it can significantly narrow the range of realized volatility, and thus give investors comfort to use their full risk budgets. This could confer a substantial benefit over the long run.

There may be an additional advantage in volatility targeting, in that it may improve the long-run SR compared to a constant-notional strategy. Empirically, it seems to work especially for the equity market premium and for momentum and trend strategies. Volatility targeting gives more stable risk if volatility is persistent (indeed, monthly autocorrelation between one-month volatilities based on daily data is 0.6–0.7 for many assets and factors), and it improves the SR if short-term expected returns do not rise when volatility rises.[15] Return enhancement via this mechanism is best viewed as possible icing on the cake, not the key reason for volatility targeting.

---

[15]For more on volatility targeting, see Huss-Maloney (2017), Moreira-Muir (2017), Bollerslev et al. (2018), Harvey et al. (2018), Lochstoer-Muir (2020), and Bongaerts et al. (2020).

Chapter 14

ESG Investing

- The interest of asset owners, managers, and corporations in ESG themes, especially climate change, is booming.
- ESG investing involves many approaches, notably, responsible asset selection (such as screening) and responsible ownership (such as activism).
- Opinions and evidence are mixed on how ESG investing affects returns. Screens or non-financial preferences should cheapen ESG sinners and eventually raise their expected returns. During a transition phase, ESG sinners may well underperform.
- Empirically, ESG investing has reduced portfolio risk and some ESG features (mainly governance and activism) have even boosted returns.
- Lack of standardization in ESG metrics makes it harder to estimate how ESG investing affects either portfolio returns or corporate activities.

Led by climate change concerns, ESG (Environmental, Social, and Governance) has become the last decade's biggest game-changer on institutional investing practices and on corporate behavior.[1] Conservative critics have questioned whether an ESG focus is a luxury good which can only be afforded in good times, while some proponents ask whether the efforts to date are more appearances than substantive changes (greenwashing). Yet, this train has kept picking up speed. It has expanded from Europe to the US, from institutions to retail investors, from equity investing to all asset classes (debt, macro, illiquids), and the topic has even risen to central bank policy agendas.

---

[1] This chapter leans heavily on the published work of my AQR colleagues Jeff Dunn, Shaun Fitzgibbons, Chris Palazzolo, Lasse Pedersen and, especially, Lukasz Pomorski – as attested by references to this chapter.

14.1. Booming ESG

The United Nations Principles for Responsible Investment (UN PRI), developed in 2006 by a group of the world's largest institutional investors, had by 2020 been signed by over 3000 institutions, with collective assets under management exceeding $100 trn. All these assets do not focus on ESG, but by any measure the asset growth has been phenomenal. Climate change concerns have been a game-changer.

ESG investing is an umbrella term that various people may interpret very differently. Even the umbrella term is debated, as ESG is almost interchangeably called responsible or sustainable or impact investing, or corporate social responsibility. Possible approaches range from excluding sinful companies to actively engaging with the same companies to change their behavior. In most cases, investments are evaluated not just on financial considerations but also through the ESG lens. While some aspects of ESG may also enrich expected return or risk forecasts and improve a portfolio's risk/return trade-off, many ESG-sensitive investors will choose to have "more ESG" in their process than would be optimal for strictly financial reasons.

Figure 14.1 tries to clarify in a consistent framework the varied terms and approaches around ESG investing. At the top, the framework considers separately responsible asset selection and responsible ownership. This split is consistent with the first two principles of the UN PRI. Principle 1 pledges to include ESG considerations into the analysis and selection of investments, while Principle 2 commits to active ownership practices once investments are made.

Responsible asset selection traditionally focused on negative screens that remove controversial stocks or industries from the investment universe, but these may now be complemented by positive screens that favor responsible companies. Increasingly, investors also apply ESG integration – viewing ESG information as one important input in an overall evaluation of an investment.

A clear advantage of screening is that it directly excludes stocks with the worst ESG profile. A disadvantage is that it reduces the breadth of the investment universe, especially when a restriction is very broad. For example, a climate-aware investor may want to reduce the emissions footprint of its portfolio. A screen may not be a good practical solution because it is not clear how many stocks to restrict (most companies produce at least some emissions), because it would be highly concentrated, and because a screen may not guarantee that the overall portfolio emits less than the benchmark. In such a situation, tilting the portfolio or adopting a portfolio-level rather than a security-level objective may be a better idea.

Tilting can be done by changing the weight of each stock in the portfolio as a function of that stock's ESG profile, perhaps through expected return assumptions. Another possibility is tilting by imposing portfolio-level ESG constraints and thus allowing an optimizer to weigh stocks

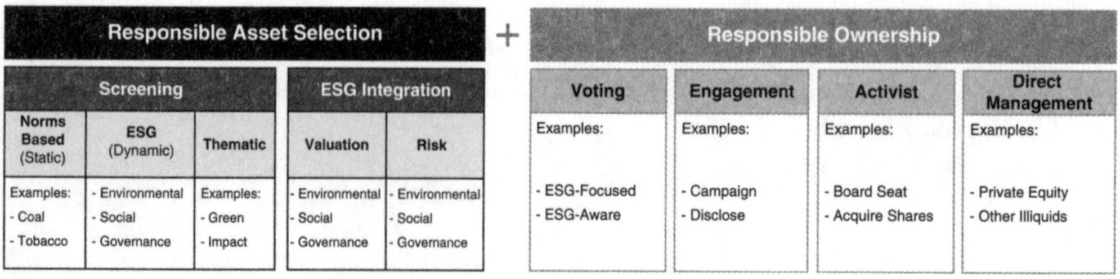

Responsible Asset Selection					+	Responsible Ownership			
Screening			ESG Integration			Voting	Engagement	Activist	Direct Management
Norms Based (Static)	ESG (Dynamic)	Thematic	Valuation	Risk		Examples:	Examples:	Examples:	Examples:
Examples:	- Environmental	Examples:	- Environmental	- Environmental		- ESG-Focused	- Campaign	- Board Seat	- Private Equity
- Coal	- Social	- Green	- Social	- Social		- ESG-Aware	- Disclose	- Acquire Shares	- Other Illiquids
- Tobacco	- Governance	- Impact	- Governance	- Governance					

Figure 14.1   Responsible, or ESG, Investing Framework
Sources: AQR, UN PRI, Dunn, Hernandez and Palazzolo (2020).

so that the overall portfolio has a higher ESG score than its benchmark. Tilting can lead to a more efficient implementation than a screen, achieving the ESG goal with less investment distortion. However, since tilting does not exclude stocks,[2] some investors may wish to combine tilting with some screening to avoid holding the very worst ESG offenders.

Responsible ownership involves expressing opinions in shareholder votes and pursuing more active methods of engagement such as acquiring a seat on the board of directors. Even passive financial investors can be active owners.

14.2. How Does ESG Affect Returns?

Does ESG investing help or hurt investment performance? This question has been debated both on logical and empirical grounds. Perhaps unsurprisingly, there is no clear answer. I first discuss the logical arguments (and will conclude "it depends"), before turning to empirical evidence (and will conclude "mixed").

The argument from ESG proponents is a wishful win-win: There is no trade-off. Many investors like the message that they can be virtuous and satisfy many constituents without sacrificing performance, maybe even boosting it. The logic is that we are in the early innings of a transition phase where pro-ESG ("green") firm stocks will keep improving growth prospects and valuations while anti-ESG ("brown") firm stocks will keep declining.[3] Investors who underestimate the bad consequences for brown companies (regulatory costs, stranded assets, etc.) and other ESG sinners are behind the curve and will get their just deserts and underperform ESG-oriented investors.

The finance textbook argument is that constraints cannot help and that adding non-financial considerations in the utility function must imply some trade-off with financially optimal holdings. If ESG is a win-win, you'd choose the same portfolio without ESG preferences.[4]

This latter perspective may admit that when investors' tastes change, there can be large inflows into ESG funds and stocks, and a related repricing. ESG assets that are increasingly shunned by investors will lose value as long as this repricing continues, but eventually they will be cheap enough to offer a "sin premium," a higher expected return on a forward-looking basis. This mechanism holds also when we think that ESG may be a proxy for material risks, for example climate risks. A similar repricing would then lower the price of riskier assets to the point where they imply a risk premium that compensates investors for holding such ESG risks. (This is of

---

[2]For example, even if a manager's expected return forecast may include ESG, other information it consists of may more than offset a stock's poor ESG profile and still produce an attractive overall evaluation.

[3]I use, for convenience, terms "green" versus "brown" firms, which are associated with climate change concerns. The arguments I make apply more generally to more versus less responsible firms, whatever ESG criteria are used.

[4]According to Asness (2017), virtuous ESG investors should recognize that to have the impact they want, they must accept lower long-run expected returns than sinful investors. The way to reduce sinful firms' activities is to raise their discount rate (this happens most obviously through the exclusions of ESG-oriented investors). The higher discount rate means that these firms will initiate fewer sinful projects, the very outcome ESG investors want to achieve. But, Cliff reminds, discount rates for a firm are expected returns for investors, and this higher discount rate will allow sinful investors without ESG preferences to earn higher long-run returns than the virtuous ESG-oriented investors by investing in the sinful companies. To be clear, both investor groups are maximizing their utilities, and the ESG-oriented investors get a reward for their virtue which compensates for their somewhat lower returns. Pastor-Stambaugh-Taylor (2020) presents a formal model with the same implications.

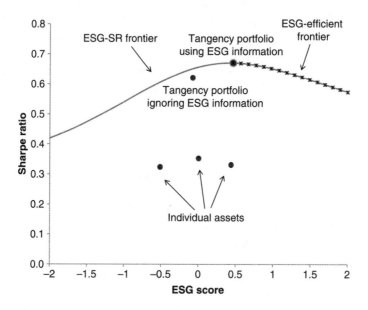

Figure 14.2   Stylized Example of an ESG–Sharpe Ratio Frontier
Source: Based on Pedersen-Fitzgibbons-Pomorski (2020), which provides further details.

course related to the discount rate effect discussed in Chapter 2 near Figure 2.1, which can make realized average returns misleading estimates of prospective returns.)

One way to reconcile these two perspectives is to see that they imply different opinions on how long the transition stage can last and whether we are today in the early or late innings. The pro-ESG camp assumes that we are still in the early innings or that the transition will end in brown firms losing all their value. The other camp assumes that we are in the later innings or at least wants to emphasize that eventually the repricing will give a long-run expected return edge to the shunned assets.

Let us now ignore the transition period and focus on the long-run case. Pedersen-Fitzgibbons-Pomorski (2020) builds a stylized ESG-Sharpe Ratio frontier which summarizes the trade-offs between ESG and performance. The frontier in Figure 14.2 shows, for each possible level of ESG score, the portfolio that maximizes the SR while at the same time satisfying that level of ESG score.

The frontier is hump-shaped. The maximum corresponds to the classic "tangency portfolio" (see Box 12.1), that is, the optimal portfolio for a mean-variance investor who is ESG-agnostic (who just accepts the ESG score of the portfolio with the highest SR).

To the left of the tangency portfolio, there is no trade-off as long as some ESG strategies enable investors to improve both the portfolio SR and ESG score. Not all ESG strategies will offer this fortuitous combination, but some may.

Investors who derive additional utility from ESG beyond mean-variance considerations will go beyond the tangency portfolio and optimally choose a portfolio to the right of it. Such portfolios, along the ESG-efficient frontier, trade off a reduction in the SR with an increase in the ESG score. Investors with ESG preferences will accept the lower SR as the price worth paying for attaining their ESG goals. For many investors who see climate change as an existential threat, the decision is easy.

So much for theory: What about empirical evidence? Can certain individual E, S or G signals or composite metrics improve long-run performance without a trade-off?

Table 14.1 Examples of ESG Themes

Environmental	Social	Governance
Climate change	Community relations	Board structure
Resource use	Employee relations	Shareowner rights
Water management	Consumer rights	Transparency
Waste management	Product safety	Accounting practices
Environmental policy	Health and safety	Executive pay

Source: Lukasz Pomorski's Yale class notes, PRI.

Table 14.1 lists some specific examples of environmental, social, and governance themes. Given the variety of themes, it is not surprising that both the proposed ESG models and the empirical verdicts on their performance are all over the place.

The literature is too broad to cover in detail, so here's an overview. Systematic investment analysis can help in quantifying the empirical relationships between ESG indicators and performance, including any trade-offs (and also help in measuring ESG indicators' ESG impact, a topic covered later).

Empirical evidence is positive on the governance signals ("G"), perhaps because they overlap with some defensive/quality factors discussed in Chapter 6.[5]

It is less clear whether environmental and social tilts have had a positive or negative return impact. There is some evidence of employee satisfaction being positively related to higher stock returns (Green et al. (2019)), but the evidence on the rewards of climate change–related or other environmental signals is at best mixed.

If only G is a win-win, it will warm few hearts, since few people feel as passionate about governance issues as about climate change or labor conditions. Someone wise said, "I rarely see demonstrators on the street waving flags on G."

Other prominent results from the literature are that (i) excluding "sin stocks" has been historically costly because tobacco, alcohol, and gambling stocks have historically outperformed (Hong-Kacperczyk (2009)) and (ii) activist investors have tended to perform well (Brav et al. (2008), Dimson-Karakis-Li (2015)). Especially the latter study suggests that influencing companies to become more ESG-oriented may have double benefits.

Investors increasingly use data from dedicated third-party providers of ESG indicators, including composite metrics. A common complaint about such data is that it is weakly correlated across providers. Composite ESG metrics have helped reduce risk but it is less clear whether they have boosted returns (Dimson-Marsh-Staunton (2020) and Dunn-Fitzgibbons-Pomorski (2018)).

A general problem is that ESG signals may not have good and consistent data coverage or clear industry standards to guide what companies report, what data is gathered, or how it is aggregated. Consequently, ESG data may suffer from a variety of weaknesses or outright biases such as short data histories, low cross-sectional coverage, stale or backfilled data, and self-reported surveys. More generally, selection biases, such as searching for positive relations, can happen also in ESG research – both for individual signals and composite metrics.

True believers may not care about such limitations or, indeed, about any historical evidence. They may have strong priors that the world is changing, historical relations can be misleading, and ESG is bound to outperform going ahead.

[5]Gompers-Ishii-Metrick (2003) documented a positive relation between their governance index and stock returns. Later studies have not found as robust result. Sloan (1996) pioneered a literature on earnings quality; high accruals predict low returns, presumably serving as a red flag on a firm's accounting practices. The broader use of quality signals and their link to ESG is discussed in Dunn-Fitzgibbons-Pomorski (2018).

14.3. ESG Impact of ESG Investing – a Case Study on Climate Change

If it is hard to quantify how ESG investing affects returns, it is even harder to estimate its ESG impact, the main goal. Some critics worry about greenwashing, that the actual impact is limited. A further concern is that the ESG metrics used are highly divergent across providers (see Dimson-Marsh-Staunton (2020) and Berg-Kölbel-Rigobon (2020)), so there is an effort to agree on a common standard of ESG metrics within the industry instead of developing novel indicators unique to the provider.

Apart from ESG metrics, there is another debate on the appropriate approach. ESG purists prefer to walk away from any ESG-sinning firms, whereas others encourage active engagement. The former approach was clearly the more popular until recently; today, ESG investors increasingly feel that screens alone cannot bring about the real-world outcomes they desire.

The common number-one concern of climate change is an excellent case study.[6] Without going into details, we can debate the metrics and approaches used. The literature focuses on carbon intensity, but purists may prefer a focus on total carbon footprint to minimize it. Either way, we can measure scope 1, 2, or 3 emissions.[7]

Once investors have a measure of carbon emissions, they can adjust their portfolio to meet their emissions goals. The most common approach involves underweighting or avoiding the "brown" (utilities, energy, or materials) industries to reduce the carbon exposure of the portfolio (or regionally avoiding emerging markets, which tend to be overweight these "brown" industries). Carbon emissions tend to be concentrated in relatively few industries and companies, so even a small adjustment can have a large impact on the portfolio's carbon exposure.

This makes it easier to build a portfolio with a desired level of emissions, but at the same time makes it difficult for the portfolio to have impact. The handful of companies that climate-aware investors tend to exclude is responsible for the bulk of emissions generated by corporations. Not holding these companies means that the investor does not have shares that give them the right to vote or make it easier to engage with the company, making it less likely that the investor can impact what the company does.

Finally, many institutions seek to make measurable impact on climate and have made aggressive (up to "net zero") carbon commitments with a certain horizon date, perhaps without considering how realistic such goals are. Just underweighting or even excluding the brown industries may not be enough because almost all companies have at least some emissions. Shortselling the worst offenders and/or trading carbon offsets and permissions may be more realistic ways to reach the most aggressive goals.[8]

---

[6]My broad book cannot do justice to this topic. I can only highlight extensive work done in the European Union, including its taxonomy of environmentally sustainable activities, and research within large institutions, such as Skancke et al. (2021).

[7]Scope 1 are emissions from company operations; Scope 2 are those from electricity, heating, steam, or cooling purchased from third-party providers; and Scope 3 are those traced back to the company's value chain (its suppliers or end-consumers). The comprehensive Scope 3 is arguably most relevant but hardest to measure (and hardest for a company to impact).

[8]See AQR Portfolio Solutions Group (2019a) and Palazzolo-Pomorski-Zhao (2021).

Chapter 15

Costs and Fees

- Cost consciousness is important but cost/fee minimization is not the goal; maximizing (risk-adjusted) net returns is.
- Trading costs have come down over time for individual investors, and new research indicates they are lower than commonly viewed also for institutions if efficient, liquidity-providing trading algorithms are used.
- Likewise, asset management fees have come down. The investor shift to passive has raised the bar among active managers. Yet investors have also raised allocations to high-fee hedge funds and illiquid asset managers.
- Fair fees between asset owners and managers recognize that bulk beta is almost free and thus belongs to asset owners, while alpha-like-returns are scarce and valuable, so asset managers have a larger claim at these.

Trading costs and asset management fees diminish investor performance. Yet, while cost consciousness is appropriate, *the goal should be to maximize net returns adjusted for risk, and not to minimize costs or fees.* For active investing, the relevant comparison is an index fund with low costs and fees. Active managers – whether public or private, systematic or discretionary – need to make a decent case for justifying and more-than-covering their higher costs and fees. Historically, this has been a tough challenge.

Growing asset owner awareness of Sharpe's (1991) arithmetic of active management as a zero-sum game before fees, and of the industry's broad track record, has led to a gradual but persistent shift from active investing to passive. Yet, the last two decades have also seen inflows into hedge funds and illiquid alternatives like private equity, with substantially higher fees. Overall, investor choices on trading activity and on active versus passive management appear more faith-based than evidence-based.

15.1. Trading Costs

For most small investors, explicit trading costs such as bid-ask spreads and commissions were traditionally a big handicap, but broker competition has brought such costs dramatically down over time. For large investors, market impact costs are the dominant part of total costs when trading stocks or other listed assets.[1]

Trading costs can be estimated for each trade and expressed as percentage of the amount traded (say, 20bps or 0.2%). However, for a given strategy it is more useful to report annual trading costs as a product of these costs per amount traded and the annual turnover rate. For example, a strategy with 200% annual turnover and 20bps average market impact (and no other costs) has a total annual cost of 40bps (0.4%).

How Trading Costs Differ Across Strategies, Assets, Investors, and over Time

Annual trading costs are higher for strategies with high turnover. For example, a momentum strategy turning fully over every quarter has higher costs than a value strategy turning over once or twice a year.[2]

The other determinant of annual trading costs – the cost per dollar traded – can vary hugely across assets, from less than one basis point to several percentage points. Liquid index futures, major currencies, and US Treasuries have lower trading costs than single stocks; small-cap stocks and emerging-market stocks have higher trading costs than US large-cap stocks; and all these costs are dwarfed by those in private assets. An investment in a private equity fund which turns over twice a decade may thus have higher annual trading costs than a large-cap momentum strategy.

Trading costs also vary a lot across investors, based on their size and execution skill. Until recently, small retail investors faced relatively high explicit trading costs, while large institutional investors faced higher market impact costs and even capacity constraints in many markets. For a given investor, costs will be higher if it trades a larger share of the daily trading volume, especially if done in a liquidity-demanding fashion. Intelligent trading algorithms often execute a given order in several smaller packages and in a patient way.[3]

Finally, trading costs for a given asset vary over time. Improving technology and liquidity has caused a downtrend in most assets' trading costs, but trading costs can spike higher during periods of heightened volatility.

---

[1] I will focus here on these costs and skip more specialized issues, such as paying for order flow, securities borrowing fees for shorts, extra costs associated with leverage, or myriad costs on private investments.

[2] Terminology gets complex with levered long/short strategies, including whether turnover is quoted as one- or two-sided and on the net asset value or the levered gross amount. These and other technical issues are beyond this book.

[3] A trading algorithm decides how patiently to trade (minutes versus days), but not what to trade. The algorithm is typically designed to trade patiently, to provide rather than demand market liquidity, by posting passive limit orders at or below the current bid price in the case of a buy, or at or above the current ask price for a sell. However, some trades may demand more immediacy (market orders) when the opportunity cost of waiting to trade is very high. Real-world algorithms are more complex and must evolve when the market infrastructure evolves. See Frazzini-Israel-Moskowitz (2018).

Naive Trading Cost Adjustments May Be Misleading

When we study the net performance of one strategy, if we naively subtract the estimated annual trading cost from the standalone gross return, the resulting net return understates the strategy's potential usefulness in at least three ways:

- Managers increasingly trade multi-factor strategies, and there will be natural netting between trades in different factors.
- Managers do not need to target the optimal portfolio in the absence of trading costs. If high turnover really hurts performance, managers can maximize net-of-costs returns by slowing down their trading. They will trade only partially *toward* the optimal portfolio.[4]
- If a factor with a very high turnover (e.g. a five-day reversal strategy) has strong gross alpha but negative net alpha, long-term investors can still use the information in this fast signal to time their trading. They do not need to overcome the cost hurdle if they use the fast signal merely to *delay* trading when the fast signal disagrees with their core slow signals.[5]

Trading Costs and Turnover Rates May Not Be Comparable Across Managers

When we compare strategies or managers, it is important to see that high trading costs or turnover are not inherently bad. If a strategy offers high gross alpha but also fast alpha decay,[6] requiring high turnover, it may still offer superior net alpha for investors with efficient execution skills. We should not accept a manager's boast of its low turnover without asking whether it is unable to benefit from some fast-alpha-decay, high-turnover strategies.

Factors vary in their alpha decay rates, thereby driving different optimal execution approaches and levels of trading costs. For example, momentum has a higher gross SR than value but a faster alpha decay, so to take advantage of the opportunity, more frequent trading is needed. Besides having a higher turnover, factors with fast alpha decay may require more aggressive trade execution, increasing their cost disadvantage to factors whose slow alpha decay affords patience in trading.

Figure 15.1 is a stylized case of how the alpha decay profile of a strategy, expected trading costs, and net alpha are related to trading frequency or intensity. A manager who just maximizes expected gross return (left side of the chart) would trade too aggressively, earning high gross returns but at high costs. Conversely, a manager who focuses on minimizing trading costs (right side of the chart) would trade too infrequently and give up some net alpha. Only by maximizing net expected returns can a manager make the appropriate trade-off between alpha decay and trading costs (the middle line).

These comparisons apply to evaluating the alpha decay speed across factors (say, fast versus slow momentum signals), the rebalancing frequency of a portfolio, or the pace of trade execution.[7] Optimal trading frequency depends on the manager's skill and size.

---

[4]Garleanu-Pedersen (2013) shows that the optimal trading strategy is to aim from the current portfolio toward a mix of the current and expected future optimal portfolios, a moving target. This is akin to skating where the puck is going, in Wayne Gretzky's language.

[5]See Israelov-Katz (2011).

[6]Alpha decay refers to the expected speed of degradation in a factor's performance over time. Say, a value opportunity today may be expected to be almost as good three months hence, whereas a momentum opportunity's expected alpha may be largely lost after a similar delay.

[7]See Hedayati-Hurst-Stamelos (2018).

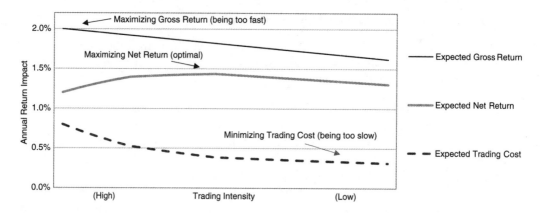

Figure 15.1   It Is not About Minimizing Cost but About Maximizing Net Return.

Empirical Estimates on Trading Costs

We have high-quality data on trading costs going back to the late 1990s. For earlier decades, any estimates are educated guesses. I focus next on one study which provides exceptional transparency on institutional equity trading costs and shows that previous estimates of trading costs had been overstated.

Frazzini-Israel-Moskowitz (2018) uses 1.7 trillion dollars of live trade execution data from a large institutional money manager (who could it be?) across 21 equity markets between 1998 and 2016. Trading costs are measured using the implementation shortfall methodology of Perold (1988). Implementation shortfall measures (i) the market impact – the difference between the market price just before the trade was initiated and the actual traded price, scaled by the amount traded – and (ii) the opportunity cost from any pre-trade moves that might occur from the time a model portfolio is generated and the time trading actually begins. Implementation shortfall thus measures the total amount of slippage a strategy might experience from its theoretical returns, including both the cost of trading and the opportunity cost of not trading. The market impact cost is empirically the largest part of the total cost of execution; the opportunity cost and any explicit costs are small in comparison.

The Frazzini et al. study provides the most comprehensive and the highest quality data on trading costs ever published. Figure 15.2 summarizes market impact costs from the full dataset.

- The mean implementation shortfall measure of all trades in all equity markets over the full sample is 11bps, of which 10bps is market impact and 1bp the difference between the intended model prices and the actual prices at the start of trading. The value-weighted mean implementation shortfall (market impact cost) is higher at 16bps (15bps), which indicates that the larger trades are more expensive, consistent with trading cost models that argue that costs increase with trade size.
- The mean market impact cost is lower for large-cap stocks at 9bps, compared to 19bps for small-cap stocks.
- Some studies compare the actual traded price not to the pre-trade price but to the volume-weighted average price (VWAP). This may make sense for small investors whose trading cannot move the markets, but it clearly understates the permanent market impact of a large manager (as a big trade pushes up both the actual traded price and the VWAP). In the

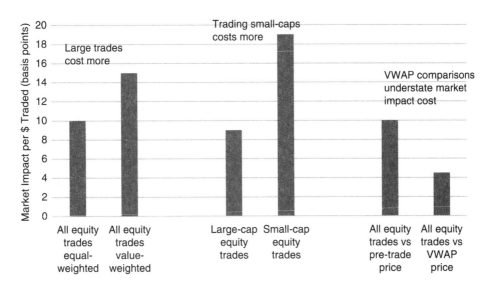

Figure 15.2 Average Market Impact Cost Estimates from Frazzini–Israel–Moskowitz (2018)
Source: Data from Frazzini-Israel-Moskowitz (2018).

Frazzini et al. study, the mean market impact measured relative to the VWAP is only 4.5bps, as the VWAP comparison misses the temporary additional price pressure the manager is exerting.

These trading cost estimates are in line with data from large brokers and a cost consultant Ancerno as well as the costs of the largest index funds. However, they are much lower than estimates found in earlier academic studies. The main reason is the shape of the price impact function with respect to trade size when modeling costs. Theories have proposed either concave or linear relationships between price impact and trade size. Academic studies often chose the linear relationship which overstates trading costs compared to the Frazzini et al. (2018) evidence of a concave relation for less liquidity-demanding traders.[8]

Lower cost estimates also matter when Frazzini, Israel, and Moskowitz (2017) study whether the factors size, value, momentum, and short-term reversal survive real-world trading costs. The results vary on the assumed fund size, but with the low estimated trading costs and the possibility to reduce turnover, the authors conclude that the main anomalies are robust, implementable, and scalable. Results vary across styles, with value and momentum being more scalable than size, and short-term reversals being the most constrained by trading costs.

---

[8]Frazzini et al. (2018) find that the most important variable determining price impact is the size of the trade – measured as the fraction of daily volume traded in a stock. Larger trades generate greater price impact, as expected, but the empirical relationship is non-linear, with price impact rising with trade size *at a decreasing rate*. The resulting trading cost estimates are substantially smaller than those in the earlier literature. Prior studies chose a linear function, perhaps because their aggregated data reflected the average trader's experience. The average trader includes informed insiders, retail traders, liquidity demanders, and otherwise impatient traders. These groups require immediacy and thus face much higher costs than patient traders. Patience requires using smaller trading sizes and efficient trading algorithms which allow trading in a liquidity-providing rather than liquidity-demanding fashion (crudely: using limit orders rather than market orders).

15.2. Asset Management Fees

Asset management fees have naturally attracted attention when many active managers' performance has disappointed asset owners, when managers have had to enhance their fee transparency, and when investors face the prospects of low future returns, gross of fees. Growing fee consciousness is mainly a good thing but can go too far. Capital owners should think about fair fees for each asset class and for the alpha/beta split. A myopic fee-minimizing goal by investors pushes them to cash and index funds, while prompting some asset managers to offer them complex structured products with hidden costs/risks or closet indexing (or, more generally, a tie-in-sale of scarce uncorrelated returns with bulk beta exposures).

Fair fees are essentially about splitting the pre-fee investment returns between the capital owner and the investment manager. At first blush, we might think that a fair split might be constant across investments. Not at all. Upon reflection, many observers would agree that passive market returns should largely belong to the capital owners, while the managers have a stronger claim on the fruits of their active investment skill.

The first hedge fund manager, A. W. Jones, argued to his investors in the 1940s that his 20% share of the upside of investment returns (apart from fixed fees) was inspired by ancient shipping practices where Phoenician merchants kept a fifth of the profits from successful voyages, leaving the rest to the capital providers. Later hedge fund managers were happy to copy this "2+20" model. When the demand for hedge funds grew in the 1990s and the 2000s, there was limited fee pressure. Only in the past decade have asset owners been able to negotiate typical hedge fund fees down to 1–1.5% fixed fee plus 10–15% performance fee. Yet the most popular hedge fund managers can still charge 2+20 or even more.

I will not focus on fixed versus performance fee for hedge funds and private asset funds but try to cover all-in fees. Mutual funds and long-only institutional funds do not charge performance fees. The classic study before the last decade, French (2008), documented that mutual fund fees and institutional fund fees edged lower between 1980 and 2006, but since investors raised the weights of high-fee hedge funds, there was no downward trend in total annual fees paid. During this period, the excess fees investors spent trying to outperform passive US indices averaged 67bp. Since 2006, the active management fees have kept edging lower, and investor allocations to passive strategies have increased – but so have allocations to costly private assets.

Virtually all fund types' fees have declined over time, a trend that is expected to continue. Here is the lay of the land from the 2010s. Expressed in typical all-in fees in recent years, most passive equity funds charge 0–30bp fees, while most active equity funds charge 30–80bp fees. Fixed income funds charge less than equity funds due to lower average returns and volatility. Typical hedge funds charge all-in 2–3% fees, while private equity funds charge all-in near 5% fees. Figure 15.3 gives one set of estimated fees among institutional investors from CEM Benchmarking surveys. The largest investors would face lower fees, retail investors clearly higher fees.

Determinants of Actual and Fair Fees

The main explanation for these fee differences is that asset owners pay very little for market exposure (institutional investors pay at most 10bp fees for equity market beta/index exposure) but much more for scarce alpha. This is as it should be. My colleagues have argued for decades

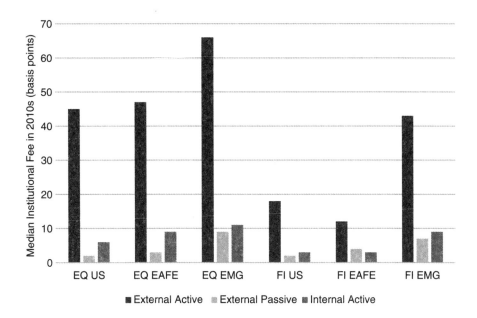

Figure 15.3 Estimates of Typical Asset Management Fees for Institutional Investors
Source: Data from Investment Cost Effectiveness Analysis (for the 10-year period ending December 31, 2019) for the
Norwegian Government Pension Fund Global by CEM Benchmarking in www.regjeringen.no.

that investors should not pay alpha fees for beta performance, and over time investors have begun
to listen.[9]

Long/short managers (hedge funds, ARP) offer other diversifying return sources than market beta; their alpha could be very valuable to asset owners. Market-neutral funds have higher
fees than long-only funds because the latter offer a blend of market risk and diversifying return
sources – and mainly the cheaply available market risk – while the former offer pure exposure
to the scarce stuff.

It is instructive to consider a long-only equity fund which combines market risk at about
15% volatility with 2% active risk from style exposures, and compare it to a market-neutral ARP
fund which uses leverage to target 10% volatility using long/short exposures to the same styles. To
simplify, the long-only fund charges a zero fee for its market beta but charges a 30bp fee for its 2%
active risk. Then a fair fee for the five times bigger active risk for the ARP fund would be 150bps.[10]

The key insight is that blending diversifying return sources with the market risk enables
managers to charge lower headline fees. Yet, these lower fees may not be fairer. Indeed, in the
above example, they offer a worse deal for the investor if a comparable ARP fund is available
at, say, 120bp fee, that is, "only" four times higher than the long-only fund fee. The same logic
applies to traditional active long-only funds, hedge funds, and PE funds, all of which blend
significant market beta with other exposures.

---

[9]See Asness-Krail-Liew (2001) and Berger-Crowell-Kabiller (2008). Also see Kahn-Scanlan-Siegel (2006) and
Siegel-Waring-Scanlan (2009) who describe the trade-off between alpha- and beta-generated return streams.
[10]Not only does the ARP fund give a purer and larger exposure to the style premia, it can also give a more efficient exposure. It does not suffer from the no-shorting constraint in the long-only fund, which meaningfully
compromises implementation efficiency.

In sum, long/short funds of a given quality should only earn "alpha" fees for their active (non-beta) risk, and then fees should be proportional to the active risk level. A manager with 10% active risk and zero beta should be broadly indifferent to halving the fixed fee it charges if it is allowed to halve the size of all its active positions (and thus have 5% volatility). This is true whether the manager replaces half of its active positions with a passive equity index or with cash.

Among long/short managers, actual fees are not directly related to volatility level or diversifying ability. Instead, hedge funds with strong performance in recent years can charge higher fees, perhaps revealing greater investor belief in multiyear performance persistence than long-run evidence warrants.

Finally, PE funds have collectively earned higher returns in recent decades, even after charging higher fees. They offer some mix of perceived manager-specific alpha, illiquidity premia, high market beta, embedded leverage, and smoothing service. High fees and ongoing inflows reveal that asset owners are willing to pay a lot for this cocktail, largely because they expect PE outperformance to persist. Whether investors expect collective outperformance due to systematic premia or are optimistic on the specific managers they select is less clear.

Evidently, the fee pressures faced by active hedge funds and mutual funds have not yet had much bite in the PE world. And yet, PE is the asset class which seems to be testing the "Asness Law." Cliff has said in some interviews that "if I could ever have a law named after me, it'd be that no investment product is so good that high enough fees cannot make it a bad investment."[11]

Overall, I conclude that differences in asset management fees reflect, first, the perceived beta versus alpha split, and second, the perceived quality of the beta-adjusted alpha returns. The observed fees across groups suggest that the perceived quality is higher for PE funds and hedge funds, so fee differentials are not only manager-specific. However, it seems that perceived manager-specific skill (often inferred from past outperformance which is expected to persist) can also justify higher fees.

Fair Split of Returns Between Asset Owners and Managers

Practitioner interviews sometimes debate what is the fair split of total gross returns between the asset (or capital) owner and the asset manager. The previous discussion reveals that there will not be a single answer. In one extreme of market beta, almost 100% of market premia should accrue to the asset owner, with small fees to the index manager. In the other extreme of pure alpha, a well-known academic model in Berk-Green (2004) argues that the skillful asset managers who provide the scarce alpha will earn 100% of it. The asset owners will compete aggressively for such managers' services and pay so high fees or offer them so large mandates as to bring asset owners' expected net alpha to zero. However, this model assumes that only the market for asset managers is perfectly competitive. If asset managers are also competing for capital from asset owners and there is broad uncertainty about managers' true skills – two abundantly realistic assumptions – the negotiating power should be more balanced, and gross returns may be split more evenly between the asset owner and the asset manager (see Garleanu-Pedersen (2018) and Chapter 7 (7.1)).

---

[11]Some large institutions have tried to reduce PE fees through coinvestments or direct investments. The evidence on improving net returns is mixed, however, as any fee savings may have been offset by "lemons risk" in coinvestments or by underperformance in direct investments by internal team (see Ivashina-Lerner (2019) and Lerner et al. (2020)). It is hard to acquire and retain best expertise in-house without ability and willingness to pay for large, highly compensated teams. Internal success is most plausible for some large Canadian pension funds willing to pay people compensation somewhat competitively with PE managers, unlike most US or European institutions.

Another situation which gives intermediate answers on the fair fee split involves the various blend products which are neither pure beta nor pure manager-specific alpha (the same applies for publicly known ARP which are not prized as highly as pure alpha). In practice, there is a continuum between the extremes. We could try to estimate fair fees based on some demystifying analysis on how much a manager's returns reflect market beta versus ARP versus pure alpha. This is a conceptually nice idea and points investors in the right direction, but there is too much noise in such estimations to narrowly pin down the fair fee level for most funds. At least remember this: Bulk beta is abundant and cheap, while perceived alpha is scarce and costly.

Box 15.1   Taxes

An old English proverb says, "There's many a slip 'twixt the cup and the lip." Taxes are among them, besides costs and fees. Following much of the literature, this book analyzes pre-tax returns, while taxable investors should of course focus on after-tax returns.

Any tax considerations vary across investor type, wealth, and location, so this book is not the right place to cover the topic. Moreover, my main audience is institutional investors like pension funds for whom tax considerations are less important than for individual investors. Here I only make a few general observations, beyond recommending everyone to consult their tax advisor.

Some assets have tax advantages, making them especially suitable for taxable investors. One example is US municipal bonds which are often exempt from federal income tax and, for local residents, also from state and local taxes.

A broad goal in tax-efficient investing is to defer taxes because tax-free compounding of investments often leads to higher final after-tax wealth.[12] The benefit is reinforced if retirees face a lower income tax rate than prime-age earners, or if long-term capital gains are taxed at a lower rate than income and short-term capital gains.

It often makes sense to prioritize contributions to retirement saving accounts which allow deductible contributions and tax-deferred growth, while matching tax-inefficient investments (which generate much taxable income) to tax-advantaged accounts.

With active investing, delaying realized capital gains and offsetting them with tax losses can help improve after-tax returns. Passive investing rarely involves selling and thus naturally defers capital gains taxes. Active strategies with high turnover are often considered problematic because they frequently realize gains. However, thoughtfully applied they also offer potential for tax loss harvesting.[13]

---

[12]Sosner-Liberman-Liu (2021) estimates the magnitude of this effect, including income and estate taxes.

[13]My colleagues have written extensively about tax-aware investing in the US which recognizes the return impact of realizing gains as tax costs and realizing losses as tax gains. For example: Sialm-Sosner (2018) highlights the benefits of short-selling in realizing well-timed capital losses (especially important for managing the higher short-term capital gains); Liberman et al. (2020) shows that separating the alpha of long/short strategies from the beta of passive indices offers tax advantages over a traditional active long-only approach; and Sosner-Gromis-Krasner (2021) studies the tax benefits of direct indexing.

Chapter 16

Tactical Timing on Medium-term Expected Returns

- Timing evidence points to humility with tactical forecasts.
- Contrarian market timing overpromises with popular visuals, while out-of-sample trading rule results underwhelm and careful statistical analyses raise questions.
- Contrarian market timing did not beat buy-and-hold equity investing in our lifetime, partly because it faced headwinds from short-term and long-term momentum.
- Combining contrarian, momentum, and other timing signals may justify humble timing endeavors ("sin a little").
- Results are comparable, not better, for timing other asset classes and long/short style premia.

The benefits of strategic diversification often trump those from tactical timing. It is worth exploring why tactical timing benefits set such a low bar. I will focus on the case of contrarian timing of US equities, but I will extend the analysis to timing bonds and long/short factors as well as to using other signals than valuations. (I describe predictive techniques briefly in Chapter 10.)

16.1. Contrarian Timing of the US Equity Market

My 2011 book *Expected Returns* emphasized humility when it comes to market timing, yet it clearly favored forward-looking (yield- or value-based) estimates of expected returns over historical average returns. Our later research has made me even more humble about contrarian market timing, as summarized in the title of our 2017 article "Market Timing: Sin a Little," co-authored with Cliff Asness and Thomas Maloney.[1] This chapter is largely based on that article, so special thanks to my coauthors.

My more cautious tone contrasts with the academic consensus shifting toward time-varying expected returns. Cochrane (2011) argued that previously academics thought returns were unpredictable, with variation in valuation ratios due to variation in expected cash flows, while now it seems all variation in valuation ratios corresponds to discount-rate variation. I wonder if the pendulum swung too far.[2]

I will focus here on the classic case of market timing the S&P500 based on the Shiller CAPE (cyclically adjusted P/E ratio), or rather its inverse: the CAEY (cyclically adjusted earnings yield). The predictive ability of this valuation indicator is typically shown with long-horizon returns, which give a visually more impressive fit than short-term returns. The better fit implies higher explanatory power (R^2) and reinforces the belief that equity markets are more predictable over long horizons than short horizons. To the extent that this statement is true, it is because it is easier to predict a meaningful fraction of smooth 10-year average returns than of jagged monthly returns. It is less clear that market timing is more effective over longer horizons.

The seductive promise of long-horizon predictability is visible in time series like Figure 16.1, in scatter plots like Figure 16.2, or in bar charts like Figure 16.3.[3] The prediction suggested being bullish near the early 1920s, the 1930s and the 1980s cheapness peaks and bearish near the rich markets of 1929 and 2000. All three visuals may make contrarian market timing look reliable, even easy. It is neither.

"In-sample" signals judge the CAEY at every point compared to the full sample of 100+ years. This implies foreknowledge that CAEYs below 4% are extremely rare, which would have been very useful information for investors in 1929 and 2000, but not truly available for them at the time. To avoid such "cheating" or "lookahead bias," we can use "out-of-sample" estimates of the CAEY compared to the history that was available at the time (here we use past 60 years).

The long-horizon return is just a chain of short-horizon returns. If you want to take a 10-year horizon, please consider how you would implement it. Would you buy once and then ignore markets until a decade has passed?[4] Or would you make the decision every month with

---

[1] Economist Paul Samuelson (1994) suggested that if you are tempted to do market timing, you can yield to the temptation, but cautiously: "sin – but only a little." We share his sentiment. Zero market timing may not be right, but overconfident aggressive market timing is almost certainly wrong. There are no old market timers in the Forbes billionaires list.

[2] Apart from our study, Boudoukh-Israel-Richardson (2019, 2020) highlights various econometric problems in long-horizon predictability regressions. Separately, De la O and Myers (2021) departs from the rational paradigm and documents that time-varying survey-based growth expectations influence time-varying equity valuations and time-varying expected returns (in line with comparable stock-specific analysis in Bordalo et al. (2019)).

[3] I focus here on the well-known CAPE as a market timing predictor. Many other predictors have been proposed and some have a better statistical fit (but all are vulnerable to the problems discussed in this chapter). Rintamäki (2021) shows that the equity share in a broader market portfolio has been empirically a better predictor of future market returns than CAPE and other candidates. Importantly (to alleviate overfitting concerns), he explains why, through a series of return decompositions and empirical tests. The equity share combines information about equity valuations with other potentially useful predictive information (the attractiveness of equities versus other markets, both through valuations and the relative size or payouts across markets). Equity share is also more robust to structural changes that affect all asset classes – for example, the general richening when required real yields have fallen in recent decades – but as a flipside it may miss the broad low expected return signal.

[4] Most investors dislike this approach, but if you do it, it is arbitrary when you start. The luck of the draw will influence outcomes quite a bit. This would be an extreme form of what Hoffstein et al. (2020) calls "rebalancing timing luck." Their method of mitigating the role of chance involves averaging across many starting dates, which is also my proposal.

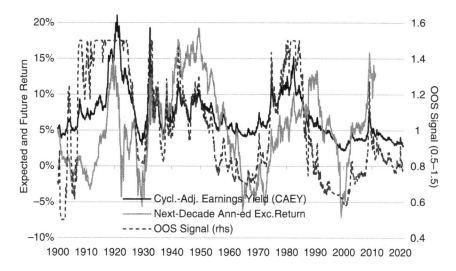

Figure 16.1   Time Series of CAEY and Next-Decade Excess Returns of US Equities, 1900–2021
Sources: AQR, Robert Shiller's website. Notes: CAEY is the cyclically adjusted earnings yield. The OOS (out-of-sample)
signal judges each month how cheap the market CAEY is compared to the previous 60 years (no lookahead bias) and gives
score 0.5–1.5 based on the current CAEY's percentile rank.

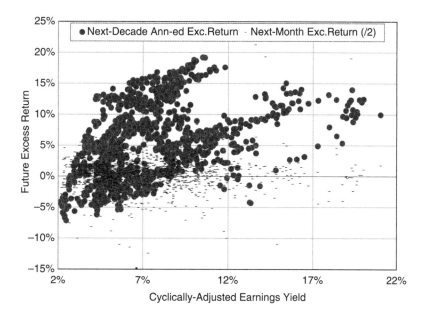

Figure 16.2   Scatter Plot of CAEY and Next-Decade (and Next-Month) Excess Returns of US
Equities, 1900–2021
Sources: AQR, Robert Shiller's website.

1/120th of your wealth? Then your total portfolio on any date would be a total of these 120 small
positions with different start months. This turns out to be equivalent to trading every month the
total portfolio by using as your value signal the average of the past decade's CAEYs. Or you can
do something in between, say, lock your money for a year at a time.

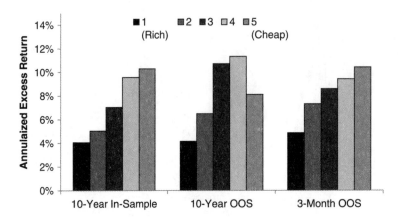

Figure 16.3 Quintile Buckets of CAEY and Future Excess Returns of US Equities, 1900–2021
Sources: AQR, Robert Shiller's website.

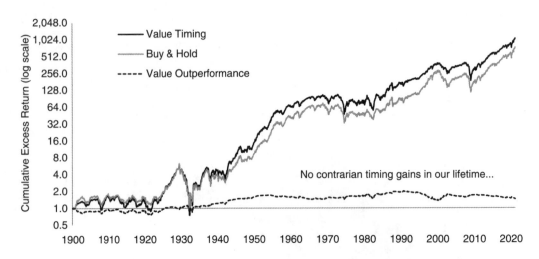

Figure 16.4 Cumulative Performance of Contrarian Market Timing Versus Buy&Hold of the
S&P500 Index, Jan 1900–Mar 2021
Sources: AQR, Robert Shiller's website.

A scatter plot in Figure 16.2 depicts a positive relation with next-decade performance (0.41 correlation in sample – and 0.30 out of sample, not shown) but a weaker relation with next-month performance (0.05 correlation).

Sorting future returns in a few buckets based on starting valuations gives the most promising picture, as it does not reveal how much variation exists within each bucket. The results in Figure 16.3 look quite compelling for in-sample evidence and surprisingly better for the OOS prediction over short than long horizons.

Now comes the bad news. When we measure the historical success of market timing strategies based on this information, the results are downright disappointing. Figure 16.4 shows the cumulative performance of a simple contrarian market timing strategy and a buy-and-hold strategy on the S&P500, as well as the relative performance between the two. Market timing did mildly beat buy-and-hold over 120 years, *but just not in our lifetime*! More recently, a mainly bearish timing signal would have left investors on the wrong side of a multi-decade bull market.

When I first saw this evidence about a decade ago, I thought there was a spreadsheet error. It took me many a sleepless night to reconcile the difference between the promising results in Figures 16.1–16.3 and the underwhelming reality in Figure 16.4.

Once we made sense of it, as explained next, I began to guiltily wonder if I had encouraged investors to sin too much by peddling promising graphs like the first three figures. Not only I, of course; this appealing long-horizon predictability evidence is widely used in academic and practitioner studies and in financial media. While my new tone is not a case of full conversion against timing, I hope that readers who have been seduced by long-horizon predictability evidence will read these pages carefully.

How can Figure 16.4 be based on the same data as the preceding graphs? For starters, there are the issues of in-sample versus out-of-sample signals and the impracticality of long-horizon trading. The trading strategy uses OOS forecasts and monthly trading (a 10-year investment would be exposed to a chain of 120 monthly returns) because they are the realistic options. But these two explanations do not explain everything, since even the OOS near-term forecasts appear good in the last bar-quintet of Figure 16.3.

So why does the contrarian timing rule have such underwhelming results?

• Contrarian signals often trigger action too early, and the old saw says: "early equals wrong." They face the headwinds from markets' tendency to trend. Indeed, performance could be improved by blindly delaying action by 6–12 months or more thoughtfully by waiting for a confirmation signal from a changing market trend. I will verify below that combining value and momentum signals is a good idea in market timing, but even the combined signal can hurt in whipsawing markets.

• Contrarian strategies also face headwinds from *long-run* trends, that is, structural changes in the market. The persistently richening market valuations between 1950 and 2000 made contrarian investors meaningfully underinvested in the equity premium. Investors expected valuation normalization, but it never came. Since the CAEY has been in the bottom quintile for much of the last quarter-century, such underinvestment has continued. Tactical signals would have to be quite good to offset the missed equity premium.

• Investors may have unrealistically high expectations on the usefulness of market timing, boosted by visuals like the figures above.[5] Ultimately the valuation signals are too coarse to help much. For example, a market timer who'd exit the equity market whenever the CAEY is in the bottom quintile would have left the market in the early 1990s and missed the nearly decade-long rally.[6] More broadly, the appealing Figure 16.3 "forgets to mention" that the timing signal was bearish almost all the time since the late 1980s. In reality, few managers could have stayed the course, and premature capitulations would have made real-world market timing results even worse than those shown in Figure 16.4.

---

[5]The illusion of hindsight makes us think too easily that we would have sold near the top and bought near the bottom at key cycles, and somehow avoided the pitfalls in structural changes. All this makes us think market timing is easier or more useful than it is.

[6]This also describes my own youthful experience in the 1990s. Having learned about the predictive ability of dividend yields from Fama-French research, I largely avoided stocks, being overconfident of the signal's market timing ability. At that time the Shiller CAPE was not yet known. In 1996, then Fed chairman Alan Greenspan was famously impressed by Shiller's presentation of CAPE valuations and warned markets about "irrational exuberance." This 1996 incident happened three and half years before the bull market ended, another case of contrarian signals being too early. The related Campbell-Shiller (1998) article came out soon afterwards. (The market dividend yield gave even more prematurely bearish timing signals. It reached historical lows already in the 1980s, partly reflecting the market richening and partly the growing use of buybacks.)

- Our 2017 article tried many of other variants of the timing model (e.g. a longer horizon or adding features like "only trade at extremes"). None made much difference to Figure 16.4; all these timing variants had long-run SRs of 0.36–0.39, compared to buy&hold SR 0.38.

Meanwhile, my more statistically oriented colleagues (Boudoukh-Israel-Richardson, 2019, 2020) have highlighted the many problems with long-horizon regressions that use persistent predictors like valuation ratios. First, long-horizon return analysis implies a small number of independent observations (e.g. ten 10-year returns over a century), and the posited remedy of shifting from non-overlapping observations to overlapping observations can only modestly increase the effective sample size. Second, typical statistical adjustments to standard errors and t-statistics, such as Newey-West (1987), underestimate the problem with overlapping observations, and thus overstate the predictability evidence. Third, extending Stambaugh (1999) analysis of small-sample biases in beta estimates of persistent (often price-scaled) predictors, reveals that the typical beta estimates in long-horizon regressions are overstated, more so with overlapping data. Overall, a careful examination of econometric challenges says that the statistical evidence on long-horizon predictability of asset returns is not very strong. This state of affairs means that priors matter a lot when judging such predictability.

Lastly, I am cautious on market timing because these strategies may tempt overfitting even more than other systematic strategies. Trading one series is poor diversification,[7] and it is easy to come up with hindsighted predictor signals that would have helped avoid a big drawdown like 2008. Perhaps related, there have been many attempts to improve CAPE's predictive ability, mainly by justifying higher equity allocations in the past two decades. It helps to use a shorter history to judge neutral value as the average CAPE has drifted up over time. Using more generous earnings than GAAP, such as Siegel's (2016) use of NIPA profits or operating earnings, also helps. In this vein, higher profit margins and increasing intangible investments may justify higher CAPE. Finally, we have the lower (real) bond yields to justify higher equity valuations.[8]

16.2. Beyond Contrarian Timing of Equities: Other Assets and Factors, Other Predictors

My caution on contrarian signals extends beyond timing the S&P500. Duration timing and long/short factor timing also prove underwhelming, largely because "early equals wrong." This problem certainly has applied to duration timing where apparently rich government bonds (based on low real yields) have become ever richer over time. When it comes to long/short style premia in stock selection, a contrarian investor would have underweighted the defensive factor in the early 2010s before its superb decade and overweighted the value factor well before its troubles in 2020.[9]

---

[7]Using only slow-moving contrarian valuations for market timing implies low breadth from three perspectives: trading one market, using one signal, and a slow one at that (without multiple independent trades every year). I like improving breadth by multiple signals (including some faster ones) and by trading multiple markets, directionally as well as cross-sectionally (global tactical asset allocation, including cross-country relative value).

[8]While this logic is fair, investors should recall that higher equity valuations imply lower expected return through carry, even if there is less pressure for valuations to mean revert. And if bond yields were to rise, the same argument implies pressure for equity valuations to fall.

[9]See Asness-Ilmanen-Maloney (2017) and Asness et al. (2017). Moreover, unpublished work shows similar results for credit-Treasury spread timing which was thought to be more amenable to timing – more cyclical without structural changes. Yet, even that strategy disappointed, due to too early bullish positioning in 2001 and 2008.

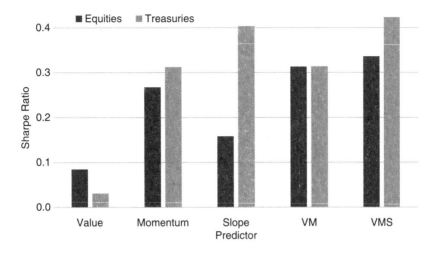

Figure 16.5   Equity and Bond Market Timing Strategy Sharpe Ratios Based on 1–3 Predictors, 1900–2021
Sources: AQR, Robert Shiller's website.

While I sound quite negative (partly to balance any too-positive impression in my earlier book), I stress that the message is not "do not sin," but "sin only a little." Tactical timing should be done with humility, not hubris, and using multiple metrics. It almost always makes sense to combine value and momentum signals (here contrarian and trend) given their complementary nature. I have discussed trend following and factor momentum earlier. Besides value and momentum signals, yield curve steepness tends to be a helpful predictor both for stocks and bonds, while the literature suggests credit growth and the variance risk premium are among other interesting candidates.[10] Since specifications matter and some fitting is allowed, it might not be hard to come up with pretty evidence!

Other timing signals tend to be more useful for predicting returns over multi-month horizons than 5- to 10-year horizons typical for capital market assumptions. For the latter, yield-based forecasts are the most useful inputs, despite all the above cautions.

For short-horizon equity and Treasury market timing, value, momentum, and yield curve steepness (slope) have all helped, and combinations have outperformed single-predictor models. Figure 16.5 shows SRs for many strategies using OOS signals – all are positive, but even the best are no higher than 0.3–0.4.

Timing analyses in other asset classes or long/short style premia have not provided more supportive evidence. Factor investing research and applications have evolved from a focus on a single factor (consistent with long-run factor premia) to strategic multi-factor diversification (consistent with diversification benefits) and more recently to explorations of tactical factor timing (consistent with time-varying factor premia). Ilmanen et al. (2021a) documents only moderately positive SRs over nearly a century when timing value, momentum, carry and defensive styles with the help of valuation ratios, factor momentum, and other predictors. Our century of

---

[10]See AQR Portfolio Solutions Group (2019b) on yield curve as a return (and recession) predictor and Greenwood et al. (2020) on credit growth as a predictor. Welch-Goyal (2008) shows that the out-of-sample predictive ability of various equity market timing indicators is pitiful, while Campbell-Thompson (2008) counters that priors-motivated constraints on coefficients improve the prediction results.

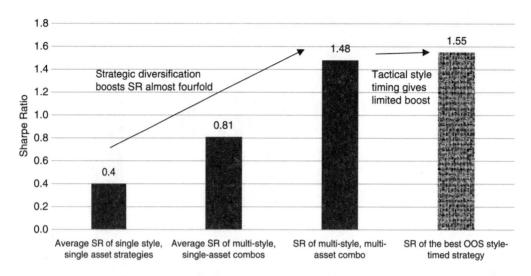

Figure 16.6   Boosting Sharpe Ratio with Factor Diversification or Factor Timing, 1926–2020
Sources: AQR, Ilmanen-Israel-Lee-Moskowitz-Thapar (2021).

evidence provides plentiful support for strategic multi-factor diversification but questions the additional benefits of tactical factor timing.

Figure 16.6 contrasts the great long-run benefits from style factor diversification and much more tenuous improvements from factor timing in historical backtests. As discussed near Figure 11.3, diversification across long/short (not long-only!) style premia can double the (gross of everything) SR, and diversification across asset classes can almost double it again. In contrast, the best out-of-sample style timing strategy using either single predictors or their composite boosted the strategic long-run SR by less than a tenth.

Neither individual timing predictors nor a multi-predictor composite could improve much on a static well-diversified composite. And while we do find some areas of supportive evidence for value-based or momentum-based factor timing, none of the documented style factor timing results were highly robust across subperiods and asset classes. Overall, the verdicts on the additivity, reliability, and practical usefulness of strategic factor diversification and tactical factor timing appear very different, in each case favoring the former. Thus, *sin (only) a little* when timing asset class or style premia.

Chapter 17

Bad Habits and Good Practices

- Good investors strive to resist common bad habits, even when it is hard. They focus on what they can control (process rather than recent results).
- Multiyear return chasing may deserve to be called the premier bad habit. Others include undersaving, underdiversification, overtrading, and cycles of fear and greed.
- Good practices include efforts to enhance discipline, patience, and good governance.

Successful investing requires good investments *and good investors*. Good investors recognize that they should resist any bad habits which hinder long-term investment performance, while they also cultivate good practices.

I focus here on what Goyal-Ilmanen-Kabiller (2015) called "the premier bad habit"[1]: multiyear return chasing, based on impatience, overextrapolation, and emotions/sentiment. Procyclic investing into strength and ill-timed capitulation after a fall can be done for the overall market, for a given factor or a manager, even for a single stock. A good strategy is one you can stick with.

Afterwards I will briefly discuss a broad set of bad habits: undersaving, underdiversification, overtrading, cycles of fear and greed; overextrapolation and underreaction as forces behind value and momentum factors; as well as lottery preferences and leverage aversion as the causes of the low-risk factor. I trace each back to certain underlying behavioral biases and preferences highlighted in the literature. Any bad habits have predictable complements as good practices which I will not dwell on. However, I will emphasize the importance of good discipline and good governance.

---

[1]Similar sentiment is expressed in Ang-Kjaer (2011), (2014a), Jones (2017), and Arnott-Kalesnik-Wu (2018).

17.1. Multiyear Return Chasing

Many investors buy multiyear winners and sell multiyear laggards – whether asset classes, strategy styles, single stocks, or funds. This is not surprising, since the human tendency to imitate and extrapolate is one of our deepest behavioral biases. Chasing winners over the past few months may actually be profitable, as financial markets tend to exhibit momentum (continuation, persistence, trends) over multi-month horizons up to a year. However, empirical evidence indicates that at multiyear horizons, financial markets tend to exhibit more mean reversion than continuation. Unfortunately, it is at this horizon that reallocation decisions tend to be made.

Several studies indicate that investor inflows/outflows or fire/hire decisions are clearly performance-chasing and often ill-timed when it comes to future returns. The poor timing of investor flows is frequently inferred from the evidence that money-weighted average returns *investors* earned tend to lag time-weighted average returns for *investments*.[2] Given the problems in this approach, I prefer more direct evidence on the lead-lag relations between investor flows and investment performance.

The most widely-quoted study on ill-timed investor flows and performance mean reversion is the Goyal-Wahal (2008) analysis of US pension plan sponsors' firing and hiring of investment managers. Figure 17.1 shows that replacing managers has been clearly procyclic (past laggards are replaced by past winners) and, more interestingly, that fired managers tended to later mildly outperform their hired replacements.

Many other studies provide evidence of procyclicality and/or poor timing in both retail and institutional flows. For example, Cornell-Hsu-Nanigian (2017) shows that past three years' winning mutual funds tend to lag past losers over the next three years.[3]

Goyal-Ilmanen-Kabiller (2015) emphasizes the tension between multiyear procyclic investor flows and multiyear mean-reverting returns across asset classes. We first study annual data from CEM Benchmarking on evolving US pension funds' asset allocations between 1990 and 2011 to

---

[2]Dichev (2007) shows that the dollar-weighted returns (internal rates of return) US stock investors earned between 1926 and 2002 were 1.3% lower than the time-weighted (buy and hold) market returns of the NYSE/AMEX indices, reflecting larger net inflows after high returns and before low returns. The gap was an even wider 5.3% for NASDAQ investors (1973–2002) mainly due to the heavy inflows during the late-1990s tech bubble. Firms such as Dalbar and Morningstar update these results regularly and attract much attention in the financial press. These analyses are typically done at the aggregate market level, but similar patterns are shown for some individual stocks, industries, countries, and even hedge funds. This type of indirect analysis has some shortcomings and may overstate the negative case; see Hayley (2012) and Pfau (2017). Much of the gap does not reflect cyclical return chasing but differential trends when inflows into markets have increased over time while average returns have declined. Thus, the gap is also quite large for index funds. Typical evidence also does not suggest that certain investor groups gain at the expense of others; net issuers might. Finally, Fried-Ma-Wang (2021) argue that the empirical performance gap between all investors' return and total equity market return is mainly due to infeasible reinvestment assumptions (all investors cannot reinvest dividends back to the market) and less to ill-timed investor flows or equity issuers' market timing ability.

[3]Frazzini and Lamont (2008) shows that retail investor money has tended to flow into mutual funds that hold stocks with low subsequent returns. Stewart-Neumann-Knittel-Heisler (2009) analyzes institutional plan sponsor allocation activity over time. They document that investment products receiving contributions subsequently underperform products experiencing withdrawals (over one- to five-year horizons). The difference is statistically significant although the gap is relatively modest. Most of the post-flow underperformance is due to product (manager) selection rather than category (asset class) reallocation, but both contribute. For more recent evidence, see Jones (2017) and Goyal-Wahal-Yamuz (2020).

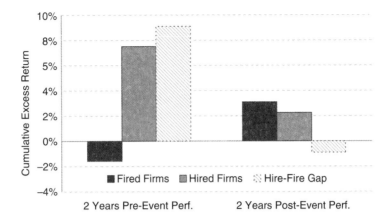

Figure 17.1 US Pension Plan Sponsors' Hire and Fire Decisions, 1996–2003
Sources: AQR, Goyal and Wahal (2008).

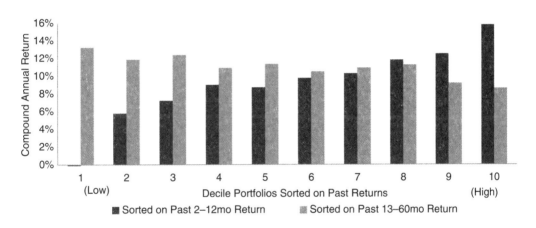

Figure 17.2 Momentum and Reversal Patterns in US Stock Returns, 1931–2018
Source: Data from Ken French Data Library. Notes: Decile-sorted portfolios formed on Momentum and portfolios formed on Long-Term Reversal, where the 10 sort refers to the highest value.

provide direct evidence on pension funds' procyclic tendencies. We then contrast such multiyear procyclic flows with the common multiyear reversal patterns in financial market returns.

Turning to stock selection and again picking a well-known example, Figure 17.2 shows evidence of multiyear reversals and one-year momentum in the performance of decile-sorted US stock portfolios. When sorting on one-year performance, the decile portfolios with high past-year returns subsequently outperform the decile portfolios with low past-year returns. When sorting on five-year performance excluding the past year, we observe the opposite pattern (albeit weaker). One-year momentum and multiyear reversal patterns are also evident in other countries, as well as in cross-country returns in many asset classes, and in overall asset class returns.[4]

Unfortunately, investors too often "act like momentum investors at reversal horizons." Some institutional investors are able to withstand underperformance for one or two years, but draw the

[4]See Figure 8.4 as well as Asness-Moskowitz-Pedersen (2013).

line at three to five years – just when such underperformance empirically predicts higher future returns. Procyclicality for institutional investors at three- to five-year horizons may be reinforced by common performance evaluation periods.

This topic overlaps with the Patience section in Chapter 9.1. Many investors understandably lack patience when facing years of underperformance – even if they are aware of the limited predictive ability in past performance and the high transition costs. The academic advice to wait even longer for statistically significant evidence is not realistic for many investors.

What else can they do? It is easier to identify the problem than to offer satisfactory solutions. Here are some constructive answers to this quandary, but even these are hard to implement. Multiyear return chasing wouldn't be so prevalent if it were otherwise.

- To realistically improve patience and to rely less on the return experience, investors need to spend even more time evaluating the merits of a strategy/manager *before* investing and only select the ones they really have faith in and ability to stick with.
- Investors should consider other decision criteria besides past performance (e.g. people, philosophy, process) and develop an understanding of the reasonable range of outcomes.
- If then a manager disappoints over a multiyear horizon, again the investor should look at other things in addition to return during the evaluation period.
- Correlations to common factors or to other managers can help assess whether the manager behaved as expected, given the mandate, or changed its approach.

More broadly, investors should ideally take a very long view to judge performance, using a portfolio perspective and focusing on ex-ante quality of decision/process, as opposed to making hindsighted, solely outcome-driven judgments. Nobody said it would be easy. Superhuman patience and serenity are hard to come by.

17.2. Other Bad Habits and Good Practices

Table 17.1 tries to trace major bad habits – or systematic investment opportunities caused by them – back to key behavioral biases and preferences.[5]

Impatience is a key reason for the problem of insufficient retirement saving. Of course, it is easier to save if you can afford to do it, but impatience can hurt even the wealthy. At almost any income level we can see people living beyond their means and quickly adjusting expenditures and aspirations to their higher income.

Overextrapolation, together with impatience and the cycle of fear and greed, is behind the multiyear return chasing, excessive fire-and-hire activity, and all kinds of momentum and value opportunities.

Moods, emotions, feelings, sentiment, reinforced by social dynamics, are widely-talked-about behavioral pitfalls. They give rise to herding, bubbles, a cycle of fear and greed ("get me out of here" versus "get rich quickly" mindsets, or irrational gloom and exuberance), FOMO ("fear of missing out") participation in bull markets, and other momentum and value opportunities.

Anchoring and conservatism contribute to the underreaction effects (gradual information diffusion) that give rise to momentum and fundamental momentum opportunities. As noted,

---

[5]These themes are discussed in influential surveys on behavioral finance literature by Nick Barberis (2013, 2017) and David Hirshleifer (2015). Note that any behavioral pattern can be seen introspectively as a bad habit we could correct or more predatorily as a potential opportunity to benefit from others' mistakes.

Table 17.1 Linking Behavioral Forces to Bad Habits and Investment Opportunities

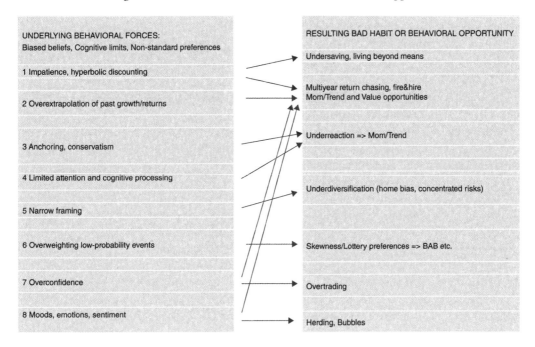

underreaction effects are weaker with highly salient, easily available news and more pronounced with bread-and-butter news.

Limited attention and limits of cognitive processing (bounded rationality) also contribute to underreaction effects, as well as to narrow framing.

The prospect theory of Kahneman-Tversky (1979) combines many features of common behavior in decision-making situations. The best-known feature, loss aversion ("losses loom larger than gains"), may not have as big investment implications[6] as narrow framing and probability weighting:

- Narrow framing is related to line-item thinking at the expense of portfolio perspective. It leads to a focus on an investment's standalone gains/losses instead of its impact on total wealth. Narrow framing contributes to different types of underdiversification (to home bias, along with ambiguity aversion; to equity concentration, along with leverage aversion; to concentrated single-stock exposures, along with overconfidence).
- Probability weighting, and especially overweighting of low-probability events, naturally explains investor preferences for lottery-like positively-skewed investments such as high-risk stocks or IPOs. Such lottery preferences can explain the relatively poor long-run performance of both investments (while leverage aversion also contributes to the former).

Overconfidence is a hugely influential bias, together with self-attribution and confirmation biases as well as overoptimism, which sustain it (as they help us maintain self-esteem and avoid

---

[6]Standard risk aversion has many similar consequences as loss aversion. Key differences include a kink at the origin (asymmetry between gains and losses) and potential risk-seeking behavior in the domain of losses (called "get-evenitis" if a successful bet could make up losses). The shape of the prospect theory value function, combined with probability weights, can also explain why we may want to buy both lotteries and insurance.

learning from mistakes).[7] Overconfidence may be the main explanation for overtrading (as well as to the popularity of active management, CEOs overpaying for mergers and acquisitions, entrepreneur underdiversification[8] – and a contributor to some momentum and reversal patterns).

Good Practices

Instead of going through the contrasting good practices that correspond to the bad habits in Table 17.1, I make some broad observations.

Try to cultivate your discipline, patience, and probabilistic thinking. Discipline helps especially against swinging moods and emotions, and this is where systematic/quant investing has a clear edge. Enhancing self-discipline through commitment devices (recall the story of Odysseus being tied to the mast when facing the sirens) can help you save more or avoid selling after a large market fall.

I already discussed patience-boosting ideas, such as evaluating investments broadly and rarely (to resist narrow framing and myopia). Also recognize that as a species we humans are drawn to stories. But when it comes to investing, decisions driven by appealing stories can be damaging to your wealth, unless you can better calibrate the impact statistical evidence and anecdotal stories have on you.

Overall, figure out what you believe in and try to stick with it. Inconsistently believing in right things might turn out even worse than consistently believing in wrong things.

For a recent quote, I like Morgan Housel's (2020) "Save like a pessimist, invest like an optimist." It is especially important to save more in a low-return world to reach any spending targets you have, and some risk taking is a must when low cash rates are at the heart of low expected returns. Another excellent Housel insight states that if you happen to get rich, you should protect your wealth (diversify) and resist adaptation (not let your expectations rise fully with income).[9]

These issues apply to an institution as much as to an individual investor, but governance issues are more complex within organizations. Governance problems highlighted in the literature include misalignment of incentives (agency problems); unclear roles between the board and the staff (e.g. a board micromanaging and spending most of its time on manager or stock selection or on market outlook instead of setting strategic investment policy); as well as related mismatches between responsibility, authority, and accountability.[10]

---

[7]Overconfidence may be the most important bias also because it feeds the other ones, just as pride (or hubris) has been called the most serious of the seven deadly sins, and the father of all sins. We may be wired to be overconfident for evolutionary reasons (good for effort and motivation, balanced by more disappointments and repeated futile efforts). This evolutionary argument rhymes with the happiness literature theme that evolution does not care whether we are happy but it wants us to pursue happiness. The US Declaration of Independence identified the pursuit as an inalienable right, not satisfying the goal. The US founding fathers had it right, as the unquenchable hunger for more is the energy that advances our collective prospects.

[8]Entrepreneurs often take very concentrated risks during their career, and they tend to have higher confidence on business success odds in their area of specialty than facts warrant, and even higher optimism regarding their own prospects. After the subset of successful (in part, lucky) entrepreneurs sell their businesses, they may have overconfident and unrealistic expectations of feasible returns. This makes them vulnerable to dream-sellers promising high expected returns if they think that even mediocre players should be able to earn double-digit returns.

[9]Given humans' incredible ability to adapt, rising standards of living raise our expectations. To resist jumping on the hedonic treadmill, it helps to recall the old quip that happiness equals the gap between reality and expectations. Balancing between striving for more and appreciating what you have is not easy. Survey evidence of the so-called happiness curve suggests that this balance shifts mid-life, making the above-50s more easily contented and happier, perhaps because their genetic duty is done. As preceding footnotes indicate, such patterns work only on average; resting on the laurels is not for everyone.

[10]See Koedijk-Slaeger-van Dam (2020) for more on the important governance topic. In their Exhibit 1 they heroically try to estimate the size of potential governance alpha from various sources. Ivashina-Lerner (2019) discusses the particular agency problems in delegated private asset management.

Chapter 18

Concluding Remarks

- The low return prospects do not obviously point to taking more risk or less risk, but many investors have chosen the former path.
- The main prescriptions in this book are meant to be timeless, even if the low-return challenge makes them more important.
- It is hard to publish an investing book with a long-term orientation when asset yields are record-low and many markets show signs of exuberance and excesses.
- I conclude by reiterating key principles of good investing and by calling for stable confidence in whatever your chosen investment approach is.

Should Investors Take More or Less Risk amid Low Expected Returns?

It is hard to escape our collective destiny when all asset classes are expensive against their own histories for a common reason: Their discount rates reflect extremely low real riskless yields (while most asset or factor premia on top of them are more or less ordinary). If investors are to make changes, should they take more risk because old liabilities or return goals cannot be met with existing portfolios – or less risk because expected returns are historically low?

It is not obvious which is preferable, though many investors have already chosen the former path. They should do it with open eyes. They are increasing portfolio risk when investments have higher valuations than in the past and may be more vulnerable to corrections (though nobody has the crystal ball to say when). Conversely, taking less risk by moving to cash is also a tough choice when negative real cash rates are at the root of the problem. Patiently staying in cash requires huge confidence in the market timing call. Chapter 16 emphasizes how hard it is to succeed.

A justifiable – yet difficult – answer is for investors to hold a broadly similar portfolio as in normal times: to stick with their long-run strategies and beliefs, serenely accepting that markets now offer less. They will need to lower expectations and reduce waste. Investing efficiently – making the most with the cards you are dealt – is arguably more important today than ever. Of course, many of us will still try to outrun others – by taking more risk, making timing calls, or applying portfolio tilts to capture relative value opportunities (say, the wide valuation gap between value and growth stocks or between US and other equity markets). This book includes my insights for such active investing, while endorsing humility.

Having essentially borrowed returns from the future through multi-decade windfall gains, we are in for low returns for the next decade or longer. Yet, it is not clear whether the low returns will materialize through slow pain (persistent low income) or fast pain (repricing toward lower valuations and higher prospective returns).

As a subjective call, I leaned for many years toward the slow-pain outcome, but writing this in mid-2021, the fast-pain scenario is becoming more plausible. We face a bubbly situation where high asset valuations are supported by central bank policies, despite rising inflation. It is all too easy to see how de-anchoring of inflation expectations could force central banks to make hard choices for the first time in ages. There are many other signs of speculative excess. Conservative investors today merely reach for yield, while the inexperienced risk-seeking meme stock buyers look for fast gains on virtually anything, with little economic analysis – and are expecting to have fun on their way to riches. A generation or two of investors do not remember inflation, rising bond yields, or persistent equity bear markets (thus, buy on dips). Their main fear is of missing out. Scary.

I confess I'd selfishly have liked things to be more "ordinary" at the end of my book's sample period. We still have near record rich equities, low bond yields, extreme value-growth spread, and so on, all of which make historical average returns biased, and major corrections soon could make the book appear quickly dated. Well, I should serenely accept I cannot alter this. At least I can debias historical average returns or study yield-based forward-looking returns when valuations are extreme at the end of the sample.

Good Investing Principles

As noted, I believe that principles of good long-term oriented investing are timeless; they just matter more in tough times. One size does not fit all, so only you can decide what works best for you or your institution. But there are some common themes that work for all of us. (Well, maybe not for all the fun-loving young speculators, but for those of us who like returns, dislike risk, and have constraints.)

- Select return sources thoughtfully (form realistic investment beliefs you can stick with; for example, I believe mainly in some long-run rewarded asset class and style premia).
- Size risks appropriately (based on risk-adjusted expected excess returns).
- Invest strategically and patiently (at most "sin a little" in tactical timing).
- Diversify boldly (construct robust portfolios that will survive most scenarios).
- Execute cost-effectively (consider costs, fees, and taxes).
- Govern well (seek good governance within your organization and with its agents).

Finally, humility rhymes with serenity. I believe both can improve long-run investment performance. That said, I do not endorse excessive humility. It generally makes sense to resist overconfidence, but here I want to make a case for *stable* confidence, resisting the impact of recent success *or* failure on confidence.

Successful outcomes depend on luck and skill. Luck often dominates the short term and especially in extreme outcomes. Skill reflects expertise and effort. Confidence grows with success, often too fast. Expertise and effort give us an anchor of stable confidence; yet, luck matters too and can give rise to a cycle of overconfidence.[1]

Overconfidence may vary over time, similar to feedback effects in financial markets – positive momentum and rubber band reversal. Random lucky outcomes raise measured success and breed overconfidence, leading to excessive risk-taking and other harmful behavior. Conversely, random outcomes are sometimes unlucky enough to breed underconfidence and loss of faith after bad draws. Such unstable risk preferences cause ill-timed exuberance and capitulations.

In the spirit of the Serenity Prayer, we should remember that we can only control the ex-ante process and recognize the role of luck in ex-post outcomes. Let's keep exploring and improving our skill, but not demanding constant validation from realized success.

Stable investment behavior is encouraged by calls for equanimity: "This too shall pass," "You are never as good as your best year, and never as bad as your worst year," or "If you can meet with triumph and disaster and treat those two impostors just the same . . . (then) . . . Yours is the Earth." A serene mindset helps make us into better, more patient, and more consistent investors – essential characteristics when a strategy is good only if you can stick with it.

---

[1] These thoughts were inspired by as diverse group as Moore (2020), Meng (2019), Duckworth (2016), Mauboussin (2012), and Gladwell (2008).

Acknowledgments

When in 2011 I published my first book, *Expected Returns,* I fully expected it to be the last one. But then I joined AQR a few months later, and to my pleasant surprise, my learning curve went up again. During my decade in AQR, we've kept pushing the envelope research-wise and education-wise.

My preacher's passion was also inflamed by the gradually worsening low expected return environment, a generational challenge to retirement savers. I felt that my first book had given the building blocks but not enough historical or institutional context, nor much discussion on how to put the pieces together.

So I began to think about a second book five years ago, partly prompted by polite requests for an update or a sequel. I knew I wanted to go both broader and shorter than in the first book, not easy. I mulled over the book but had no time to write it until Covid-19 lockdowns and the pause in business travel gave a window. I got the opportunity to work part-time, and I took it. This also means that while this book is hugely influenced by my AQR colleagues' work, it is a private effort and the responsibility for errors is all mine.

I have so much gratitude toward AQR colleagues, not just for this book's contents but more generally for the common learning experience. The list is too long so I choose to high-light colleagues with whom I have co-authored at least a couple of articles: Cliff Asness, Swati Chandra, Ronen Israel, Thom Maloney, Toby Moskowitz, Ashwin Thapar, and Dan Villalon.[1] And besides crediting the co-founders Cliff, David, and John for their ongoing support, I want to acknowledge the evolving Portfolio Solutions Group "family" over the years: AdamB, Dan, Brad, Arthur, Alex, Thom, April, Forrest, Adrienne, Swati, AdamA, Liza, Nick, Pete, Paras, Max, Jason, Ing-Chea, Jack, Alfie, Kelvin, Emily, Justin, Noah, Ekin, and Vik.

---

[1] None of the articles are directly used in this book, but of course I draw on their content. Notably, parts of Chapters 9 and 16 rely heavily on the work with Thom Maloney, my co-author and collaborator since 2005. Chapter 14 on ESG benefited a lot from Lukasz Pomorski's help. And if you think I could write a chapter on trading costs or even boxes on machine learning and taxes without using my colleagues' expertise, think again.

I also thank many clients, peers, and academic researchers for dialogue and inspiration. Given this book's breadth, I cannot include a history of thought on each topic. I cannot even do justice to AQR's own lengthy research list, so attempting to do so for the exhaustive research done by others would be futile. I acknowledge that research is collaborative and influenced by ideas from an array of contributors. I apologize to the many worthy authors for only including select references. Overall, I ended up with 500+ references, among them about a quarter from AQR-affiliated authors. All the latter references are available at aqr.com, as are some historical series used in this book (see AQR Data Library). Among others, I prioritize the most relevant new research as well as good overviews. Undoubtedly, this book gives an AQR-tinted view on good investing, but I try to offer both sides on important topics of debate and let readers judge for themselves.

Most sources I contacted outside AQR generously shared with me the data I requested: David Chambers, Magnus Dahlquist, Elroy Dimson, Ralph Koijen, Coleman Long, Michael Mauboussin, Mikhail Samonov, Bernd Scherer, Philip Straehl, and Laurens Swinkels. I thank them all, together with their co-authors or colleagues. I also appreciate my other data sources, both outside AQR and inside (Kris, Sarah, Hernan, Rachel, Sham, Alfie, Nick, Ekin, and especially Justin).

I am again indebted to Cliff for the characteristically witty Foreword and for much influence on my thinking. Many people gave their time to review and comment on the whole manuscript (Victor Haghani, Matti Ilmanen, Knut Kjaer, Thom Maloney, Paul Rintamäki, Dan Villalon) or some sections (Andrew Ang, Gabriel Baracat, Chiam Swee Chiang, Elroy Dimson, Pete Hecht, Doug Huggins, Bryan Kelly, Mikko Niskanen, Lasse Pedersen, Lukasz Pomorski, Scott Richardson, Rudi Schadt, Nathan Sosner, Larry Swedroe, Ingrid Tierens). They helped me greatly to improve the book but bear no responsibility for any faults.

I warmly thank my editors Bill Falloon and Purvi Patel and the rest of the Wiley team.

Finally, I am grateful to my families in Finland and Germany for their unwavering support.

Antti Ilmanen
October 2021

Author Bio

Antti Ilmanen is a principal and global co-head of the Portfolio Solutions Group at AQR Capital Management. He manages the team responsible for advising institutional investors and sovereign wealth funds and develops the firm's broad investment ideas. Prior to joining AQR in 2011, Antti spent seven years as a senior portfolio manager at Brevan Howard and a decade in a variety of roles at Salomon Brothers/Citigroup. He began his career as a central bank portfolio manager in Finland. Over the years, he has advised many institutional investors, including Norway's Government Pension Fund Global and the Government of Singapore Investment Corporation. Antti has published extensively in finance and investment journals and has received a Graham and Dodd Award, the Harry M. Markowitz Special Distinction Award, and multiple Bernstein Fabozzi/Jacobs Levy awards for his articles. His first book, *Expected Returns* (Wiley, 2011), is a broad synthesis of the central issues in investing. He also received the CFA Institute's 2017 Leadership in Global Investment Award. Antti earned M.Sc. degrees in economics and law from the University of Helsinki and a Ph.D. in finance from the University of Chicago.

Acronyms

T his list does not include acronyms that were only used in the paragraph or equation where they were introduced.*

A/L	asset/liability
AM	arithmetic mean
ARP	alternative risk premia
AUM	assets under management
B/P	book/price
BRP	bond risk premium
CAEY	cyclically adjusted earnings yield
CAPE	cyclically adjusted price/earnings ratio (also called the Shiller P/E)
CAPM	Capital Asset Pricing Model
DB	defined benefit
DC	defined contribution
DPS	dividends per share
DY	dividend yield
EPS	earnings per share*
E(R)	expected return*
ESG	environmental, social, and governance (also called responsible or sustainable investing)
ETF	exchange-traded fund
FAMAG	Facebook, Apple, Microsoft, Amazon, Google

FI	fixed income
FLAM	fundamental law of active management
FR	funding ratio (value of assets/liabilities)
g	growth (of dividends, earnings, or broader payouts)
GFC	Global Financial Crisis (2008)
GM	geometric mean
HF	hedge fund
HY	high yield
IG	investment grade
IR	information ratio
IRR	internal rate of return
k	payout ratio (dividends/earnings)
L/S	long/short
MRP	market risk premia
MVO	mean–variance optimization
OAS	option–adjusted spread
OOS	out of sample
PE	private equity
SR	Sharpe ratio
VC	venture capital

*Note that E may mean earnings or the expectations operator; should be clear from the context. And then there's the E in ESG.

References

Accominotti, Olivier; Jason Cen; David Chambers; and Ian Marsh (2019), "Currency regimes and the carry trade," *Journal of Financial and Quantitative Analysis* **54**(5), 2233–2260.

Acharya, Viral; and Lasse H. Pedersen (2005), "Asset pricing with liquidity risk," *Journal of Financial Economics* **77**, 375–410.

Adrian, Tobias; Richard Crump; and Emanuel Moench (2013): "Pricing the term structure with linear regressions", *Journal of Financial Economics* **110**(1), 110–38.

Aggarwal, Rajesh K.; and Philippe Jorion (2010), "Hidden survivorship in hedge fund returns," *Financial Analysts Journal* **66**(2), 69–74.

Alquist, Ron; Andrea Frazzini; Antti Ilmanen; and Lasse H. Pedersen (2020), "Fact and fiction about low-risk investing," *Journal of Portfolio Management* **46**(6), 72–92.

Alquist, Ron; Ronen Israel; and Tobias Moskowitz (2018), "Fact, fiction and the size effect," *Journal of Portfolio Management* **45**(1), 34–61.

Amato, Livia; and Harald Lohre (2020), "Diversifying macroeconomic factors – for better or for worse," SSRN working paper.

Amenc, Noël; Felix Goltz; and Ben Luyten (2020), "Intangible capital and the value factor: Has your value definition just expired?" *Journal of Portfolio Management* **46**(7), 83–9.

Amihud, Yakov (2002), "Illiquidity and stock returns: Cross-section and time-series effects," *Journal of Financial Markets* **5**(1), 31–56.

Amihud, Yakov; Haim Mendelson; and Lasse H. Pedersen (2012), *Market Liquidity: Asset Pricing, Risk, and Crises*, Cambridge University Press.

Andonov, Aleksandar; and Joshua D. Rauh (2020), "The return expectations of institutional investors," SSRN working paper.

Andonov, Aleksandar; Rob Bauer; and Martijn Cremers (2017), "Pension fund asset allocation and liability discount rates," *Review of Financial Studies* **30**(8), 2555–2595.

Andonov, Aleksandar; Roman Kräussl; and Joshua D. Rauh (2021), "Institutional investors and infrastructure investing," SSRN working paper.

Ang, Andrew (2014), *Asset Management: A Systematic Approach to Factor Investing*, Oxford University Press.

Ang, Andrew; and Angela Maddaloni (2003), "Do demographic changes affect risk premiums? Evidence from international data." *NBER working paper* 9677.

Ang, Andrew; and Knut Kjaer (2011), "Investing for the long run," in *A Decade of Challenges: A Collection of Essays on Pensions and Investments* (ed. by Tomas Franzen), 94–111, AP2.

Ang, Andrew; Dimitris Papanikolaou; and Mark M. Westerfield (2014), "Portfolio choice with illiquid assets," *Management Science* **60**(11), 2737–2761.

Ang, Andrew; Joseph Chen; and Yuhang Xing (2006), "Downside risk," *Review of Financial Studies* **19**(4), 1191–1239.

Ang, Andrew; Neil Nabar; and Samuel Wald (2013), "Searching for a common factor in public and private real estate returns," SSRN working paper.

Ang, Andrew; Robert Hodrick; Yuhang Xing; and Xiaoyan Zhang (2006), "The cross-section of volatility and expected returns," *Journal of Finance* **61**, 259–299.

AQR Portfolio Solutions Group (2013), "Putting returns in perspective," AQR white paper.

AQR Portfolio Solutions Group (2015), "Strategic portfolio construction," *AQR Alternative Thinking*.

AQR Portfolio Solutions Group (2017a). "Capital market assumptions for major asset classes." *AQR Alternative Thinking*.

AQR Portfolio Solutions Group (2017b), "Systematic vs. discretionary," *AQR Alternative Thinking*.

AQR Portfolio Solutions Group (2018), "Active and passive investing: The long-run evidence," *AQR Alternative Thinking*.

AQR Portfolio Solutions Group (2019a), "Responsible asset selection: ESG in investment decisions," *AQR Alternative Thinking*.

AQR Portfolio Solutions Group (2019b). "Inversion anxiety: Yield curves, economic growth, and asset prices," *AQR Alternative Thinking*.

AQR Portfolio Solutions Group (2020a), "Fire and ice: Confronting the twin perils of inflation and deflation," *AQR Alternative Thinking*.

AQR Portfolio Solutions Group (2020b), "Was that intentional? Ways to improve your active risk," AQR Alternative Thinking.

AQR Portfolio Solutions Group (2021), "Capital market assumptions," *AQR Alternative Thinking*.

Arnott, Rob: Vitali Kalesnik; and Lilian Wu (2018), "The folly of hiring winners and firing losers," *Journal of Portfolio Management* **45**(1), 71–84.

Arnott, Robert D.; and Denis Chaves (2012), "Demographic changes, financial markets, and the economy," *Financial Analysts Journal* **68**(1), 23–46.

Arnott, Robert D.; and Peter L. Bernstein (2002), "What risk premium is 'normal'?" *Financial Analysts Journal* **58**(2), 64–85.

Arnott, Robert D.; Campbell R. Harvey; Vitali Kalesnik, and Juhani T. Linnainmaa (2021), "Reports of value's death may be greatly exaggerated," *Financial Analysts Journal* **77**(1), 44–67.

Asness, Clifford S. (1994), "Variables that explain stock returns," dissertation, University of Chicago.

Asness, Cliff (2014a), "My top 10 peeves," *Financial Analysts Journal* **70**(1), 22–30.

Asness, Cliff (2014b), "Our model goes to six and saves value from redundancy along the way," *Cliff's Perspectives*, aqr.com.

Asness, Cliff (2015), "Don't go for the exacta," *Cliff's Perspectives*, aqr.com.

Asness, Cliff (2016), "My factor Philippic," *Cliff's Perspectives*, aqr.com.

Asness, Cliff (2017), "Virtue is its own reward or one man's ceiling is another man's floor," *Cliff's Perspectives*, aqr.com.

Asness, Cliff (2019a), "Looking for the intuition underlying multi-factor stock selection," *Cliff's Perspectives*, aqr.com.

Asness, Cliff (2019b), "The illiquidity discount," *Cliff's Perspectives*, aqr.com.

Asness, Cliff (2020), "Is (systematic) value investing dead?" *Cliff's Perspectives*, aqr.com.

Asness, Cliff (2021), "The long run is lying to you," *Cliff's Perspectives*, aqr.com.

Asness, Cliff; Swati Chandra; Antti Ilmanen; and Ronen Israel (2017), "Contrarian factor timing is deceptively difficult," *Journal of Portfolio Management* **43**(5), 72–87.

Asness, Cliff; and Andrea Frazzini (2013), "The devil in HML's details," *Journal of Portfolio Management* 39(4), 49–68.

Asness, Clifford; Andrea Frazzini; Niels J. Gormsen; and Lasse H. Pedersen (2020), "Betting against correlation: Testing theories of the low-risk effect," *Journal of Financial Economics* **135**(3), 629–652.

Asness, Clifford; Andrea Frazzini; Ronen Israel; and Tobias Moskowitz (2014), "Fact, fiction and momentum investing," *Journal of Portfolio Management* **40**(5), 75–92.

Asness, Clifford; Andrea Frazzini; Ronen Israel; and Tobias Moskowitz (2015), "Fact, fiction and value investing," *Journal of Portfolio Management*, **42**(1), 34–52.

Asness, Clifford; Antti Ilmanen; Ronen Israel; and Tobias Moskowitz (2015), "Investing with style," *Journal of Investment Management* **13**(1), 27–63.

Asness, Cliff; Antti Ilmanen; and Thomas Maloney (2017), "Market timing: Sin a little," *Journal of Investment Management*, **15**(3): 23–40.

Asness, Cliff; Antti Ilmanen; Tobias Moskowitz; Lukasz Pomorski; and Lei Xie (2022), "Who is on the other side?" AQR white paper, forthcoming.

Asness, Clifford; Roni Israelov; and John Liew (2011), "International diversification works (eventually)," *Financial Analysts Journal* **67**(3), 24–38.

Asness, Clifford; Robert Krail; and John Liew (2001), "Do hedge funds hedge?" *Journal of Portfolio Management* **28**(1), 6–19.

Asness, Clifford S.; Tobias J. Moskowitz; and Lasse H. Pedersen (2013), "Value and momentum everywhere," *Journal of Finance* **68**(3), 929–985.

Asvanunt, Attakrit; and Scott Richardson (2017), "The credit risk premium," *Journal of Fixed Income* **26**(3), 6–24.

Avdis, Efstathios; and Jessica A. Wachter (2017), "Maximum likelihood estimation of the equity premium," *Journal of Financial Economics*, **125**(3), 589–609.

Ayres, Ian; and Barry Nalebuff (2010), *Lifecycle Investing: A New, Safe, and Audacious Way to Improve the Performance of Your Retirement Portfolio*, Basic Books.

Babu, Abhilash; Brendan Hoffman; Ari Levine; Yao Hua Ooi; Sarah Schroeder; and Erik Stamelos (2020), "You Can't Always Trend When You Want," *Journal of Portfolio Management* **46**(4), 52–68.

Bacchetta, Philippe; Elmar Mertens; and Eric van Wincoop (2009), "Predictability in financial markets: What do survey expectations tell us?" *Journal of International Money and Finance* **28**(3), 406–426.

Bailey, David; and Marcos Lopez de Prado (2014), "The deflated Sharpe ratio: correcting for selection bias, backtest overfitting, and non-normality," *Journal of Portfolio Management* **40**(5), 94–107.

Bain (2021), *Global Private Equity Report 2021*.

Bakshi, Gurdip S.; and Zhiwu Chen (1994), "Baby boom, population aging, and capital markets," *Journal of Business* **67**(2), 165–202.

Bali, Turan G.; Nusret Cakici; and Robert F. Whitelaw (2011), "Maxing out: Stocks as lotteries and the cross-section of expected returns." *Journal of Financial Economics* **99**(2), 427–446.

Bali, Turan G.; Stephen J. Brown; Scott Murray; and Yi Tang (2017), "A lottery-demand-based explanation of the beta anomaly." *Journal of Financial and Quantitative Analysis* **52**(6), 2369–2397.

Baltas, Nick; and Bernd Scherer (2019), "Tail risk in the cross section of alternative risk premium strategies," *Journal of Portfolio Management* **45**(2), 93–104.

Baltussen, Guido; Laurens Swinkels; and Pim van Vliet (2019), "Global factor premiums," *Journal of Financial Economics, forthcoming.*

Baltussen, Guido; Bart van Vliet; and Pim van Vliet (2021), "The cross-section of stock returns before 1926 (and beyond)," SSRN working paper.

Baltzer, Markus; Stephan Jank; and Esad Smajlbegovic (2015), "Who trades on momentum?" SSRN working paper.

Banz, Rolf W. (1981), "The relationship between return and market value of common stocks," *Journal of Financial Economics*, **9**(1), 3–18,

Barberis, Nicholas (2013), "Thirty years of prospect theory in economics: a review and assessment," *Journal of Economic Perspectives* **27**(1), 173–196.

Barberis, Nicholas (2017), "*Behavioral finance: Asset prices and investor behavior,*" American Economic Association lectures, https://www.aeaweb.org/content/file?id=2978

Barberis, Nicholas; and Ming Huang (2008), "Stocks as lotteries: The implications of probability weighting for security prices," *American Economic Review* **98**, 2066–2100.

Barberis, Nicholas; and Richard Thaler (2003), "A survey of behavioral finance," in the *Handbook of the Economics of Finance* (Constantinides, G., Harris, M., Stulz, R. eds.), North Holland.

Barberis, Nicholas; Andrei Shleifer; and Robert Vishny (1998), "A model of investor sentiment," *Journal of Financial Economics* **49**, 307–345.

Barberis, Nicholas; Lawrence J. Jin; and Baolian Wang (2021), "Prospect theory and stock market anomalies," *Journal of Finance, forthcoming.*

Barroso, Pedro; and Pedro Santa-Clara (2015), "Momentum has its moments," *Journal of Financial Economics* **116**, 111–120.

Barth, Daniel; Juha Joenvaara; Mikko Kauppila; and Russ Wermers (2020), "The hedge fund industry is bigger (and has performed better) than you think," SSRN working paper.

Bauer, Michael D.; and Glenn D. Rudebusch (2020), "Interest rates under falling stars," *American Economic Review* **110**(5), 1316–54.

Bawa, Vijay S.; and Eric Lindenberg (1977), "Capital market equilibrium in a mean, lower partial moment framework," *Journal of Financial Economics* **5**, 189–200.

Baz, Jamil; Steve Sapra; Christian Stracke; and Wentao Zhao (2021), "Valuing a lost opportunity: An alternative perspective on the illiquidity discount," *Journal of Portfolio Management* **47**(3), 112–121.

Beath, Alexander D.; Betermier, Sebastien; Chris Flynn; and Quentin Spehner (2021), "The Canadian pension fund model: A quantitative portrait," *Journal of Portfolio Management* **47**(5), 159–177.

Beath, Alexander; and Christopher Flynn (2020), "Benchmarking the performance of private equity portfolios of the world's largest institutional investors: A view from CEM Benchmarking, *Journal of Investing* **30**(1), 67–87.

Bekaert, Geert; and George Panayotov (2020), "Good carry, bad carry," *Journal of Financial and Quantitative Analysis* **55**(4), 1063–1094.

Ben Dor, Arik: Albert Desclee: Lev Dynkin: Jay Hyman; Simon Polbennikov (2021), Systematic Investing in Credit, Wiley.

Benartzi, Shlomol and Richard Thaler (1995), "Myopic loss aversion and the equity premium puzzle," *Quarterly Journal of Economics* **110**(1), 73–92.

Berg, Florian; Julian Kölbel; and Roberto Rigobon (2020), "Aggregate confusion: The divergence of ESG ratings," MIT working paper.

Berger, Adam; Brian Crowell; and David G. Kabiller (2008), "Is alpha just beta waiting to be discovered?" AQR white paper (revised 2012).

Berk, Jonathan B; and Richard C. Green (2004), "Mutual fund flows and performance in rational markets," *Journal of Political Economy* **112**, 1269–1295.

Berk, Jonathan; and Jules van Binsbergen (2015), "Measuring skill in the mutual fund industry," *Journal of Financial Economics* **118**(1), 1-20.

Berkin, Andrew L.; and Larry E. Swedroe (2016), *Your Complete Guide to Factor-Based Investing: The Way Smart Money Invests Today*, Buckingham.

Bernanke, Ben S. (2005), "*The global saving glut and the US current account deficit*," Federal Reserve Board speech.

Bernstein, William (2013), *Deep Risk: How History Informs Portfolio Design, Efficient Frontier*.

Bernstein, William J. (2021), *The Delusions of Crowds: Why People Go Mad in Groups*, Atlantic Monthly Press.

Bessembinder, Hendrik (2018), "Do stocks outperform treasury bills?" *Journal of Financial Economics*, **129**(3), 440–457.

Best, Peter; Alistair Byrne; and Antti Ilmanen (1998), "What really happened to US bond yields?" *Financial Analysts Journal* **54**(3), 41–49.

Bhansali, Vineer (2014), *Tail Risk Hedging: Creating Robust Portfolios for Volatile Markets*, McGraw-Hill.

Bhardwaj, Geetesh; Rajkumar Janardanan; and K. Geert Rouwenhorst (2019), "The commodity futures risk premium: 1871–2018," SSRN working paper.

Black, Fischer (1972), "Capital Market Equilibrium with Restricted Borrowing," *Journal of Business* **45**(3), 444–455.

Black, Fischer (1993), "Beta and return," *Journal of Portfolio Management* **20**(1), 8–18.

Black, Fischer; and Robert Litterman (1992), "Global portfolio optimization." *Financial Analysts Journal* **48**(5), 28–43.

Black, Fischer; Michael Jensen; and Myron Scholes (1972), "The capital asset pricing model: some empirical tests," in *Studies in the Theory of Capital Markets*. Praeger, Jensen, Michael (ed.): 79–121.

Blake, David; Alberto G. Rossi; Allan Timmermann; Ian Tonks; and Russ Wermers (2013), "Decentralized investment management: Evidence from the pension fund industry," *Journal of Finance* **68**(3), 1133–1178.

Blitz, David (2018), "Are hedge funds on the other side of the low-volatility trade?" *Journal of Alternative Investments* **21**(1). 17–26.

Blitz, David; Pim van Vliet; and Guido Baltussen (2020), "The volatility effect revisited," *Journal of Portfolio Management* **46**(2), 45–63.

Bodie, Zvi; Robert C. Merton; and William Samuelson (1992), "Labor supply flexibility and portfolio choice in a life-cycle model," *Journal of Economic Dynamics and Control* 16(3-4), 427–449.

Bollen, Nicolas; Juha Joenvaara; and Mikko Kauppila (2021), "Hedge fund performance: End of an era?" *Financial Analysts Journal, forthcoming*.

Bollerslev, Tim: Benjamin Hood; John Huss; and Lasse H. Pedersen (2018), "Risk everywhere: Modeling and managing volatility," *Review of Financial Studies* **31**(7), 2729–2773.

Bongaerts, Dion; Xiaowei Kang; and Mathijs A. van Dijk (2020), "Conditional volatility targeting," *Financial Analysts Journal* **76**(4), 54–71.

Bordalo, Pedro; Nicola Gennaioli; and Andrei Shleifer (2013), "Salience and asset prices," *American Economic Review* **103**(3), 623–28.

Bordalo, Pedro; Nicola Gennaioli; Rafael LaPorta; and Andrei Shleifer (2019), "Diagnostic expectations and stock returns," *Journal of Finance* **74**(6), 2839–2874.

Borio, Claudio; Piti Disyatat; Mikael Juselius; and Phurichai Rungcharoenkitkul (2017), "Why so low for so long? A long-term view of real interest rates," *BIS working paper* 685.

Boudoukh, Jacob; Matthew Richardson; Ashwin Thapar; and Franklin Wang (2019), "Optimal currency hedging for international equity portfolios," *Financial Analysts Journal* **75**(4), 65–83.

Boudoukh, Jacob; Ronen Israel; and Matthew Richardson (2019), "Long-horizon predictability: A cautionary tale," *Financial Analysts Journal* **75**(1), 17–30.

Boudoukh, Jacob; Ronen Israel; and Matthew Richardson (2020), "Biases in long-horizon predictive regressions," SSRN working paper.

Brav, Alon; Wei Jiang; Frank Partnoy; and Randall Thomas (2008), "Hedge fund activism, corporate governance, and firm performance," *Journal of Finance* **63**(4), 1729–1775.

Broeders, Dirk; and Kristy Jansen (2021), "Pension funds and drivers of heterogeneous investment strategies," SSRN working paper.

Broeders, Dirk; Kristy Jansen; and Bas Werker (2021), "Pension fund's illiquid assets allocation under liquidity and capital requirements," *Journal of Pension Economics & Finance* **20**(1), 102–124.

Brooks, Jordan (2017), "A half century of macro momentum," AQR white paper.

Brooks, Jordan (2021), "What drives bond yields," AQR white paper.

Brooks, Jordan; Severin Tsuji; and Daniel Villalon (2018), "Superstar investors," *Journal of Investing.* **28**(1), 124–135.

Brooks, Jordan; Tony Gould; and Scott Richardson (2020), "Active fixed income illusions," *Journal of Fixed Income* **29**(4), 5–19.

Brown, Aaron (2011), *Red-Blooded Risk*, Wiley.

Brown, Aaron (2015), *Financial Risk Management for Dummies*, For Dummies.

Brown, Gregory W.; and Steven N. Kaplan (2019). "Have private equity returns really declined?" *Journal of Private Equity* **22**(4), 11–18.

Brown, Gregory; Wendy Hu; and Bert-Klemens Kuhn (2021), "Private investments in diversified portfolios," UNC working paper.

Butler, Adam, et al. (2018), weblink https://advisoranalyst.com/etfs/2018/09/07/skis-and-bikes-the-untold-story-of-diversification-2/.

Calluzzo, Paul; Fabio Moneta; and Selim Topaloglu (2019), "When anomalies are publicized broadly, do institutions trade accordingly?" *Management Science* **65**(10), 4555–4574.

Campbell John Y.; Sunderam Adi; and Viceira Luis M. (2017), "Inflation bets or deflation hedges? The changing risks of nominal bonds," *Critical Finance Review.* 6, 263–301.

Campbell, John Y. (2019), *Financial Decisions and Markets: A Course in Asset Pricing*, Princeton University Press.

Campbell, John Y.; and Robert J. Shiller (1998), "Valuation ratios and the long-run stock market outlook," *Journal of Portfolio Management* **24**(2), 11–26.

Campbell, John Y.; and Samuel B. Thompson (2008), "Predicting excess stock returns out of sample: Can anything beat the historical average?" *Review of Financial Studies* **21**, 1509–1531.

Campbell, John Y; and Roman Sigalov (2020), "Portfolio choice with sustainable spending: A model of reaching for yield," *NBER working paper* 27025.

Carney, Mark (2021), *Value(s): Building a Better World for All*, PublicAffairs.

Case, Karl E.; and Robert J Shiller (1990), "Forecasting prices and excess returns in the housing market," *Real Estate Economics* **18**(3), 253–273.

CEM Benchmarking (2020), "Investment cost effectiveness analysis (for the 10-year period ending Dec. 31, 2019) for the Norwegian Government Pension Fund Global" in www.regjeringen.no.

Chambers, David; and Elroy Dimson (2015), "The British origins of the US endowment model," *Financial Analysts Journal* **71**(2), 8–12.

Chambers, David; and Elroy Dimson (2016), *Financial Market History: Reflections on the Past for Investors Today*, CFA Institute Research Foundation.

Chambers, David; Christophe Spaenjers; and Eva Steiner (2021), "The rate of return on real estate: Long-run micro-level evidence," *Review of Financial Studies* **34**(8), 3572–3607.

Chambers, David; Elroy Dimson; and Antti Ilmanen (2012), "The Norway model," *Journal of Portfolio Management* **38**(2), 67–81.

Chambers, David; Elroy Dimson; and Antti Ilmanen (2021), "The Norway model in perspective," *Journal of Portfolio Management* **47**(5), 178–187.

Chambers, David; Elroy Dimson; and Charikleia Kaffe (2020), "Seventy-five years of investing for future generations," *Financial Analysts Journal* **76**(4), 5–21.

Chan, Louis K.C.; Narasimhan Jegadeesh; and Josef Lakonishok (1996), "Momentum strategies," *Journal of Finance* **51**(5), 1681–1713.

Chen, Joseph S. (2019), "Currency investing throughout recent centuries," SSRN working paper.

Chen, Nai-Fu; Richard Roll; and Stephen A. Ross (1986), "Economic forces and the stock market," *Journal of Business* **59**, 383–403.

Christiansen, Charlotte; Angelo Ranaldo, and Paul Soderlind (2011), "The time-varying systematic risk of carry trade strategies," *Journal of Financial and Quantitative Analysis* **46**(4), 1107–1125.

Chua, David; Mark Kritzman; and Sébastien Page (2009), "The myth of diversification," *Journal of Portfolio Management* **36**(1), 26–35.

Cieslak, Anna (2018), "Short-rate expectations and unexpected returns in treasury bonds," *Review of Financial Studies* **31**(9), 3265–3306.

Cieslak, Anna; Adair Morse; and Annette Vissing-Jorgensen (2019), "Stock returns over the FOMC cycle," *Journal of Finance* **74**(5), 2201–2248.

Cieslak, Anna; and Pavol Povala (2015), "Expected returns in Treasury bonds," *Review of Financial Studies* **28**(10), 2859–2901.

Clarke, Roger; Harindra de Silva; and Steven Thorley (2006a), "Minimum-variance portfolios in the US equity market," *Journal of Portfolio Management* **33**(1), 10–24.

Clarke, Roger; Harindra de Silva; and Steven Thorley (2002), "Portfolio constraints and the fundamental law of active management," *Financial Analysts Journal* **58**(5), 48–66.

Clarke, Roger; Harindra de Silva; and Steven Thorley (2006b), "The fundamental law of active management," *Journal of Investment Management* **4**(3), 54–72.

Clowes, Michael J. (2000), *The Money Flood: How Pension Funds Revolutionized Investing*, Wiley.

Cochrane, John (2005), *Asset Pricing*, Princeton University Press.

Cochrane, John H. (1999), "Portfolio advice for a multifactor world," CRSP working paper.

Cochrane, John H. (2011). "Presidential address: Discount rates," *Journal of Finance* **66**, 1047–1108.

Coggan, Philip (2020), *More: A History of the World Economy from the Iron Age to the Information Age*, Economist.

Cohen, Lauren; and Andrea Frazzini (2008), "Economic links and predictable returns," *Journal of Finance* **63**, 1977–2011.

Cornell, Bradford (2010), "Economic growth and equity Investing," *Financial Analysts Journal* **66**(1), 54–64.

Cornell, Bradford; Jason Hsu; and David Nanigian (2017), "Does past performance matter in investment manager selection?" *Journal of Portfolio Management* **43**(4), 33–43.

Cremers, Martin; Jon Fulkerson; and Timothy Riley (2019), "Challenging the conventional wisdom on active management: A review of the past 20 years of academic literature on actively managed mutual funds," *Financial Analysts Journal* **75**(4), 8–35.

Crump, Richard; Stefano Eusepi; and Emanuel Moench (2018). "The term structure of expectations and bond yields," Staff report 775, Federal Reserve Bank of New York.

Czasonis, Megan; William Kinlaw; Mark Kritzman; and David Turkington (2020), "Private equity and the leverage myth," *Journal of Alternative Investments* **23**(3), 21–31.

Da, Zhi; Umit G. Gurun; and Mitch Warachka (2014), "Frog in the pan: Continuous information and momentum," *Review of Financial Studies* **27**(7), 2171–2218.

Dahlquist, Magnus; Adam Farago; and Roméo Tédongap (2017), "Asymmetries and portfolio choice," *Review of Financial Studies* **30**, 667–702.

Dahlquist, Magnus; and Markus Ibert (2021), "How cyclical are stock market return expectations? Evidence from capital market assumptions," Swedish House of Finance research paper 21-1.

D'Amico Stefania; and Athanasios Orphanides (2014), "Inflation uncertainty and disagreement in bond risk premia," Federal Reserve Bank of Chicago working paper 2014-24.

Damodaran, Aswath (2021), "Equity risk premiums (ERP): Determinants, estimation and implications – The 2021 Edition," SSRN working paper.

Daniel, Kent D.; David Hirshleifer; and Avanidhar Subrahmanyam (1998), "Investor psychology and security market under- and overreactions," *Journal of Finance* **53**, 1839–1885.

Daniel, Kent; and Sheridan Titman (1998), "Characteristics or covariances?" *Journal of Portfolio Management* 24(4), 24–33.

Daniel, Kent; and Tobias J. Moskowitz (2016), "Momentum crashes," *Journal of Financial Economics* **122**(2), 221–247.

Daniel, Kent; Robert Hodrick; and Zhongjin Lu (2017), "The carry trade: Risks and drawdowns," *Critical Finance Review* **6**(2), 211–262.

Davis, Morris A.; Andreas Lehnert; and Robert F. Martin (2008), "The rent-price ratio for the aggregate stock of owner-occupied housing," *Review of Income and Wealth* **54**(2), 279–284.

De la O, Ricardo; and Sean Myers, Sean (2021), "Subjective cash flow and discount rate expectations," *Journal of Finance forthcoming.*

De Long, J. Bradford; Andrei Shleifer; Lawrence H. Summers; and Robert J. Waldmann (1990), "Positive feedback investment strategies and destabilizing rational speculation," *Journal of Finance* 45, 375–395.

Demers, Andrew; and Andrea L. Eisfeldt (2021), "Total returns to single family rentals," SSRN white paper.

DeMiguel, Victor; Lorenzo Garlappi; and Ramon Uppal (2009), "Optimal versus naive diversification: How inefficient is the 1/N portfolio strategy?" *Review of Financial Studies* **22**(5), 1915–1953,

Dhillon, Jusvin; Antti Ilmanen; and John Liew (2016), "Balancing on the Life Cycle: Target-Date Funds Need Better Diversification," *Journal of Portfolio Management* **42**(4), 12–27.

Dichev. Ilia (2007), "What are stock investors' actual historical returns? Evidence from dollar-weighted returns," *American Economic Review* 97(1), 386–401.

Dimensional (2020), "Why worry about survivorship bias?" *Insights* Oct 2, 2020.

Dimson, Elroy; Oguzhan Karakas; and Xi Li (2015), "Active ownership," *Review of Financial Studies* **28**(12), 3225–3268.

Dimson, Elroy; Paul Marsh; and Mike Staunton (2002), *Triumph of the Optimists: 101 Years of Global Investment Returns,* Princeton University Press.

Dimson, Elroy; Paul Marsh; and Mike Staunton (2005), *Global Investment Returns Yearbook 2005,* ABN.

Dimson, Elroy; Paul Marsh; and Mike Staunton (2010), *Global Investment Returns Yearbook 2010.* Credit Suisse Research Institute.

Dimson, Elroy; Paul Marsh; and Mike Staunton (2018), *Global Investment Returns Yearbook 2018.* Credit Suisse Research Institute.

Dimson, Elroy; Paul Marsh; and Mike Staunton (2020), "Divergent ESG ratings," *Journal of Portfolio Management* **47**(1), 75–87.

Dimson, Elroy; Paul Marsh; and Mike Staunton (2021), *Global Investment Returns Yearbook 2021.* Credit Suisse Research Institute.

Ding, Zhuanxin; and R. Douglas Martin (2017), "The fundamental law of active management: Redux," *Journal of Empirical Finance* **43**, 91–114.

Doeswijk, Ronald; Trevin Lam; and Laurens Swinkels (2014), "The global multi-asset market portfolio, 1959–2012," *Financial Analysts Journal* **70**(2), 26–41.

Døskeland, Trond M.; and Per Strömberg (2018), "Evaluating investments in unlisted equity for the Norwegian Government Pension Fund Global (GPFG)." Report for the Norwegian Ministry of Finance.

Drechsler, Itamar; and Qingyi Drechsler (2016), "Shorting premium and asset pricing anomalies;" SSRN working paper.

Duckworth, Angela (2016), *Grit: The Power of Passion and Perseverance,* Scribner.

Duke, Annie (2018), *Thinking in Bets: Making Smarter Decisions When You Don't Have All the Facts,* Portfolio.

Dunn, Jeff; Marisol Hernandez; and Chris Palazzolo (2020), "Clearing the air: Responsible investment," *Journal of Portfolio Management* **46**(3), Special Issue on Ethical Investing.

Dunn, Jeff; Shaun Fitzgibbons; and Lukasz Pomorski (2018), "Assessing risk through environmental, social, and governance exposures," *Journal of Investment Management* 16(1), 4–17.

Dyck, Alexander; Karl Lins; and Lukasz Pomorski (2013), "Does active management pay? New international evidence," *Review of Asset Pricing Studies* 3(2), 200–228.

Edelen, Roger M.; Ozgur Ince; and Gregory B. Kadlec (2016), "Institutional investors and stock returns anomalies," *Journal of Financial Economics* **119**, 472–488.

Ehsani, Sina; and Juhani T. Linnainmaa (2019). "Factor momentum and the momentum factor," NBER working paper 25551.

Eichholtz, Piet; Matthijs Korevaar; and Thies Lindenthal (2018), "500 years of urban rents, housing quality and affordability," Maastricht University working paper.

Eichholtz, Piet; Matthijs Korevaar; Thies Lindenthal; and Ronan Tallec (2021), "The total return and risk to residential real estate," *Review of Financial Studies* **34**(8), 3608–3646.

Eisfeldt, Andrea L; Edward Kim; and Dimitris Papanikolaou (2020), "Intangible value," *NBER working paper* 28056.

Elton, Edwin J.; Gruber, Martin J.; and Blake Christopher R. (2012), "Does mutual fund size matter? The relationship between size and performance," *Review of Asset Pricing Studies* **2**(1), 31–55.

Engelberg Joseph; David McLean; and Jeffrey Pontiff (2018), "Anomalies and news," *Journal of Finance* **73**(5), 1971–2001.

Engle, Robert F.; Stefano Gihlio; Bryan Kelly; Heebum Lee; and Johannes Stroebel (2020), "Hedging climate change news," *Review of Financial Studies* **33**(3), 1184–1216.

Ennis, Richard M. (2020), "Institutional investment strategy and manager choice: A Critique." *Journal of Portfolio Management* **46**(5), 104–117.

Ennis, Richard M. (2021), "Failure of the endowment model," *Journal of Portfolio Management* **47**(5) 128–143.

Erb, Claude B.; and Campbell R. Harvey (2006), "The tactical and strategic value of commodity futures," *Financial Analysts Journal* **62**(2), 69–97.

Erb, Claude B.; Campbell R. Harvey; and Tadas E. Viskanta (2020), "Gold, the golden constant, and déjà vu," *Financial Analysts Journal,* **76**(4), 134–142.

Etula, Erkko; Kalle Rinne; Matti Suominen; and Lauri Vaittinen (2020), "Dash for cash: Monthly market impact of institutional liquidity needs," *Review of Financial Studies* **33**(1), 75–111.

Faber, Mebanr (2015), *Global Asset Allocation: A Survey of the World's Top Asset Allocation Strategies,* Mebane Faber.

Falkenstein, Eric (2012), *The Missing Risk Premium: Why Low Volatility Investing Works,* CreateSpace Independent Publishing.

Fallon, William; James Park; and Danny Yu (2015), "Asset allocation implications of the global volatility premium," *Financial Analysts Journal* **71**(5), 38–56.

Fama, Eugene F. (1998), "Market efficiency, long-term returns, and behavioral finance," *Journal of Financial Economics* **49**(3), 283–306.

Fama, Eugene F.; and James D. MacBeth (1973), "Risk, return, and equilibrium: empirical tests." *Journal of Political Economy* **81**(3), 607–636.

Fama, Eugene F.; and Kenneth R. French (1992), The cross-section of expected stock returns," *Journal of Finance* **47**, 427–465.

Fama, Eugene F.; and Kenneth R. French, (1993), "Common risk factors in the returns on stocks and bonds," *Journal of Financial Economics* **33**, 3–56.

Fama, Eugene F.; and Kenneth R. French (2010), "Luck versus skill in the cross-section of mutual fund returns," *Journal of Finance* **65**(5), 1915–1947.

Fama, Eugene F.; and Kenneth R. French (2020), "Comparing cross-section and time-series factor models," *Review of Financial Studies* **33**(5), 1891–1926.

Fama, Eugene F.; and Kenneth R. French, (2007), "Disagreement, tastes, and asset prices," *Journal of Financial Economics* **83**(3), 667–689.

Fama, Eugene F.; and Kenneth R. French. (2015). "A five-factor asset pricing model." *Journal of Financial Economics* **116**(1), 1–22.

Francis, Jack Clark; and Roger G. Ibbotson (2020), "Real estate returns," *Journal of Alternative Investments* **23**(2), 111–126.

Frazzini, Andrea (2006), "The disposition effect and underreaction to news," *Journal of Finance* **61**(4), 2017–2046.

Frazzini, Andrea; and Lasse H. Pedersen (2014), "Betting against beta," *Journal of Financial Economics* **111**(1), 1–25.

Frazzini, Andrea; and Owen A. Lamont (2008), "Dumb money: mutual fund flows and the cross-section of stock returns," *Journal of Financial Economics* **88**, 299–322.

Frazzini, Andrea; and Owen Lamont (2007), "The earnings announcement premium and trading volume," *NBER working paper* 13090.

Frazzini, Andrea; David Kabiller; and Lasse H. Pedersen (2018), "Buffett's alpha," *Financial Analysts Journal* **74**(4), 35–55.

Frazzini, Andrea; Ronen Israel; and Tobias J. Moskowitz (2017), "Trading costs of asset pricing anomalies," SSRN working paper.

Frazzini, Andrea; Ronen Israel; and Tobias J. Moskowitz (2018), "Trading costs," SSRN working paper.

Fried, Jesse; Paul Ma; and Charles Wang (2021), "Stock investors' returns are exaggerated," SSRN working paper.

Gabaix, Xavier; and Ralph Koijen (2020), "In search of the origins of financial fluctuations: The inelastic markets hypothesis," SSRN working paper.

Gadzinski, Gregory; Markus Schuller; and Andrea Vacchino (2018), "The global capital stock: Finding a proxy for the unobservable global market portfolio," *Journal of Portfolio Management* **44**(7), 12–23.

Garg, Ashish; Christian Goulding; Campbell R. Harvey; and Michele Mazzoleni (2020), "Breaking bad trends," SSRN working paper.

Garleanu, Nicolae; and Lasse H. Pedersen (2013), "Dynamic trading with predictable returns and transaction costs," *Journal of Finance* **68**(6), 2309–2340.

Garleanu, Nicolae; and Lasse H. Pedersen (2018), "Efficiently inefficient markets for assets and asset management," *Journal of Finance* **73**(4), 1663–1712.

Garleanu, Nicolae; and Lasse H. Pedersen (2021), "Active and passive investing: Understanding Samuelson's dictum," *Review of Asset Pricing Studies, forthcoming.*

Geczy, Christopher C.; and Mikhail Samonov (2016), "Two centuries of price-return momentum," *Financial Analysts Journal* 72(5), 32–56.

Geczy, Christopher C.; and Mikhail Samonov (2017), "Two centuries of multi-asset momentum (Equities, bonds, currencies, commodities, sectors and stocks)," SSRN working paper.

Gerakos, Joseph; Juhani Linnainmaa; and Adair Morse (2016), "Asset managers: institutional performance and smart betas," SSRN working paper.

Giglio, Stefano; Matteo Maggiori; Johannes Stroebel; and Stephen Utkus (2021), "Five facts about beliefs and portfolios," *American Economic Review* 111(5), 1481–1522.

Gladwell, Malcolm (2008), *Outliers: The Story of Success*, Little, Brown.

Goetzmann, William N. (2016), *Money Changes Everything: How Finance Made Civilization Possible*, Princeton University Press.

Goetzmann, William N.; Christophe Spaenjers; and Stijn Van Nieuwerburgh (2021), "Real and private-value assets," *NBER working paper* 28580.

Goyal, Amit (2004), "Demographics, stock market flows, and stock returns." *Journal of Financial and Quantitative Analysis*, 39(1), 115–142.

Goyal, Amit; Antti Ilmanen; and David Kabiller (2015), "Bad habits and good practices," *Journal of Portfolio Management* **41**(4), 97–107.

Goyal, Amil; and Sunil Wahal (2008), "The selection and termination of investment management firms by plan sponsors," *Journal of Finance* 63, 1805–1847.

Goyal, Amit; Sunil Wahal; and Deniz Yavuz (2020), "Choosing investment managers," *Swiss Finance Institute Research Paper* 20-63.

Graham, Benjamin; and David L. Dodd (1934), *Security Analysis*, McGraw Hill.

Graham, John R.; and Harvey, Campbell R. (2018), "*The equity risk premium in 2018*," Duke University working paper.

Gray, Wesley; and Jack Vogel (2016), *Quantitative Momentum, Wiley.*

Gray, Wesley; and Tobias Carlisle (2012), *Quantitative Value, Wiley.*

Green, Clifton; Ruoyan Huang; Quan Wen; and Dexin Zhou (2019), "Crowdsourced employer reviews and stock returns," *Journal of Financial Economics* **134**(1), 236–251.

Greenwood, Robin M.; Samuel G. Hanson; Andrei Shleifer; and Jakob Sørensen, (2020), "Predictable financial crises," *NBER working paper* 27396.

Greenwood, Robin; and Andrei Shleifer (2014). "Expectations of returns and expected returns," *Review of Financial Studies* **27**(3), 714–746.

Greenwood, Robin; Samuel G. Hanson; Joshua S. Rudolph; and Lawrence H. Summers (2014), "*Government debt management at the zero lower bound*," Brookings Paper.

Greyserman, Alex; and Kathryn Kaminski (2014), *Trend Following with Managed Futures: The Search for Crisis Alpha*, Wiley.

Grinold, Richard C. (1989), "The fundamental law of active management," *Journal of Portfolio Management* **15**(3), 30–37.

Grinold, Richard; and Ronald Kahn (1999), *Active Portfolio Management: A Quantitative Approach for Producing Superior Returns and Controlling Risk,* McGraw Hill.

Grinold, Richard; and Ronald Kahn (2019), *Advances in Active Portfolio Management: New Developments in Quantitative Investing,* McGraw-Hill.

Grossman, Sanford J.; and Joseph E. Stiglitz (1980), "On the impossibility of informationally efficient markets," *American Economic Review,* **70**(3), 393–08.

Gu, Shihao; Bryan Kelly; and Dacheng Xiu (2020), "Empirical asset pricing via machine learning," *Review of Financial Studies* **33**(5), 2223–2273.

Gupta, Tarun; and Bryan Kelly (2019), "Factor momentum everywhere," *Journal of Portfolio Management* **45**(3), 13–36.

Haghani, Victor; and James White (2021). "*A practical guide to family wealth decisions,*" Elm Funds white paper.

Hallerbach, Winfried G.; and Patrick Houweling (2013), "Ibbotson's default premium: Risky data," *Journal of Investing* **22**(2), 95–105.

Hamilton, James D.; Ethan Harris; Jan Hatzius; and Kenneth D. West (2016), "The Equilibrium real funds rate: Past, present, and future," *IMF Economic Review* **64**(4), 660–707.

Hammond, Dennis (2020), "A better approach to systematic outperformance? 58 years of endowment performance," *Journal of Investing* **29**(5), 6–30.

Hammond, P. Brett; Martin L. Leibowitz; and Laurence B. Siegel (editors) (2012), "*Rethinking the equity risk premium,*" Research Foundation of CFA Institute.

Harris, Robert S.; Tim Jenkinson; and Steven N. Kaplan (2014), "Private equity performance: what do we know?" *Journal of Finance* **69**(5), 1851–1882.

Harris, Robert S.; Tim Jenkinson; and Steven N. Kaplan (2016), "How do private equity investments perform compared to public equity?" *Journal of Investment Management* **14**(3), 1–24.

Harris, Robert S.; Tim Jenkinson; Steven N. Kaplan; and Rudiger Stucke (2020), "Has persistence persisted in private equity? Evidence from buyout and venture capital funds," *NBER working paper* 28109.

Harris, Robert S.; Tim Jenkinson; and Rudiger Stucke (2012), "Are too many private equity funds top quartile?" *Journal of Applied Corporate Finance* **24**(4), 77–89.

Harvey, Campbell R.; and Akhtar Siddique (2000), "Conditional skewness in asset pricing tests," *Journal of Finance* **55**, 1263–1295.

Harvey, Campbell R.; Edward Hoyle; Russell Korgaonkar; Sandy Rattray; Matthew Sargaison; and Otto Van Hemert (2018), "The impact of volatility targeting," *Journal of Portfolio Management* **45**(1), 14–33.

Harvey, Campbell R.; Yan Liu; and Heqing Zhu (2016), "… And the cross-section of expected returns," *Review of Financial Studies* **29**, 5–68.

Harvey, Campbell R.; Sandy Rattray; and Otto Van Hemert (2021), *Strategic Risk Management: Designing Portfolios and Managing Risk,* Wiley Finance.

Hayley, Simon (2012), "Measuring investors' historical returns: Hindsight bias in dollar-weighted returns," Cass Business School working paper.

Hedayati, Saied; Brian K. Hurst; and Erik Stamelos (2018), "Transactions costs: Practical application," AQR white paper.

Hershfield, Hal E.; Daniel Goldstein; William F. Sharpe; Jesse Fox; Leo Yeykelis; Laura Carstensen; and Jeremy Bailenson (2011), "Increasing saving behavior through age-progressed renderings of the future self," *Journal of Marketing Research* **48**, S23–S37.

Hertwig, Ralph; and Ido Erev (2009), "The description–experience gap in risky choice," *Trends in Cognitive Sciences* **13**(12), 517–523.

Heston, Steven L.; and Ronnie Sadka (2008), "Seasonality in the cross-section of expected stock returns," *Journal of Financial Economics* **87**, 418–445.

Hirshleifer, David (2015), "Behavioral finance," *Annual Review of Financial Economics* **7**, 133–159.

Hoffstein, Corey; Nathan Faber; and Steven Braun (2020), "Rebalance Timing Luck: The (Dumb) Luck of Smart Beta," SSRN white paper.

Homer, Sidney; and Richard Sylla (2006), *A History of Interest Rates,* Rutgers University Press.

Hong, Harrison; and Marcin Kacperczyk (2009), "The price of sin: The effects of social norms on markets," *Journal of Financial Economics* **93**, 15–36.

Hou, Kewei; Chen Xue; and Lu Zhang (2015), "Digesting anomalies: An investment approach," *Review of Financial Studies* **28**(3), 650–705.

Hou, Kewei; Chen Xue; and Lue Zhang (2020), "Replicating anomalies," *Review of Financial Studies* **33**(5), 2019–2133.

Housel, Morgan (2020), *The Psychology of Money: Timeless Lessons on Wealth, Greed, and Happiness*, Harriman House.

Huber, Phil (2021), *The Allocator's Edge: The Modern Guide to Alternative Investments and the Future of Diversification*, Harriman House.

Hurst, Brian; Yao Hua Ooi; and Lasse H. Pedersen (2017), "A century of evidence on trend-following investing," *Journal of Portfolio Management* **44**(1), 15–29.

Huss, John; and Thomas Maloney (2017), "Portfolio rebalancing; Common misconceptions," AQR white paper.

Ibbotson, Roger G.; and Laurence. B. Siegel (1983), "The world market wealth portfolio," *Journal of Portfolio Management* **9**(2), 5–17.

Ibbotson, Roger G.; Peng Chen; and Kevin X. Zhu (2010), "The ABCs of hedge funds: Alphas, betas, & costs," *Financial Analysts Journal* **67**(1), 15–25.

Ibbotson, Roger; and Peng Chen (2003), "Stock market returns in the long run: Participating in the real economy," *Financial Analysts Journal* **59**(1), 88–98.

Ilmanen, *Antti* (1995), "Time varying expected bond returns in international bond markets." *Journal of Finance* **50**, 481–506.

Ilmanen, Antti (1996), "Market rate expectations and forward rates," *Journal of Fixed Income* **6**(2), 8–22,

Ilmanen, Antti (2011), *Expected Returns: An Investor's Guide to Harvesting Market Rewards*, John Wiley and Sons.

Ilmanen, Antti (2012), "Do financial markets reward buying or selling insurance and lottery tickets?" *Financial Analyst Journal* **68**(5): 26–36.

Ilmanen, Antti (2013), "'Do financial markets reward buying or selling insurance and lottery tickets?' Author Response," *Financial Analyst Journal* **69**(2), 19–21.

Ilmanen, Antti (2016), "Who is on the other side?" Q-group presentation at https://www.q-group.org/wp-content/uploads/2016/10/ILMANEN_pp.pdf.

Ilmanen, Antti (2020), "The impact of smoothness on private equity expected returns," *Journal of Investing* **30**(1), 63–66.

Ilmanen, Antti; Swati Chandra; and Lars Nielsen (2015), "Are defensive stocks expensive? A closer look at value spreads," AQR white paper.

Ilmanen, Antti; Swati Chandra; and Nicholas McQuinn (2019), "Demystifying illiquid assets: Expected returns for real estate," AQR white paper.

Ilmanen, Antti; Swati Chandra; and Nicholas McQuinn (2020), "Demystifying illiquid assets: Expected returns for private equity," *Journal of Alternative Investments* **22**(3), 8–22.

Ilmanen, Antti; Ronen Israel; Rachel Lee; Tobias Moskowitz; and Ashwin Thapar (2021a), "How do factor premia vary over time? A century of evidence," *Journal of Investment Management* **19**(2), 15–57.

Ilmanen, Antti; David Kabiller; Laurence B. Siegel; and Rodney Sullivan (2017), "Defined contribution retirement plans should look and feel more like defined benefit plans," *Journal of Portfolio Management* **43**(2) 61–76.

Ilmanen, Antti; and Jared Kizer (2012), "The death of diversification has been greatly exaggerated," *Journal of Portfolio Management* **38**(3), 15–27.

Ilmanen, Antti; and Thomas Maloney (2015), "Portfolio rebalancing, part 1: Strategic asset allocation," AQR white paper.

Ilmanen, Antti; Thomas Maloney; and Adrienne Ross (2014), "Exploring macroeconomic sensitivities," *Journal of Portfolio Management* **40**(3), 87–99.

Ilmanen, Antti; and Matthew Rauseo (2018), "Intelligent risk taking" *in How Persistent Low Returns Will Shape Saving and Retirement* (2018); edited by Olivia Mitchell, Robert Clark, and Raimond Maurer; Oxford University Press.

Ilmanen, Antti; Matthew Rauseo; and Liza Truax (2016), "How much should DC savers worry about expected returns?" *Journal of Retirement* **4**(2), 44–53.

Ilmanen, Antti; Ashwin Thapar; Harsha Tummala; and Dan Villalon (2021b), "Tail risk hedging: Contrasting put and trend strategies," *Journal of Systematic Investing* **1**(1), 111–124.

Ilmanen, Antti; and Daniel Villalon (2012), "Alpha beyond expected returns," AQR white paper.

Innocenti, Robert (1969), "The stock-bond split decision for pension funds," **25**(6), 97–102.

Israel, Ronen; Sarah Jiang; and Adrienne Ross (2018), "Craftsmanship alpha: An application to style investing," *Journal of Portfolio Management* **44**(2), 23–39.

Israel, Ronen; Bryan Kelly; and Tobias Moskowitz (2020). "Can machines "learn" finance" *Journal of Investment Management* **18**(2), 23–36.

Israel, Ronen; Kristoffer Laursen; and Scott Richardson (2021), "Is (systematic) value investing dead?" *Journal of Portfolio Management* **47**(2), 38–62.

Israel, Ronen; Diogo Palhares; and Scott Richardson (2018.) "Common factors in corporate bond returns." *Journal of Investment Management* **16**(2), 17–46.

Israelov, Roni; and Michael Katz (2011), "To trade or not to trade? Informed trading with high-frequency signals for long-term investors," *Financial Analysts Journal* **67**(5), 23–36.

Ivashina, Victoria; and Josh Lerner (2019), *Patient Capital: The Challenges and Promises of Long-Term Investing,* Princeton University Press.

Jacobs, Bruce I.; and Kenneth N. Levy (2021), "Factor modeling: The benefits of disentangling cross-sectionally for explaining stock returns," *Journal of Portfolio Management* **47**(6), 33–50.

Jacobs, Heiko; and Sebastian Muller (2020), "Anomalies across the globe: Once public, no longer existent?" *Journal of Financial Economics* **135**(1), 213–230.

Jegadeesh, Narasimhan; and Sheridan Titman (1993), "Returns to buying winners and selling losers: Implications for stock market efficiency." *Journal of Finance* **48**(1), 65–91.

Jensen, Theis I.; Bryan Kelly; and Lasse H. Pedersen (2021), "Is there a replication crisis in finance?" NBER working paper 28432.

Jones, Brad (2017), "Leaning with the wind: Long-term asset owners and procyclical investing," *Journal of Investment Management* **15**(2), 16–38.

Jones, Robert C.; and Russ Wermers (2011), "Active management in mostly efficient markets," *Financial Analysts Journal* **67**(6), 29–45.

Jorda Òscar; Katharina Knoll; Dmitry Kuvshinov; Moritz Schularick; and Alan M Taylor (2019), "The rate of return on everything, 1870–2015," *Quarterly Journal of Economics* **134**(3), 1225–1298.

Jorda Òscar; Sanjay R. Singh; and Alan M Taylor (2020), "Longer-run economic consequences of pandemics," NBER working paper 26934.

Jurek, Jakub (2014), "Crash-neutral currency carry trades," *Journal of Financial Economics* **113**, 325–347.

Kahn, Ronald N.; Matthew H. Scanlan; and Laurence B. Siegel (2006), "Five myths about fees," *Journal of Portfolio Management* **32**(3,) 56–64.

Kahneman, Daniel (2011), *Thinking, Fast and Slow,* Farrar, Straus and Giroux.

Kahneman, Daniel; and Amos Tversky (1979), "Prospect theory: An analysis of decision under risk," *Econometrica* **47**(2), 263–291.

Kahneman, Daniel; and Dan Lovallo (1993), "Timid choices and bold forecasts: A cognitive perspective on risk taking," *Management Science* **39**(1), 17–31.

Kaminski, Kathryn (2011), "In search of crisis alpha: A short guide to investing in managed futures," CME Group white paper.

Kaplan Steven N.; and Antoinette Schoar (2005), "Private equity performance: Returns, persistence, and capital flows," *Journal of Finance* **60**, 1791–1823.

Kaplan, Steven N.; and Per Strömberg (2009), "Leveraged buyouts and private equity," *Journal of Economic Perspectives* **23**(1), 121–146.

Kartashova, Katya (2014), "Private equity premium puzzle revisited," *American Economic Review* **104**(10), 3297–3334.

Kay, John; and Mervyn King (2020), *Radical Uncertainty,* Little, Brown.

Keloharju, Matti; Juhani T. Linnainmaa; and Peter Nyberg (2016), "Return seasonalities," *Journal of Finance* **71**(4), 1557–1590.

Kessler, Stephan; Bernd Scherer; and Jan P. Harries (2020), "Value by design?" *Journal of Portfolio Management* **46**(2), 25–43.

Kim, Don H.; and Jonathan H. Wright (2005), "An arbitrage-free three-factor term structure model and the recent behavior of long-term yields and distant-horizon forward rates," FEDS working paper 2005-33, Board of Governors of the Federal Reserve System.

Kinlaw, Will; Mark Kritzman; and Jason Mao (2015), "The components of private equity performance: Implications for portfolio choice," *Journal of Alternative Investments* **18**(2), 25–38.

Kinlaw, William; Mark P. Kritzman; Sebastien Page; and David Turkington (2021), "The myth of diversification reconsidered," *Journal of Portfolio Management* **47**(8), 124–137.

Kinlaw, William; Mark P. Kritzman; and David Turkington (2017), *A Practitioner's Guide to Asset Allocation*, Wiley.

Kizer, Jared; Sean Grover; and Corey Hendershot (2019), "Re-examining the credit premium," SSRN working paper.

Knoll, Katharina; Moritz Schularick; and Thomas Steger (2017), "No price like home: Global house prices, 1870–2012," *American Economic Review* **107**(2), 331–53.

Koedijk, Kees; Alfred Slaeger; and Jaap van Dam (2020), *Achieving Investment Excellence: A Practical Guide for Trustees of Pension Funds, Endowments and Foundations*, Wiley.

Koedijk, Kees; and Alfred Slager (2021), "New perspective on investment models," *Journal of Portfolio Management* **47**(5), 15–23.

Koijen, Ralph S.; Tobias J. Moskowitz; Lasse H. Pedersen; and Evert B. Vrugt (2018), "Carry," *Journal of Financial Economics* **127**(2), 197–225.

Kolm, Petter; Gordon Ritter; and Joseph Simonian (2021), "Black–Litterman and beyond: The Bayesian paradigm in investment management," *Journal of Portfolio Management* **47**(5), 91–113.

Kopecky, Joseph; and Alan Taylor (2020), "The murder-suicide of the rentier: population aging and the risk premium," NBER working paper 26943.

Korevaar, Matthijs (2021), "Reaching for yield: How investors amplify housing booms and busts," SSRN working paper.

Kozicki, Sharon; and Peter A. Tinsley (2006), "Survey-based estimates of the term structure of expected US inflation," Bank of Canada working paper 06-46.

Kritzman, Mark P. (2000), *Puzzles of Finance: Six Practical Problems and Their Remarkable Solutions*, Wiley.

Kritzman, Mark; Sebastien Page; and David Turkington (2010), "In defense of optimization: The fallacy of 1/N," *Financial Analysts Journal* **66**(2), 3139.

Kuvshinov, Dmitry; and Kaspar Zimmermann (2021), "The big bang: Stock market capitalization in the long run," *Journal of Financial Economics, forthcoming*.

L'Her, Jean-Francois; Rossitsa Stoyanova; Kathryn Shaw; William Scott; and Charissa Lai (2016), "A bottom-up approach to the risk-adjusted performance of the buyout fund market." *Financial Analysts Journal* **72**(4), 36–48.

L'Her, Jean-François; Tarek Masmoudi; and Ram Karthik Krishnamoorthy (2018), "Net buybacks and the seven dwarfs," *Financial Analysts Journal* **74**(4), 57–85.

Lakonishok, Josef; Andrei Shleifer; and Robert W. Vishny (1994), "Contrarian investment, extrapolation, and risk," *Journal of Finance* **49**(5), 1541–1578.

Leibowitz, Martin L.; Anthony Bova; and P. Brett Hammond (2010), *The Endowment Model of Investing: Return, Risk, and Diversification*, Wiley Finance.

Leibowitz, Martin; Anthony Bova; and Stanley Kogelman (2014), "Long-term bond returns under duration targeting," *Financial Analysts Journal*, **70**(1), 31–51.

Leibowitz, Martin L.; and Antti Ilmanen (2016), "US corporate DB pension plans—Today's challenges," *Journal of Portfolio Management Special* Issue, 54–66.

Lemperiere, Yves; Cyril Deremble; Trung-Tu Nguyen; Philip Seager; Marc Potters; and Jean-Philippe Bouchaud (2017), "Risk premia: asymmetric tail risks and excess returns," *Quantitative Finance* **17**(1), 1–14.

Lerner, Josh; Jason Mao; Antoinette Schoar; and Nan Zhang (2020), "Investing outside the box: Evidence from alternative vehicles in private equity," Harvard Business School Finance working paper 19-012.

Lettau, Martin; Matteo Maggiori; and Michael Weber (2015), "Conditional risk premia in currency markets and other asset classes," *Journal of Financial Economics* **114**, 197–225.

Lettau, Martin; Sydney Ludvigson; and Paulo Manoel (2019), "Characteristics of mutual fund portfolios: Where are the value funds?" NBER working paper 25381.

Lev, Baruch I.; and Anup Srivastava (2019), "Explaining the recent failure of value investing," SSRN working paper.

Levine, Ari; Yao Hua Ooi; Matthew Richardson; and Caroline Sasseville (2018), "Commodities for the long run," *Financial Analysts Journal* **74**(2), 55–68.

Lewellen, Jonathan (2011), "Institutional investors and the limits of arbitrage," *Journal of Financial Economics* **102**, 62–82.

Liberman Joseph; Clemens Sialm; Nathan Sosner; and Liu Wang (2020), "The tax benefits of separating alpha from beta." *Financial Analysts Journal* **76**(1), 38–61.

Litterman, Bob (2003), *Modern Investment Management: An Equilibrium Approach*, Wiley.

Lo, Andrew W.; and Stephen R. Foerster (2021), *In Pursuit of the Perfect Portfolio: The Stories, Voices, and Key Insights of the Pioneers Who Shaped the Way We Invest*, Princeton University Press.

Lo, Andrew W.; Egor Matveyev; and Stefan Zeume (2021), "The risk, reward, and asset allocation of nonprofit endowment funds," MIT Sloan research paper 6163-20.

Lochstoer, Lars; and Tyler Muir (2020), "Volatility expectations and returns," NBER working paper 28102.

Lopez de Prado, *Marcos* (2018), *Advances in Financial Machine Learning*, Wiley.

Lou, Dong; Christopher Polk; and Spyros Skouras (2019), "A tug of war: Overnight versus intraday expected returns," *Journal of Financial Economics* **134**(1), 192–213.

Lozada, Gabriel A. (2016), "Constant-duration bond portfolios' initial (rolling) yield forecasts return best at twice duration," University of Utah working paper.

Lu, Lina; Matthew Pritsker; Andrei Zlate; Kenechukwu Anadu; and James Bohn (2019), "Reach for yield by US public pension funds," FRB Boston Risk and Policy Analysis Unit Paper 19-2.

Luo, Cheng; Enrichetta Ravina; Marco Sammom; and Luis M. Viceira (2020), "Retail investors' contrarian behavior around news and the momentum effect," SSRN working paper.

Lussier, Jacques (2013), *Successful Investing Is a Process: Structuring Efficient Portfolios for Outperformance*, Bloomberg Press.

Lustig, Hanno; Nikolai Roussanov; and Adrien Verdelhan (2011), "Common risk factors in currency markets," *Review of Financial Studies* **24**, 3731–3777.

Malmendier, Ulrike; and Stefan Nagel (2011), "Depression babies: Do macroeconomic experiences affect risk-taking?" *Quarterly Journal of Economics* **126**(1), 373–416.

Malmendier, Ulrike; Stefan Nagel; and Zhen Yan (2021), "The making of hawks and doves," *Journal of Monetary Economics* **117**, 19–42.

Maloney, Thomas; and Tobias J. Moskowitz (2021), "Value and interest rates: Are rates to blame for value's torments?" *Journal of Portfolio Management* **47**(6), 65–87.

Markowitz, Harry M. (1952), "Portfolio selection," *Journal of Finance* **7**(1), 77–91.

Mauboussin, Michael J. (2009), *Think Twice: Harnessing the Power of Counterintuition*, Harvard Business Review Press.

Mauboussin, Michael J. (2012), *The Success Equation: Untangling Skill and Luck in Business, Sports, and Investing*, Harvard Business Review Press.

Mauboussin, Michael; and Dan Callahan (2020), *Public to Private Equity in the United States: A Long-Term Look*, Consilient Observer, Counterpoint Global Insights.

McKinsey (2021), "A year of disruption in the private markets," *McKinsey Global Private Markets Review 2021*.

McLean, David; and Jeffrey Pontiff (2016), "Does academic research destroy stock return predictability?" *Journal of Finance* **71**(1), 5–32.

McLean, David; Jeffrey Pontiff; and Christopher Reilly (2020), "Taking sides on return predictability," SSRN working paper.

McQuarrie, Edward F. (2020), "When do corporate bond investors earn a premium for bearing risk? A test spanning the Great Depression of the 1930s," SSRN working paper.

McQuarrie, Edward F. (2021), "New lessons from market history: Sometimes bonds win," SSRN working paper.

McQuinn, Nicholas; Ashwin Thapar; and Dan Villalon (2021), "Portfolio protection? It's a long (term) story." *Journal of Portfolio Management* **47**(3), 35–50.

Mee, Kristjan (2017), "GDP and earnings growth in emerging markets – a loose connection," *Schroders*.

Meng, Yu (Ben) (2019), "The success equation," *Journal of Investment Management* 17(4), 5–8.

Menkhoff, Lukas; Lucio Sarno; Mark Schmeling; and Andreas Schrimpf (2012), "Carry trades and global foreign exchange volatility," *Journal of Finance* **67**, 681–718.

Mercer CFA Institute (2020), Global Pension Index, Mercer Australia.

Merton, Robert C. (1973), "An Intertemporal Capital Asset Pricing Model," *Econometrica,* **41**(5), 867–887.

Misirli, Efdal; Daniela Scida; and Mikhail Velikov (2020), "Peer momentum," SSRN working paper.

Mitchell, Olivia S. (2020), "Building better retirement systems in the wake of the global pandemic," SSRN working paper.

Morecroft, Nigel; and Craig Turnbull (2019), "Institutional equity investing in Britain from 1900 to 2000," *Financial History Review* **26**(1), 1–19.

Moore, Don A. (2020), *Perfectly Confident: How to Calibrate Your Decisions Wisely*, Harper Business.

Moreira, Alan; and Tyler Muir (2017), "Volatility-managed portfolios," *Journal of Finance* **72**(4), 1611–1644.

Moskowitz, Tobias J.; and Kaushik Vasudevan (2021), "What can betting markets tell us about investor preferences and beliefs? Implications for low risk anomalies," SSRN white paper.

Moskowitz, Tobias J.; Yao Hua Ooi; and Lasse H. Pedersen (2012), "Time series momentum," *Journal of Financial Economics* **104**(2), 228–250.

Munday, Shawn; Wendy Hu; Tobias True; and Jian Zhang (2018), "Performance of private credit funds: A first look," *Journal of Alternative Investments* **21**(2), 31–51.

Ng, Kwok Yuen; and Bruce Phelps (2011), "Capturing credit spread premium," *Financial Analysts Journal*, **67**(3), 63–75.

Nicholas, Tom (2019), *VC: An American History,* Harvard University Press.

Novick, Barbara; S. Cohen; A. Madhavan; T. Bunzel; J. Sethi; and S. Matthews (2017), "Index investing supports vibrant capital markets," *BlackRock Viewpoint.*

Novy-Marx, Robert; and Joshua D. Rauh (2009), "The liabilities and risks of state-sponsored pension plans," *Journal of Economic Perspectives* **23**(4), 191–210.

Osband, Kent (2011), *Pandora's Risk: Uncertainty at the Core of Finance,* Columbia Business School Publishing.

Page, Sebastien (2021), *Beyond Diversification: What Every Investor Needs to Know About Asset Allocation,* McGraw-Hill.

Pagliari, Joseph L. (2017), "Some thoughts on real estate pricing," *Journal of Portfolio Management* **34**(6), 44–61.

Palazzolo, Christopher; Lukasz Pomorski; and Alice Zhao (2021), "(Car)Bon voyage," AQR white paper.

Palhares, Diogo; and Scott Richardson (2020), "Looking under the hood of active credit managers," *Financial Analysts Journal* **76**(2), 63–75.

Parikh, Harsh (2019), "Institutional gold," SSRN working paper.

Parikh, Harsh; Karen McQuiston; and Sujian Zhi (2018), "The impact of market conditions on active equity management," *Journal of Portfolio Management* **44**(3), 89–101.

Pastor, Lubos; and Robert F. Stambaugh (2003), "Liquidity risk and expected stock returns," *Journal of Political Economy* **111**(3), 642–685.

Pastor, Lubos; and Robert F. Stambaugh (2009), "Are stocks really less volatile in the long run?" *NBER working paper* 14757.

Pastor, Lubos; Robert F. Stambaugh; and Luke Taylor (2014), "Scale and skill in active management," *Journal of Financial Economics* **116**(1), 23–45.

Pastor, Lubos; Robert F. Stambaugh; and Luke Taylor (2020), "Sustainable investing in equilibrium," SSRN working paper.

Pedersen Lasse H. (2018), "Sharpening the arithmetic of active management," *Financial Analysts Journal* **74**(1), 21–36.

Pedersen, Lasse H. (2015), *Efficiently Inefficient: How Smart Money Invests & Market Prices Are Determined.* Princeton University Press.

Pedersen, Lasse H.; Abhilash Babu; and Ari Levine (2021), "Enhanced portfolio optimization," *Financial Analysts Journal* **77**(2), 124–151.

Pedersen, Lasse H.; Shaun Fitzgibbons; and Lukasz Pomorski (2020), "Responsible investing: The ESG-efficient frontier," *Journal of Financial Economics, forthcoming.*

Perold, Andre F. (1988), "The implementation shortfall: Paper vs. reality," *Journal of Portfolio Management* **14**, 4–9.

Perold, Andre F.; and William F. Sharpe (1988), "Dynamic strategies for asset allocation." *Financial Analysts Journal* **44**(1), 16–27.

Pfau, Wade (2017). "A warning to the advisory profession: Dalbar's math is wrong," *Advisor Perspectives,* March 6.

Phalippou, Ludovic (2014), "Performance of private equity revisited?" *Review of Finance* **18**(1), 189–218.

Phalippou, Ludovic (2019), *Private Equity Laid Bare, Independent.*

Phalippou, Ludovic (2020), "An inconvenient fact: Private equity returns and the billionaire factory," *Journal of Investing* **30**(1), 11–39.

Phalippou, Ludovic; and Oliver Gottschalg. 2009. "The performance of private equity funds," *The Review of Financial Studies* **22**(4): 1747–1776.

Piketty, Thomas (2013), *Capital in the Twenty First Century,* Harvard University Press.

Podkaminer, Eugene; Wylie Tollette; and Laurence B. Siegel (2020), "Real interest rate shocks and portfolio strategy," *Journal of Investing* **29**(6), 23–41.

Poterba, James M. (2001), "Demographic structures and asset returns." *Review of Economics and Statistics* **83**(4), 565–584.

PwC (2020), "Asset and wealth management revolution: The power to shape the future," a PwC Global report.

Qian, Edward E. (2018), *Portfolio Rebalancing,* Chapman and Hall.

Qian, Edward; Ronald Hua; and Eric Sorensen (2007), *Quantitative Equity Portfolio Management: Modern Techniques and Applications*, Chapman and Hall.

Rabin, Matthew; and Richard H. Thaler (2001), "Anomalies: Risk aversion," *Journal of Economic Perspectives* **15**(1), 219–232.

Rachel, Lukasz; and Lawrence H. Summers (2019), "On secular stagnation in the industrialized world," *NBER working paper* 26198.

Randl, Otto; Arne Westerkamp; and Josef Zechner (2018), "Equilibrium policy portfolios when some assets are non-tradable," SSRN working paper.

Rattray, Sandy; Nick Granger; Campbell R. Harve; and Otto Van Hemert (2020), "Strategic rebalancing," *Journal of Portfolio Management* **46**(6), 10–31.

Richardson, Scott; and Diogo Palhares (2019), "(Il)liquidity premium in credit markets: A myth?" *Journal of Fixed Income* **28**(3), 5–23.

Rintamäki, Paul (2021), "Total wealth portfolio composition and stock market returns," Aalto University working paper.

Ritter, Jay R. (2005), "Economic growth and equity returns," *Pacific-Basin Finance Journal* **13**(5), 489–503.

Ritter, Jay R. (2012), "Is economic growth good for investors?" *Journal of Applied Corporate Finance* **24**(3), 8–18.

Rizova, Savina; and Namiko Saito (2020), "Intangibles and expected stock returns," SSRN working paper.

Roncalli, Thierry (2013), *Introduction to Risk Parity and Budgeting*, Chapman & Hall.

Ross, Stephen (1976), "The arbitrage theory of capital asset pricing," *Journal of Economic Theory* **13**(3), 341–360.

Ruff, Jon (2007), "Commercial real estate: New paradigm or old story?" *Journal of Portfolio Management Special Real Estate Issue*, 27–36.

Samonov, Mikhail (2020), "Two centuries of value and momentum" in https://www.twocenturies.com/blog/2020/5/26/value-and-momentum.

Samuelson, Paul A. (1994), "The long-term case for equities," *Journal of Portfolio Management* **21**(1), 15–24.

Savor, Pavel; and Mungo Wilson (2014), "Asset pricing: A tale of two days," *Journal of Financial Economics* **113**(2), 171–201.

Scheidel, Walter (2017), *The Great Leveler: Violence and the History of Inequality from the Stone Age to the Twenty-First Century*, Princeton University Press.

Scherer, Bernd (2015), *Portfolio Construction and Risk Budgeting*, Risk Books.

Schmelzing, Paul (2020), "Eight centuries of global real interest rates, R-G, and the 'suprasecular' decline, 1311–2018," *Bank of England Working Paper No. 845*.

Sexauer, Stephen C.; and Laurence B. Siegel (2013), "A pension promise to oneself," *Financial Analysts Journal* **69**(6), 13–32.

Sharpe, Wiliiam F. (1964). "Capital asset prices: A theory of market equilibrium under conditions of risk," *Journal of Finance* **19**, 425–442.

Sharpe, William F. (1981), "Decentralized investment management," *Journal of Finance* **36**, 217–234.

Sharpe, William F. (1991), "The Arithmetic of active management," *Financial Analysts' Journal* **47**(1), 7–9.

Sharpe, William F. (2005), "Insights from a pioneer in portfolio theory and practice: A talk with Nobel laureate William F. Sharpe." *Journal of Investment Consulting* **7**(2), 10–20.

Shleifer, Andrei (2019), "The return of survey expectations," *NBER Reporter* No.1, 14–17.

Shleifer, Andrei; and Robert W. Vishny (1997), "The limits of arbitrage," *Journal of Finance* **52**(1), 35–55.

Sialm, Clemens; and Nathan Sosner (2018), "Taxes, shorting, and active management," *Financial Analysts Journal* **74**(1), 88–107.

Siegel, Jeremy J. (1994), *Stocks for the Long Run*, McGraw Hill.

Siegel, Jeremy J. (2016), "The Shiller CAPE ratio: A new look," *Financial Analysts Journal* **72**(3), 41–50.

Siegel, Laurence B.; Barton Waring; and Matthew Scanlan (2009), "Five principles to hold onto (even when your boss says the opposite)," *Journal of Portfolio Management* **35**(2), 25–41.

Skancke, Martin; Kristin Halvorsen; Tone Hanstad; Karin Thorburn; and Thomas Ekeli (2021), "Climate risk and the Government Pension Fund Global: Managing risks associated with climate change and the green transition," Report from an expert group appointed by the Ministry of Finance in www.regjeringen.no.

Sloan, Richard G. (1996), "Do stock prices fully reflect information in accruals and cash flows about future earnings?" *The Accounting Review* **71**(3), 289–315.

Smith, Edgar Lawrence (1924), *Common Stocks as Long Term Investments*, MacMillan.

Sosner, Nathan; Michael Gromis; and Stanley Krasner (2021), "The tax benefits of direct indexing," *Journal of Index Investing*, forthcoming.

Sosner, Nathan; Joseph Liberman; and Steven Liu (2021), "Integration of income and estate tax planning," *Journal of Wealth Management* **24**(1), 78–104.

Stafford, Erik (2017), "Replicating private equity with value investing, homemade leverage, and hold-to-maturity accounting," HBS working paper.

Stambaugh, Robert F.; and Yu Yuan (2017), "Mispricing factors," *Review of Financial Studies* **30**(4), 1270–1315.

Stewart, Scott D.; John J. Neumann; Christopher R. Knitte; and Jeffrey Heisler, (2009), "Absence of value: An analysis of investment allocation decisions by institutional plan sponsors," *Financial Analysts Journal* **65**(6), 34–51.

Straehl, Philip U.; and Roger Ibbotson (2017), "The long-run drivers of stock returns: Total payouts and the real economy," *Financial Analysts Journal* **73**(3), 32–52.

Stucke, Rüdiger (2011), "Updating history," SSRN working paper.

Suhonen, Antti; Matthias Lennkh; and Fabrice Perez (2017), "Quantifying backtest overfitting in alternative beta strategies," *Journal of Portfolio Management* **43**(2), 90–104.

Sullivan, Rodney (2021), "Hedge fund alpha: Cycle or sunset?" *Journal of Alternative Investments* **23**(3), 55–79.

Swedroe, Larry (2018) *Temperament Trumps Intelligence: Seven Keys to Investment Discipline,* Buckingham.

Swedroe, Larry; and Andrew Berkin (2015), *The Incredible Shrinking Alpha: And What You Can Do to Escape Its Clutches,* Buckingham.

Swensen, David (2009). *Pioneering Portfolio Management: An Unconventional Approach to Institutional Investment,* Free Press.

Taleb, Nassim N. (2013), "'Do financial markets reward buying or selling insurance and lottery tickets?': A Comment," *Financial Analyst Journal* **69**(2), 17–19.

Taleb, Nassim Nicholas (2001), *Fooled by Randomness: The Hidden Role of Chance in the Markets and Life, Texere.*

Taleb, Nassim Nicholas (2020), *Statistical Consequences of Fat Tails: Real World Preasymptotics, Epistemology, and Applications,* STEM Academic Press.

Thinking Ahead Institute (2021), "*Global pension assets study – 2021,*" Willis Towers Watson report.

Tostevin, Paul (2017), "*How much is the world worth?*" The Savills Blog.

Towle, Margaret M. (ed.) (2014), *Masters of Finance: Interviews with Some of the Greatest Minds in Investing and Economics, Investments & Wealth Institute.*

Turnbull, Craig (2017), *A History of British Actuarial Thought,* Palgrave MacMillan.

Van Vliet, Pim; and Jan de Koning (2016), *High Returns from Low Risk: A Remarkable Stock Market Paradox,* Wiley.

Vatanen, Kari; and Antti Suhonen (2019), "A framework for risk premia investing: Anywhere to hide?" SSRN working paper.

Vissing-Jorgensen, Annette; and Tobias J. Moskowitz (2002), "The returns to entrepreneurial investment. A private equity premium puzzle?" *American Economic Review* **92**(4), 745–778.

Vollrath, Dietrich (2020), *Fully Grown: Why a Stagnant Economy Is a Sign of Success,* University of Chicago Press.

Welch, Ivo; and Goyal, Amit (2008), "A comprehensive look at the empirical performance of equity premium prediction," *Review of Financial Studies* **21**, 1455–1508.

Wright, Jonathan H. (2011), "Term premiums and inflation uncertainty: Empirical evidence from an international panel dataset," *American Economic Review* **101**(4), 1514–34.

Index